Psychotherapy for Prolonged and Traumatic Grief

Psychotherapy for Prolonged and Traumatic Grief integrates evidence-based, cognitive-behavioral treatment interventions for prolonged grief disorder (PGD), posttraumatic stress disorder (PTSD), and depressive disorder. These interventions can be applied in bereaved people following different types of traumatic loss, including those bereaved by suicide or disasters, military veterans, first responders, refugees, and others.

This groundbreaking volume is an ambitious and essential first: a truly global integration of scholarly perspectives on prolonged and traumatic grief. Covering all age groups with remarkable sensitivity, it is the go-to guide for mental health practitioners worldwide. From precise, state-of-the-art diagnostic planning to nuanced, culturally sensitive implementation of evidence-based interventions, the book empowers clinicians to assist people with prolonged and traumatic grief. By seamlessly integrating cognitive behavioral and meaning-oriented approaches, it provides a comprehensive and compassionate framework for prevention and treatment.

Geert E. Smid, MD, PhD, is a psychiatrist and professor of psychotrauma, loss, and grief at the University of Humanistic Studies, Utrecht, and ARQ National Psychotrauma Centre, Diemen, the Netherlands.

Hannah Comtesse, PhD, is a clinical psychologist and professor of clinical and health psychology at the University of Hagen, Germany.

Paul A. Boelen, PhD, is a clinical psychologist and full professor of clinical psychology at Utrecht University and ARQ National Psychotrauma Centre, the Netherlands.

"The scope of this comprehensive guide for mental health professionals transcends previous contributions of a similar kind, bringing us squarely up to date with 21st-century developments. It is theory-based, research-informed, and culturally sensitive, but it is also thought-provoking, with awareness of current limitations to understanding about grief complications, which adds to its value. This is a book that all those concerned with the care of bereaved persons can turn to, and I am glad to have this scholarly yet accessible source at hand for consultation."

Margaret Stroebe, PhD, *professor emeritus of clinical psychology, Utrecht University and University of Groningen, The Netherlands*

"Traumatic deaths are particularly embedded in cultural narratives, making it essential for treatment of prolonged grief and related mental health issues to be culturally informed. This book is an indispensable resource for practitioners working with patients from diverse cultural backgrounds who deal with grief-related distress. A must-read book, it provides a comprehensive range of therapeutic strategies and tools meticulously tailored to address the unique needs of these patients."

Cyrille Kossigan Kokou-Kpolou, PhD, *assistant professor of clinical and health psychology, Université Laval, Quebec, Canada*

"Timely, comprehensive, up to date, evidence based, culturally sensitive, covering the life span development from childhood to old age: This book is much needed and a must read for all therapists!"

Ulrich Schnyder, MD, *professor emeritus of psychiatry and psychotherapy, University of Zurich, Switzerland*

Psychotherapy for Prolonged and Traumatic Grief

A Guide for Mental Health Professionals

Edited by Geert E. Smid, Hannah Comtesse, and Paul A. Boelen

NEW YORK AND LONDON

Designed cover image: Getty Images

First published 2026
by Routledge
605 Third Avenue, New York, NY 10158

and by Routledge
4 Park Square, Milton Park, Abingdon, Oxon, OX14 4RN

Routledge is an imprint of the Taylor & Francis Group, an informa business

For Product Safety Concerns and Information please contact our EU representative GPSR@taylorandfrancis.com. Taylor & Francis Verlag GmbH, Kaufingerstraße 24, 80331 München, Germany.

ISBN: 978-1-032-46483-1 (hbk)
ISBN: 978-1-032-46480-0 (pbk)
ISBN: 978-1-003-42977-7 (ebk)

DOI: 10.4324/9781003429777

Typeset in Galliard
by KnowledgeWorks Global Ltd.

Contents

Contributors

Anaïs Aeschlimann, PhD, University of Zurich, Switzerland

Lauren Alvis, PhD, Trauma and Grief Center, Meadows Mental Health Policy Institute, Houston, Texas

Paul A. Boelen, PhD, Utrecht University and ARQ National Psychotrauma Centre, Diemen, the Netherlands

Eric Bui, MD, PhD, Normandy University and Normandy University Hospital, Caen, France and Massachusetts General Hospital, Boston, MA, USA

Hannah Comtesse, PhD, University of Hagen, Germany

Simon Groen, PhD, De Evenaar, GGZ Drenthe, Beilen, the Netherlands

Muriel A. Hagenaars, PhD, Utrecht University and Altrecht Centre for Personality Disorders, the Netherlands

Louisa Heinzl, MSc, Freie Universität Berlin, Germany

Julie B. Kaplow, PhD, Trauma and Grief Center, Meadows Mental Health Policy Institute, Houston, Texas; Tulane University School of Medicine, New Orleans, LA

Clare Killikelly, PhD, University of Zurich, Switzerland

Jeroen W. Knipscheer, PhD, Utrecht University and ARQ National Psychotrauma Centre, Diemen, the Netherlands

Katrine B. Komischke-Konnerup, MSc, Aarhus University, Denmark

Franziska Lechner-Meichsner, PhD, University of Wuppertal, Germany

Fiona Maccallum, PhD, University of Queensland, Australia

Robert A. Neimeyer, PhD, University of Memphis and Portland Institute for Loss and Transition, Portland, OR, USA

Maja O'Connor, PhD, Aarhus University, Denmark

Benjamin Oosterhoff, PhD, Trauma and Grief Center, Meadows Mental Health Policy Institute, Houston, Texas

Lyanne Reitsma, PhD, Utrecht University, the Netherlands

Rita Rosner, PhD, Catholic University of Eichstätt-Ingolstadt, Germany

Geert E. Smid, MD, PhD, University of Humanistic Studies, Utrecht, and ARQ National Psychotrauma Centre, Diemen, the Netherlands

Nadine Stammel, PhD, Freie Universität Berlin, Germany

Charles Tesnières, MD, Normandy University and Normandy University Hospital, Caen, France

Anna Vogel, PhD, Rosenheim Technical University of Applied Sciences, Germany

Oscar Widales-Benitez, PhD, Trauma and Grief Center, Meadows Mental Health Policy Institute, Houston, Texas

Introduction

Geert E. Smid, Hannah Comtesse, and Paul A. Boelen

Why this book?

It has long been recognized that grief following the death of a loved one may cause long-standing and impairing suffering. However, prolonged grief disorder (PGD) is a condition only recently included in international diagnostic classification systems. This condition is newly included in the eleventh edition of the International Classification of Diseases (ICD-11; World Health Organization [WHO], 2022) and the text revision of the fifth Diagnostic and Statistical Manual of Mental Disorders (DSM-5-TR; American Psychiatric Association [APA], 2022). According to criteria in ICD-11 and DSM-5-TR, a PGD diagnosis applies if manifestations of grief are accompanied by severe suffering or functional impairment for at least 6–12 months after the death and go beyond cultural norms of grief responses.

The recognition of PGD facilitates access to specialized care for those suffering from pervasive and disruptive grief. However, the new classification has generated controversy, notably the concern that normal grief might be pathologized (Prigerson et al., 2024), underscoring the importance of accurate diagnosis. Despite this debate, the inclusion of PGD emphasizes approaching mental health within the context of individual life experiences, such as traumatic events, stressors, and losses. A person-centered and humanistic perspective in mental healthcare prioritizes the individual's experience in relation to their values, beliefs, and cultural context and recognizes the individual's inherent worth, search for meaning, and capacity for growth.

In today's world, grief has become a central theme. Global population is projected to peak well before the century's end, with statistical models estimating a peak of 9.73 billion in 2064, followed by a decline to 8.79 billion by 2100 (Vollset et al., 2020). Population aging and decline may introduce challenges related to grief in the future. In a world facing crisis—marked by international conflicts, climate change, and poverty—tragic losses of loved ones are likely to increase. This book seeks to equip mental

DOI: 10.4324/9781003429777-1

health professionals with the tools to help bereaved individuals cope with prolonged and traumatic grief.

Defining prolonged and traumatic grief

Bereavement can trigger several mental disorders beyond PGD, notably posttraumatic stress disorder (PTSD) and major depressive disorder. The DSM-5-TR (but not ICD-11) criteria for these disorders include specific considerations for bereavement. As for PTSD, being confronted with a person's actual or threatened death has been defined as a potentially traumatic event capable of causing PTSD (APA, 2022). Unlike DSM-5-TR, ICD-11 provides a list of factors influencing health status, enabling the clinician to specify several distinct problems associated with the absence, loss, or death of others (WHO, 2022).

Critically, learning about the death of a loved one qualifies as a traumatic event only if the death was violent or accidental, i.e., stemming from events such as accidents, disasters, homicide, war, other violence, and suicide. As for major depressive disorder, the DSM-5-TR acknowledges the similarity between responses to bereavement and a major depressive episode. While symptoms such as intense sadness, rumination, insomnia, appetite changes, and weight loss may be understood as responses to loss, the manual urges clinicians to carefully evaluate the presence of a major depressive episode. Many studies have found that the co-occurrence of PGD with PTSD, depression, and anxiety is common following bereavement, with some research suggesting that traumatic death may influence this co-occurrence (Djelantik et al., 2020; Komischke-Konnerup et al., 2021). This book uses the term "traumatic grief" to refer to PGD accompanied by (symptoms of) PTSD and/or major depressive disorder following the traumatic death of a loved one. Box 1 summarizes definitions of key terms as used in this book.

A meaning-oriented understanding of grief

Confrontation with death has consistently been highlighted as one of the existential experiences capable of profoundly affecting spiritual and mental well-being (Yalom, 1980). Acute grief encompasses several symptoms related to existential concerns, such as confronting death and mortality, experiencing a disrupted sense of self, feeling a lack of meaning-in-life, and struggling with intense loneliness or isolation.

Meaning-in-life operates on multiple levels. Existentially, it involves feeling connected to something larger than oneself, a sense of belonging to a meaningful whole that transcends individual existence. This often involves cultural, spiritual, or religious values, beliefs, and traditions. This

Box 1 Definitions of prolonged grief, traumatic grief, and traumatic death

Prolonged grief refers to a clinical diagnosis of PGD according to current criteria in DSM-5-TR and ICD-11.

Traumatic grief refers to a clinical diagnosis of PGD with comorbid (symptoms of) PTSD and/or major depressive disorder following confrontation with the traumatic death of a loved one.

Traumatic death refers to the death of a loved one in the context of (a) potentially traumatizing (i.e., threatening, unexpected) event(s), e.g., homicide, suicide, violence, an accident, a disaster, or life-threatening illness or injury in the absence of adequate medical care.

transcendence, the human capacity to transform both self and world, is rooted in the belief that change, creativity, and the growth of meaning are possible (Johnson, 2012). Cognitively, affectively, and motivationally, meaning-in-life is characterized by coherence (a sense of comprehensibility), significance (a feeling that life is important and valuable), and purpose (having core goals and direction) (Martela & Steger, 2016). Socially, meaning-in-life is bidirectionally linked to social connectedness, which bolsters community resilience after trauma and loss (Hobfoll et al., 2007; Stavrova & Luhmann, 2016). Somatically, meaning-in-life is vital for mental and physical well-being, health, and quality of life (Haugan & Dezutter, 2021). A meta-analysis has even demonstrated a link between physical health and meaning-in-life, specifically meaning-related feelings of harmony, peace, and well-being (Czekierda et al., 2017).

The loss of loved ones causes the world of the bereaved and the place of the bereaved survivor in it to change irreversibly. These changes impact on existential/cultural, cognitive, affective, motivational, social, and somatic levels of meaning-in-life. On the existential level, these changes lead to a stage of ***liminality*** (from the Latin ***limen*** meaning threshold or margin). Drawing on anthropological research (Van Gennep, 2013), liminality describes the transitional middle phase of a "rite of passage" in tribal societies. These rites typically involve three stages: separation from one's social group, the liminal period itself, and subsequent reintegration. During this transition, people become "liminal entities" who are "betwixt and between the positions assigned and arrayed by law, custom, convention, and ceremonial" (Turner, 1969, p. 95). Following bereavement, people may experience their sense of identity, reality, and being in the world have been suspended (Pearce, 2019).

On the cognitive-affective level, the loss of a loved one brings about experiences of ambiguity and ambivalence. The grieving person may experience a fundamental ambiguity between the presence and absence of the deceased, between living in the present and the past worlds. The loved one is present in a still ongoing past, from which the alienated present has separated in a desynchronized strand of time (Fuchs, 2018). Part of this ambiguity is often a sense of "unrealness" about the loss (Boelen, 2017) and an "as-if presence" of the deceased that may cause a conflict between affects and cognitions: encounters with the deceased that may occur in dreams or when bereaved persons report having seen, heard, felt, smelled, or talked with the deceased.

Bereaved individuals often experience ambivalence, torn between the desire to maintain a connection with the deceased and the need to move forward. This creates a double bind, as clinging to the past can hinder the development of a new identity (Pearce, 2019). Ambivalence toward reminders of the loved one's death and the wish to avoid those may lead to life changes (e.g., move from the home where a loved one died by homicide). On the motivational and social levels, experiential avoidance and social withdrawal may result from the loss of a shared world, habits, and practices. If these reactions persist, corresponding symptoms of PGD include avoidance of reminders that the person is dead and difficulties in moving on with life, e.g., withdrawal from contacts and activities. Social withdrawal may be associated with emotional loneliness and detachment from others.

Somatic distress may include headaches, dizziness, indigestion, chest pain, and fatigue, along with elevated rates of disability, illness, and mortality (Stroebe et al., 2007, 2017). In his classic description of grief, Lindemann (1994) noted somatically experienced "pangs" of grief that comprises "feeling of tightness in the throat, choking with shortness of breath, need for sighing, an empty feeling in the abdomen, lack of muscular power, and an intense subjective distress described as tension or mental pain" (Lindemann, 1994, p. 141).

In sum, the loss of a loved one may affect the bereaved person's sense of meaning-in-life on different levels. If acute and impairing grief persists beyond social and cultural norms, prolonged grief may develop. PGD, as defined by DSM-5-TR, is characterized by separation distress manifesting as yearning for and/or preoccupation with the deceased and additional symptoms such as identity disruption, disbelief, avoidance, intense emotional pain, difficulties moving on, emotional numbness, a sense of meaninglessness, and loneliness. ICD-11 PGD similarly comprises yearning/preoccupation and intense emotional pain, but specifies a broader range of additional symptoms such as guilt, denial, and blame.

Acknowledging and understanding the multilayered experience of grief is particularly important in traumatic grief. A strictly trauma-focused approach to traumatic grief, while valuable, risks reducing the experience of traumatic loss to simply a "traumatic event." This narrow lens can inadvertently overlook the essential dimensions of grief and the individual's unique and evolving experience of its meaning. A comprehensive approach to traumatic grief integrates the trauma perspective with an understanding of separation distress characteristic of prolonged grief and the individual's search for meaning within their personal and cultural context.

Approaching the treatment of prolonged and traumatic grief

This book aims to integrate evidence-based, cognitive-behavioral treatment interventions for PGD, PTSD, and major depressive disorder with meaning-oriented, culturally sensitive experiential interventions. Cognitive behavioral therapy (CBT) has demonstrated promising results for PGD. A seminal study compared grief-focused CBT with interpersonal psychotherapy, finding grief-focused CBT significantly more effective (Shear et al., 2005). This initial grief-focused CBT approach involved grief reduction through imaginal and in vivo exposure (focusing on the death scene and avoided situations, respectively), addressing unresolved issues with the deceased, increasing activity levels, and goal setting. Subsequent research has confirmed and extended these findings (Komischke-Konnerup et al., 2024).

Contemporary CBT for PGD builds on these foundations and typically incorporates several key elements (Bryant et al., 2024; Rosner et al., 2024). The therapy often begins with psychoeducation about PGD, explaining its physiological, emotional, and cognitive impact, and the development of an individualized understanding of the disorder, including the interplay of grief and any co-occurring symptoms. Exposure therapy, a core component, involves revisiting distressing memories of the loss, mostly related to the circumstances of the death or other significant events (e.g., the funeral). Cognitive restructuring techniques are used to identify and challenge negative (maladaptive) thoughts and beliefs related to the loss, trauma, self, and future, employing methods like Socratic questioning, behavioral experiments, and formulating helpful thoughts. Communication with the deceased, often through letter writing, can facilitate this cognitive restructuring process. Goal setting, focusing on social reengagement and other life activities, is also emphasized. Positive memories of the deceased are enhanced and integrated into the therapy. Finally, relapse prevention strategies are taught, including identifying potential triggers and practicing coping mechanisms.

Recent approaches also integrate systemic elements (e.g., genograms) and experiential exercises (e.g., reenacting the graveside visit) and emphasize establishing a healthy connection with the deceased. The final sessions focus on consolidating gains, establishing new goals, and integrating emotional learning (Rosner et al., 2025).

Culturally sensitive care for prolonged and traumatic grief benefits from a meaning-oriented approach for several interconnected reasons, elaborated in this book. First, grief is embedded in cultural contexts. A meaning-oriented approach acknowledges diverse cultural interpretations of grief and tailors interventions to align with them (Smid et al., 2018). Second, a meaning-oriented exploration of the individual's unique understanding of the loss supports them in finding ways to make sense of it within their cultural framework (Neimeyer, 2019; Smid & Boelen, 2021). Third, a culturally sensitive approach recognizes cultural variations in attribution of meaning (Killikelly & Maercker, 2022). Fourth, meaning-oriented interventions can be culturally adapted (Aeschlimann et al., 2024), allowing therapists to provide culturally sensitive care that is tailored to the individual's specific needs and beliefs.

For whom this book is meant

This book is intended both for educators and practitioners, including therapists, psychologists, psychiatrists, counselors, chaplains, and social workers. Bereavement is increasingly recognized as a significant public health concern (Lichtenthal et al., 2024). A public health model suggests a tiered approach to bereavement care, estimating that 60% of bereaved individuals are at low risk of distress, 30% at moderate risk, and 10% at high risk (Aoun et al., 2015; Killikelly et al., 2021). Research confirms varying experiences and needs corresponding to these levels of support (Aoun et al., 2018). While informal support networks (family, friends, and funeral providers) are the most frequently utilized and perceived as most helpful, professional support sources are the least used (Aoun et al., 2018). A public health approach, such as the compassionate communities model, is therefore crucial for supporting the majority of bereaved individuals (Aoun et al., 2018). Compassionate communities can be strengthened by a bereavement care network, that facilitates provider collaboration through training, consultation, and referral.

What this book has to offer

This book offers a comprehensive exploration of prolonged and traumatic grief, encompassing diagnosis, risk factors, theoretical models, treatment strategies, and approaches for special populations.

Part I: Diagnosing Prolonged and Traumatic Grief lays the groundwork for understanding prolonged and traumatic grief. Chapter 1 examines the diagnostic criteria for PGD as defined in the DSM and ICD, explores differential diagnoses, and discusses prevalence and comorbidity. It also addresses the complexities of bereavement research and care and introduces a staging typology that provides a framework to describe the trajectory from healthy to unhealthy grief, the factors influencing this trajectory, and corresponding interventions. Chapter 2 focuses on the practical application of diagnostic procedures, emphasizing the value of structured approaches and sensitivity to special populations while navigating the delicate distinction between normal and disordered grief. Chapter 3 addresses risk and protective factors associated with prolonged and traumatic grief, considering the nature of the loss (e.g., traumatic, sudden), the relationship with the deceased, individual vulnerabilities (e.g., age, gender, attachment style, personal history), and the influence of social and cultural contexts (e.g., social support, cultural beliefs, rituals). Chapter 4 explores prominent theoretical models of grief, emphasizing the process of adapting to loss through self-concept revision and the search for meaning. It elucidates how stalled adaptation, negative appraisals, and maladaptive coping mechanisms can contribute to PGD, and it also considers the impact of traumatic circumstances and co-occurring mental health conditions.

Part II: Psychotherapy for Prolonged and Traumatic Grief details therapeutic interventions for prolonged and traumatic grief. Chapter 5 highlights the importance of psychoeducation in providing information about grief reactions to enhance understanding and treatment engagement. Chapter 6 focuses on memory processes involved in prolonged and traumatic grief and examines the use of different exposure techniques to mitigate emotional distress following loss. Chapter 7 explores the processes of meaning-making, reengagement, and activation, focusing on helping individuals find meaning in their loss and reintegrate into life. Chapter 8 discusses symbolic interactions, employing creative methods like writing, imagery rescripting, and rituals to address unresolved issues. Chapter 9 describes internet- and mobile-based interventions for delivering accessible grief support. Finally, Chapter 10 considers the role of pharmacotherapy in managing comorbid conditions such as PTSD and depression.

Part III: Special Populations addresses approaches to grief in specific populations. Chapter 11 explores the unique challenges of ambiguous loss, focusing on interventions for those dealing with the disappearance of a loved one. Chapters 12 and 13 examine the diagnosis and treatment of grief in children and adolescents, respectively. Chapter 14 discusses adapting therapeutic approaches for older adults experiencing loss. Finally, Chapter 15 explores the complexities of grief in migrants and refugees, considering the intersection of trauma and cultural transition.

References

Aeschlimann, A., Heim, E., Killikelly, C., Arafa, M., & Maercker, A. (2024). Culturally sensitive grief treatment and support: A scoping review. *SSM - Mental Health*, 5, 100325. https://doi.org/10.1016/j.ssmmh.2024.100325

American Psychiatric Association. (2022). *Diagnostic and Statistical Manual of Mental Disorders, Fifth Edition, Text Revision (DSM-5-TR)*. APA. https://doi.org/10.1176/appi.books.9780890425787

Aoun, S. M., Breen, L. J., Howting, D. A., Rumbold, B., McNamara, B., & Hegney, D. (2015). Who needs bereavement support? A population based survey of bereavement risk and support need. *PLoS ONE, 10*(3), e0121101. https://doi.org/10.1371/journal.pone.0121101

Aoun, S. M., Breen, L. J., White, I., Rumbold, B., & Kellehear, A. (2018). What sources of bereavement support are perceived helpful by bereaved people and why? Empirical evidence for the compassionate communities approach. *Palliative Medicine, 32*(8), 1378–1388. https://doi.org/10.1177/0269216318774995

Boelen, P. A. (2017). "It feels as if she might return one day": A sense of unrealness as a predictor of bereavement-related emotional distress / "Tengo la sensación de que ella puede volver algún día": la sensación de irrealidad como un predictor del sufrimiento emocional relacionado con la pérdida. *Studies in Psychology, 38*(3), 734–751. https://doi.org/10.1080/02109395.2017.1340140

Bryant, R. A., Azevedo, S., Yadav, S., Cahill, C., Kenny, L., Maccallum, F., Tran, J., Choi-Christou, J., Rawson, N., Tockar, J., Garber, B., Keyan, D., & Dawson, K. S. (2024). Cognitive behavior therapy vs mindfulness in treatment of prolonged grief disorder: A randomized clinical trial. *JAMA Psychiatry, 81*(7), 646-654. https://doi.org/10.1001/jamapsychiatry.2024.0432

Czekierda, K., Banik, A., Park, C. L., & Luszczynska, A. (2017). Meaning in life and physical health: Systematic review and meta-analysis. *Health Psychology Review, 11*(4), 387–418. https://doi.org/10.1080/17437199.2017.1327325

Djelantik, A. A. A. M. J., Robinaugh, D. J., Kleber, R. J., Smid, G. E., & Boelen, P. A. (2020). Symptomatology following loss and trauma: Latent class and network analyses of prolonged grief disorder, posttraumatic stress disorder, and depression in a treatment-seeking trauma-exposed sample. *Depression and Anxiety, 37*, 26–34. https://doi.org/10.1002/da.22880

Fuchs, T. (2018). Presence in absence. The ambiguous phenomenology of grief. *Phenomenology and the Cognitive Sciences, 17*(1), 43–63. https://doi.org/10.1007/s11097-017-9506-2

Haugan, G., & Dezutter, J. (2021). Meaning-in-life: A vital salutogenic resource for health. In G. Haugan & M. Eriksson (Eds.), *Health promotion in health care – Vital theories and research* (pp. 85–101). Springer International Publishing. https://doi.org/10.1007/978-3-030-63135-2_8

Hobfoll, S. E., Watson, P., Bell, C. C., Bryant, R. A., Brymer, M. J., Friedman, M. J., Friedman, M., Gersons, B. P. R., De Jong, J. T. V. M., Layne, C. M., Maguen, S., Neria, Y., Norwood, A. E., Pynoos, R. S., Reissman, D., Ruzek, J. I., Shalev, A. Y., Solomon, Z., Steinberg, A. M., & Ursano, R. J. (2007). Five essential elements of immediate and mid-term mass trauma intervention: Empirical evidence. *Psychiatry, 70*(4), 283–315. https://doi.org/10.1521/psyc.2007.70.4.283

Johnson, M. (2012). *The meaning of the body: Aesthetics of human understanding*. University of Chicago Press.

Killikelly, C., & Maercker, A. (2022). The cultural supplement: A new method for assessing culturally relevant prolonged grief disorder symptoms. *Clinical Psychology in Europe, 5*(1), 1–14. https://doi.org/10.32872/cpe.7655

Killikelly, C., Smid, G. E., Wagner, B., & Boelen, P. A. (2021). Responding to the ICD-11 prolonged grief disorder during the COVID-19 pandemic: Uniting clinicians and researchers with a new bereavement network and outline for a three-tiered model of care. *Public Health, 191*, 85–90. https://doi.org/10.1016/j.puhe.2020.10.034

Komischke-Konnerup, K. B., Zachariae, R., Boelen, P. A., Marello, M. M., & O'Connor, M. (2024). Grief-focused cognitive behavioral therapies for prolonged grief symptoms: A systematic review and meta-analysis. *Journal of Consulting and Clinical Psychology*, *92*(4), 236–248. https://doi.org/10.1037/ccp0000884

Komischke-Konnerup, K. B., Zachariae, R., Johannsen, M., Nielsen, L. D., & O'Connor, M. (2021). Co-occurrence of prolonged grief symptoms and symptoms of depression, anxiety, and posttraumatic stress in bereaved adults: A systematic review and meta-analysis. *Journal of Affective Disorders Reports*, *4*, 100140. https://doi.org/10.1016/j.jadr.2021.100140

Lichtenthal, W. G., Roberts, K. E., Donovan, L. A., Breen, L. J., Aoun, S. M., Connor, S. R., & Rosa, W. E. (2024). Investing in bereavement care as a public health priority. *The Lancet Public Health*, *9*(4), e270–e274. https://doi.org/10.1016/S2468-2667(24)00030-6

Lindemann, E. (1994). Symptomatology and management of acute grief. *American Journal of Psychiatry*, *151*(6), 155–160. (Original work published 1944)

Martela, F., & Steger, M. F. (2016). The three meanings of meaning in life: Distinguishing coherence, purpose, and significance. *The Journal of Positive Psychology*, *11*(5), 531–545. https://doi.org/10.1080/17439760.2015.1137623

Neimeyer, R. A. (2019). Meaning reconstruction in bereavement: Development of a research program. *Death Studies*, *43*(2), 79–91. https://doi.org/10.1080/07481187.2018.1456620

Pearce, C. (2019). *The public and private management of grief: Recovering normal*. Springer International Publishing. https://doi.org/10.1007/978-3-030-17662-4

Prigerson, H. G., Singer, J., & Killikelly, C. (2024). Prolonged grief disorder: Addressing misconceptions with evidence. *The American Journal of Geriatric Psychiatry*, *32*(5), 527–534. https://doi.org/10.1016/j.jagp.2023.10.020

Rosner, R., Rau, J., Kersting, A., Rief, W., Steil, R., Rummel, A.-M., Vogel, A., & Comtesse, H. (2025). Grief-specific cognitive behavioral therapy vs present-centered therapy: A randomized clinical trial. *JAMA Psychiatry*, *82*(2), 109–117. https://doi.org/10.1001/jamapsychiatry.2024.3409

Shear, M. K., Frank, E., Houck, P. R., & Reynolds, C. F. (2005). Treatment of complicated grief: A randomized controlled trial. *JAMA: The Journal of the American Medical Association*, *293*(21), 2601–2608. https://doi.org/10.1001/jama.293.21.2601

Smid, G. E., & Boelen, P. A. (2021). Culturally sensitive approaches to finding meaning in traumatic bereavement. In R. A. Neimeyer (Ed.), *New techniques of grief therapy: Bereavement and beyond*. Routledge.

Smid, G. E., Groen, S., De la Rie, S. M., Kooper, S., & Boelen, P. A. (2018). Toward cultural assessment of grief and grief-related psychopathology. *Psychiatric Services*, *69*(10), 1050–1052. https://doi.org/10.1176/appi.ps.201700422

Stavrova, O., & Luhmann, M. (2016). Social connectedness as a source and consequence of meaning in life. *The Journal of Positive Psychology*, *11*(5), 470–479. https://doi.org/10.1080/17439760.2015.1117127

Stroebe, M., Schut, H., & Stroebe, W. (2007). Health outcomes of bereavement. *The Lancet*, *370*(9603), 1960–1973. https://doi.org/10.1016/S0140-6736(07)61816-9

Stroebe, M., Stroebe, W., Schut, H., & Boerner, K. (2017). Grief is not a disease but bereavement merits medical awareness. *The Lancet*, *389*(10067), 347–349. https://doi.org/10.1016/S0140-6736(17)30189-7

Turner, V. (1969). *The ritual process: structure and anti-structure.* Cornell University Press.

Van Gennep, A. (2013). *The rites of passage.* Routledge. (Original work published 1909)

Vollset, S. E., Goren, E., Yuan, C.-W., Cao, J., Smith, A. E., Hsiao, T., Bisignano, C., Azhar, G. S., Castro, E., Chalek, J., Dolgert, A. J., Frank, T., Fukutaki, K., Hay, S. I., Lozano, R., Mokdad, A. H., Nandakumar, V., Pierce, M., Pletcher, M., & Murray, C. J. L. (2020). Fertility, mortality, migration, and population scenarios for 195 countries and territories from 2017 to 2100: A forecasting analysis for the Global Burden of Disease Study. *The Lancet, 396*(10258), 1285–1306. https://doi.org/10.1016/S0140-6736(20)30677-2

World Health Organization [WHO]. (2022). *International classification of diseases, eleventh revision (ICD-11).* WHO. https://icd.who.int/browse11/l-m/en

Yalom, I. D. (1980). *Existential psychotherapy.* Hachette UK.

Part I

Diagnosing Prolonged and Traumatic Grief

Chapter 1

Prolonged and traumatic grief

Symptoms, staging, and stepped care

Paul A. Boelen

Most people confronted with the death of a close person experience transient symptoms of sadness and grief but rapidly return to the emotional balance before the loss (Galatzer-Levy et al., 2018). In a significant minority though, the death activates or intensifies pre-existing symptoms of mental disorders or leads to a grief response that gradually develops into persistent distressing and disabling grief (Djelantik et al., 2020b; Keyes et al., 2014; Lundorff et al., 2017). The growing acknowledgment that grief may culminate into persistent disturbance has led to the inclusion of prolonged grief disorder (PGD) as a new condition in the eleventh edition of the International Classification of Diseases (ICD-11; World Health Organization [WHO], 2022) and the text revision of the *Diagnostic and Statistical Manual of Mental Disorders*, Fifth Edition, Text Revision (DSM-5-TR; APA, 2022). In this chapter, we address criteria for PGD, differential diagnostic considerations, and prevalence and comorbidity. We also consider challenges for bereavement research and care—some of which associated with the artificial binary distinction between healthy/normal and unhealthy/disordered grief. We introduce a staging typology that offers a framework to understand the longitudinal development of healthy and unhealthy grief, factors affecting this development, and different interventions.

PGD in DSM-5-TR and ICD-11

Separation distress is at the heart of grief. Separation distress has emotional, cognitive, and behavioral elements. Emotional elements include yearning and longing for the lost person—sometimes accompanied by pangs of panic and (existential) despair, a sense of being lost, and feelings of meaninglessness, emptiness, and loneliness. Cognitive elements include disbelief and "unrealness", a sense that the person is just temporarily gone. This may be accompanied by a sense that one hears or sees the lost person. Meanwhile, people may find themselves immersed in memories of their lost loved one, experiencing a confusing and ambiguous blend of painful awareness of the

DOI: 10.4324/9781003429777-3

separation and disbelief that it is permanent. Behavioral aspects of separation distress include seeking proximity through actions like visiting places the deceased used to be present, arranging the home as if they might return at any moment, and "searching" for them, despite knowing it is in vain.

Although separation distress is a normal response, it can turn into a grief disorder if it persists for a long period of time and if it disturbs a person's psychological functioning many months or years after the loss. Indeed, separation distress is a key element of PGD, both according to DSM-5-TR (APA, 2022) and ICD-11 criteria (WHO, 2022). Specifically, in terms of DSM-5-TR, adults can be diagnosed with PGD when they experienced the death of a close person, at least 12 months earlier and experience at least one of two separation distress symptoms (yearning/longing and/or preoccupation) and at least three of eight additional symptoms (identity disruption, disbelief, avoidance, intense emotional pain, difficulties moving on, emotional numbness, a sense of meaninglessness, and loneliness). In terms of ICD-11, someone can be diagnosed with PGD when they experienced the death of a loved one, at least 6 months ago, and experiences yearning/longing and/or preoccupation accompanied by "intense emotional pain", as manifesting in sadness, guilt, anger, denial, blame, difficulties accepting the death, feeling that a part of self is lost, inability to experience positive mood, numbness, and/or difficulties engaging in social or other activities. Both DSM-5-TR and ICD-11 further require that for a diagnosis of PGD, the grief reactions exceed social, cultural, and religious norms and cause significant distress and dysfunction.

Differential diagnostic considerations

There are similarities between the clinical presentation of PGD and that of posttraumatic stress disorder (PTSD) and depression, two conditions frequently observed in individuals who struggle to move through their grief. All three disorders are characterized by difficulties to downregulate negative emotions and upregulate positive emotions, negative thinking patterns (related to, e.g., the self, life, the future), and difficulties to engage in effective coping behaviors that could mitigate distress. There are also differences between these conditions. In terms of emotional symptoms, separation distress is central to PGD, anxiety and hypervigilance are central to PTSD, and dysphoria and reduced positive affect are central to depression. In terms of memory phenomena, PGD is characterized by frequent reliving of memories of the deceased and the circumstances of the death. PTSD is characterized by intrusive memories of threatening events associated with the loss. In the case of traumatic, unnatural deaths, these are often related to the circumstances of the death. Depression may be accompanied by broader negative self-referential memories, not tied with specific events, or memories of earlier negative life experiences. In terms of behaviors, PGD is associated with both approach behaviors, where individuals engage in proximity-seeking behaviors to maintain a sense of closeness to the lost person, and avoidance behaviors, where they avoid cues that remind them the separation is permanent. PTSD is characterized by avoidance of cues that remind of (or announce the recurrence of) the threatening event. Depression is characterized by inactivity and withdrawal. PGD can be considered as a chronic activation of the attachment system (driving a continues search for the lost person); PTSD involves a chronic activation of the fear network (driving a pervasive sense of current threat, hypervigilance, and avoidance); depression is a chronic disturbance in mood and approach motivation (maintaining negative self-focus and withdrawal).

The distinction between PGD, PTSD, and depression has been confirmed in research. For example, network, factor analytic, and latent class analysis have shown that symptoms of PGD, PTSD, and depression represent distinct phenomena (e.g., Djelantik et al., 2020a). In addition, emerging evidence suggests that the three conditions are associated with distinct neural mechanisms (e.g., Bryant et al., 2021). Furthermore, elevated PGD symptoms have been found to predict later impaired functioning and mental health, independent of PTSD and depression (e.g., Boelen & Prigerson, 2007). Treatment studies indicated that PGD symptoms do not respond sufficiently to therapies focused on PTSD and depression and, therefore, should be treated with specific grief-focused interventions (cf. Reynolds et al., 1999). Despite their differences, PGD, PTSD, and depression often co-occur. Evidence indicates that roughly one in two people reporting clinically significant PGD also experienced clinically significant PTSD and/or depression (Komischke-Konnerup et al., 2021). This book posits "traumatic grief" as a common combination of separation distress, traumatic distress, and dysphoria; this concept reflects that, particularly in the face of deaths happening in potentially traumatizing circumstances, comorbidity is the rule and not the exception.

Prevalence of PGD and other emotional problems following loss

Figures on PGD prevalence differ between studies. Two meta-analyses reported pooled PGD prevalence rates of 9.8% (Lundorff et al., 2017) and 49% (Djelantik et al., 2020b) in people confronted with natural losses and unnatural losses, respectively. However, these figures should be interpreted with caution, as studies included in these reviews largely relied on non-representative samples, outdated criteria for PGD, and a range of measures to assess PGD. Rosner et al. (2021) examined PGD prevalence in a representative sample of the German general population and found that, among bereaved persons, prevalence rates were 4.2% (ICD-11 criteria) and 3.3% (DSM-5-TR criteria). Slightly higher rates of 5.4% (ICD-11) and 4.7% (DSM-5-TR) were found in a different representative German sample studied by Treml et al. (2024). Shevlin et al. (2023) reported prevalence rates of ICD-11 PGD in a representative UK sample of 2.4% and 7.9%, based on "strict criteria" (i.e., symptoms scored ≥4, on a 5-point scale) and "moderate criteria" (i.e., symptoms scored ≥3 on that same scale), respectively. Boelen and Adamkovič (2024) reported ICD-11-based PGD rates of 7.8% in a representative Slovak sample, bereaved 6–12 months earlier. A recent study comparing PGD rates across countries found that, paradoxically, PGD rates are lower in lower-resourced countries compared to higher-resourced ones; however, more research is needed to compare rates across different countries and cultures (Comtesse et al., 2024).

Importantly, losses may precipitate PGD, PTSD, and depression but many other disorders too. In an epidemiological study, Keyes et al. (2014) found that, in a representative US sample, one in two people reported that they ever suffered an unexpected loss. Not only was sudden loss the most frequently occurring life event, but it was also associated with the onset of different mental health problems, including depression, panic disorder, manic episodes, alcohol use, and PTSD.

Challenges for bereavement research and care

Thirty years after Prigerson et al.'s (1995) influential study showing that "complicated grief" is truly different from depression, there is now widespread recognition that not all grief is normal. Since then, research into causes, consequences, and treatments of disordered grief has grown substantially. Nonetheless, the field of bereavement research and care still faces challenges. A first set of challenges involves the *distinction* between normal, integrated, or "healthy" grief and pathological, disordered, or "unhealthy" grief. For instance, there are still differing perspectives on the nature and number of grief reactions needed to differentiate PGD from "normal grief". This is reflected in differences between PGD in DSM-5-TR and ICD-11, which feature partially (but not completely) overlapping symptom criteria and differing temporal thresholds (≥12 months in DSM-5-TR; ≥6 months in ICD-11). In addition, some writers worry that the PGD label is stigmatizing, may create new markets for medication, and break down normal grieving rituals (e.g., Bandini, 2015). These claims remain largely unproven (Prigerson et al., 2024) but may hinder recognition that not all grief is healthy and discourage bereaved individuals experiencing persistent emotional pain from seeking help.

A second group of challenges has to do with risk and protective factors. As discussed below, some consistent predictors of pervasive grief have been identified, including sociodemographic characteristics (e.g., female gender), characteristics of the loss (e.g., unexpectedness of the death), and additional stress in the loss's aftermath (e.g., limited support). In addition, individual factors, including pre-loss mental vulnerability and cognitive behavioral variables (rigid negative cognitions and avoidant coping) have been found to predict poorer outcomes (e.g., Buur et al., 2024 and Chapter 3 of this volume). However, several issues remain unexplored. For example, knowledge is still limited regarding differences and overlap in risk factors for early versus later onset PGD, the significance of pre-loss versus post-loss risk factors, and how various risk factors interact in predicting grief. Further, limited knowledge exists regarding protective factors that facilitate adjustment, yet the absence of such factors may be just as influential in shaping recovery from loss as the presence of risk factors (cf. Wood & Tarrier, 2010).

A third set of challenges pertains to *treatment*. Evidence shows that care is not so useful for individuals with mild grief reactions (Johannsen et al., 2019), possibly because treatment may interfere with the natural recovery processes of these people (Currier et al., 2008). On the other hand, postponing bereavement care for those experiencing pervasive, disabling grief can lead to chronic conditions that eventually require more intensive treatment. Finding a balance between overtreating healthy grief and undertreating unhealthy grief is essential. There is also an urgent need to enhance options for effective preventive bereavement care. In many western countries, there is a wide offer of universal and selective preventive interventions, targeting the general population of bereaved people or high-risk groups, respectively (Killikelly et al., 2021). However, there is no clear evidence that such interventions accelerate recovery (Currier et al., 2008; Johannsen et al., 2019). Promisingly, studies have shown that internet-based cognitive behavioral therapy, offered to individuals with elevated PGD in the early months of bereavement, can lead to long-term reductions in PGD symptoms (Litz et al., 2014; Reitsma et al., 2023). It appears crucial to further develop these interventions and expand their accessibility. Similarly, there is a need to improve curative interventions for those with full-blown PGD. Current treatments successfully mitigate PGD in only 40–60% of patients (Johannsen et al., 2019), leaving a substantial portion of individuals insufficiently benefitting from treatment.

Clinical staging, profiling, and stepped care

The field of bereavement research and care faces challenges in increasing knowledge about the phenomenology, risk and protective factors, prevention, and treatment of emotional problems following loss. A clinical staging approach to grief could provide a framework for integrating existing knowledge on clinical manifestations, underlying mechanisms, and treatment of unhealthy grief, while also helping to identify and address knowledge gaps. Clinical staging offers a template to distinguish stages in the temporal development of a disorder and to characterize inflection points during this development. Clinical staging can be combined with ***profiling***. Profiling involves connecting stages in the course of a disorder with clinical characteristics and risk and protective factors, to distinguish people in different stages and to predict disorder improvement, progression, and extension (cf. Voshaar et al., 2015). Staging and profiling offer a heuristic tool for a stepped (or tiered) model of bereavement care, in which interventions are offered that align with the nature, intensity, and maintaining mechanisms of the presenting problems. Below, we will outline our emerging staging approach.

Clinical stages of PGD

Influential authors in psychiatry have laid the foundation for a general clinical staging model in which five stages are distinguished along the continuum of the course of a disorder (cf. Cosci & Fava, 2013; McGorry et al., 2006). Stage 0 is characterized by an at-risk state with no or few symptoms. In Stage 1, a person has symptoms yielding mild distress and disability that are either general and undifferentiated or suggestive of a specific disorder. These symptoms may culminate into Stage 2 where a diagnostic threshold is passed for a full episode of a circumscribed disorder with moderate-severe distress and disability. This may be followed by Stage 3 that is characterized by incomplete remission and persistent symptoms of the Stage 2 disorder with ongoing impairment or relapses. Eventually, a Stage 4 may be reached, characterized by persistent, unremitting disorder causing severe distress and disability.

Drawing from this general framework and literature on PTSD (McFarlane & Bryant, 2017), we provided a nascent formulation of a clinical staging framework of disordered grief (Boelen et al., 2019). This framework distinguishes four stages in the development of grief from mild responses to severe, unremitting disturbance (see Table 1.1). *Stage 0* refers to the experience of individuals who have lost a close person with whom they shared a meaningful relationship; they experience mild signs of grief, occurring transiently in many bereaved people, in the context of some risk factors, which could amplify the risk of worsening of symptoms if insufficiently countered by protective factors. *Stage 1* is characterized by non-specific symptoms and/or subclinical signs of PGD. At this stage, individuals may experience diffuse signs of depression (e.g., absence of positive affect, low mood, a sense of worthlessness or hopelessness) or anxiety (growing worry, hypervigilance, and agitation). In addition, an exacerbation of symptoms of acute separation distress and traumatic distress may be experienced, with these symptoms becoming more distressing, disabling, and uncontrollable.

Table 1.1 Hypothetical staging, profiling, and stepped care model for prolonged grief disorder

Stage	*Characteristics*	*Clinical characteristics*	*Risk and protective factors*	*Interventions*
0	Confronted with the death of a close person; signs of acute separation distress (e.g., sadness, yearning)		Loss: Low risk (single, timely, natural loss). Social context: Supporting, moderate-high socioeconomic status (SES).	None or community support.
1	a) Undifferentiated symptoms of grief, dysphoria, and/or anxiety	Distress: mild. Functional impairment: mild. Timing: >3 months since death.	Personality: Some vulnerable personality traits. Loss: Low risk (e.g., anticipated death). Social context: Supporting, moderate-high SES.	Self-help, psycho-education, watchful waiting.
	b) Subsyndromal signs of PGD (e.g., increasing or non-improving separation distress, avoidance, difficulties accepting the loss)	Distress: mild. Functional impairment: mild. Timing: >3 months since death.	Personality: Some vulnerable personality traits. Loss: Low risk with additional stressors or high-risk (sudden, untimely, and/or traumatic loss). Social context: Supporting, low-moderate SES.	Non-assisted online interventions, counselling, social work.
2	First episode of full-threshold PGD	Distress: moderate-severe. Functional impairment: moderate-severe, in multiple areas. Timing: >6 months since death. Comorbidity: increasing internalizing and/or externalizing symptoms.	Personality: Vulnerable personality, previous loss experiences. Loss: High-risk. Social Context: Impaired support, low SES.	Psychotherapy (e.g., "prolonged grief treatment", cognitive behavioral therapy).

(*Continued*)

Table 1.1 (Continued)

Stage	*Characteristics*	*Clinical characteristics*	*Risk and protective factors*	*Interventions*
3	Persistent (fluctuating) PGD symptoms, in the form of a) Incomplete remission of first episode b) Recurrence or relapse, persistent impairments c) Multiple relapses or worsening following incomplete treatment response	Distress: severe. Functional impairment: severe, in multiple areas. Timing: >12 months since death Comorbidity: clinically significant internalizing and/ or externalizing symptoms.	Personality: Vulnerable personality, previous loss experiences. Loss: High-risk, multiple, and/ or violent or unnatural loss. Social context: Lack of support, migration, low SES.	Psychotherapy. Day patient treatment. Medication.
4	Unremitting PGD of increasing chronicity	Distress: severe. Functional impairment: severe, in multiple areas. Timing: >12 months since death. Comorbidity: unremitting internalizing and/or externalizing symptoms.	Personality: Vulnerable personality, previous loss experiences, childhood adversity Loss: High-risk, traumatic, and multiple Context: Lack of social support, migration, low SES.	Day patient/ inpatient treatment, medication.

In a minority, Stage 1 may culminate in *Stage 2* where the person passes the diagnostic threshold for PGD, either with or without accompanying symptoms of traumatic distress (e.g., a sense of current threat, re-experiencing threatening events), depression (e.g., lack of positive affect, anhedonia), or with other emotional symptoms (e.g., impaired impulse control or substance use). At this stage, symptoms cause moderate to severe distress, impairing functioning in multiple domains. Considering the time since the death occurred, we propose that individuals can only enter Stage 2 beyond the first half year of bereavement. Severe PGD symptoms causing profound distress and dysfunction in the first six months after a loss would then be classified as Stage 1 grief.

Stage 2 may be followed by *Stage 3*, characterized by the persistence of PGD, yielding severe distress and functional disability in multiple areas, and clinically significant levels of accompanying internalizing or externalizing symptoms. In accord with general staging models, Stage 3 PGD may manifest as (a) incompletely remitted severe PGD, (b) recurrence of an episodes of full-blown PGD after a period of significant symptom reduction and improved functioning, or (c) multiple recurring episodes of intense PGD with persistent functional impairments in multiple areas, with (more often than not) comorbid symptomatology. Clinical experience suggests that Stage 3 disordered grief is typically marked by relatively steady levels of PGD rather than symptom fluctuations. However, identifying the symptom patterns of this stage, the inflection point where PGD becomes chronic, and the role of comorbid symptoms remain areas for future research.

Once the Stage 3 symptoms have been entrenched and insufficient symptom reduction has occurred following treatment, the probability rises that people enter *Stage 4*. In this preliminary formulation of this staging model, we propose that this most serious stage in the development of loss-related psychopathology is characterized by unremitting PGD and comorbid mental disorders, combined with severe manifestations of distress (e.g., uninterrupted emotional pain) and disability (e.g., inability to function in almost all areas, suicidality, impaired self-care).

Profiling hypothesized stages of PGD

Profiling refers to the process of assigning descriptive characteristics to each disorder stage. It also encompasses the identification of risk and protective factors associated with disorder progression and improvement, including static sociodemographic and loss-related variables, as well as contextual factors and biopsychological mechanisms amenable to change (cf. Voshaar et al., 2015). Profiling PGD and its hypothesized stages helps to create a more comprehensive picture of the phenomenology of PGD and its possible development over time. Moreover, it allows for better assessment of unhealthy grief, improves the timely identification of vulnerable groups, and helps to define targets for treatment tailored to individual needs and risks. Below, we will provide examples of clinical characteristics, static risk and protective factors, and potentially modifiable biopsychosocial mechanisms that could have a place in this nascent model.

Clinical characteristics

Clinical characteristics include the nature, duration, frequency, and intensity of symptoms, and the distress and disability caused by these symptoms. For example, while separation distress occurs at all stages, it tends to be more prolonged, frequent, and pervasive at advanced stages. Occasional avoidance behavior is healthy and only becomes indicative of disordered grief when it is not balanced by moments of confronting the loss, or when it is accompanied by intense fear and withdrawal. Similarly, seeking proximity to reminders of the lost person is healthy, unless the individual is reluctant to acknowledge the irreversibility of the loss and consistently avoids focusing on the future without the lost person. Distress and disability are two further clinical characteristics signifying disorder progression. More than by the nature of specific symptoms, the worsening of grief is characterized by increased mental suffering and by greater difficulties to perform daily routines and function effectively in different contexts. Social functioning is critical. Relevant dimensions include the extent of social participation versus isolation, social inclusion versus exclusion, and occupational functioning versus disengagement. It is conceivable that more advanced stages of disordered grief are characterized by fewer social resources and greater social vulnerability (McGorry et al., 2006). Time since loss is important. Arguably, we should avoid referring to full-blown Stage 2 PGD before the first six months have passed since a death, and only consider referring to grief as Stage 3 PGD beyond the first anniversary of the loss. The nature of grief reactions matters, with more obscure and bizarre responses (e.g., complete denial of the death, impaired reality testing on confrontation with hallucinatory grief experiences) signaling a possible worsening of the grief (cf. Kamp et al., 2020). Comorbidity is important with the likelihood of individuals experiencing severe comorbid disorders alongside the grief increasing progressively from Stage 2 to Stage 3 to Stage 4. Response to treatment is another key clinical characteristic. A favorable response to treatment at a given stage suggests that progression to a more severe stage of grief is less likely. And caution may be applied in suggesting that someone is approaching a more severe stage of grief before effective treatments have been applied at the current stage.

Relatively static risk and protective factors

Apart from clinical characteristics that are *descriptive* more than *predictive* of stages, some static risk and protective factors may be predictive more than descriptive of how grief may develop (also see Buur et al., 2024; Heeke et al., 2019; and Chapter 3). These include sociodemographic variables, pre-loss vulnerabilities, characteristics of the loss, and circumstances in the loss's aftermath. Regarding sociodemographic variables, evidence indicates that bereavement outcomes are worse for women, elderly people, and people with lower education and lower socioeconomic status. Pre-loss vulnerabilities include mental and physical health problems existing before the loss occurred, increased neuroticism, attachment insecurity, and attachment anxiety. Regarding characteristics of the loss, there is evidence that the loss of a closer attachment figure, dependency in the relationship, deaths that occur suddenly, and deaths from unnatural and violent causes increase the risk of disabling grief. Relevant aspects of the loss's aftermath are socioeconomic declines (e.g., when the deceased was the breadwinner), tedious legal procedures (e.g., when others are accountable for the death), negative social support, and perceived stigmatization. Relatively static protective factors are, to some extent, the inverse of certain risk factors. Sociodemographic protective factors include male gender, younger age, higher educational attainment, and better socioeconomic status. Additionally, social and relational protective factors encompass greater pre-loss mental and physical health, stable attachment relationships, and robust social support systems. Loss-related and cultural protective factors include the foreseeability of the loss and the ability to engage in desired preparatory activities.

Modifiable biopsychosocial mechanisms

Predicting and influencing people's movement across disorder stages is a (or *the*) key goal of clinical staging (cf. Cosci & Fava, 2013). Knowledge about neurobiological, psychological, and social variables that are amenable to change is imperative to this goal. Knowledge about neurobiological variables is limited. There is evidence that protracted grief relates to increased brain activity in the neurobiological reward system, reduction of serotonergic brain activity, and altered diurnal cortisol profiles (Kakarala et al., 2020; O'Connor, 2021). Current knowledge in this area is too limited to allow treatment implications. However, gaining a deeper understanding of the neurobiological mechanisms associated with PGD and its stages is valuable, particularly for informing the development of pharmacological interventions (see also Chapter 10).

More is known about psychological variables. Grief theories (Chapter 4) have linked the intensification and persistence of grief with too much loss-oriented coping and too little restoration orientation (Stroebe & Schut, 1999), rigid negative appraisals and depressive and anxious avoidance strategies (Boelen et al., 2006), and other unhelpful coping behaviors (Boddez, 2018), a merged identity with the deceased (Maccallum & Bryant, 2013), inadequate integration of the loss into one's self-concept and relationship model to accommodate the separation (Boelen et al., 2006; Shear & Shair, 2005), and inability to attribute adaptive meanings to a loss (Milman et al., 2017; Smid, 2020). These theories differ in focus and terminology, but all suggest that acute grief persists due to a mismatch between one's internal understanding of self and the relationship with the lost person and external reality, along with maladaptive appraisals and avoidant coping. While the relationship between psychological variables and stages requires further investigation, it is plausible that as disordered grief progresses, appraisals and meanings become increasingly negative, rigid, and stable, while avoidant coping may affect a broader range of life domains, including social interactions, work, and leisure activities.

The relationship between risk factors and grief remains an area for future investigation. It seems plausible that an individual with a greater number of risk factors and fewer protective factors may be more susceptible to advance to a more severe stage of grief. It is also possible that certain factors (e.g., losing one's only child, violent mode of death) have a stronger impact on grief than others (e.g., sociodemographic variables). Moreover, risk factors are likely to interact, such as when the loss of an only child has a devastating impact that can be significantly exacerbated if it was caused by violence and further inflated by tumultuous publicity, legal trials, and lack of social support. The relationship between external, static factors (the death's circumstances) and individual, dynamic factors (e.g., appraisals, coping behaviors) also warrants further exploration, with the latter likely exerting a stronger influence on the grief process than the former (Haehner et al., 2024). Table 1.1 includes examples of possible combinations of stages and profiling characteristics.

Stepped bereavement care

This nascent formulation of clinical stages and profiling characteristics creates a template for a stepped or tiered approach to bereavement care, where each stage in the progression of disordered grief relates to its own set of interventions (cf. Aoun et al., 2017; Killikelly et al., 2021). Several principles underlie the distinction between different interventions within this framework. First, interventions offered in early stages are less intense and invasive than interventions for later stages. Second, interventions should optimally influence malleable biopsychosocial variables affecting the grief at each stage. Third, interventions are evaluated in terms of their ability to mitigate current symptoms as well as to prevent progression to more advanced stages of the disorder (McGorry et al., 2006).

In our emerging model, stages can be combined with various interventions. At *Stage 0*, informal support from family and friends may suffice for most people. Public health interventions, such as awareness campaigns to increase grief literacy (Breen et al., 2022), could help make the social environment more attuned to the needs of bereaved individuals and encourage them to communicate these needs. Ideally, there should be a variety of resources available, tailored to the individual characteristics of each mourner. For those with stronger intellectual and social resources, psycho-education, self-help books, and unassisted online support may be suitable. For individuals who are more intellectually and socially vulnerable, "watchful waiting" by a family doctor (monitoring symptoms to enable timely intervention) and participation in a peer support group might be recommended.

At *Stage 1*, care by more professionally trained clinical workers is indicated. That should be focused both on mitigating the current distress and preventing exacerbation of symptoms. Stage 1 presents a crucial window of opportunity for preventative care to reduce the risk of a full-blown disorder. Ideally, multiple options for such care are available, allowing individuals to obtain optimal care aligning with their profiling characteristics. For instance, peer-support groups led by trained non-mental health specialists (e.g., nurses) or experts by experience may suffice for specific groups united by a similar type of loss (e.g., loss to suicide, late-life spousal loss). Individuals experiencing subsyndromal PGD may benefit from self-guided or therapist-guided online cognitive behavioral therapy which appears to be effective in preventing the progression of grief (e.g., Reitsma et al., 2023). Individuals experiencing more diffuse subclinical mental health issues should ideally be offered transdiagnostic preventative interventions, targeting commonalities of different emotional symptoms (cf. Moses & Barlow, 2006).

At *Stage 2*, the diagnostic threshold for PGD is passed. Then, evidence-based treatments delivered by trained health care professionals are indicated. Several such treatments have been developed, including "prolonged grief treatment" (Shear et al., 2005, 2014, 2016), cognitive behavioral therapy (Boelen et al., 2007; Bryant et al., 2014, 2024; Rosner et al., 2014, 2025), and internet-based CBT (Treml et al., 2021; Wagner et al., 2006). For people with vulnerable social contexts, group or systemic interventions may be preferred over individual therapies (e.g., Kealy et al., 2017; Sandler et al., 2016). At this stage too, multiple treatment options are ideally available. Access to interventions tailored to specific clinical features and circumstances of the loss would be beneficial. It is worth noting that some cognitive behavioral treatments have been developed and tested, tailored to subgroups of people experiencing traumatic loss, including loss due to homicide (Van Denderen et al., 2018), suicidal loss (Treml et al., 2021), and traffic accidents (Lenferink et al., 2023). CBT-based approaches to the treatment of PGD in other subgroups such as children, older adults, and refugees are described elsewhere in this book.

At *Stage 3*, the clinical picture is more complex. At this stage, an adequate dose, duration, and application of evidence-based PGD-focused Stage 2 treatment has not led to full remission. Ongoing psychological treatment is likely indicated for incompletely remitted and persistent grief at this stage. This should possibly be supplemented by other treatment modalities to achieve further symptom reduction, such as pharmacological treatment (in case of severe additional depression or anxiety), systemic interventions (when dysfunctional family dynamics contribute to the maintenance of symptoms), or support from a social worker (when difficulties in psychosocial rehabilitation are a contributing factor). In case the Stage 3 grief is characterized by frequent relapses, some form of maintenance treatment is indicated, focused on monitoring warning signs of relapse, maintaining activities that enhance stable functioning, and taking appropriate measures to prevent relapse.

Stage 4 grief is the most debilitating manifestation of grief. Specialized care services are needed to remediate the grief at this stage. This requires a patient-centered care approach in which clinical features of the most severe symptoms, current conditions that maintain the symptoms, and social resources, as well as the interplay between them, are unraveled and mapped. Based on this, interventions are deployed that can achieve optimal stability or improvement. Examples of interventions include maintenance pharmacotherapy for symptoms for which medication is proven effective (Chapter 10), rehabilitation-focused treatments (fostering connectedness, hope, identity, meaning, and empowerment; Leamy et al., 2011), and multimodal treatments synergizing with the person grief's clinical characteristics and maintaining mechanisms. The key aims of Stage 4 interventions are to enhance functioning, support social participation (e.g., physical activity, work, caregiving, recreation), and halt further mental and physical deterioration and self-neglect.

Conclusions and discussion

The inclusion of PGD in DSM-5-TR and ICD-11 has brought bereavement research and care at a tipping point. The awareness that bereavement can cause serious mental health problems has grown, and clinicians and researchers face the challenge to improve options for the timely identification and treatment of disordered grief (Killikelly et al., 2021). As noted above, studies indicate that approximately 3%–5% of people develop PGD, making disordered grief the exception rather than the norm. However, for the obvious reason that deaths occur frequently, in absolute terms, large numbers of people are affected by this disorder each year. Additionally, Keyes et al.'s (2014) study shows that unexpected deaths can precipitate various other emotional disorders. Thus, not every loss results in a psychological disorder, but when disorders occur, losses often play a significant role in activating or intensifying them. Taken together, emotional problems following loss are a significant public health issue.

We addressed several challenges for bereavement research and care and introduced a nascent formulation of a clinical staging model of grief. This approach has the potential to address some of these challenges and may serve as a roadmap for future developments in this research and care. Specifically, with respect to the artificial distinction between healthy and unhealthy grief, the staging approach permits the distinction between different positions along the continuum of transient to chronic/pervasive grief. It permits combining a dimensional and categorical approach. That is, it characterizes the course of grief along a dimension from transient to severe and unremitting grief, while recognizing that, at some point, people meet criteria for full PGD as per DSM-5-TR or ICD-11.

Regarding challenges related to risk and protective factors, the staging typology may help identify knowledge gaps. Relevant questions pertain to how factors interact in affecting grief, what factors determine the movement from one stage to the next, and what variables determine extensively protracted (e.g., Stage 4) grief. The framework could guide the study of unexplored psychobiosocial variables, focusing on variables that are amenable to change and thus potential targets for intervention. For instance, research has so far mostly concentrated on negative, maladaptive processes predicting problematic grief, but may benefit from focusing on appraisals and coping behaviors conferring protection to such grief. An increased understanding of the neurobiological mechanisms underlying protracted grief may aid in the development of pharmacological interventions (cf. McFarlane & Bryant, 2017). A deeper understanding of the social mechanisms involved in grief may expand the range of available systematic or community interventions (cf. Maciejewski et al., 2022).

A broader understanding of clinical characteristics is important. It seems clear that as grief progresses into full-blown PGD and, in some cases, further into chronicity, there is a corresponding increase in emotional distress, disability, and dysfunction across multiple domains. But more work is needed to understand, e.g., the nature of "illness extension" across stages, referring to increased complexity and comorbid problems beyond the initial PGD symptoms. For instance, akin to staging in PTSD, extension may be marked by marked deterioration in information processing and stress regulation (cf. Nijdam et al., 2023). Furthermore, evidence suggests that progression of

PGD is associated with increased risk of comorbid internalizing symptoms (anxiety, depression; Komischke-Konnerup et al., 2021) and sleep dysregulation (Lancel et al., 2020). However, an outstanding question is to what extent PGD progression coincides with externalizing problems (impaired impulse control, substance use). More fundamentally, the staging model proposed here has a disorder-specific approach, implying that PGD symptoms are at the heart of post-loss psychopathology, to which other problems may be added as extensions of the problems. Ultimately however, it may turn out that a transdiagnostic model, that describes a range of psychopathology for which the death of close persons is an etiological factor, offers a more accurate reflection of emotional problems after loss (cf. McFarlane & Bryant, 2017).

Looking at the third challenge, to improve bereavement care, the staging approach moves away from the binary distinction between healthy/normal and unhealthy/pathological/disordered grief. This creates space to develop low-threshold interventions that can be offered outside the medical realm of psychiatric care. Moreover, this could increase recognition that interventions with a light touch suffice for some, but definitely not for all forms of grief. More knowledge about the manifestations and underlying mechanisms of the earliest stage of disturbed grief is critical to improve much-needed public health and community-based interventions. Likewise, increased knowledge about undifferentiated or preclinical manifestations of problematic grief could inform the development of preventive interventions and help identify who does and does not require early care. There is a reason to believe that some individuals—such as those experiencing intense and disabling grief following the sudden loss of a minor child—may benefit from targeted therapy even within the first few months after the loss.

A key aim of applying a clinical staging approach is to improve options for bereavement care and treatment that is proportional to the needs and suffering of mourners at different stages. This implies offering light interventions for benign grief and more intense treatment to those who need it. Arguably, so far, too few people with full-blown (Stage 2) PGD benefit from good treatments. This is likely due to a combination of factors, including the poor identification of these individuals (because in clinical practice, there is still little knowledge about PGD and about tools measuring it properly) and the fact that interventions that have proven effective (e.g., exposure, "prolonged grief treatment") have not been widely disseminated. It is promising, however, that clinicians are increasingly developing interventions tailored to specific subgroups, distinguished by the circumstances of the loss (e.g., specialized cognitive behavioral therapy for those bereaved by suicide), demographic characteristics (e.g., approaches for the elderly and children, as discussed elsewhere in this book), and care needs (e.g., low-intensity approaches using eHealth, and intensive face-to-face therapy). One major task of the field of bereavement research and care is to disseminate effective treatments, to make these more readily available. Another major challenge is improving care for individuals in Stage 4 grief, who are chronically and profoundly affected by the loss of an attachment figure.

Broader adaptation of the concept of staging in bereavement care has yet to occur. With the recent inclusion of PGD in DSM-5-TR and ICD-11, alongside persistent concerns that the dichotomous classification of normal and disordered grief may stigmatize individuals experiencing prolonged grief, there is a pressing need for a framework that accounts for the fluidity of grief, facilitates timely preventive interventions, and enables targeted treatment for those most severely affected. The staging model introduced here offers such a framework. It is a prototype, an initial formulation of how grief may progress. Profiling characteristics should gradually be added to the model to create a more comprehensive description of the phenomenology, clinical features, and underlying mechanisms of different manifestations and levels of grief, enabling proportional bereavement care.

Acknowledgment

The author used ChatGPT (OpenAI, Version 4.0) to improve the grammar and fluency of the English language in the manuscript. No content was generated by the tool; all ideas, interpretations, and conclusions are the authors' own.

References

American Psychiatric Association (2022). *Diagnostic and statistical manual of mental disorders, fifth edition, text revision (DSM-5-TR)*. APA. https://doi.org/10.1176/appi.books.9780890425787

Aoun, S. M., Rumbold, B., Howting, D., Bolleter, A., & Breen, L. J. (2017). Bereavement support for family caregivers: The gap between guidelines and practice in palliative care. *PloS One*, *12*(10), e0184750. https://doi.org/10.1371/journal.pone.0184750

Bandini, J. (2015). The medicalization of bereavement: (Ab)normal grief in the DSM-5. *Death Studies*, *39*(6), 347–352. https://doi.org/10.1080/07481187.2014.951498

Boddez, Y. (2018). The presence of your absence: A conditioning theory of grief, *Behaviour Research and Therapy*, *106*, 18–27. https://doi.org/10.1016/j.brat.2018.04.006

Boelen, P. A., & Adamkovič, M. (2024). Prevalence and correlates of ICD-11-based prolonged grief disorder in a representative Slovakian sample of recently bereaved adults. *European Journal of Psychotraumatology*, *15*(1), 2381368. https://doi.org/10.1080/20008066.2024.2381368

Boelen, P. A., de Keijser, J., van den Hout, M. A., & van den Bout, J. (2007). Treatment of complicated grief: A comparison between cognitive-behavioral therapy and supportive counseling. *Journal of Consulting and Clinical Psychology*, *75*(2), 277–284. https://doi.org/10.1037/0022-006X.75.2.277

Boelen, P. A., Olff, M., & Smid, G. E. (2019). Traumatic loss: Mental health consequences and implications for treatment and prevention. *European Journal of Psychotraumatology*, *10*(1). https://doi.org/10.1080/20008198.2019.1591331

Boelen, P. A., & Prigerson, H. G. (2007). The influence of symptoms of prolonged grief disorder, depression, and anxiety on quality of life among bereaved adults: A prospective study. *European Archives of Psychiatry and Clinical Neuroscience*, *257*(8), 444–452. https://doi.org/10.1007/s00406-007-0744-0

Boelen, P. A., van den Hout, M. A., & van den Bout, J. (2006). A cognitive-behavioral conceptualization of complicated grief. *Clinical Psychology: Science and Practice*, *13*(2), 109–128. https://doi.org/10.1111/j.1468-2850.2006.00013.x

Breen, L. J., Kawashima, D., Joy, K., Cadell, S., Roth, D., Chow, A., & Macdonald, M. E. (2022). Grief literacy: A call to action for compassionate communities. *Death Studies*, *46*(2), 425–433. https://doi.org/10.1080/07481187.2020.1739780

Bryant, R. A., Andrew, E., & Korgaonkar, M. S. (2021). Distinct neural mechanisms of emotional processing in prolonged grief disorder. *Psychological Medicine*, *51*(4), 587–595. https://doi.org/10.1017/S0033291719003507

Bryant, R. A., Azevedo, S., Yadav, S., Cahill, C., Kenny, L., Maccallum, F., Tran, J., Choi-Christou, J., Rawson, N., Tockar, J., Garber, B., Keyan, D., & Dawson, K. S. (2024). Cognitive behavior therapy vs mindfulness in treatment of prolonged grief disorder: A randomized clinical trial. *JAMA Psychiatry*, *81*(7), 646–654.

Bryant, R. A., Kenny, L., Joscelyne, A., Rawson, N., Maccallum, F., Cahill, C., Hopwood, S., Aderka, I., & Nickerson, A. (2014). Treating prolonged grief disorder: A randomized clinical trial. *JAMA Psychiatry*, *71*(12), 1332–1339. https://doi.org/10.1001/jamapsychiatry.2014.1600

Buur, C., Zachariae, R., Komischke-Konnerup, K. B., Marello, M. M., Schierff, L. H., & O'Connor, M. (2024). Risk factors for prolonged grief symptoms: A systematic review and meta-analysis, *Clinical Psychology Review*, *107*, 102375. https://doi.org/10.1016/j.cpr.2023.102375

Comtesse, H., Smid, G. E., Rummel, A. M., Spreeuwenberg, P., Lundorff, M., & Dückers, M. L. A. (2024). Cross-national analysis of the prevalence of prolonged grief disorder. *Journal of Affective Disorders*, *350*, 359–365. https://doi.org/10.1016/j.jad.2024.01.094

Cosci, F., & Fava, G. A. (2013). Staging of mental disorders: Systematic review. *Psychotherapy and Psychosomatics*, *82*(1), 20–34. https://doi.org/10.1159/000342243

Currier, J. M., Neimeyer, R. A., & Berman, J. S. (2008). The effectiveness of psychotherapeutic interventions for bereaved persons: A comprehensive quantitative review. *Psychological Bulletin*, *134*(5), 648–661. https://doi.org/10.1037/0033-2909.134.5.648

Djelantik, A. A. A. M. J., Robinaugh, D. J., Kleber, R. J., Smid, G. E., & Boelen, P. A. (2020a). Symptomatology following loss and trauma: Latent class and network analyses of prolonged grief disorder, posttraumatic stress disorder, and depression in a treatment-seeking trauma-exposed sample. *Depression and Anxiety*, *37*(1), 26–34. https://doi.org/10.1002/da.22880

Djelantik, A. A. A. M. J., Smid, G. E., Mroz, A., Kleber, R. J., & Boelen, P. A. (2020b). The prevalence of prolonged grief disorder in bereaved individuals following unnatural losses: Systematic review and meta regression analysis. *Journal of Affective Disorders*, *265*, 146–156, https://doi.org/10.1016/j.jad.2020.01.034

Galatzer-Levy, I. R., Huang, S. H., & Bonanno, G. A. (2018). Trajectories of resilience and dysfunction following potential trauma: A review and statistical evaluation. *Clinical Psychology Review*, *63*, 41–55, https://doi.org/10.1016/j.cpr.2018.05.008

Haehner, P., Würtz, F., Kritzler, S., Kunna, M., Luhmann, M., & Woud, M. L. (2024). The relationship between the perception of major life events and depression: A systematic scoping review and meta-analysis. *Journal of Affective Disorders*, *349*, 145–157, https://doi.org/10.1016/j.jad.2024.01.042

Heeke, C., Kampisiou, C., Niemeyer, H., & Knaevelsrud, C. (2019). A systematic review and meta-analysis of correlates of prolonged grief disorder in adults exposed to violent loss. *European Journal of Psychotraumatology*, *10*(1), 1583524. https://doi.org/10.1080/20008198.2019.1583524

Johannsen, M., Damholdt, M. F., Zachariae, R., Lundorff, M., Farver-Vestergaard, I., & O'Connor, M. (2019). Psychological interventions for grief in adults: A systematic review and meta-analysis of randomized controlled trials. *Journal of Affective Disorders*, *253*, 69–86.

Kakarala, S. E., Roberts, K. E., Rogers, M., Coats, T., Falzarano, F., Gang, J., Chilov, M., Avery, J., Maciejewski, P. K., Lichtenthal, W. G., & Prigerson, H. G. (2020). The neurobiological reward system in prolonged grief disorder (PGD): A systematic review. *Psychiatry Research Neuroimaging*, *303*, 111135. https://doi.org/10.1016/j.pscychresns.2020.111135

Kamp, K. S., Steffen, E. M., Alderson-Day, B., Allen, P., Austad, A., Hayes, J., Larøi, F., Ratcliffe, M., & Sabucedo, P. (2020). Sensory and quasi-sensory experiences of the deceased in bereavement: An interdisciplinary and integrative review. *Schizophrenia Bulletin*, *46*(6), 1367–1381. https://doi.org/10.1093/schbul/sbaa113

Kealy, D., Sierra-Hernandez, C. A., Piper, W. E., Joyce, A. S., Weideman, R., & Ogrodniczuk, J. S. (2017). Short-term group therapy for complicated grief: The relationship between Patients' in-session reflection and outcome. *Psychiatry*, *80*(2), 125–138. https://doi.org/10.1080/00332747.2016.1220231

Keyes, K. M., Pratt, C., Galea, S., McLaughlin, K. A., Koenen, K. C., & Shear, M. K. (2014). The burden of loss: Unexpected death of a loved one and psychiatric disorders across the life course in a national study. *American Journal of Psychiatry*, *171*, 864–871.

Killikelly, C., Smid, G. E., Wagner, B., & Boelen, P. A. (2021). Responding to the new international classification of diseases-11 prolonged grief disorder during the COVID-19 pandemic: A new bereavement network and three-tiered model of care. *Public Health*, *191*, 85–90. https://doi.org/10.1016/j.puhe.2020.10.034

Komischke-Konnerup, K. B., Zachariae, R., Johannsen, M., Nielsen, L. D., & OConnor, M. (2021). Co-occurrence of prolonged grief symptoms and symptoms of depression, anxiety, and posttraumatic stress in bereaved adults: A systematic review and meta-analysis. *Journal of Affective Disorders Reports*, *4*, 100140. https://doi.org/10.1016/j.jadr.2021.100140

Lancel, M., Stroebe, M., & Eisma, M. C. (2020). Sleep disturbances in bereavement: A systematic review. *Sleep Medicine Reviews*, *53*, 101331. https://doi.org/10.1016/j.smrv.2020.101331

Leamy, M., Bird, V., Le Boutillier, C., Williams, J., & Slade, M. (2011). Conceptual framework for personal recovery in mental health: Systematic review and narrative synthesis. *The British Journal of Psychiatry*, *199*(6), 445–452. https://doi.org/10.1192/bjp.bp.110.083733

Lenferink, L. I. M., Eisma, M. C., Buiter, M. Y., de Keijser, J., & Boelen, P. A. (2023). Online cognitive behavioral therapy for prolonged grief after traumatic loss: A randomized waitlist-controlled trial. *Cognitive Behaviour Therapy*, *52*(5), 508–522. https://doi.org/10.1080/16506073.2023.2225744

Litz, B. T., Schorr, Y., Delaney, E., Au, T., Papa, A., Fox, A. B., Morris, S., Nickerson, A., Block, S., & Prigerson, H. G. (2014). A randomized controlled trial of an internet-based therapist-assisted indicated preventive intervention for prolonged grief disorder. *Behaviour Research and Therapy*, *61*, 23–34. https://doi.org/10.1016/j.brat.2014.07.005

Lundorff, M., Holmgren, H., Zachariae, R., Farver-Vestergaard, I., & O'Connor, M. (2017). Prevalence of prolonged grief disorder in adult bereavement: A systematic review and meta-analysis. *Journal of Affective Disorders*, *212*, 138–149. https://doi.org/10.1016/j.jad.2017.01.030

Maccallum, F., & Bryant, R. A. (2013). A cognitive attachment model of prolonged grief: Integrating attachments, memory, and identity. *Clinical Psychology Review*, *33*(6), 713–727. https://doi.org/10.1016/j.cpr.2013.05.001

Maciejewski, P. K., Falzarano, F. B., She, W. J., Lichtenthal, W. G., & Prigerson, H. G. (2022). A micro-sociological theory of adjustment to loss. *Current Opinion in Psychology*, *43*, 96–101. https://doi.org/10.1016/j.copsyc.2021.06.016

McFarlane, A. C., & Bryant, R. A. (2017). PTSD: The need to use emerging knowledge to improve systems of care and clinical practice in Australia. *Australasian Psychiatry: Bulletin of Royal Australian and New Zealand College of Psychiatrists*, *25*(4), 329–331. https://doi.org/10.1177/1039856217716297

McFarlane, A. C., Lawrence-Wood, Van Hooff, M., Malhi, G. S., & Yehuda, R. (2017). The need to take a staging approach to the biological mechanisms of PTSD and its treatment. *Current Psychiatry Reports*, *19*(2017), 10.

McGorry, P. D., Hickie, I. B., Yung, A. R., Pantelis, C., & Jackson, H. J. (2006). Clinical staging of psychiatric disorders: A heuristic framework for choosing earlier, safer and more effective interventions. *The Australian and New Zealand Journal of Psychiatry*, *40*(8), 616–622. https://doi.org/10.1080/j.1440-1614.2006.01860.x

Milman, E., Neimeyer, R. A., Fitzpatrick, M., MacKinnon, C. J., Muis, K. R., & Cohen, S. R. (2017). Prolonged grief symptomatology following violent loss: The mediating role of meaning. *European Journal of Psychotraumatology*, *8*(Supp 6), 1503522. https://doi.org/10.1080/20008198.2018.1503522

Moses, E. B., & Barlow, D. H. (2006). A new unified treatment approach for emotional disorders based on emotion science. *Current Directions in Psychological Science*, *15*(3), 146–150. https://doi.org/10.1111/j.0963-7214.2006.00425.x

Nijdam, M. J., Vermetten, E., & McFarlane, A. C. (2023). Toward staging differentiation for posttraumatic stress disorder treatment. *Acta Psychiatrica Scandinavica*, *147*(1), 65–80. https://doi.org/10.1111/acps.13520

O'Connor, M. F. (2021). *The grieving brain: The surprising science of how we learn from love and loss.* HarperOne.

Prigerson, H. G., Frank, E., Kasl, S. V., Reynolds, C. F. III, Anderson, B., Zubenko, G. S., Houck, P. R., George, C. J., & Kupfer, D. J. (1995). Complicated grief and bereavement-related depression as distinct disorders: Preliminary empirical validation in elderly bereaved spouses. *The American Journal of Psychiatry*, *152*(1), 22–30. https://doi.org/10.1176/ajp.152.1.22

Prigerson, H. G., Singer, J., & Killikelly, C. (2024). Prolonged grief disorder: Addressing misconceptions with evidence. *The American Journal of Geriatric Psychiatry*, *32*(5), 527–534. https://doi.org/10.1016/j.jagp.2023.10.020

Reitsma, L., Boelen, P. A., de Keijser, J., & Lenferink, L. I. M. (2023). Self-guided online treatment of disturbed grief, posttraumatic stress, and depression in adults bereaved during the COVID-19 pandemic: A randomized controlled trial. *Behaviour Research and Therapy*, *163*, 104286. https://doi.org/10.1016/j.brat.2023.104286

Reynolds, C. F. III, Miller, M. D., Pasternak, R. E., Frank, E., Perel, J. M., Cornes, C., Houck, P. R., Mazumdar, S., Dew, M. A., & Kupfer, D. J. (1999). Treatment of bereavement-related major depressive episodes in later life: A controlled study of acute and continuation treatment with nortriptyline and interpersonal psychotherapy. *The American Journal of Psychiatry*, *156*(2), 202–208. https://doi.org/10.1176/ajp.156.2.202

Rosner, R., Comtesse, H., Vogel, A., & Doering, B. K. (2021). Prevalence of prolonged grief disorder. *Journal of Affective Disorders*, *287*, 301–307. https://doi.org/10.1016/j.jad.2021.03.058

Rosner, R., Pfoh, G., Kotoučová, M., & Hagl, M. (2014). Efficacy of an outpatient treatment for prolonged grief disorder: A randomized controlled clinical trial. *Journal of Affective Disorders*, *167*, 56–63. https://doi.org/10.1016/j.jad.2014.05.035

Rosner, R., Rau, J., Kersting, A., Rief, W., Steil, R., Rummel, A. M., Vogel, A., & Comtesse, H. (2025). Grief-specific cognitive behavioral therapy vs present-centered therapy: A randomized clinical trial. *JAMA Psychiatry*, *82*(2), 109–117. https://doi.org/10.1001/jamapsychiatry.2024.3409

Sandler, I., Tein, J. Y., Cham, H., Wolchik, S., & Ayers, T. (2016). Long-term effects of the Family Bereavement Program on spousally bereaved parents: Grief, mental health problems, alcohol problems, and coping efficacy. *Development and Psychopathology*, *28*(3), 801–818. https://doi.org/10.1017/S0954579416000328

Shear, K., Frank, E., Houck, P. R., & Reynolds, C. F. III. (2005). Treatment of complicated grief: A randomized controlled trial. *JAMA*, *293*(21), 2601–2608. https://doi.org/10.1001/jama.293.21.2601

Shear, M. K., Reynolds, C. F. III, Simon, N. M., Zisook, S., Wang, Y., Mauro, C., Duan, N., Lebowitz, B., & Skritskaya, N. (2016). Optimizing treatment of complicated grief: A randomized clinical trial. *JAMA Psychiatry*, *73*(7), 685–694. https://doi.org/10.1001/jamapsychiatry.2016.0892

Shear, M. K., & Shair, H. (2005). Attachment, loss, and complicated grief. *Developmental Psychobiology*, *47*, 253–267. https://doi.org/10.1002/dev.20091

Shear, M. K., Wang, Y., Skritskaya, N., Duan, N., Mauro, C., & Ghesquiere, A. (2014). Treatment of complicated grief in elderly persons: A randomized clinical trial. *JAMA Psychiatry*, *71*(11), 1287–1295. https://doi.org/10.1001/jamapsychiatry.2014.1242

Shevlin, M., Redican, E., Hyland, P., Murphy, J., Karatzias, T., McBride, O., Bennett, K., Butter, S., Hartman, T. K., Vallières, F., & Bentall, R. P. (2023). Symptoms and levels of ICD-11 prolonged grief disorder in a representative community sample of UK adults. *Social Psychiatry and Psychiatric Epidemiology*, *58*(10), 1535–1547. https://doi.org/10.1007/s00127-023-02469-1

Smid, G. E. (2020). A framework of meaning attribution following loss. *European Journal of Psychotraumatology*, *11*(1), 1776563. https://doi.org/10.1080/20008198.2020.1776563

Stroebe, M., & Schut, H. (1999). The dual process model of coping with bereavement: Rationale and description. *Death Studies*, *23*(3), 197–224. https://doi.org/10.1080/074811899201046

Treml, J., Linde, K., Brähler, E., & Kersting, A. (2024). Prolonged grief disorder in ICD-11 and DSM-5-TR: Differences in prevalence and diagnostic criteria. *Frontiers in Psychiatry*, *15*, 1266132. https://doi.org/10.3389/fpsyt.2024.1266132

Treml, J., Nagl, M., Linde, K., Kündiger, C., Peterhänsel, C., & Kersting, A. (2021). Efficacy of an internet-based cognitive-behavioural grief therapy for people bereaved by suicide: A randomized controlled trial. *European Journal of Psychotraumatology*, *12*(1), 1926650. https://doi.org/10.1080/20008198.2021.1926650

Van Denderen, M., de Keijser, J., Stewart, R., & Boelen, P. A. (2018). Treating complicated grief and posttraumatic stress in homicidally bereaved individuals: A randomized controlled trial. *Clinical Psychology & Psychotherapy*, *25*(4), 497–508. https://doi.org/10.1002/cpp.2183

Voshaar, R. C., Beekman, A. T., & Pachana, N. (2015). Clinical staging and profiling of late-life anxiety disorders; the need for collaboration and a life-span perspective. *International Psychogeriatrics*, *27*(7), 1057–1059. https://doi.org/10.1017/S1041610215000599

Wagner, B., Knaevelsrud, C., & Maercker, A. (2006). Internet-based cognitive-behavioral therapy for complicated grief: A randomized controlled trial. *Death Studies*, *30*(5), 429–453. https://doi.org/10.1080/07481180600614385

Wood, A. M., & Tarrier, N. (2010). Positive clinical psychology: A new vision and strategy for integrated research and practice. *Clinical Psychology Review*, *30*(7), 819–829. https://doi.org/10.1016/j.cpr.2010.06.003

World Health Organization [WHO] (2022). *International classification of diseases eleventh revision (ICD-11)*. WHO. https://icd.who.int/browse11/l-m/en

Chapter 2

Practice of clinical assessment of prolonged and traumatic grief

Anna Vogel, Hannah Comtesse, and Rita Rosner

Advantages of a structured diagnostic procedure for bereaved individuals

Diagnostics are a powerful tool for understanding bereaved persons and their symptomatology and thus provide crucial information for a tailored treatment. Implementing a standardized diagnostic procedure that allows for screening for prolonged and traumatic grief (PTG) in everyday clinical practice has several advantages.

First, direct questions regarding events of loss and their consequences send important messages to the bereaved person: "There is room for your experiences here, I am familiar with experiences like this and open to them." After an initial period of broad sympathy, many bereaved individuals often experience at some point that their environment becomes less open to their needs. Therefore, asking them directly about their experiences conveys signs of professionalism in dealing with loss events as well as empathy and compassion.

Second, direct questioning of loss events may impede avoidance tendencies at an early stage – on the part of both the interviewee and the interviewer. Since avoidance is a relevant symptom in both prolonged grief disorder (PGD) and posttraumatic stress disorder (PTSD), this is also commonly observed in interview interactions: loss events may not be reported spontaneously or only hesitantly or without distressing details. A structure can encourage the interviewers to ask clear, direct questions, especially if they are unsure of how to exactly address issues of loss and grief.

Finally, structured diagnostics allow interviewers to feel confident in conducting an interview without distressing the bereaved to an ethically unacceptable extent. Research (Andriessen et al., 2018; Jaffe et al., 2015) shows that discussing traumatic or loss events is stressful but not harmful in the long term. Therefore, it is ethically justifiable from a cost-benefit perspective. Focusing on validated diagnostic tools ensures that interviewers explore only necessary aspects, thus maintaining this cost-benefit ratio.

DOI: 10.4324/9781003429777-4

In the following paragraphs, we provide some insights into the diagnostic procedure that we have established in our outpatient clinic over the past years.

Practical guideline for diagnostics with persons with suspected PTG

The following is a step-by-step guide to the tasks required for a comprehensive diagnostic process.

Implement a screening question for loss events by default in your initial interview

Questions about traumatic events and significant loss should be included in every initial interview. Many bereaved persons may not associate their symptoms with a mental disorder and may not report loss events spontaneously. Some individuals avoid talking about symptoms because they are afraid, ashamed, or in pain. It is important to actively ask about loss events and thus signal a willingness to talk about them. Possible screening questions are listed in Box 2.1. The initial interview should provide enough time to explore participants' narratives. They may also talk about other losses, like losing a pet or a partner due to divorce. These losses do not meet PGD event criteria, but empathy is key for understanding the distress and symptoms they can cause.

It is important to adapt the procedure to the particular setting. In facilities that specifically support bereaved persons or offer specialized treatment of trauma- and stressor-related disorders, a loss is often the reason for (self-) referral. In these facilities, information about the loss and possible PGD symptoms can be obtained during registration, possibly from referring specialists, making the initial interview more precise.

In general mental health care facilities, however, it is crucial to ask questions about traumatic and loss experiences during the initial interview, even

Box 2.1 Formulation aids for loss-related screening questions in the initial interview

Have you lost one or more loved ones through death?

If so, to what extent does this loss still affect you today? In the past month, did you find yourself longing or yearning for the deceased and feel bad about the longing?

when participants are referred by other health care providers without any initial suspicion of stress due to (traumatic) loss.

Record stressful (loss) events in a structured way

A structured recording of stressful loss and life events is always advisable, even if prior information is available, e.g., from referring specialists, because not all persons spontaneously report all the stressful events that are decisive for the symptoms. The questions listed in Box 2.2 have proven to be useful in the specialty grief consultation hours of our outpatient clinic for the structured recording of individual loss events. To allow for more personal questions, it is recommended to ask the deceased's first name at the time of the initial interview and, if culturally appropriate, to use it thereafter.

Some of this information is also important for the valid evaluation of diagnostic results. Therefore, it is crucial to identify important anniversaries (e.g., anniversary of the loss, holidays, birthday of the deceased) and specific triggers that increase symptom distress. Stress levels may be higher than usual in the immediate vicinity of such events and might therefore decrease diagnostic validity.

Furthermore, the possibility and manner of saying goodbye to the deceased is often formative for those left behind. Limited opportunities to say goodbye, commemorate, or perform morning rituals, which is especially relevant for persons after (forced) migration, have been shown to be associated with ongoing distress (Smid et al., 2018a) and should therefore be recorded as part of the diagnostic process.

In the case of multiple or ambiguous losses, structured assessment using specifically designed checklists may be helpful, such as the Traumatic Grief

Box 2.2 Questions for the structured recording of loss-related data

- Name and relationship to the deceased?
- When did it happen?
- How old was [name] when [they] died?
- Was the death unexpected?
- What was the cause of death?
- Were you present when [name] died?
- Was it possible to say goodbye?
- Are there any missing loved ones?

Inventory Self Report Plus (TGI-SR+) version for multiple loss (Lenferink et al., 2022, available at https://osf.io/dpxcy) or the Ambiguous Loss Inventory Plus (Comtesse et al., 2023). The use of a trauma checklist, such as the Life Events Checklist for DSM-5 (LEC-5; Weathers et al., 2013), is recommended for the structured recording of traumatic events. In general, it is worthwhile to assess checklists embedded in a personal interview or in conjunction with specific assessment procedures to avoid overestimating rates of potentially traumatic events (Schoenleber et al., 2018).

Use a questionnaire to screen for PTG

Any time a participant reports a significant loss in the initial interview and expresses distress or impact on daily life as a result, the interviewer should introduce a screening instrument for PTG symptoms. In this chapter, instruments that focus on PGD are presented in more detail. In the case of traumatic loss, it is also advisable to use additional questionnaires and interviews that focus on PTSD symptoms.

Focusing on self-report measures that allow for screening for PGD according to DSM-5-TR and/or ICD-11, the measures listed in Table 2.1 currently exist. However, as research into the assessment of PGD is an evolving and dynamic field, it can be assumed that further research will supplement these preliminary findings in the near future.

While facilities specializing in PTG treatment may distribute screening questionnaires to patients before their initial interview to enhance diagnostic efficiency, we have found that bereaved individuals are more willing to disclose their symptoms in a personal appointment. Additionally, screening instruments appear to be more valid in face-to-face interactions.

Especially for institutions that support bereaved persons after acute loss, it is advisable to wait six months after the loss before interpreting the results of screening instruments for PTG according to ICD-11 (World Health Organization [WHO], 2022) criteria.

Discuss the results of the screening with the participant

In order to avoid the impression that diagnostic results disappear into a "black box" for professionals, the interviewer should report the results of a screening back to the participant promptly and categorize them in terms of their meaning. After normalizing symptoms, classify participants' results using the given cutoff values. If the results are above the cutoff, initiate further diagnostics, emphasizing the limited validity of screening questionnaires.

If results are below the cutoff, encourage participants in their grieving process, emphasize their resources explored and that therapeutic help is not indicated at this time and praise them in detail for their strength in coping

Table 2.1 Overview of current self-report instruments according to DSM-5-TR and ICD-11 PGD criteria

Instrument	*Target concepts*	*Items, Scale*	*Psychometric properties*	*Special characteristics*
Aarhus PGD scale (A-PGDs; O'Connor et al., 2023)	ICD-11 and DSM-5-TR PGD	20 items 5-point Likert scale No cutoff and diagnostic algorithm established (yet)	Reliability and validity shown in a first non-clinical sample (N = 349; O'Connor et al., 2023)	Bottom-up approach in the development of the scale
International Grief Questionnaire (IGQ; Hyland et al., 2024)	ICD-11 PGD	7 items 5-point Likert scale Diagnostic algorithm defined, no cutoff established (yet)	Reliability and validity shown in two first non-clinical samples (N = 2023; Hyland et al., 2024)	Total score tries to reflect a balanced ratio of core to additional symptoms
International Prolonged Grief Disorder Scale (IPGDS; Killikelly et al., 2020)	ICD-11 PGD	15 items standard scale 19 items cultural supplement 5-point Likert scale Diagnostic algorithms defined, cutoffs proposed	Reliability and validity shown in several non-clinical international samples (Killikelly et al., 2020; Killikelly et al., 2021; Killikelly et al., 2023)	Includes a cultural supplement module to capture culture-specific grief experiences (Killikelly & Maercker, 2023)
Prolonged Grief Scale 13 Revised (PG-13-R; Prigerson et al., 2021)	DSM-5-TR PGD	13 Items 5-point Likert scale Diagnostic algorithm defined, cutoff of ≥ 30 suggests clinically significant PGD symptoms	Reliability and validity shown in three first non-clinical samples (N = 672; Prigerson et al., 2021), but await further formal psychometric evaluation	Revised version of the PG-13
Traumatic Grief Inventory Self Report Plus (TGI-SR+; Lenferink et al., 2022)	ICD-11 and DSM-5-TR PGD	22 Items 5-point Likert scale Diagnostic algorithms defined, cutoffs proposed	Reliability and validity shown in several non-clinical and clinical international samples (Kokou-Kpolou et al., 2022; Lenferink et al., 2022; Lenferink et al., 2023)	Revised version of the TGI-SR

with the loss. While many participants are relieved by such an outcome, some may be disappointed. In these cases, carefully explore and validate their needs (e.g., desire to talk about the deceased), and, if possible, meet them, e.g., by referring to lower-threshold services. It may also be helpful to point out that there is no evidence of the effectiveness of psychotherapeutic interventions for subthreshold PGD symptoms (Wittouck et al., 2011): "Science tells us that therapeutic support is not helpful for individuals who are already coping well despite a loss. You wouldn't benefit from treatment".

Plan a clinical interview in the case of suspected PTG

Clinical judgement, not merely reaching cutoff scores in self-report questionnaires, is crucial to establish the diagnostic status of PGD. The need for (structured) clinical interviews becomes even more apparent when one considers that some studies indicate only modest concordance between self-report instruments and clinical interviews (e.g., Eaton et al., 2000; Unterhitzenberger et al., 2019).

While most of the widely used clinical interviews capture earlier definitions of PGD (e.g., Bui et al., 2015; Prigerson et al., 2009), currently, three clinical interviews exist that offer an assessment corresponding to the ICD-11 and/or DSM-5-TR (American Psychiatric Association [APA], 2022) PGD definition.

First, the Traumatic Grief Inventory-Clinician Administered (TGI-CA; Lenferink et al., 2023) has been developed based on the TGI-SR+ to assess DSM-5-TR and ICD-11 PGD severity and probable caseness. A first validation study has proven good psychometric properties in a non-clinical sample when the TGI-CA was conducted via telephone (N = 433; Lenferink et al., 2023), but further validation should focus on clinical samples and face-to-face settings.

Second, the International Interview for PGD according to ICD-11 (I-PGD-11) has been introduced lately, following the PG-13-R and allows to assess both the diagnostic status and the severity of PGD ICD-11 symptoms. There was good psychometric performance in the first study in a clinical inpatient sample (N = 101; Rueger et al., 2024).

Third, the Aarhus PGD Interview (A-PGDi) was recently evaluated in a subclinical sample of N=124 as a first structured interview according to DSM-5-TR and ICD-11 PGD criteria. It allows diagnosis and intensity assessment with promising validity and reliability (O'Connor et al., 2025).

Further research will likely result in the development and further validation of clinical interviews for assessing PGD. Existing clinical interviews vary in complexity. The A-PGDi, for example, provides extensive information on administration and symptom differentiation, while the TGI-CA provides more limited information and differs only in response format from the screening questionnaire from which it was derived. This variation in complexity affects the length of training and administration for the interviewer, but also shows that a previous screening instrument can be used as a clinical interview with few modifications. This can save time and resources for valid diagnostics in limited capacities.

Regardless of the interview used, the interviewer decides whether the reported phenomenon is functional or dysfunctional. This may not always be easy, so it may be useful to reflect on various aspects of the diagnostic information listed in Box 2.3.

Consider comorbidities

Traumatic loss is a risk factor for many mental health problems (Heeke et al., 2019). Symptoms of PGD can be similar to, but distinct from, symptoms of other mental health conditions, such as bereavement-related depression or PTSD (Lenferink et al., 2021; Shear et al., 2011). However, many individuals with PGD also have high rates of comorbidity with anxiety, bereavement-related depression, or PTSD (Komischke-Konnerup et al., 2021), especially in the case of traumatic loss, see Chapter 1. Accordingly, a thorough differential diagnosis is crucial to differentiate whether a bereaved person is suffering from PGD alone, from another mental health condition alone, or from multiple disorders. These diagnostic findings are particularly important for planning appropriate treatment. Therefore, we recommend that instruments to assess comorbid symptoms should always be included in the diagnostic process with bereaved individuals, ideally in the form of a structured broadband interview, such as the Structured Clinical Interview for the DSM (First et al., 2016).

Some indications help distinguish PGD symptoms from those of other disorders. Intrusions are common to both PGD and PTSD. To distinguish between the two, examine the intrusions' content and associated emotions. PTSD often involves reliving a horrific situation with fear, horror, and shock. In contrast, PGD involves memories of farewell situations or happy moments with the deceased, associated with emotions that are more bittersweet. The source of stress also differs between the two: in PTSD, it is often the fear of the next re-experience, and in PGD, it is the absence of the deceased.

PGD and depression often share the experience of sadness or emotional numbness. On a cognitive level, PGD may involve self-blame and self-criticism specifically related to the loss. Depression involves a critical and negative view of the loss and its circumstances, as well as a more general negative view of oneself, the world, and the future, according to the cognitive triad sensu Beck. Suicidal thoughts and actions are also not typical in PGD. The strong longing for the deceased may include a desire to be

Box 2.3 Reference points for assessing the clinical relevance of PGD symptoms

1 Concepts of emotions: There are a few disorders that list as many different emotional concepts as possible symptoms as PGD, e.g., grief, sadness, anger, bitterness, guilt, self-blame, loneliness. Keep in mind that not everyone is able to label their own emotional life. In addition, certain emotional words, such as bitterness, may be unfamiliar to some respondents, leading to false positives or negatives. Therefore, ensure you and the respondent are talking about the same emotion by asking for specific examples and defining terms.
2 Symptom intensity: Many interviews use scales to assess symptom intensity, but further exploration is often needed to determine clinical relevance. For example, if longing is experienced as overwhelming and persistent, it may indicate a dysfunctional form of grief. If the longing is constant but fades during relevant daily activities, it is likely a healthy form of grief. In addition, pay attention to the appropriateness of emotional reactions, as very inappropriate ones may indicate dysfunctional grief.
3 Level of functioning: When asking about limitations in level of functioning, also ask for specific examples: How has communication in the couple's relationship worked since the loss? Can they grieve together? Since the loss, who has taken care of the tax return, who cooks balanced meals, who mows the lawn?
4 Dysfunctional cognitions: Ask about thoughts associated with symptoms. Maladaptive cognitions may manifest in extreme or distorted thoughts that may also limit the validity of diagnostic findings, such as believing that one will never be better without the deceased.
5 Coping strategies: Ask about specific strategies the person uses to cope with grief. Those who cope effectively usually adopt strategies that are flexible and adaptable to their needs and daily demands. For instance, occasionally distracting oneself from grief can be beneficial for daily functioning. Conversely, persistently avoiding reminders of the loss indicates inflexibility and may signal a dysfunctional grief process.
6 Multifaceted nature of avoidance: Avoidance can take many forms. Do not just ask about avoidance of certain places, activities, situations, or thoughts and feelings. Constant preoccupation

with the deceased, such as visiting the grave, looking at pictures, or reminiscing, can also constitute avoidance if it is an attempt to avoid the fact that the deceased is no longer there. If this preoccupation hinders the bereaved's daily life, pathological grief may be present.

7 Grief history: Find out how long the person has been grieving and if there have been any changes in their grief reactions. Also, take into account losses that occurred before the index loss. Prolonged stagnation in grief processing may be a sign of dysfunctional grief, while highly fluctuating grief trajectories may be more indicative of other disorders, such as recurrent depression.

reunited with them in the afterlife, but this is usually not associated with suicidal tendencies, which would rather indicate the presence of depressive symptoms.

In general, concentration and sleep disturbances are not typical symptoms of PGD, and should always be investigated and discussed with regard to other disorders.

Give Feedback on the diagnostic results to the bereaved person

The formal conclusion of any diagnostic procedure is the feedback of the results to the participant. To make this understandable to the participant, the following steps have proven helpful:

- Provide a detailed overview of the symptoms of each diagnosis with specific examples. This is the first step in allowing the patients to become experts on their problems.
- Begin your feedback by praising the participants – for their courage, openness, and perseverance in answering all the questions.
- Visualize given diagnoses and explain their meaning in a language appropriate to the participant. Provide initial psychoeducational information about etiological concepts or therapeutic principles, e.g., exposure, guided by the participant's questions (see Chapter 5).
- Obtain feedback from the participant on the diagnoses identified and discuss possible inconsistencies.
- If clinical disorders have been identified, this session is the ideal time to promote hope. Point out the positive aspects to the current situation: The participant has taken the first step and thanks to the diagnostic results, the right form of help can now be recommended.

- In the case of a treatment recommendation: Provide detailed information and clarify motivation and readiness for treatment. In addition to time or organizational barriers, are there any concerns? Ambivalence is not uncommon in grief-focused treatment and is often based on false assumptions (e.g., "Treatment means I have to forget the deceased"). Therefore, it is important to uncover these early on: "We know from many patients that although they want help, they are often ambivalent about therapy. They may have fears about what it might do to them if they actually get better. Do you know this about yourself?"
- Provide information about any framework related to your treatment recommendations, such as cost, procedure, and duration. Control and predictability provide participants with important structure, contrasting to the supposedly uncontrollable feelings of grief.
- If no treatment is indicated, the feedback should be based on the points already mentioned for reporting subthreshold screening results. If indicated, an adequate referral should be prepared accordingly.

Dealing with special situations during the diagnostic process

When working with bereaved individuals, the interviewer may face unique clinical challenges. With the right strategies, however, it is possible to ensure valid diagnostic results, and to create a comfortable atmosphere for the participant.

Diagnostics with individuals from other cultural backgrounds

How one deals with loss is influenced by the norms of one's cultural identity. Both DSM-5-TR and the ICD-11 PGD criteria include a cultural caveat stating that symptoms of PGD must be beyond cultural norms of grief response and not be better explained by culturally specific mourning rituals (APA, 2022; WHO, 2022; see also Chapter 15). Therefore, a culturally sensitive assessment of losses and grief is critical for a comprehensive evaluation and the determination of an appropriate treatment recommendation. To this end, the Bereavement and Grief Cultural Formulation Interview (BG-CFI; Smid et al., 2018b) was developed as a complementary module to the DSM-5 Cultural Formulation Interview (Lewis-Fernández et al., 2020). It aims to facilitate clinical exploration of cultural aspects of grief and bereavement through ten person-centered, open-ended questions on (1) death, bereavement, and mourning, and (2) help-seeking and coping. Thus, the BG-CFI is a useful tool for validating the diagnosis of PGD, enhancing understanding, and tailoring appropriate interventions, e.g., by helping to integrate meaningful rituals into subsequent treatment (Smid et al., 2018b).

Diagnostics with individuals suffering from severe avoidance

Avoidance in interviews can manifest in various ways, such as talking about the deceased in the present tense as if they were still alive, or discussing other topics extensively (see also Chapter 6). By following a structured interview process, which can provide a good basis for limiting content, and by clearly stating facts, the interviewer can counter these forms of avoidance early in the diagnostic process. However, avoidance can also manifest in silence or brief responses. Addressing this issue immediately is crucial in these cases. Sometimes, motivational interviewing techniques (Miller & Rollnick, 2023) can be helpful in motivating the person to overcome avoidance. Certain formulation aids can prove helpful when dealing with avoidant participants; see Box 2.4.

Box 2.4 Formulation aids for dealing with avoidance

- Address and validate avoidance: "I know very well that bereaved persons find it very difficult to talk about their loss, and that's exactly what I'm experiencing with you. Am I right? I understand how stressful the situation must be for you. Do you have any ideas on how we can make it easier for you?"
- Motivate to continue the interview: "You've already taken the hardest step - you've realized you need support. That's great! However, I notice that you are finding it more and more difficult to talk to me about your loss. I can understand that. But what will happen if you don't continue the interview with me?"
- Emphasize the participant's autonomy, offer interruptions: "It's entirely up to you to decide what and how much you want to tell me. We can take a break or continue our interview at another time."
- Narrow down the content: "Some bereaved persons find it difficult to talk about their loss events. Therefore, it is important for me to tell you that we are not going to discuss exactly what happened, but to get an overview of what loss events you experienced and how you felt afterwards. You can think of it like moving boxes: we imagine that the experiences of your life are in individual boxes. My goal today is to see what headings we can write on the moving boxes, not to open the boxes."

Diagnostics with individuals suffering from severe emotional distress

It is not uncommon for the disclosure of stressful life and/or loss events to result in intense internal tension and/or the expression of strong feelings.

During initial interviews, it is important to create an open atmosphere for bereaved individuals to express their grief. Therapeutic interventions are usually not necessary when dealing with crying, and the interviewer should wait and be patient. Many individuals apologize for their tears, but a direct invitation to show their feelings can help dispel feelings of shame.

Particularly in the case of comorbid PTSD symptoms, some participants may experience strong states of tension when asked about loss events, leading to dissociative symptoms like derealization or depersonalization. These may be expressed by a sudden change in conversational behavior: Freezing, interrupted conversation, loss of eye contact, suddenly delayed or absent responses, altered body tone. While managing dissociative states should be part of an individualized treatment plan (for which reference should be made to specific treatment manuals, e.g., Linehan, 2014), initial strategies can be applied during the diagnostic process to reduce tension and help participants remain grounded in the present. Based on our clinical experience, the following low-threshold strategies can be used at any time without additional materials:

- Address participants by name
- Ask participants to open their eyes, stamp their feet, stand up, and walk around the room
- Draw the participants' attention to sensory impressions in the room (e.g., visual, acoustic) and have them describe them
- Ask participants to write something down (e.g., next appointment to continue the interview)

As the interviewer, remain calm and view the dissociation as important diagnostic information. Discuss the situation at the next appointment to further explore the participant's behavior and prepare for future treatment.

Dealing with unexpected behavior in the diagnostic process

In rare cases, bereaved participants may present pictures of the deceased or gravesite during interviews, bring extensive police reports, or report unusual alternative treatment methods (e.g., consultation with a medium). For the interviewer, it is crucial to approach these situations openly and nonjudgmentally. While such behavior may initially be validated (e.g., by thanking participants for their openness and the opportunity to gain a deeper insight), a structured diagnostic process helps avoid irritation and quickly returns to prescribed steps and questions of the diagnostic procedure. In our experience, the examples mentioned can often be clinical indications of certain symptoms, e.g., preoccupation with the deceased, and can be revisited as examples later in the interview and thus be used diagnostically.

Conclusion and outlook

Diagnostics with bereaved persons can be challenging. However, we have personally experienced it to be very enriching on many occasions. Therefore, we encourage professionals to view diagnostics as a valuable opportunity to understand the participant's story and find the best support option. The inclusion of PGD in international classification systems has stimulated extensive research, with the expectation of further validation and development of additional diagnostic tools for traumatic loss. It is hoped that this will not only lead to valid results in clinical trials, but that user-friendly instruments and increasing opportunities for training will encourage practitioners to implement structured diagnostic processes in their work.

References

American Psychiatric Association. (2022). *Diagnostic and Statistical Manual of Mental Disorders, Fifth Edition, Text Revision (DSM-5-TR)*. APA. https://doi.org/10.1176/appi.books.9780890425787

Andriessen, K., Krysinska, K., Draper, B., Dudley, M., & Mitchell, P. B. (2018). Harmful or helpful? A systematic review of how those bereaved through suicide experience research participation. *Crisis*, *39*(5), 364–376. https://doi.org/10.1027/0227-5910/a000515

Bui, E., Mauro, C., Robinaugh, D. J., Skritskaya, N. A., Wang, Y., Gribbin, C., Ghesquiere, A., Horenstein, A., Duan, N., Reynolds, C., Zisook, S., Simon, N. M., & Shear, M. K. (2015). The structured clinical interview for complicated grief: Reliability, validity, and exploratory factor analysis. *Depression and Anxiety*, *32*(7), 485–492. https://doi.org/10.1002/da.22385

Comtesse, H., Killikelly, C., Hengst, S. M. C., Lenferink, L. I. M., de la Rie, S. M., Boelen, P. A., & Smid, G. E. (2023). The Ambiguous Loss Inventory Plus (ALI+): Introduction of a measure of psychological reactions to the disappearance of a loved one. *International Journal of Environmental Research and Public Health*, *20*(6), 5117. https://doi.org/10.3390/ijerph20065117

Eaton, W. W., Neufeld, K., Chen, L. S., & Cai, G. (2000). A comparison of self-report and clinical diagnostic interviews for depression: Diagnostic interview schedule and schedules for clinical assessment in neuropsychiatry in the Baltimore epidemiologic catchment area follow-up. *Archives of General Psychiatry*, *57*(3), 217–222. https://doi.org/10.1001/archpsyc.57.3.217

First, M. B., Williams, J. B. W., Karg, R. S., & Spitzer, R. L. (2016). *Structured clinical interview for DSM-5 disorders: SCID-5-CV clinician version*. American Psychiatric Association.

Heeke, C., Kampisiou, C., Niemeyer, H., & Knaevelsrud, C. (2019). A systematic review and meta-analysis of correlates of prolonged grief disorder in adults exposed to violent loss. *European Journal of Psychotraumatology*, *10*(1), 1583524. https://doi.org/10.1080/20008198.2019.1583524

Hyland, P., Redican, E., Karatzias, T., & Shevlin, M. (2024). The international grief questionnaire (IGQ): A new measure of ICD-11 prolonged grief disorder. *Journal of Traumatic Stress*, *37*(1), 141–153. https://doi.org/10.1002/jts.22986

Jaffe, A. E., DiLillo, D., Hoffman, L., Haikalis, M., & Dykstra, R. E. (2015). Does it hurt to ask? A meta-analysis of participant reactions to trauma research. *Clinical Psychology Review*, *40*, 40–56, https://doi.org/10.1016/j.cpr.2015.05.004

Killikelly, C., Kagialis, A., Henneman, S., Coronado, H., Demanarig, D., Farahani, H., Özdoğru, A. A., Yalçın, B., Yockey, A., Gosnell, C. L., Jia, F., Maisel, M., Stelzer, E., Wilson, D., Anderson, J., Charles, K., Cummings, J. P., Faas, C., Knapp, B., & Irgens, M. S. (2023). Measurement and assessment of grief in a large international sample. *Journal of Affective Disorders*, *327*, 306–314. https://doi.org/10.1016/j.jad.2023.01.095

Killikelly, C., & Maercker, A. (2023). The cultural supplement: A new method for assessing culturally relevant prolonged grief disorder symptoms. *Clinical Psychology in Europe*, *5*(1), e7655. https://doi.org/10.32872/cpe.7655

Killikelly, C., Merzhvynska, M., Zhou, N., Stelzer, E. M., Hyland, P., Rocha, J., Ben-Ezra, M., & Maercker, A. (2021). Examination of the new ICD-11 prolonged grief disorder guidelines across five international samples. *Clinical Psychology in Europe*, *3*(1), e4159. https://doi.org/10.32872/cpe.4159

Killikelly, C., Zhou, N., Merzhvynska, M., Stelzer, E. M., Dotschung, T., Rohner, S., Sun, L. H., & Maercker, A. (2020). Development of the international prolonged grief disorder scale for the ICD-11: Measurement of core symptoms and culture items adapted for Chinese and German-speaking samples. *Journal of Affective Disorders*, *277*, 568–576. https://doi.org/10.1016/j.jad.2020.08.057

Kokou-Kpolou, C. K., Lenferink, L. I. M., Brunnet, A. E., Park, S., Megalakaki, O., Boelen, P., & Cénat, J. M. (2022). The ICD-11 and DSM-5-TR prolonged grief criteria: Validation of the traumatic grief inventory-self report plus using exploratory factor analysis and item response theory. *Clinical Psychology & Psychotherapy*, *29*(6), 1950–1962. https://doi.org/10.1002/cpp.2765

Komischke-Konnerup, K. B., Zachariae, R., Johannsen, M., Nielsen, L. D., & O'Connor, M. (2021). Co-occurrence of prolonged grief symptoms and symptoms of depression, anxiety, and posttraumatic stress in bereaved adults: A systematic review and meta-analysis. *Journal of Affective Disorders Reports*, *4*, 100140, https://doi.org/10.1016/j.jadr.2021.100140

Lenferink, L. I. M., Eisma, M. C., Smid, G. E., de Keijser, J., & Boelen, P. A. (2022). Valid measurement of DSM-5 persistent complex bereavement disorder and DSM-5-TR and ICD-11 prolonged grief disorder: The traumatic grief inventory-self report plus (TGI-SR+). *Comprehensive Psychiatry*, *112*, 152281. https://doi.org/10.1016/j.comppsych.2021.152281

Lenferink, L. I. M., Franzen, M., ten Klooster, P. M., Knaevelsrud, C., Boelen, P. A., & Heeke, C. (2023). The traumatic grief inventory-clinician administered: A psychometric evaluation of a new interview for ICD-11 and DSM-5-TR prolonged grief disorder severity and probable caseness. *Journal of Affective Disorders*, *330*, 188–197. https://doi.org/10.1016/j.jad.2023.03.006

Lenferink, L. I. M., van den Munckhof, M. J. A., de Keijser, J., & Boelen, P. A. (2021). DSM-5-TR prolonged grief disorder and DSM-5 posttraumatic stress disorder are related, yet distinct: Confirmatory factor analyses in traumatically bereaved people. *European Journal of Psychotraumatology*, *12*(1), 1–14. https://doi.org/10.1080/20008198.2021.2000131

Lenferink, L. I. M., van Dijk, I., Eisma, M. C., Eklund, R., Boelen, P. A., & Sveen, J. (2023). Psychometric evaluation of the Swedish Traumatic Grief Inventory Self-Report Plus (TGI-SR+) in bereaved parents. *Clinical Psychology & Psychotherapy*, *31*, e2922. https://doi.org/10.1002/cpp.2922

Lewis-Fernández, R., Aggarwal, N. K., & Kirmayer, L. J. (2020). The cultural formulation interview: Progress to Date and future directions. *Transcultural Psychiatry*, *57*(4), 487–496. https://doi.org/10.1177/1363461520938273

Linehan, M. M. (2014). *DBT skills training manual, second edition*. Guilford Publications.

Miller, W. R., & Rollnick, S. (2023). *Motivational interviewing: Helping people change* (4th ed.). *Applications of motivational interviewing*. The Guilford Press.

O'Connor, M., Vang, M., Bryant, R., Buur, C., Komischke-Konnerup, K., Frostholm, L., & Ladegaard, N. (2025). Development and validation of the Aarhus Structured Clinical Interview for Prolonged Grief Disorder in ICD-11 and DSM-5-TR (A-PGDi). *European Journal of Psychotraumatology*, *16*(1). https://doi.org/10.1080/20008066.2025.2511373

O'Connor, M., Vang, M. L., Shevlin, M., Elklit, A., Komischke-Konnerup, K. B., Lundorff, M., & Bryant, R. (2023). Development and validation of the Aarhus PGD scale for operationalizing ICD-11 and DSM-5-TR TR prolonged grief disorder. *Journal of Affective Disorders*, *342*, 201–209. https://doi.org/10.1016/j.jad.2023.09.022

Prigerson, H. G., Boelen, P. A., Xu, J., Smith, K. V., & Maciejewski, P. K. (2021). Validation of the new DSM-5-TR criteria for prolonged grief disorder and the PG-13-revised (PG-13-r) scale. *World Psychiatry*, *20*(1), 96–106. https://doi.org/10.1002/wps.20823

Prigerson, H. G., Horowitz, M. J., Jacobs, S. C., Parkes, C. M., Aslan, M., Goodkin, K., Raphael, B., Marwit, S. J., Wortman, C., Neimeyer, R. A., Bonanno, G. A., Bonanno, G., Block, S. D., Kissane, D., Boelen, P., Maercker, A., Litz, B. T., Johnson, J. G., First, M. B., & Maciejewski, P. K. (2009). Prolonged grief disorder: Psychometric validation of criteria proposed for DSM-v and ICD-11. *PLoS Medicine*, *6*(8), e1000121. https://doi.org/10.1371/journal.pmed.1000121

Rueger, M. S., Lechner-Meichsner, F., Kirschbaum, L., Lubik, S., Roll, S. C., & Steil, R. (2024). Prolonged grief disorder in an inpatient psychiatric sample: Psychometric properties of a new clinical interview and preliminary prevalence. *BMC Psychiatry*, *24*(1), 333. https://doi.org/10.1186/s12888-024-05784-2

Schoenleber, M., Milanak, M. E., Schuld, E., & Berenbaum, H. (2018). Rating procedures for improving identification of exposure to potentially traumatic events when using checklist measures. *Journal of Aggression, Maltreatment & Trauma*, *27*(10), 1090–1109.

Shear, M. K., Simon, N., Wall, M., Zisook, S., Neimeyer, R., Duan, N., Reynolds, C., Lebowitz, B., Sung, S., Ghesquiere, A., Gorscak, B., Clayton, P., Ito, M., Nakajima, S., Konishi, T., Melhem, N., Meert, K., Schiff, M., O'Connor, M., & Keshaviah, F. (2011). Complicated grief and related bereavement issues for DSM-5. *Depression and Anxiety*, *28*(2), 103–117. https://doi.org/10.1002/da.20780

Smid, G. E., Drogendijk, A. N., Knipscheer, J., Boelen, P. A., & Kleber, R. J. (2018a). Loss of loved ones or home due to a disaster: Effects over time on distress in immigrant ethnic minorities. *Transcultural Psychiatry*, *55*(5), 648–668. https://doi.org/10.1177/1363461518784355

Smid, G. E., Groen, S., de La Rie, S. M., Kooper, S., & Boelen, P. A. (2018b). Toward cultural assessment of grief and grief-related psychopathology. *Psychiatric Services*, *69*(10), 1050–1052. https://doi.org/10.1176/appi.ps.201700422

Unterhitzenberger, J., Wintersohl, S., Lang, M., König, J., & Rosner, R. (2019). Providing manualized individual trauma-focused CBT to unaccompanied refugee minors with uncertain residence status: A pilot study. *Child and Adolescent Psychiatry and Mental Health, 13*(1), 288. https://doi.org/10.1186/s13034-019-0282-3

Weathers, F. W., Blake, D. D., Schnurr, P. P., Kaloupek, D. G., Marx, B. P., & Keane, T. M. (2013). *The Life Events Checklist for DSM-5 (LEC-5)*. Instrument available from the National Center for PTSD at www.ptsd.va.gov

Wittouck, C., Van Autreve, S., Jaegere, E., de, Portzky, G., & van Heeringen, K. (2011). The prevention and treatment of complicated grief: A meta-analysis. *Clinical Psychology Review, 31*(1), 69–78. https://doi.org/10.1016/j.cpr.2010.09.005

World Health Organization [WHO]. (2022). *International Classification of Diseases Eleventh Revision (ICD-11)*. WHO. https://icd.who.int/browse11/l-m/en

Chapter 3

Risk and protective factors for prolonged and traumatic grief

Louisa Heinzl, Nadine Stammel, and Geert E. Smid

The occurrence and severity of prolonged and traumatic grief symptoms are influenced by risk and protective factors that may operate prior to, during, or following the death of a loved one. Understanding risk factors allows for early identification of vulnerable individuals, enabling timely intervention and preventative strategies to mitigate the development or persistence of psychopathology. It is important to note that the term risk factor in the literature often refers to correlates. True risk factors must precede and be associated with the outcome, and potential sources of systematic error (e.g., selection bias and confounding variables) need to be considered (Buur et al., 2024).

There are several theoretical frameworks that group risk and protective factors along different dimensions. The following overview adapts a framework of potential risk and protective factors (Smid et al., 2021), organizing them across five dimensions: loss-related factors, relationship with the deceased, individual factors, social factors, and cultural factors. Given the potential overlap between these categories, this framework should be considered flexible, allowing for the addition or recategorization of factors as needed.

The current framework has some similarities with the framework by Parkes and Prigerson (2010), which organizes "determinants of grief" along four categories: kinship, gender, and age; mode of death; personal vulnerability; and social, religious, and cultural influences. Compared with the framework by Stroebe et al. (2006), that incorporates loss-related stressors, intra- and interpersonal risk and protective factors, and appraisal and coping processes, the current framework emphasizes several distinct factors related to the relationship with the deceased and cultural factors that may operate by impacting on coping behavior, cognitions, and meanings following the loss.

As shown in Table 3.1, risk and protective factors may operate at different times: preceding ("preloss"), surrounding ("periloss"), and following the loss ("postloss"). The risk and protective factors mentioned in the table will be elaborated in the following paragraphs.

DOI: 10.4324/9781003429777-5

Table 3.1 Overview of risk and protective factors of prolonged and traumatic grief and time of operation

Domain	*Description*	*Time of operation*		
Loss-related factors	Cause of death and context of the loss		Periloss	
	Pre-existing and early symptoms	Preloss	Periloss	Postloss
	Coping behaviors, cognitions, and meanings	Preloss	Periloss	Postloss
Factors related to the relationship with the deceased	Nature and quality of the relationship	Preloss		Postloss
	Farewell	Preloss	Periloss	Postloss
	Involvement in the death		Periloss	
Individual factors	Gender and age	Preloss		
	Attachment and personality	Preloss		
	Personal and intergenerational history	Preloss		Postloss
	Neurobiological and immunological correlates		Periloss	Postloss
Social factors	Social environment	Preloss	Periloss	Postloss
	Economic and environmental context	Preloss		Postloss
	Juridical and political situation			Postloss
	Media coverage			Postloss
Cultural factors	Explanatory models, spirituality, and faith	Preloss		Postloss
	Migration	Preloss		Postloss
	End-of-life care and bereavement care experiences	Preloss	Periloss	Postloss
	Rituals	Preloss	Periloss	Postloss

Note: Factors may increase the risk of and/or protect against prolonged and traumatic grief. The time of operation of factors is hypothesized.

Loss-related factors

Cause of death and context of the loss

The cause of death has consistently been shown to influence the risk of prolonged and traumatic grief. The term traumatic grief has therefore been defined in this book as prolonged grief disorder (PGD) with comorbid (symptoms of) posttraumatic stress disorder (PTSD) and/or depression, following a loved one's unnatural death in a traumatic context (e.g., homicide, suicide, accident, disaster, terrorism, war). The death of a loved one due to natural causes, e.g., a chronic illness, is less frequently associated with prolonged grief. The pooled prevalence of PGD among bereaved individuals was 5% in a meta-analysis of probability samples (Comtesse et al., 2024). In people bereaved due to unnatural death, the prevalence of PGD is higher – a meta-analysis reported a pooled prevalence of probable PGD as high as 49% (Djelantik et al., 2020). Traumatic loss is often experienced in the context of other losses or other traumatic events, which further elevate the risk of developing PGD and PTSD (Heeke et al., 2019; Lobb et al., 2010). However, losses of loved ones due to a natural disaster were associated with lower rates of PGD compared to other causes of unnatural loss (Djelantik et al., 2020).

Unnatural deaths usually occur unexpectedly, which is a further risk factor for the development of PGD. Indeed, the unexpected death of a loved one due to natural causes (e.g., a stroke) also constitutes a risk factor for PGD (Buur et al., 2024). The impact of an expected death on the bereaved person's mental health may be mitigated by *preparedness*, a concept that encompasses a caregiver's cognitive, behavioral, and emotional preparation in the multiple loss situation of the impending death (Nielsen et al., 2016).

Pre-existing and early symptoms

People reporting preloss depressive or grief symptoms are more likely to develop PGD postloss (Buur et al., 2024). Although *anticipatory grief*, a concept introduced by Lindemann (1994), has been thought to be capable of promoting adaptation to a loss, this pertains only to preparedness for the death and not to pre-loss grief reactions. High levels of pre-loss grief combined with low levels of preparedness during caregiving predict prolonged grief reactions (Nielsen et al., 2016).

Following the death of a loved one, most people go through a period of more or less intense grief, with grief-related distress gradually decreasing over time (see also Chapter 1). Prospective studies exploring groups with distinct symptom trajectories identified two to five trajectories (Pociunaite et al., 2023). One such study that combined data from two countries up to five years postloss (N = 398) found four PGD symptom trajectories characterized by stable high symptoms (6% of the sample), quick recovery (10%), slow recovery (35%), and stable low symptoms (49%); unnatural causes of death increased the likelihood of being in the stable high and slow recovery trajectories compared to the low symptoms trajectory (Pociunaite et al., 2023). In a study of 1138 participants who lost a partner due to a terminal illness, five grief trajectories were identified within a 3-year timeframe: low (34% of the sample), moderate/decreasing (30%), high/decreasing (20%), high (7%), and late grief (10%). Thus, people with prolonged and traumatic grief have typically experienced early symptoms.

Importantly, these early symptoms may include symptoms of PTSD, depression, anxiety, disturbed sleep, substance use, and impaired functioning. Meta-analyses show that PGD often co-occurs with other mental health problems, specifically, depressive, anxiety, and PTSD symptoms (Heeke et al., 2019; Komischke-Konnerup et al., 2021). In longitudinal studies assessing co-occurring symptoms, prolonged grief symptoms more consistently predicted symptoms of depression and PTSD than vice versa, suggesting that prolonged grief may be a *transdiagnostic* risk factor for depressive and PTSD symptoms (Janshen & Eisma, 2024). A systematic review found initial evidence of bidirectional causal relationships between prolonged grief and sleep disturbances (Lancel et al., 2020). Bereaved individuals with substance misuse are at increased risk for subsequent development of prolonged grief, particularly when increases in substance consumption preceded bereavement; conversely, prolonged grief may predict increases in smoking and alcohol dependence (Parisi et al., 2019). Besides early symptoms, self-perceived impairment during the first year after the loss has been found to increase the risk for elevated PGD symptoms later on (Specht et al., 2022).

Coping behaviors, cognitions, and meanings

Coping behaviors, cognitions, and meanings mediate risk and protective factor effects on prolonged and traumatic grief. Coping behaviors such as experiential avoidance and rumination increase the risk of prolonged grief (Eisma & Stroebe, 2021). People bereaved by violent losses appear to have higher symptom levels of PGD, PTSD, and depression than persons bereaved by nonviolent losses (Boelen et al., 2015), and linkages between violent loss and elevated symptom levels are mediated by "unrealness", negative cognitions, and avoidance. Meanings are also implicated in the risk of prolonged and traumatic grief. Losses due to violent and accidental causes may disrupt fundamental beliefs about the world as a safe and just place where events follow a certain predictability and happen for a reason (Kristensen et al., 2012). In a prospective study (Milman et al., 2019), the effects of violent loss on PGD symptoms were partially mediated by meanings attributed to the loss, including a sense of peace and continuing bonds. Chapters 4 and 7 elaborate on these aspects.

Factors related to the relationship with the deceased

Nature and quality of the relationship

The loss of a close family member as compared to the loss of a distant family member has been consistently identified as a risk factor for PGD. As elaborated in Chapter 4, closeness of the relationship may result in a merging of selves, contributing to the risk of prolonged and traumatic grief following the loved one's death. Particularly strong evidence exists for the loss of a spouse or a child (Burke & Neimeyer, 2013; Buur et al., 2024), especially if the deceased child was the parents' only child (Djelantik et al., 2020; Heeke et al., 2019). Higher PGD symptom severity has also been associated with a younger age of the deceased (Parro-Jiménez et al., 2021). In terms of the quality of the relationship, marital dependency is associated with a higher risk for the severity and persistence of PGD when losing a spouse (Burke & Neimeyer, 2013).

Farewell

Saying goodbye – referring to both a pre-death farewell and a farewell during a funeral or other rituals (see discussion of rituals in the paragraph below) – facilitates understanding and accepting the reality of the loss and can thereby support grief processing. Saying goodbye pre-death implies a shared awareness of the finiteness of the relationship (Smid, 2020). Research suggests that openness related to the end of life during end-of-life care has a favorable influence on the grief process (Swarte et al., 2003; Wright et al., 2008). Saying goodbye is not possible if loved ones go missing. This situation of ambiguous loss is discussed further in Chapter 11.

Involvement in the death

The concept of survivor guilt was introduced to the psychiatric literature by Niederland, who described the intense suffering of Holocaust survivors who carried with them "the ever present feeling of guilt, as accompanied by conscious or unconscious dread of punishment, for having survived the very calamity to which their loved ones succumbed" (Niederland, 1961, p. 238). If a care relationship existed with the loved one – for example, parents of a child – the death can be experienced as a failure of caregiving (Shear et al., 2007). The death of a loved one by suicide is among the most frequent causes of traumatic grief. In suicide bereaved people, the perception that one somehow has directly caused the death is common. In a longitudinal study of suicide survivors followed up 6 months to 2 years after the loss (Kõlves et al., 2020), feelings of responsibility for the suicide, guilt, stigmatization, and feelings of rejection were higher than in survivors after other sudden losses.

Besides suicide, people with a wish to die may consider the option of physician-assisted dying (PAD; BMA, 2021) that is legally permitted under strict conditions in a growing number of countries. Symptoms of PGD and PTSD in bereaved persons may be lower following PAD than following a natural loss (Andriessen et al., 2020). Clinical care aimed at good dying may contribute to the prevention of PGD. In a Dutch mixed-methods study of grief following PAD or suicide due to a mental disorder in bereaved life partners, PAD was found to convey less grief-related distress than suicide (Snijdewind et al., 2022b). The social environment's understanding of the irremediable and unbearable suffering of the deceased contributed to a lower risk of prolonged grief and other mental distress following PAD compared with suicide (Snijdewind et al., 2022a). However, in the absence of broad cultural acceptance of PAD, its impact on grief may be less favorable. For example, in a study among 85 Swiss relatives or friends who had been present during assisted suicide, bereaved persons who perceived social disapproval of PAD, often causing them to maintain secrecy regarding the cause of death, reported higher PTSD and PGD symptoms (Wagner et al., 2011).

Individual factors

Gender and age

Although gender differences in the likelihood of developing PGD are not consistently reported (Djelantik et al., 2020; Lundorff et al., 2017), research shows a slight tendency for women to be more frequently affected by PGD (Buur et al., 2024; Heeke et al., 2019). Different socializations might be a cause for gender differences in grief reactions and processes (Lundorff et al., 2020), although there are many commonalities between grief reactions of men and women (Farver-Vestergaard et al., 2023). In old age, the likelihood of losing loved ones increases. On top of that, there is fairly consistent evidence that people who lose a loved one at an older age are more likely to suffer from PGD (Comtesse et al., 2024; Lundorff et al., 2017; Newson et al., 2011). Thus, clinicians working with older adults need to consider the presence of prolonged grief.

Attachment and personality

Early experiences with caregivers shape how relationships are formed, maintained, and resolved later in life (Bowlby, 1973). Attachment theory describes different insecure attachment styles that are connected to negative beliefs, expectations, and associated behaviors in close relationships. While persons with *attachment anxiety* tend to feel dependent on their partners and feel strong negative emotions when separated, people with *attachment avoidance* are reluctant to engage in close relationships and tend to suppress negative emotions related to separation (Eisma et al., 2023; Mikulincer & Shaver, 2008). It has been shown that higher attachment anxiety is related to PGD (Buur et al., 2024; Eisma et al., 2023; Heeke et al., 2019) while results on attachment avoidance are more mixed (Buur et al., 2024; Eisma et al., 2023; Heeke et al., 2019). However, an analysis of long-term studies concludes that while PGD symptoms and attachment insecurities often occur simultaneously in bereaved people, there is no conclusive evidence that specific attachment styles are a cause for the development or increase of PGD symptoms after a loss (Eisma et al., 2023). Nevertheless, it can be helpful for clinicians to consider the overlap between attachment insecurities and bereavement-related psychopathology (Mikulincer & Shaver, 2022). Wijngaards-de Meij et al. (2007) found that besides and above attachment insecurity, higher neuroticism was associated with a poorer adjustment to bereavement. Further studies have found neuroticism to be related to maladaptive grief reactions (Gegieckaite & Kazlauskas, 2022; Goetter et al., 2019).

Personal and intergenerational history

Persons who have experienced prior and/or multiple losses have an increased risk to develop PGD (Buur et al., 2024; Heeke et al., 2019). There is some indication from qualitative interviews that grief reactions take longer and are more difficult to cope with when losses occur simultaneously than when losses occur further apart in time (Mercer & Evans, 2006). Furthermore, in a meta-analysis, lifetime experience of traumatic events and the presence of physical symptoms or illness were associated with an elevated risk of PGD in adults exposed to violent loss (Heeke et al., 2019).

There is preliminary evidence that PGD symptoms might be passed on intergenerationally from parents to their children, thus that grief reactions or grief patterns of the parents are related to the severity of children's PGD symptoms (Lenferink & O'Connor, 2023, but see Boelen & Spuij, 2024) or children's emotional coping (Bryant et al., 2021). This relationship was found in underage as well as already grown-up children.

Neurobiological and immunological correlates

There is a growing body of evidence on neurobiological and immunological correlates of bereavement and PGD. A systematic review of 24 studies examining reward-related brain regions in PGD found that compared to normal grief, PGD involves an altered activity pattern in the amygdala and orbitofrontal cortex, likely also in parts of the cingulate cortex and more generally in the basal ganglia, including the nucleus accumbens and possibly also in the insula (Kakarala et al., 2020). These regions are also known to be active in substance addiction, which arises from dysregulation of the neural reward system (Prigerson et al., 2021). In a systematic review of 20 studies on neuroendocrine correlates of grief and bereavement, the majority of the studies reported cortisol as the outcome measure and found elevated mean cortisol levels, elevated morning cortisol, and flattened diurnal cortisol slopes in bereaved compared with nonbereaved groups. Cortisol alterations were moderated by grief and depressive symptoms, closeness to the deceased, and age or gender (Hopf et al., 2020). In a systematic review of the association between bereavement and biomarkers of immune function, most of the included 33 studies supported the association between bereavement and maladaptive changes in immune parameters, both in healthy and nonhealthy populations, and most studies examining grief symptom severity reported associations with maladaptive changes in immune parameters (Knowles et al., 2019). Future research is needed to indicate to what extent comprehensive individual neurobiological profiles (e.g., based on neuroendocrine, immunological, and functional neuroimaging findings) contribute to improved clinical staging (see also Chapter 1).

Social factors

Social environment

There is good evidence that social support may protect against the development of PGD (Mason et al., 2020). Having a close and supportive social network might buffer psychopathological effects of a loss, while living alone has been shown to be a risk factor (Sanderson et al., 2022). A loss usually affects not just one person but entire family systems and social networks. Literature on couples' reactions to dealing with the loss of a child reveals that the loss can influence the quality of the relationship on different levels and in different directions (Albuquerque et al., 2015). In addition, research suggests that individual adjustment to the loss of a child may be influenced by the quality of the bereaved couple's partnership (Albuquerque et al., 2015). While a well-functioning relationship thus may act as a protective factor, family conflicts before the loss as well as a family having difficulties accepting the loss were related to more severe grief symptoms (Mason et al., 2020).

Some bereaved persons might face stigma within their social network due to their prolonged reactions to the loss and experience a loss of support. Several vignette-based studies showed that participants had negative attributions and emotions about a fictional person with PGD symptoms and expressed a desire to socially distance themselves from the described person (e.g., Gonschor et al., 2020; Johnson et al., 2009; Kahler et al., 2021). Therefore, it is important to be aware of the social environment of a bereaved person and its potential changes after a loss to detect resources in the form of social support but also signs for disconnect and isolation.

Economic and environmental context

Meta-analyses show that a lower level of education or a lower socioeconomic status of the bereaved are associated with more severe symptoms of PGD (Buur et al., 2024; Heeke et al., 2019). In a study that combined data from 24 PGD prevalence studies and data about country vulnerability as predictors of PGD, lower country vulnerability was associated with higher PGD rates. A possible explanation is that in more vulnerable countries, loss and bereavement are more universal experiences that are less likely to cause a severe disruption of an individual's assumptive world, loss of meaning, and development of PGD (Comtesse et al., 2024).

A significant loss can lead to a worsened and insecure economic situation for the bereaved (Smid et al., 2018). While there is insufficient evidence to conclude that economic hardship is a risk factor for prolonged grief (Buur et al., 2024), a mixed-methods study of changes in financial circumstances and economic roles following death of a life partner found that economic changes, and the practicalities of dealing with such transitions, shaped individual responses to the death, and a perceived decline in financial well-being was associated with increased risk of poor psychological health following bereavement (Corden & Hirst, 2013).

Juridical and political situation

Especially after a violent or traumatic loss, there may be criminal investigations and court proceedings, and participating in a criminal trial may increase the likelihood of experiencing symptoms of prolonged and traumatic grief. Indeed, higher PGD, PTSD, and depression levels were reported by people who delivered a personal statement during a court hearing than those who did not (Nijborg et al., 2023). In homicidally bereaved persons, a still ongoing criminal process, compared to the conviction of the perpetrator, was associated with higher PGD and PTSD symptoms (van Denderen et al., 2016). In a retrospective naturalistic study among 929 homicide bereaved individuals who received traumatic grief-focused psychotherapy through the UK National Homicide Therapeutic Service, the status of the verdict was predictive of change in PGD and PTSD symptoms. The verdict being spoken during therapy compared to before therapy was associated with smaller reductions in

PTSD and PGD symptoms, and no verdict being spoken was associated with smaller reductions in PTSD symptoms only (Soydas et al., 2020).

Media coverage

Besides criminal investigations, a violent death as well as the mourning process of the bereaved can become part of media coverage in the weeks following the incident. Initial results suggest that bereaved persons with a higher exposure to media coverage also reported higher PGD symptoms (Kristensen et al., 2016). The way in which an affected person is confronted with press and media coverage, their coping with it as well as characteristics of the specific media representation of the death may further affect how it influences the bereaved.

Cultural factors

Culture shapes the way grief is processed, what is considered to be a normal reaction to a loss and what rituals are usually performed after death. Accordingly, prevalence rates and risk factors may also vary by culture. For example, no PGD was found in bereaved relatives in a study in Bali (Djelantik et al., 2021). While Kokou-Kpolou et al. (2020) observed similar PGD prevalence in a French and Togolese sample of conjugally bereaved, only recent bereavement was a risk factor across both samples. Other predictors varied between cultures: traumatic death, low education, and employment status were correlates of PGD in the French, while male gender and high education levels were predictors in the Togolese sample. This highlights that some PGD risk factors may be culture-specific, demanding careful consideration when treating diverse patients.

Explanatory models, spirituality, and faith

Cultural explanations, spirituality, and rituals can indirectly influence prolonged and traumatic grief by affecting coping behaviors, cognitions, and meanings attributed to the loss and the subsequent grief reactions. Culturally shaped *explanatory models* influence how a bereaved person understands and interprets individual symptoms and which forms of coping and help-seeking they consider appropriate (Kim et al., 2017). For example, Hinton et al. (2013) found that Cambodians have a complex system of interpretation of dreams of the deceased that frequently causes those dreams to give rise to great distress. Specifically, Cambodian refugees connected frequent dreams of people they had lost with concerns about the spiritual status of the deceased, thereby increasing their distress. Higher spirituality was shown to constitute a protective factor in two studies (Kokou-Kpolou et al., 2021; Schaal et al.,

2010). However, this might depend on the specific beliefs or spirituality that play a role in relation to loss and grief symptoms (Neimeyer & Burke, 2011).

Migration

Migration and associated stressors (e.g., ethnic minority stress; Smid et al., 2018) might put persons at a higher risk of developing PGD. Following migration, cultural customs in the host country may be experienced as less helpful in dealing with the loss of loved ones, and such cultural incongruity may contribute to increased distress following the loss of a loved one (Smid et al., 2018). Special attention should be given to refugees, as they often live through several traumatic events and traumatic losses, and can be affected by many of the above-mentioned risk factors (Bryant et al., 2021). In addition, the PGD risk might be heightened due to post-migration stress caused by insecurities and adversities in the host country (Comtesse & Rosner, 2019).

End-of-life care and bereavement care experiences

Ideas about a good death vary across cultures and interact with the way palliative and end-of-life care are defined and organized within a country and specific medical field. Within different countries, ethical debates about aspects of good death are ongoing. Contrary to the impact of traumatic circumstances of the death on grief, a good death may have favorable effects on the grief process. A systematic review on conditions of good death from the perspectives of patients, loved ones, and care providers revealed the most significant themes being preferred place of death, relief from pain and psychological distress, emotional support from loved ones, autonomy in decision making, avoidance of being a burden to others, right to assisted dying, effective communication with professionals, and performance of rituals (Zaman et al., 2021). Circumstances related to end-of-life care may impact grief. Across studies, higher levels of PGD and/or depression were associated with the following aspects of end-of-life care: major impact of care on one's schedule (Thomas et al., 2014), aggressive terminal care, i.e., ventilation and/or resuscitation (Wright et al., 2008), little preparation for death and little symptom control (Mah et al., 2022), dissatisfaction with the explanation of the expected outcome for the patient, unreasonable healthcare costs, and perception that the deceased had not achieved a sense of life completion (Miyajima et al., 2014). Being informally involved in a loved one's end-of-life care may also impact post-bereavement grief. Informal caregivers reported higher grief levels following the death of their loved one than non-caregivers, up to 10 months after death (Breen et al., 2020). The effects of care and support, both pre- and post-bereavement, may mitigate grief severity. Following the death of a loved one, cultural norms influence an individual's decisions to seek help or support from family, religious leaders, the community, and/or professional care (Good & Hinton, 2016; Smid et al., 2018).

Rituals

Across cultures, the death of a beloved person is often followed by specific mourning rituals or practices. Many reasons, such as the lack of mortal remains, an ongoing war, restrictions related to the Covid-19 pandemic, or personal reasons, can affect whether mourning rituals can be held or make participating in them impossible. Not being able to perform or participate in specific mourning rituals might cause distress in bereaved persons (Hinton et al., 2013; Lechner-Meichsner & Comtesse, 2022), especially if the performance of these rituals is thought to be connected to enabling a positive spiritual state of the deceased (Hinton et al., 2013). Guilt related to not performing rituals may contribute to PGD symptoms, as research on the suspension of funerals in the course of the Covid-19 pandemic has documented (Neimeyer & Lee, 2022; see also Chapter 7). However, longitudinal research in a bereaved population found no significant association between evaluation of the funeral, usage of grief rituals, and grief reactions (Mitima-Verloop et al., 2021). Pandemic-related qualitative evidence suggests that the benefit of death rituals depends on the ability of the bereaved to shape those rituals and say goodbye in a way which is meaningful for them (Burrell & Selman, 2022), and a study suggests looking beyond symptom levels when studying the importance of funeral and grief rituals (Mitima-Verloop et al., 2022). However, the studies differ in which aspect of mourning rituals they focus on (e.g., being involved in the planning of a funeral, funeral attendance, evaluation of the funeral, and the number of rituals). Furthermore, the effect of such rituals may depend on how a bereaved person can make use of them to say goodbye to their loved person, make meaning of a loss, or receive social support (Burrell & Selman, 2022; Mitima-Verloop et al., 2021). Therapeutic rituals are often part of grief therapy, with some preliminary evidence for their effectiveness (Wojtkowiak et al., 2021; see also Chapter 8). Although the current state of research still leaves many questions unanswered, taking into account how individuals could participate in mourning rituals, evaluating them or their absence, or the personal role they had in them might be helpful to detect distress related to a loss (Mitima-Verloop et al., 2022).

Concluding remarks

Practitioners evaluating risk and protective factors for prolonged and traumatic grief need to consider factors related to the relationship with the deceased, circumstances of the death, and individual, social, and cultural factors. Scientific insights into the nature and time of operation of risk and protective factors for prolonged and traumatic grief are evolving. Many of the studies to date were based on selective and relatively small samples, using different and not always validated outcome measures, and relying on cross-sectional designs. Interaction and mediation effects on prolonged and traumatic grief outcomes involving two or more risk or protective factors during the post-loss phase have received scarce research attention (see also Chapter 1). Some risk or protective factor effects may interact with mental health treatment, e.g., judicial procedures or therapeutic rituals. To increase insight into effects that are mediated through coping behaviors, cognitions, and meanings, future research needs to be context sensitive and may benefit from mixed-method designs to deepen insights further.

References

Albuquerque, S., Pereira, M., & Narciso, I. (2015). Couple's relationship after the death of a child: A systematic review. *Journal of Child and Family Studies*, *25*(1), 30–53. https://doi.org/10.1007/s10826-015-0219-2

Andriessen, K., Krysinska, K., Castelli Dransart, D. A., Dargis, L., & Mishara, B. L. (2020). Grief after euthanasia and physician-assisted suicide. *Crisis*, *41*(4), 255–272. https://doi.org/10.1027/0227-5910/a000630

BMA. (2021). *Physician-assisted dying legislation around the world*. https://www.bma.org.uk/media/6706/bma-where-is-pad-permitted-internationally.pdf

Boelen, P. A., de Keijser, J., & Smid, G. E. (2015). Cognitive-behavioral variables mediate the impact of violent loss on post-loss psychopathology. *Psychological Trauma: Theory, Research, Practice, and Policy*, *7*(4), 382–390. https://doi.org/10.1037/tra0000018

Boelen, P. A., & Spuij, M. (2024). Individual and systemic variables associated with prolonged grief and other emotional distress in bereaved children. *PloS One*, *19*(4), e0302725. https://doi.org/10.1371/journal.pone.0302725

Bowlby, J. (1973). *Attachment and loss. Volume II. Separation, anxiety and anger*. Basic Books.

Breen, L. J., Aoun, S. M., O'Connor, M., Johnson, A. R., & Howting, D. (2020). Effect of caregiving at end of life on grief, quality of life and general health: A prospective, longitudinal, comparative study. *Palliative Medicine*, *34*(1), 145–154. https://doi.org/10.1177/0269216319880766

Bryant, R. A., Creamer, M., Edwards, B., Felmingham, K. L., Forbes, D., Hadzi-Pavlovic, D., McFarlane, A. C., Nickerson, A., O'Donnell, M., Silove, D., Steel, Z., & van Hooff, M. (2020). A population study of prolonged grief in refugees. *Epidemiology and Psychiatric Sciences*, *29*, e44. https://doi.org/10.1017/S2045796019000386

Bryant, R. A., Edwards, B., Creamer, M., O'Donnell, M., Forbes, D., Felmingham, K. L., Silove, D., Steel, Z., McFarlane, A. C., Van Hooff, M., Nickerson, A., & Hadzi-Pavlovic, D. (2021). Prolonged grief in refugees, parenting behaviour and children's mental health. *Australian & New Zealand Journal of Psychiatry*, *55*(9), 863–873. https://doi.org/10.1177/0004867420967420

Burke, L. A., & Neimeyer, R. A. (2013). Prospective risk factors for complicated grief: A review of the empirical literature. In M. Stroebe, H. Schut, & J. van den Bout (Eds.), *Complicated grief: Scientific foundations for health care professionals* (pp. 145–161). Routledge/Taylor & Francis Group.

Burrell, A., & Selman, L. E. (2022). How do funeral practices impact bereaved relatives' mental health, grief and bereavement? A mixed methods review with implications for COVID-19. *Omega*, *85*(2), 345–383. https://doi.org/10.1177/0030222820941296

Buur, C., Zachariae, R., Komischke-Konnerup, K. B., Marello, M. M., Schierff, L. H., & O'Connor, M. (2024). Risk factors for prolonged grief symptoms: A systematic review and meta-analysis. *Clinical Psychology Review*, *107*, 102375. https://doi.org/10.1016/j.cpr.2023.102375

Comtesse, H., & Rosner, R. (2019). Prolonged grief disorder among asylum seekers in Germany: The influence of losses and residence status. *European Journal of Psychotraumatology*, *10*(1), 1591330. https://doi.org/10.1080/20008198.2019.1591330

Comtesse, H., Smid, G. E., Rummel, A.-M., Spreeuwenberg, P., Lundorff, M., & Dückers, M. L. A. (2024). Cross-national analysis of the prevalence of prolonged grief disorder. *Journal of Affective Disorders*, *350*, 359–365.

Corden, A., & Hirst, M. (2013). Economic components of grief. *Death Studies*, *37*(8), 725–749. https://doi.org/10.1080/07481187.2012.692456

Djelantik, A., Smid, G. E., Mroz, A., Kleber, R. J., & Boelen, P. A. (2020). The prevalence of prolonged grief disorder in bereaved individuals following unnatural losses: Systematic review and meta regression analysis. *Journal of Affective Disorders*, *265*, 146–156. https://doi.org/10.1016/j.jad.2020.01.034

Djelantik, A. A. A. M. J., Aryani, P., Boelen, P. A., Lesmana, C. B. J., & Kleber, R. J. (2021). Prolonged grief disorder, posttraumatic stress disorder, and depression following traffic accidents among bereaved Balinese family members: Prevalence, latent classes and cultural correlates. *Journal of Affective Disorders*, *292*, 773–781. https://doi.org/10.1016/j.jad.2021.05.085

Eisma, M. C., Bernemann, K., Aehlig, L., Janshen, A., & Doering, B. K. (2023). Adult attachment and prolonged grief: A systematic review and meta-analysis. *Personality and Individual Differences*, *214*, 112315. https://doi.org/10.1016/j.paid.2023.112315

Eisma, M. C., & Stroebe, M. S. (2021). Emotion regulatory strategies in complicated grief: A systematic review. *Behavior Therapy*, *52*(1), 234–249. https://doi.org/10.1016/j.beth.2020.04.004

Farver-Vestergaard, I., Johannsen, M., Lundorff, M., Maccallum, F., & O'Connor, M. (2023). An exploration of gender and prolonged grief symptoms using network analysis. *Psychological Medicine*, *53*(5), 1770–1777. https://doi.org/10.1017/S0033291721003391

Gegieckaite, G., & Kazlauskas, E. (2022). Do emotion regulation difficulties mediate the association between neuroticism, insecure attachment, and prolonged grief? *Death Studies*, *46*(4), 911–919. https://doi.org/10.1080/07481187.2020.1788667

Goetter, E., Bui, E., Horenstein, A., Baker, A. W., Hoeppner, S., Charney, M., & Simon, N. M. (2019). Five-factor model in bereaved adults with and without complicated grief. *Death Studies*, *43*(3), 204–209. https://doi.org/10.1080/07481187.2018.1446059

Gonschor, J., Eisma, M. C., Barke, A., & Doering, B. K. (2020). Public stigma towards prolonged grief disorder: Does diagnostic labeling matter? *PLoS One*, *15*(9), e0237021. https://doi.org/10.1371/journal.pone.0237021

Good, B., & Hinton, D. E. (2016). The culturally sensitive assessment of trauma: Eleven analytic perspectives, a typology of errors, and the multiplex models of distress generation. In D. E. Hinton & B. Good (Eds.), *Culture and PTSD: Trauma in global and historical perspective* (pp. 50–114). University of Pennsylvania Press.

Heeke, C., Kampisiou, C., Niemeyer, H., & Knaevelsrud, C. (2019). A systematic review and meta-analysis of correlates of prolonged grief disorder in adults exposed to violent loss. *European Journal of Psychotraumatology*, *10*(1), 1583524. https://doi.org/10.1080/20008198.2019.1583524

Hinton, D. E., Peou, S., Joshi, S., Nickerson, A., & Simon, N. M. (2013). Normal grief and complicated bereavement among traumatized Cambodian refugees: Cultural context and the Central role of dreams of the dead. *Culture, Medicine, and Psychiatry*, *37*(3), 427–464. https://doi.org/10.1007/s11013-013-9324-0

Hopf, D., Eckstein, M., Aguilar-Raab, C., Warth, M., & Ditzen, B. (2020). Neuroendocrine mechanisms of grief and bereavement: A systematic review and implications for future interventions. *Journal of Neuroendocrinology*, *32*(8), e12887. https://doi.org/10.1111/jne.12887

Janshen, A., & Eisma, M. C. (2024). Bidirectional associations between prolonged grief symptoms and depressive, anxiety, and posttraumatic stress symptoms: A systematic review. *Journal of Traumatic Stress*, *37*(6), 825–836. https://doi.org/10.1002/jts.23061

Johnson, J. G., First, M. B., Block, S., Vanderwerker, L. C., Zivin, K., Zhang, B., & Prigerson, H. G. (2009). Stigmatization and receptivity to mental health services among recently bereaved adults. *Death Stud*, *33*(8), 691–711. https://doi.org/10.1080/07481180903070392

Kahler, J., Papa, A., Epstein, E., & Levin, C. (2021). Attributions about bereaved spouses: Testing the myths of coping with loss. *OMEGA - Journal of Death and Dying*, *84*(1), 307–334. https://doi.org/10.1177/0030222819890974

Kakarala, S. E., Roberts, K. E., Rogers, M., Coats, T., Falzarano, F., Gang, J., Chilov, M., Avery, J., Maciejewski, P. K., Lichtenthal, W. G., & Prigerson, H. G. (2020). The neurobiological reward system in prolonged grief disorder (PGD): A systematic review. *Psychiatry Research. Neuroimaging*, *303*, 111135. https://doi.org/10.1016/j.pscychresns.2020.111135

Kim, J., Tol, W. A., Shrestha, A., Kafle, H. M., Rayamajhi, R., Luitel, N. P., Thapa, L., & Surkan, P. J. (2017). Persistent complex bereavement disorder and culture: Early and prolonged grief in Nepali widows. *Psychiatry*, *80*(1), 1–16. https://doi.org/10.1080/00332747.2016.1213560

Knowles, L. M., Ruiz, J. M., & O'Connor, M.-F. (2019). A systematic review of the association between bereavement and biomarkers of immune function. *Biopsychosocial Science and Medicine*, *81*(5), 415. https://doi.org/10.1097/PSY.0000000000000693

Kokou-Kpolou, C. K., Cenat, J. M., Noorishad, P. G., Park, S., & Bacque, M. F. (2020). A comparison of prevalence and risk factor profiles of prolonged grief disorder among French and Togolese bereaved adults. *Social Psychiatry and Psychiatric Epidemiology*, *55*(6), 757–764. https://doi.org/10.1007/s00127-020-01840-w

Kokou-Kpolou, C. K., Park, S., Lenferink, L. I. M., Iorfa, S. K., Fernández-Alcántara, M., Derivois, D., & Cénat, J. M. (2021). Prolonged grief and depression: A latent class analysis. *Psychiatry Research*, *299*, 113864. https://doi.org/10.1016/j.psychres.2021.113864

Kõlves, K., Zhao, Q., Ross, V., Hawgood, J., Spence, S. H., & de Leo, D. (2020). Suicide and sudden death bereavement in Australia: A longitudinal study of family members over 2 years after death. *Australian & New Zealand Journal of Psychiatry*, *54*(1), 89–98. https://doi.org/10.1177/0004867419882490

Komischke-Konnerup, K. B., Zachariae, R., Johannsen, M., Dyrvig Nielsen, L., & O'Connor, M. (2021). Co-occurrence of prolonged grief symptoms and symptoms of depression, anxiety, and posttraumatic stress in bereaved adults: A systematic review and meta-analysis. *Journal of Affective Disorders Reports*, *4*. https://doi.org/10.1016/j.jadr.2021.100140.

Kristensen, P., Dyregrov, K., Dyregrov, A., & Heir, T. (2016). Media exposure and prolonged grief: A study of bereaved parents and siblings after the 2011 Utøya Island terror attack. *Psychological Trauma: Theory, Research, Practice, and Policy*, *8*(6), 661–667. https://doi.org/10.1037/tra0000131

Kristensen, P., Weisæth, L., & Heir, T. (2012). Bereavement and mental health after sudden and violent losses: A review. *Psychiatry*, *75*(1), 76–97. https://doi.org/10.1521/psyc.2012.75.1.76

Lancel, M., Stroebe, M., & Eisma, M. C. (2020). Sleep disturbances in bereavement: A systematic review. *Sleep Medicine Reviews*, *53*, 101331. https://doi.org/10.1016/j.smrv.2020.101331

Lechner-Meichsner, F., & Comtesse, H. (2022). Beliefs about causes and cures of prolonged grief disorder among Arab and Sub-Saharan African refugees. *Frontiers in Psychiatry*, *13*. https://doi.org/10.3389/fpsyt.2022.852714

Lenferink, L. I. M., & O'Connor, M. (2023). Grief is a family affair: Examining longitudinal associations between prolonged grief in parents and their adult children using four-wave cross-lagged panel models. *Psychological Medicine*, *53*(15), 7428–7434. https://doi.org/10.1017/S0033291723001101

Lindemann, E. (1994). Symptomatology and management of acute grief. *American Journal of Psychiatry*, *151*(6), 155–160. (Original work published 1944)

Lobb, E. A., Kristjanson, L. J., Aoun, S. M., Monterosso, L., Halkett, G. K., & Davies, A. (2010). Predictors of complicated grief: a systematic review of empirical studies. *Death Studies*, *34*(8), 673–698. https://doi.org/10.1080/07481187.2010.496686

Lundorff, M., Bonanno, G. A., Johannsen, M., & O'Connor, M. (2020). Are there gender differences in prolonged grief trajectories? A registry-sampled cohort study. *Journal of Psychiatric Research*, *129*, 168–175. https://doi.org/10.1016/j.jpsychires.2020.06.030

Lundorff, M., Holmgren, H., Zachariae, R., Farver-Vestergaard, I., & O'Connor, M. (2017). Prevalence of prolonged grief disorder in adult bereavement: A systematic review and meta-analysis. *Journal of Affective Disorders*, *212*, 138–149. https://doi.org/10.1016/j.jad.2017.01.030

Mah, K., Swami, N., Pope, A., Earle, C. C., Krzyzanowska, M. K., Nissim, R., Hales, S., Rodin, G., Hannon, B., & Zimmermann, C. (2022). Caregiver bereavement outcomes in advanced cancer: Associations with quality of death and patient age. *Supportive Care in Cancer*, *30*(2), 1343–1353. https://doi.org/10.1007/s00520-021-06536-8

Mason, T. M., Tofthagen, C. S., & Buck, H. G. (2020). Complicated grief: Risk factors, protective factors, and interventions. *Journal of Social Work in End-of-Life & Palliative Care*, *16*(2), 151–174. https://doi.org/10.1080/15524256.2020.1745726

Mercer, D., & Evans, J. (2006). The impact of multiple losses on the grieving process: An exploratory study. *Journal of Loss and Trauma*, *11*(3), 219–227. https://doi.org/10.1080/15325020500494178

Mikulincer, M., & Shaver, P. R. (2008). An attachment perspective on bereavement. In M. S. Stroebe, R. O. Hansson, & W. Stroebe (Eds.), *Handbook of bereavement research and practice: Advances in theory and intervention* (pp. 87–112). American Psychological Association. https://doi.org/10.1037/14498-005

Mikulincer, M., & Shaver, P. R. (2022). An attachment perspective on loss and grief. *Current Opinion in Psychology*, *45*, 101283. https://doi.org/10.1016/j.copsyc.2021.11.003

Milman, E., Neimeyer, R. A., Fitzpatrick, M., MacKinnon, C. J., Muis, K. R., & Cohen, S. R. (2019). Prolonged grief and the disruption of meaning: Establishing a mediation model. *Journal of Counseling Psychology*, *66*(6), 714–725. https://doi.org/10.1037/cou0000370

Mitima-Verloop, H. B., Mooren, T. T. M., & Boelen, P. A. (2021). Facilitating grief: An exploration of the function of funerals and rituals in relation to grief reactions. *Death Studies*, *45*(9), 735–745. https://doi.org/10.1080/07481187.2019. 1686090

Mitima-Verloop, H. B., Mooren, T. T. M., Kritikou, M. E., & Boelen, P. A. (2022). Restricted mourning: Impact of the COVID-19 pandemic on funeral services, grief rituals, and prolonged grief symptoms. *Front Psychiatry*, *13*, 878818. https://doi.org/10.3389/fpsyt.2022.878818

Miyajima, K., Fujisawa, D., Yoshimura, K., Ito, M., Nakajima, S., Shirahase, J., Mimura, M., & Miyashita, M. (2014). Association between quality of end-of-life care and possible complicated grief among bereaved family members. *Journal of Palliative Medicine*, *17*(9), 1025–1031. https://doi.org/10.1089/jpm.2013.0552

Neimeyer, R. A., & Burke, L. A. (2011). Complicated grief in the aftermath of homicide: Spiritual crisis and distress in an African American sample. *Religions*, *2*(2), 145–164. https://doi.org/10.3390/rel2020145

Neimeyer, R. A., & Lee, S. A. (2022). Circumstances of the death and associated risk factors for severity and impairment of COVID-19 grief. *Death Studies*, *46*(1), 34–42. https://doi.org/10.1080/07481187.2021.1896459

Newson, R. S., Boelen, P. A., Hek, K., Hofman, A., & Tiemeier, H. (2011). The prevalence and characteristics of complicated grief in older adults. *Journal of Affective Disorders*, *132*(1-2), 231–238. https://doi.org/10.1016/j.jad.2011.02.021

Niederland, W. G. (1961). The problem of the survivor. *Journal of the Hillside Hospital*, *10*(3–4), 233–247.

Nielsen, M. K., Neergaard, M. A., Jensen, A. B., Bro, F., & Guldin, M.-B. (2016). Do we need to change our understanding of anticipatory grief in caregivers? A systematic review of caregiver studies during end-of-life caregiving and bereavement. *Clinical Psychology Review*, *44*, 75–93. https://doi.org/10.1016/j.cpr.2016.01.002

Nijborg, L. C. J., Kunst, M. J. J., Westerhof, G. J., de Keijser, J., & Lenferink, L. I. M. (2023). Grief and delivering a statement in court: a longitudinal mixed-method study among homicidally bereaved people. *European Journal of Psychotraumatology*, *15*(1), 2297541. https://doi.org/10.1080/20008066.2023.2297541

Parisi, A., Sharma, A., Howard, M. O., & Blank Wilson, A. (2019). The relationship between substance misuse and complicated grief: A systematic review. *Journal of Substance Abuse Treatment*, *103*, 43–57. https://doi.org/10.1016/j.jsat.2019.05.012

Parkes, C. M., & Prigerson, H. G. (2010). *Bereavement: Studies of grief in adult life* (4th ed.). Penguin.

Parro-Jiménez, E., Morán, N., Gesteira, C., Sanz, J., & García-Vera, M. P. (2021). Complicated grief: A systematic review of the prevalence, diagnosis, risk and protective factors in the adult population of Spain. *Anales De Psicologia*, *37*, 189–201.

Pociunaite, J., van Dijk, I., Reitsma, L., Nordström, E. E. L., Boelen, P. A., & Lenferink, L. I. M. (2023). Latent trajectories of DSM-5-TR-based prolonged grief disorder: Findings from a data pooling project MARBLES. *European Journal of Psychotraumatology*, *14*(2). https://doi.org/10.1080/20008066.2023.2281183

Prigerson, H. G., Kakarala, S., Gang, J., & Maciejewski, P. K. (2021). History and status of prolonged grief disorder as a psychiatric diagnosis. *Annual Review of Clinical Psychology*, *17*(1), 109–126. https://doi.org/10.1146/annurev-clinpsy-081219-093600

Sanderson, E. A. M., Humphreys, S., Walker, F., Harris, D., Carduff, E., McPeake, J., Boyd, K., Pattison, N., & Lone, N. I. (2022). Risk factors for complicated grief among family members bereaved in intensive care unit settings: A systematic review. *PLoS One*, *17*(3), e0264971. https://doi.org/10.1371/journal.pone.0264971

Schaal, S., Jacob, N., Dusingizemungu, J.-P., & Elbert, T. (2010). Rates and risks for prolonged grief disorder in a sample of orphaned and widowed genocide survivors. *BMC Psychiatry*, *10*(1), 55. https://doi.org/10.1186/1471-244X-10-55

Shear, M. K., Monk, T., Houck, P., Melhem, N., Frank, E., Reynolds, C., & Sillowash, R. (2007). An attachment-based model of complicated grief including the role of avoidance. *European Archives of Psychiatry and Clinical Neurosciences*, *257*(8), 453–461. https://doi.org/10.1007/s00406-007-0745-z

Smid, G. E. (2020). A framework of meaning attribution following loss. *European Journal of Psychotraumatology*, *11*(1), 1776563. https://doi.org/10.1080/20008198.2020.1776563

Smid, G. E., Drogendijk, A. N., Knipscheer, J., Boelen, P. A., & Kleber, R. J. (2018). Loss of loved ones or home due to a disaster: Effects over time on distress in immigrant ethnic minorities. *Transcultural Psychiatry*, *55*(5), 648–668. https://doi.org/10.1177/1363461518784355

Smid, G. E., Groen, S., De la Rie, S. M., Kooper, S., & Boelen, P. A. (2018). Toward cultural assessment of grief and grief-related psychopathology. *Psychiatric Services*, *69*(10), 1050–1052. https://doi.org/10.1176/appi.ps.201700422

Smid, G. E., Killikelly, C., & Wagner, B. (2021). Editorial: Grief disorders: Clinical, cultural, and epidemiological aspects. *Frontiers in Psychiatry*, *12*, 681523. https://doi.org/10.3389/fpsyt.2021.681523

Snijdewind, M. C., de Keijser, J., Casteelen, G., Boelen, P. A., & Smid, G. E. (2022a). "I lost so much more than my partner" – Bereaved partners' grief experiences following suicide or physician-assisted dying in case of a mental disorder. *BMC Psychiatry*, *22*(1), 454. https://doi.org/10.1186/s12888-022-04098-5

Snijdewind, M. C., de Keijser, J., Casteelen, G., Boelen, P. A., & Smid, G. E. (2022b). "Only one way out" – Partners' experiences and grief related to the death of their loved one by suicide or physician-assisted dying due to a mental disorder. *Frontiers in Psychiatry*, *13*, 894417. https://doi.org/10.3389/fpsyt.2022.894417

Soydas, S., Smid, G. E., Goodfellow, B., Wilson, R., & Boelen, P. A. (2020). The UK National Homicide Therapeutic Service: A retrospective naturalistic study among 929 bereaved individuals. *Frontiers in Psychiatry*, *11*, 878. https://doi.org/10.3389/fpsyt.2020.00878

Specht, F., Vöhringer, M., Knaevelsrud, C., Wagner, B., Stammel, N., & Böttche, M. (2022). Prolonged grief disorder in Arabic-speaking treatment-seeking populations: Relationship with socio-demographic aspects, loss- and trauma-related characteristics, and mental health support. *Frontiers in Psychiatry*, *13*. https://doi.org/10.3389/fpsyt.2022.933848

Stroebe, M. S., Folkman, S., Hansson, R. O., & Schut, H. (2006). The prediction of bereavement outcome: Development of an integrative risk factor framework. *Social Science & Medicine*, *63*(9), 2440–2451. https://doi.org/10.1016/j.socscimed.2006.06.012

Swarte, N. B., van der Lee, M. L., van der Bom, J. G., Van den Bout, J., & Heintz, A. P. (2003). Effects of euthanasia on the bereaved family and friends: A cross sectional study. *British Medical Journal*, *327*(7408), 189. https://doi.org/10.1136/bmj.327.7408.189

Thomas, K., Hudson, P., Trauer, T., Remedios, C., & Clarke, D. (2014). Risk factors for developing prolonged grief during bereavement in family carers of cancer patients in palliative care: A longitudinal study. *Journal of Pain and Symptom Management*, *47*(3), 531–541. https://doi.org/10.1016/j.jpainsymman.2013.05.022

van Denderen, M., de Keijser, J., Huisman, M., & Boelen, P. A. (2016). Prevalence and correlates of self-rated posttraumatic stress disorder and complicated grief in a community-based sample of homicidally bereaved individuals. *Journal of Interpersonal Violence*, *31*(2), 207–227. https://doi.org/10.1177/0886260514555368

Wagner, B., Keller, V., Knaevelsrud, C., & Maercker, A. (2011). Social acknowledgement as a predictor of post-traumatic stress and complicated grief after witnessing assisted suicide. *International Journal of Social Psychiatry*, *58*(4), 381–385. https://doi.org/10.1177/0020764011400791

Wijngaards-de Meij, L., Stroebe, M., Schut, H., Stroebe, W., van den Bout, J., van der Heijden, P., & Dijkstra, I. (2007). Neuroticism and attachment insecurity as predictors of bereavement outcome. *Journal of Research in Personality*, *41*(2), 498–505. https://doi.org/10.1016/j.jrp.2006.06.001

Wojtkowiak, J., Lind, J., & Smid, G. E. (2021). Ritual in therapy for prolonged grief: A scoping review of ritual elements in evidence-informed grief interventions. *Frontiers in Psychiatry*, *11*. https://doi.org/10.3389/fpsyt.2020.623835

Wright, A. A., Zhang, B., Ray, A., Mack, J. W., Trice, E., Balboni, T., Mitchell, S. L., Jackson, V. A., Block, S. D., Maciejewski, P. K., & Prigerson, H. G. (2008). Associations between end-of-life discussions, patient mental health, medical care near death, and caregiver bereavement adjustment. *JAMA: The Journal of the American Medical Association*, *300*(14), 1665–1673. https://doi.org/10.1001/jama.300.14.1665

Zaman, M., Espinal-Arango, S., Mohapatra, A., & Jadad, A. R. (2021). What would it take to die well? A systematic review of systematic reviews on the conditions for a good death. *The Lancet Healthy Longevity*, *2*(9), e593–e600. https://doi.org/10.1016/S2666-7568(21)00097-0

Chapter 4

Conceptualizations of prolonged grief and traumatic grief

Fiona Maccallum

The death of a close loved one has the potential to upend one's entire life. Understanding how individuals adapt to such losses, including the factors that facilitate or hinder adaptation, has been the focus of much scientific attention in recent years. This interest has been driven both by the inclusion of prolonged grief disorder (PGD) within psychiatric diagnostic systems and by the COVID-19 pandemic. Empirical studies have investigated a wide range of potential maintaining mechanisms, including cognitive, behavioural, memory, emotion regulation and attachment processes. Although theoretical models developed to explain PGD (e.g., Boddez, 2018; Boelen et al., 2006; Maccallum & Bryant, 2013; Shear et al., 2007; Stroebe et al., 2010) differ in their emphasis, they share the basic premise that adapting to a bereavement requires updating one's self-concept in a way that acknowledges the reality of the death. This involves relinquishing or modifying life goals and roles that were dependent on the physical presence of the deceased and developing new sources of purpose and meaning in life (see Maccallum & Bryant, 2013, Table 4.1 for a comparison of the major models). Integrating the reality of the death is considered of primary importance, as it places the death as something that has happened in the past, reducing the sense of shock and disbelief on recalling the loss and facilitating a revision of life goals and roles. A block in this process is thought to lead to "complicated" or prolonged grief reactions, whereby the individual becomes "stuck" in a state of acute grief, and experiences a persistent reactions reflected by the diagnostic criteria for PGD as outlined in Chapter 1.

As previously discussed, the likelihood of developing PGD increases following an unexpected, violent or "unnatural" death, or where the death is of a child or spouse, suggesting rates of PGD may be higher in some subpopulations (see Chapter 3). Comorbidity is also common, though not universal (e.g., posttraumatic stress disorder (PTSD), major depression; see Chapters 1 and 2) necessitating careful clinical consideration of how best to conceptualize grief reactions within each individual (Eberle & Maercker, 2023). Three processes are hypothesized to interact and contribute to the

DOI: 10.4324/9781003429777-6

development of PGD: (1) Autobiographical processes involving the self and memory, (2) negative cognitions about one's grief reactions, self, the world, and the future, and (3) avoidant and approach-seeking coping strategies. It is argued that interactions among these three processes inhibit integration of the death, hinder the development of new sources of meaning in life and keep the bereaved person focused on their loss.

This chapter outlines the theoretical proposals and empirical evidence relevant to each of these processes and then discusses how models can be extended for working with subgroups of individuals bereaved in traumatic circumstances or experiencing comorbid reactions. A model adapted from Maccallum and Bryant (2013) is outlined in Figure 4.1.

The self and autobiographical memory processes

Within cognitive and affective science, the self is conceived of as a complex set of interacting processes containing information relevant to the short- and long-term self and autobiographical memories are defined as memories for events from one's own life (Conway, 2005). Memory retrieval is viewed as a reconstructive process influenced by different facets of the self (e.g., personal goals, values, schemas, and beliefs). Conway and Pleydell-Pearce's (2000) self-memory system model proposes a reciprocal relationship between the self and the autobiographical knowledge database, arguing that the goals of the self mediate encoding and retrieval of autobiographical knowledge, and autobiographical knowledge shapes the content of one's goals (Addis et al., 2010; Conway, 2005; Conway & Pleydell-Pearce, 2000). Specifically, external events congruent with one's goals are more easily encoded and retrieved, while external events incongruent with goals are less easily integrated and are either distorted to fit with the working goals or inhibited. Numerous studies have supported the idea that memories associated with dominant goals of the self are preferenced within the autobiographical knowledge database (see Conway, 2005; Conway & Pleydell-Pearce, 2000; Moberly & MacLeod, 2006). In turn, autobiographical knowledge shapes the goals of the self; goals we remember achieving are relinquished, and goals that are inconsistent or unachievable in the context of our self-knowledge are unlikely to be set. In this way the system seeks to maintain a self-concept that corresponds with external realities (correspondence) but is also coherent over time (coherence).

The self-memory system posits that distress and memory disturbances arise when there is a discrepancy between our goals and reality, as can exist immediately following the death of a close person. Supporting this proposition, failure to disengage from previously valued goals (King & Raspin, 2004), and a discrepancy between one's goals and current life situations have been associated with various forms of emotional distress (James et al., 2024;

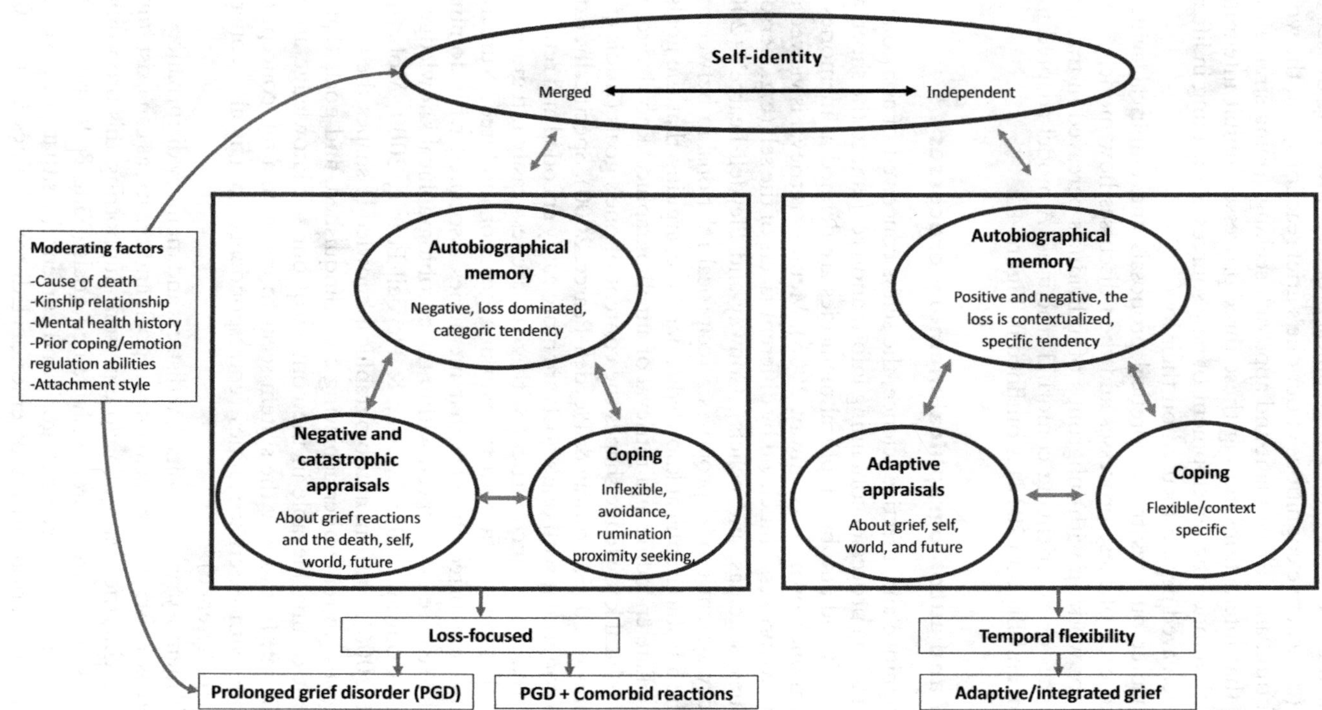

Figure 4.1 Cognitive attachment model of prolonged grief disorder. Adapted from Maccallum and Bryant (2013).

Strauman, 1992). In bereavement, the magnitude of the initial discrepancy will be determined by the degree to which a person's sense of self and working goals were intertwined with the deceased or directly impacted by the death. Such an intertwining of goals may develop in the context of an intimate relationship, where the planning of a shared future, the partitioning of roles within the relationship, and the emergence of shared past over time facilitates the merging of selves ("we" rather than "I"). In other situations, non-deceased (independent) goals and roles may have been deliberately relinquished in favour of deceased-related goals, for example, for the purposes of caring for a spouse or parent living with dementia, or to meet the care needs of a child. Secondary losses stemming from bereavement (e.g., financial, social connections) may also introduce external impediments to retaining independent goals and routines, further challenging the ability to maintain self-coherence. The extent to which an individual is able to relinquish now unachievable goals and roles and develop new goals and a sense of purpose that correspond with their new reality is thought to mediate ongoing distress. When roles and goals continue to exist independently of the deceased, they may bolster self-coherence in the face of the loss by providing access to memories and self-aspects unrelated to the deceased, allowing some respite and facilitating oscillation between engaging with the reality of the loss and its implications, and setting aside the loss to manage other aspects of life (see also Stroebe & Schut, 1999).

Investigating these propositions, Boelen et al. (2012) found that bereavement coincided with reduced self-concept clarity and was linked with symptom severity immediately after the loss. Furthermore, the degree to which distress decreased over the first month of bereavement was related to increases in self-concept clarity, rather than the extent of the initial decline (see also Papa & Lancaster, 2016). Bellet et al. (2020) found that compared to participants without PGD, those with PGD provided fewer self-concept descriptors from fewer categories, suggesting a narrower, less diverse, sense of self. PGD severity was also positively related to the percentage of loss/deceased focused descriptors. Additionally, Maccallum and Bryant (2008) found individuals with PGD were more likely to provide self-defining memories that involved the deceased than individuals without PGD. Harrison et al. (2022) found that participants with PGD reported a sense of current interpersonal closeness with the deceased that was greater than both the closeness felt by those without PGD and the closeness they felt towards a living close person (see also Harris et al., 2023). Boelen (2012) found that the more the loss had become central to the person's identity the more severe their symptoms of PGD, PTSD and depression, concurrently and one year later. Robinaugh and McNally (2013) found that participants with PGD were more easily able to recall autobiographical memories involving the deceased than memories for events that didn't involve the deceased. The same pattern of findings was observed for imaged future events. Similarly, Maccallum and Bryant (2010) observed a relative bias for participants with PGD to recall loss-related memories. They were also more likely to describe grief-related goals and imagine loss-related future events than bereaved participants without PGD (Maccallum & Bryant, 2011b). It is important to recognize, however, that this work is predominantly cross-sectional, and as such, causal relationships cannot be established. Nonetheless, the overall pattern of findings suggests that PGD is associated with a relative bias in the content of the self, personal memories, and future imaginings which likely perpetuates distress by keeping the person focused on the loss.

PGD has also been associated with bias towards recalling "overgeneral" memories (Boelen et al., 2010; Golden et al., 2007; Maccallum & Bryant, 2010). Overgeneral memories are also observed in individuals with PTSD (Ono et al., 2016), depression, and suicidality (Weiss-Cowie et al., 2023; Williams & Broadbent, 1986). This is an important clinical phenomenon given its association with increased vulnerability to developing symptoms following stressful life events (Bryant et al., 2007), poorer response to treatment, vulnerability for relapse in depression, deficits imagining the future in a specific way, and impaired social problem-solving ability (see Williams, 2006; Williams et al., 2007). In PGD, overgeneral recall has also been associated with impaired ability to imagine the future in a positive way (Maccallum & Bryant, 2011b). An increase in the ability to recall specific positive memories across treatment has been linked to better outcomes (Maccallum & Bryant, 2011a). However, those with PGD may not show reduced specificity when recalling memories of the loss (Golden et al., 2007; Smith & Ehlers, 2021). This may reflect the salience of loss-related memories in PGD; however, based on current evidence, it is not possible to determine whether overgeneral memory in PGD predates the bereavement or arises after the death, due to executive functioning limitations associated with grief reactions or coping strategies employed to manage bereavement distress (e.g., avoidance and rumination; see Williams, 2006; Williams et al., 2007). Further longitudinal studies are needed to establish causal relationships.

Negative appraisals about the self, the world, and the future

A growing number of studies have investigated the relationship between appraisals and bereavement outcomes. Overall, these studies support the proposition that PGD is associated with negative appraisals about the self, life, the world, the future, and one's grief reactions (e.g., Boelen et al., 2003, 2006, 2010; Boelen et al., 2016; Smith & Ehlers, 2020). Appraisals involving negative interpretations of one's own grief reactions (e.g., "If I allow my feelings to come, I will lose control", "I don't mourn the way I should") and self-blame (e.g., "I should have prevented the death") appear particularly relevant for the persistence of PGD (e.g., Boelen et al., 2006; Boelen et al., 2016), and have been implicated in poorer treatment outcomes (Bryant et al., 2019; Lechner-Meichsner et al., 2022; Skritskaya et al., 2020). PGD severity has also been associated with a tendency to engage in upward counterfactual thinking about the loss, that is, thinking about how things could have turned out better (Golden & Dalgleish, 2012; Xu et al., 2023), and with a tendency to spend time ruminating about the death and the loss (Eisma & Stroebe, 2021). In contrast, general negative cognitions about the self ("since [–] is dead, I think I am worthless"), the world ("the death of [–] has taught me the world is unjust") and the future ("life has got nothing to offer me anymore") have been linked with multiple bereavement outcomes including PGD, depression and PTSD (Boelen et al., 2006; Maccallum & Bryant, 2019c).

Together, these findings suggest that while some belief patterns may be linked uniquely to PGD, others have transdiagnostic relevance. Within theoretical models, aspects of the self and relationship with the deceased may increase the likelihood of catastrophic appraisals, especially when the deceased met the (anxious) attachment needs of the bereaved or where there are few independent self-goals, making the task of processing the loss seem overwhelming. Conversely, these catastrophic beliefs are likely to encourage avoidance of the reality of the loss, hindering its integration and maintaining PGD. Additionally, the belief that one will not be able to cope if they think about the loss may also foster hypervigilance towards grief reactions and reminders of loss (as a safety behaviour), likely perpetuating rumination and avoidance while preventing engagement in restoration activities. This may compound secondary problems and reinforce beliefs that one cannot cope without the deceased. Furthermore, global beliefs about the self, the world and the future may reduce motivations to engage with social networks and new activities that could facilitate the development of new goals and roles to reduce the "threat" to the self-posed by the death and contributing to an ongoing sense of hopelessness and depression.

Emotion regulation and coping strategies

A range of coping strategies have also been linked with bereavement outcomes (Eisma & Stroebe, 2021). Two broad categories are considered most relevant to models of PGD: Avoidance and approach seeking coping. Overall, questionnaire-based studies have demonstrated a strong relationship between loss-related avoidance behaviour (e.g., suppression of thoughts and emotions, avoiding situations,) and poorer bereavement outcomes, both cross sectionally and longitudinally (Baker et al., 2016;

Boelen & Eisma, 2015; Boelen et al., 2010). These types of loss related avoidance have also been linked with poorer treatment outcomes (Bryant et al., 2019; Lechner-Meichsner et al., 2022). Grief-related rumination (repetitive thinking about the causes and consequences of the loss) is also conceptualized as a form of avoidance, as it often involves persistent counterfactual thinking (e.g., ways the death could have been prevented), or existential questions without answers ("why?"). Thus, while the individual may appear to spend a lot of time contemplating the death, they are actually thinking "around" it, avoiding the specific reality and it's implications for their life. Grief-related rumination has also been associated with more severe PGD (Doering (Doering et al., 2018; Eisma et al., 2014). However, results for more general forms of avoidance and rumination (ie., not loss-specific) are less consistent (for review, see Eisma & Stroebe, 2021). Notably, interventions for PGD that include specific exposure-based activities involving revisiting memories of the death to help the person engage with and integrate the reality of the death show superior outcomes compared to waitlist and alternative active treatments (e.g., Boelen et al., 2007; Bryant et al., 2014; Bryant et al., 2024; Shear et al., 2016). Reductions in both loss specific and non-loss specific forms of rumination have been associated with positive treatment responses (Boelen et al., 2011; Eisma et al., 2015). Overall, these findings provide strong evidence for the role of avoidance in PGD. However, it is important to note that avoidance is only considered maladaptive to the extent it interferes with processing of the reality of death. There are some circumstances in which avoidance may be adaptive, for example, when employed to facilitate development and engagement with goals that are restoration-focused (Boelen et al., 2006; Gupta & Bonanno, 2011; Maccallum & Bryant, 2013; Stroebe et al., 2010).

Approach behaviour, also termed proximity-seeking, describes cognitive and/or behavioural attempts to achieve a sense of closeness or maintain a bond with the deceased. This can include seeking out reminders, holding on to possessions, or becoming absorbed in reminiscing. These behaviours are also known as "continuing bonds". Some studies have found that concrete, tangible strategies (e.g., maintaining the deceased's possessions) are linked with poorer outcomes, while symbolic, internalized strategies (e.g., cherishing memories) are associated with better outcomes (Field & Filanosky, 2010; Field et al., 2003). However, in the context of PGD, internalized behaviours have also been linked with poorer outcomes (Schut et al., 2006). This has led to more nuanced theoretical hypotheses about the relationship between approach behaviours and bereavement outcomes, highlighting the need to understand the motivations underlying these behaviours (Stroebe et al., 2010). From this perspective, concrete or symbolic approach behaviours that seek to restore physical proximity with the deceased (e.g., behaviours associated with attachment anxiety) are considered problematic, whereas behaviours that acknowledge the reality death and the now symbolic nature of the relationship with the deceased are not considered problematic.

More recently, empirical investigations have moved beyond self-report methods to examine avoidance and proximity-seeking using behavioural measures. This approach allows for the indexing of responses that are less amenable to self-report but may have significant implications for theory and practice. For example, PTSD has been associated with self-reported deliberate avoidance of trauma reminders but an automatic attentional bias towards fear-relevant stimuli (see Harvey et al., 2004). This bias is thought to develop in order to enable early avoidance of threatening stimuli (Onnis et al., 2011). Ironically, however, it appears to result in greater processing of threatening information (Harvey et al., 2004). In the context of bereavement, PGD has been associated with attentional and motivational biases towards reminders of the deceased (Maccallum & Bryant, 2019a; Michel et al., 2023; Schneck et al., 2018). Theoretical models propose that this may contribute to yearning and proximity-seeking (e.g., Boddez, 2018; Maccallum & Bryant, 2013).

Theoretically, these findings suggest a pattern whereby some individuals are simultaneously drawn to reminders of the (living) deceased person while attempting to avoid reminders of their death (see also Eisma et al., 2014). This pattern is hypothesized to perpetuate distress in several ways. On the one hand, reminders of the deceased are likely to evoke thoughts of their death, leading to shock and disbelief. On the other hand, avoiding thoughts of the death prevents individuals from learning that they can cope with such thoughts and from engaging in activities which could help them develop alternate aspects of themselves.

Implications of the nature of the loss for understanding bereavement outcomes.

Rates of PGD are higher in the wake of a traumatic loss and death of a child or spouse (e.g., suicide, homicide, accident; Djelantik et al., 2020; Guldin et al., 2017; Lobb et al., 2010; Smith & Ehlers, 2020). Theoretical models suggest that one major reason for the increased risk of developing PGD following a traumatic death is the difficulty individuals have integrating the unexpected trauma into their autobiographical memory database; this information is often so discordant with their existing cognitive schemas (Boelen et al., 2015; Maccallum & Bryant, 2013). A traumatic death may also be more difficult for a person to integrate where there is a strong dependency on the deceased to provide coherence to one's sense of self. For example, those who experience the death of a child are considered at greater risk for PGD because the death violates one's self-construct as a parent with primary responsibility as a caregiver for the child, which includes goals and expectations intertwined with the child's identity and future. Additionally, the death may violate their assumptive world, such as the belief that children should outlive their parents.

The nature of the death may also sensitize the bereaved person to concerns for their own safety, leading to increased avoidance. Supporting these propositions, several studies have demonstrated that traumatic deaths predict the development of comorbid PGD/PTSD symptom patterns (Djelantik et al., 2017; Nickerson et al., 2014). Violent loss has also been associated with greater disbelief at the death (Djelantik et al., 2020). Further research is needed to determine the extent to which patterns of comorbidity are associated with different appraisals. Maccallum and Bryant (2019c) found that participants reporting PGD or PGD/PTSD both endorsed higher levels of self-blame compared to those with low symptoms. However, in the context of comorbid depression, Boelen et al. (2016) found that negative beliefs about the self, the world, and the future predicted comorbid PGD/Depression but not PGD alone.

In addition to psychological factors, different interacting psychobiological systems, such as neuroendocrinological and psycho-immunological systems, may bring about stress sensitization, i.e., increased reactivity to stressors, that may underlie fluctuations in distress over time following trauma and traumatic loss (e.g., Smid et al., 2022). Consistent with the stress sensitization model, bereaved individuals with elevated PGD levels may be more likely to experience exacerbations of PTSD and depression symptoms when confronted with loss-related stimuli (Lenferink et al., 2019). The stress sensitization model highlights contextual effects in explaining the trajectory of distress over time. For example, stressors associated with ethnic minority status may contribute to persistence of distress over time in disaster-affected residents who lost a loved one (Smid et al., 2018; see also Nickerson et al., 2014). Smid et al. (2015) describe a cognitive stress model of traumatic grief which integrates these psychobiological, and contextual aspects within an attachment-based, cognitive-behavioural framework of PGD.

Conclusions

This chapter has outlined the role of self-related processes, appraisals, and coping strategies in shaping adaptation to bereavement. A central proposition underlying the development of PGD is that these three process interact and reinforce each other, perpetuating and potentially exacerbating distress (Maccallum & Bryant, 2013, 2019b). Contextual factors, such as the cause of death or the post-bereavement environment, can further influence these reactions and contribute to the development of PTSD and/or depression, either independently or as comorbid conditions. Understanding these mechanisms and their reciprocal relationships will facilitate the development of individual case formulations to facilitate treatment planning and progress monitoring.

References

Addis, D. R., Musicaro, R., Pan, L., & Schacter, D. L. (2010). Episodic simulation of past and future events in older adults: Evidence from an experimental recombination task. *Psychology and Aging*, *25*, 369–376. https://doi.org/10.1037/a0017280

Baker, A. W., Keshaviah, A., Horenstein, A., Goetter, E. M., Mauro, C., Reynolds, C. F., & Simon, N. M. (2016). The role of avoidance in complicated grief: A detailed examination of the grief-related avoidance questionnaire (GRAQ) in a large sample of individuals with complicated grief. *Journal of Loss & Trauma*, *21*, 533–547. https://doi.org/10.1080/15325024.2016.1157412

Bellet, B. W., LeBlanc, N. J., Nizzi, M.-C., Carter, M. L., van der Does, F. H. S., Peters, J., & McNally, R. J. (2020). Identity confusion in complicated grief: A closer look. *Journal of Abnormal Psychology*, *129*, 397–407. https://doi.org/10.1037/abn0000520

Boddez, Y. (2018). The presence of your absence: A conditioning theory of grief. *Behaviour Research and Therapy*, *106*, 18–27. https://doi.org/10.1016/j.brat.2018.04.006

Boelen, P. A. (2012). A prospective examination of the association between the centrality of a loss and post-loss psychopathology. *Journal of Affective Disorders*, *137*, 117–124.

Boelen, P. A., de Keijser, J., van den Hout, M. A., & van den Bout, J. (2007). Treatment of complicated grief: A comparison between cognitive-behavioral therapy and supportive counseling. *Journal of Consulting and Clinical Psychology*, *75*, 277–284. https://doi.org/10.1037/0022-006x.75.2.277

Boelen, P. A., de Keijser, J., van den Hout, M. A., & van den Bout, J. (2011). Factors associated with outcome of cognitive–behavioural therapy for complicated grief: A preliminary study. *Clinical Psychology & Psychotherapy*, *18*, 284–291. https://doi.org/10.1002/cpp.720

Boelen, P. A., De Keijser, J., & Smid, G. E. (2015). Cognitive–behavioral variables mediate the impact of violent loss on post-loss psychopathology. *Psychological Trauma: Theory, Research, Practice, and Policy*, *7*, 382.

Boelen, P. A., & Eisma, M. C. (2015). Anxious and depressive avoidance behavior in post-loss psychopathology: A longitudinal study. *Anxiety, Stress, & Coping*, *28*, 587–600. https://doi.org/10.1080/10615806.2015.1004054

Boelen, P. A., Huntjens, R. J. C., van Deursen, D. S., & van den Hout, M. A. (2010). Autobiographical memory specificity and symptoms of complicated grief, depression, and posttraumatic stress disorder following loss. *Journal of Behavior Therapy and Experimental Psychiatry*, *41*, 331–337. https://doi.org/10.1016/j.jbtep.2010.03.003

Boelen, P. A., Keijsers, L., & van den Hout, M. A. (2012). The role of self-concept clarity in prolonged grief disorder. *Journal of Nervous and Mental Disease*, *200*, 56–62. https://doi.org/10.1097/NMD.0b013e31823e577f

Boelen, P. A., Reijntjes, A. J., Djelantik, A. A. A. M., & Smid, G. E. (2016). Prolonged grief and depression after unnatural loss: Latent class analyses and cognitive correlates. *Psychiatry Research*, *240*, 358–363. https://doi.org/10.1016/j.psychres.2016.04.012

Boelen, P. A., van den Bout, J., & van den Hout, M. A. (2003). The role of cognitive variables in psychological functioning after the death of a first degree relative. *Behaviour Research and Therapy*, *41*, 1123–1136. https://doi.org/10.1016/s0005-7967(02)00259-0

Boelen, P. A., van den Bout, J., & van den Hout, M. A. (2006). Negative cognitions and avoidance in emotional problems after bereavement: A prospective study. *Behaviour Research and Therapy*, *44*, 1657–1672. https://doi.org/10.1016/j.brat.2005.12.006

Boelen, P. A., van den Bout, J., & van den Hout, M. A. (2010). A prospective examination of catastrophic misinterpretations and experiential avoidance in emotional distress following loss. *Journal of Nervous and Mental Disease*, *198*, 252–257. https://doi.org/10.1097/NMD.0b013e3181d619e4

Boelen, P. A., van den Hout, M. A., & van den Bout, J. (2006). A cognitive-behavioral conceptualization of complicated grief. *Clinical Psychology: Science and Practice*, *13*, 109–128. https://doi.org/10.1111/j.1468-2850.2006.00013.x

Bryant, R. A., Azevedo, S., Yadav, S., Cahill, C., Kenny, L., Maccallum, F., & Dawson, K. S. (2024). Cognitive behavior therapy vs mindfulness in treatment of prolonged grief disorder: A randomized clinical trial. *Jama Psychiatry*, *81*, 646–654. https://doi.org/10.1001/jamapsychiatry.2024.0432

Bryant, R. A., Kenny, L., Joscelyne, A., Rawson, N., Maccallum, F., Cahill, C., & Nickerson, A. (2014). Treating prolonged grief disorder: A randomized controlled trial. *JAMA: Psychiatry*, *71*, 1332–1339. https://doi.org/10.1001/jamapsychiatry.2014.1600

Bryant, R. A., Kenny, L., Joscelyne, A., Rawson, N., Maccallum, F., Cahill, C., & Nickerson, A. (2019). Predictors of treatment response for cognitive behavior therapy for prolonged grief disorder. *European Journal of Psychotraumatology*, 8, 1556551.

Bryant, R. A., Sutherland, K., & Guthrie, R. M. (2007). Impaired specific autobiographical memory as a risk factor for posttraumatic stress after trauma. *Journal of Abnormal Psychology*, *116*, 837–841. https://doi.org/10.1037/0021-843x.116.4.837

Conway, M. A. (2005). Memory and the self. *Journal of Memory and Language*, *53*, 594–628. https://doi.org/10.1016/j.jml.2005.08.005

Conway, M. A., & Pleydell-Pearce, C. W. (2000). The construction of autobiographical memories in the self-memory system. *Psychological Review*, *107*, 261–288. https://doi.org/10.1037/0033-295x.107.2.261

Djelantik, A., Robinaugh, D. J., Kleber, R. J., Smid, G. E., & Boelen, P. A. (2020). Symptomatology following loss and trauma: Latent class and network analyses of prolonged grief disorder, posttraumatic stress disorder, and depression in a treatment-seeking trauma-exposed sample. *Depression and Anxiety*, *37*, 26–34. https://doi.org/10.1002/da.22880

Djelantik, A., Smid, G. E., Kleber, R. J., & Boelen, P. A. (2017). Symptoms of prolonged grief, post-traumatic stress, and depression after loss in a Dutch community sample: A latent class analysis. *Psychiatry Research*, *247*, 276–281. https://doi.org/10.1016/j.psychres.2016.11.023

Djelantik, A., Smid, G. E., Mroz, A., Kleber, R. J., & Boelen, P. A. (2020). The prevalence of prolonged grief disorder in bereaved individuals following unnatural losses: Systematic review and meta regression analysis. *Journal of Affective Disorders*, *265*, 146–156. https://doi.org/10.1016/j.jad.2020.01.034

Doering, B. K., Barke, A., Friehs, T., & Eisma, M. C. (2018). Assessment of grief-related rumination: Validation of the German version of the Utrecht grief rumination scale (UGRS). *BMC Psychiatry*, *18*. https://doi.org/10.1186/s12888-018-1630-1

Eberle, D. J., & Maercker, A. (2023). Stress-associated symptoms and disorders: A transdiagnostic comparison. *Clinical Psychology and Psychotherapy*, *30*, 1047–1057. https://doi.org/10.1002/cpp.2858

Eisma, M. C., Boelen, P. A., van den Bout, J., Stroebe, W., Schut, H. A. W., Lancee, J., & Stroebe, M. S. (2015). Internet-based exposure and behavioral activation for complicated grief and rumination: A randomized controlled trial. *Behavior Therapy*, *46*, 729–748. https://doi.org/10.1016/j.beth.2015.05.007

Eisma, M. C., Schut, H. A. W., Stroebe, M. S., van den Bout, J., Stroebe, W., & Boelen, P. A. (2014). Is rumination after bereavement linked with loss avoidance? Evidence from eye-tracking. *PLoS ONE*, *9*. https://doi.org/10.1371/journal.pone.0104980

Eisma, M. C., & Stroebe, M. S. (2021). Emotion regulatory strategies in complicated grief: A systematic review. *Behavior Therapy*, *52*, 234–249. https://doi.org/10.1016/j.beth.2020.04.004

Field, N. P., & Filanosky, C. (2010). Continuing bonds, risk factors for complicated grief, and adjustment to bereavement. *Death Studies*, *34*, 1–29. https://doi.org/10.1080/07481180903372269

Field, N. P., Gal-Oz, E., & Bonanno, G. A. (2003). Continuing bonds and adjustment at 5 years after the death of a spouse. *Journal of Consulting and Clinical Psychology*, *71*, 110–117. https://doi.org/10.1037/0022-006x.71.1.110

Golden, A.-M. J., & Dalgleish, T. (2012). Facets of pejorative self-processing in complicated grief. *Journal of Consulting and Clinical Psychology*, *80*, 512–524.

Golden, A.-M. J., Dalgleish, T., & Mackintosh, B. (2007). Levels of specificity of autobiographical memories and of biographical memories of the deceased in bereaved individuals with and without complicated grief. *Journal of Abnormal Psychology*, *116*, 786–795. https://doi.org/10.1037/0021-843x.116.4.786

Guldin, M. B., Ina Siegismund Kjaersgaard, M., Fenger-Grøn, M., Thorlund Parner, E., Li, J., Prior, A., & Vestergaard, M. (2017). Risk of suicide, deliberate self-harm and psychiatric illness after the loss of a close relative: A nationwide cohort study. *World Psychiatry*, *16*, 193–199. https://doi.org/10.1002/wps.20422

Gupta, S., & Bonanno, G. A. (2011). Complicated grief and deficits in emotional expressive flexibility. *Journal of Abnormal Psychology*, *120*, 635–643. https://doi.org/10.1037/a0023541

Harris, C. B., Brookman, R., & O'Connor, M. (2023). It's not who you lose, it's who you are: Identity and symptom trajectory in prolonged grief. *Current Psychology*, *42*, 11223–11233. https://doi.org/10.1007/s12144-021-02343-w

Harrison, O., Windmann, S., Rosner, R., & Steil, R. (2022). Inclusion of the other in the self as a potential risk factor for prolonged grief disorder: A comparison of patients with matched bereaved healthy controls. *Clinical Psychology & Psychotherapy*, *29*, 1101–1112. https://doi.org/10.1002/cpp.2697

Harvey, A. G., Watkins, E., Mansell, W., & Shafran, R. (2004). *Cognitive behavioural processes across psychological disorders: A transdiagnostic approach to research and treatment*. Oxford University Press.

James, K. E., McKimmie, B. M., & Maccallum, F. (2024). When we fail to live up to our own standards: The relationship between self-discrepancy and moral injury. *Anxiety Stress Coping*, 1–10. https://doi.org/10.1080/10615806.2024.2387607

King, L. A., & Raspin, C. (2004). Lost and found possible selves, subjective well-being, and ego development in divorced women. *Journal of Personality*, *72*, 603–632.

Lechner-Meichsner, F., Mauro, C., Skritskaya, N. A., & Shear, M. K. (2022). Change in avoidance and negative grief-related cognitions mediates treatment outcome in older adults with prolonged grief disorder. *Psychotherapy Research*, *32*, 91–103. https://doi.org/10.1080/10503307.2021.1909769

Lenferink, L. I. M., Nickerson, A., de Keijser, J., Smid, G. E., & Boelen, P. A. (2019). Reciprocal associations among symptom levels of disturbed grief, posttraumatic stress, and depression following traumatic loss: A four-wave cross-lagged study. *Clinical Psychological Science*, *7*, 1330–1339. https://doi.org/10.1177/2167702619858288

Lobb, E. A., Kristjanson, L. J., Aoun, S. M., Monterosso, L., Halkett, G. K. B., & Davies, A. (2010). Predictors of complicated grief: A systematic review of empirical studies. *Death Studies*, *34*, 673–698. https://doi.org/10.1080/07481187.2010.496686

Maccallum, F., & Bryant, R. A. (2008). Self-defining memories in complicated grief. *Behaviour Research and Therapy*, *46*, 1311–1315. https://doi.org/10.1016/j.brat.2008.09.003

Maccallum, F., & Bryant, R. A. (2010). Impaired autobiographical memory in complicated grief. *Behaviour Research and Therapy*, *48*, 328–334. https://doi.org/10.1016/j.brat.2009.12.006

Maccallum, F., & Bryant, R. A. (2011a). Autobiographical memory following cognitive behaviour therapy for complicated grief. *Journal of Behavior Therapy and Experimental Psychiatry*, *42*, 26–31. https://doi.org/10.1016/j.jbtep.2010.08.006

Maccallum, F., & Bryant, R. A. (2011b). Imagining the future in complicated grief. *Depression and Anxiety*, *28*, 658–665. https://doi.org/10.1002/da.20866

Maccallum, F., & Bryant, R. A. (2013). A cognitive attachment model of prolonged grief: Integrating attachments, memory, and identity. *Clinical Psychology Review*, *33*, 713–727. https://doi.org/10.1016/j.cpr.2013.05.001

Maccallum, F., & Bryant, R. A. (2019a). An investigation of approach behaviour in prolonged grief. *Behaviour Research and Therapy*, *119*, 103405. https://doi.org/10.1016/j.brat.2019.05.002

Maccallum, F., & Bryant, R. A. (2019b). A network approach to understanding quality of life impairments in prolonged grief disorder. *Journal of Traumatic Stress*, *33*, 106–115. https://doi.org/10.1002/jts.22383

Maccallum, F., & Bryant, R. A. (2019c). Symptoms of prolonged grief and posttraumatic stress following loss: A latent class analysis. *Australian and New Zealand Journal of Psychiatry*, *53*, 59–67. https://doi.org/10.1177/0004867418768429

Michel, C. A., Galfalvy, H. C., Mann, J. J., & Schneck, N. (2023). Attentional bias during acute grief predicts clinical outcome in suicide-related bereavement. *Journal of Affective Disorders*, *328*, 6–12. https://doi.org/10.1016/j.jad.2023.02.009

Moberly, N. J., & MacLeod, A. K. (2006). Goal pursuit, goal self-concordance, and the accessibility of autobiographical knowledge. *Memory*, *14*, 901–915. https://doi.org/10.1080/09658210600859517

Nickerson, A., Liddell, B. J., Maccallum, F., Steel, Z., Silove, D., & Bryant, R. A. (2014). Posttraumatic stress disorder and prolonged grief in refugees exposed to trauma and loss. *Bmc Psychiatry*, *14*. https://doi.org/10.1186/1471-244x-14-106

Onnis, R., Dadds, M. R., & Bryant, R. A. (2011). Is there a mutual relationship between opposite attentional biases underlying anxiety? *Emotion*, *11*, 582–594. https://doi.org/10.1037/a0022019

Ono, M., Devilly, G. J., & Shum, D. H. (2016). A meta-analytic review of overgeneral memory: The role of trauma history, mood, and the presence of posttraumatic stress disorder. *Psychol Trauma*, *8*, 157–164. https://doi.org/10.1037/tra0000027

Papa, A., & Lancaster, N. (2016). Identity continuity and loss after death, divorce, and job loss. *Self and Identity*, *15*, 47–61. https://doi.org/10.1080/15298868.2015.1079551

Robinaugh, D. J., & McNally, R. J. (2013). Remembering the past and envisioning the future in bereaved adults with and without complicated grief. *Clinical Psychological Science*, *1*, 290–300. https://doi.org/10.1177/2167702613476027

Schneck, N., Tu, T., Michel, C. A., Bonanno, G. A., Sajda, P., & Mann, J. J. (2018). Attentional bias to reminders of the deceased as compared with a living attachment in grieving. *Biological Psychiatry: Cognitive Neuroscience and Neuroimaging*, *3*, 107–115. https://doi.org/10.1016/j.bpsc.2017.08.003

Schut, H. A. W., Stroebe, M. S., Boelen, P. A., & Zijerveld, A. M. (2006). Continuing relationships with the deceased: Disentangling bonds and grief. *Death Studies*, *30*, 757–766. https://doi.org/10.1080/07481180600850666

Shear, M. K., Monk, T., Houck, P., Melhem, N., Frank, E., Reynolds, C., & Sillowash, R. (2007). An attachment-based model of complicated grief including the role of avoidance. *European Archives of Psychiatry and Clinical Neuroscience*, *257*, 453–461.

Shear, M. K., Reynolds, C. F., Simon, N. M., Zisook, S., Wang, Y. J., Mauro, C., & Skritskaya, N. (2016). Optimizing treatment of complicated grief: A randomized clinical trial. *Jama Psychiatry*, *73*, 685–694. https://doi.org/10.1001/jamapsychiatry.2016.0892

Skritskaya, N. A., Mauro, C., de la Garza, A. G., Meichsner, F., Lebowitz, B., Reynolds, C. F., & Shear, M. K. (2020). Changes in typical beliefs in response to complicated grief treatment. *Depression and Anxiety*, *37*, 81–89. https://doi.org/10.1002/da.22981

Smid, G. E., Drogendijk, A. N., Knipscheer, J., Boelen, P. A., & Kleber, R. J. (2018). Loss of loved ones or home due to a disaster: Effects over time on distress in immigrant ethnic minorities. *Transcultural Psychiatry*, *55*, 648–668. https://doi.org/10.1177/1363461518784355

Smid, G. E., Kleber, R. J., de la Rie, S. M., Bos, J. B., Gersons, B. P., & Boelen, P. A. (2015). Brief Eclectic Psychotherapy for Traumatic Grief (BEP-TG): Toward integrated treatment of symptoms related to traumatic loss. *European Journal of Psychotraumatology*, *6*, 27324. https://doi.org/10.3402/ejpt.v6.27324

Smid, G. E., Lind, J., & Bonde, J. P. (2022). Neurobiological mechanisms underlying delayed expression of posttraumatic stress disorder: A scoping review. *World J Psychiatry*, *12*, 151–168. https://doi.org/10.5498/wjp.v12.i1.151

Smith, K. V., & Ehlers, A. (2020). Cognitive predictors of grief trajectories in the first months of loss: A latent growth mixture model. *Journal of Consulting and Clinical Psychology*, *88*, 93–105. https://doi.org/10.1037/ccp0000438

Smith, K. V., & Ehlers, A. (2021). Prolonged grief and posttraumatic stress disorder following the loss of a significant other: An investigation of cognitive and behavioural differences. *PLoS ONE*, *16*, 1–18. https://doi.org/10.1371/journal.pone.0248852

Strauman, T. J. (1992). Self-guides, autobiographical memory, and anxiety and dysphoria: Toward a cognitive model of vulnerability to emotional distress. *Journal of Abnormal Psychology*, *101*, 87–95. https://doi.org/10.1037/0021-843X.101.1.87

Stroebe, M. S., & Schut, H. (1999). The dual process model of coping with bereavement: Rationale and description. *Death Studies*, *23*, 197–224. https://doi.org/10.1080/074811899201046

Stroebe, M. S., Schut, H., & Boerner, K. (2010). Continuing bonds in adaptation to bereavement: Toward theoretical integration. *Clinical Psychology Review*, *30*, 259–268. https://doi.org/10.1016/j.cpr.2009.11.007

Weiss-Cowie, S., Verhaeghen, P., & Duarte, A. (2023). An updated account of overgeneral autobiographical memory in depression. *Neuroscience & Biobehavioral Reviews*, *149*, 105157. https://doi.org/10.1016/j.neubiorev.2023.105157

Williams, J. M. G. (2006). Capture and rumination, functional avoidance, and executive control (CaRFAX): Three processes that underlie overgeneral memory. *Cognition and Emotion*, *20*, 548–568. https://doi.org/10.1080/02699930500450465

Williams, J. M. G., Barnhofer, T., Crane, C., Herman, D., Raes, F., Watkins, E., & Dalgleish, T. (2007). Autobiographical memory specificity and emotional disorder. *Psychological Bulletin*, *133*, 122–148. https://doi.org/10.1037/0033-2909.133.1.122

Williams, J. M. G., & Broadbent, K. (1986). Autobiographical memory in suicide attempters. *Journal of Abnormal Psychology*, *95*, 144–149. https://doi.org/10.1037/0021-843x.95.2.144

Xu, X., Zou, X., Tang, R., Jiao, K., Qian, W., Shen, X., & Skritskaya, N. A. (2023). Latent class analysis of grief-related beliefs among recently bereaved adults. *Scandinavian Journal of Psychology*, *64*, 552–562. https://doi.org/10.1111/sjop.12916

Part II

Psychotherapy for Prolonged and Traumatic Grief

Chapter 5

Psychoeducation about prolonged and traumatic grief

Geert E. Smid, Simon Groen, and Hannah Comtesse

Psychoeducation about grief is essential in situations where bereaved people need the support of care providers. Discussing reactions to loss and symptoms of prolonged and traumatic grief serves to increase the patient's and their social environment's awareness of these. Such awareness provides the basis for *grief literacy*, that has been defined as "the capacity to access, process, and use knowledge regarding the experience of loss" (Breen et al., 2022, p. 427). Grief literacy is multidimensional, as it comprises "knowledge to facilitate understanding and reflection, skills to enable action, and values to inspire compassion and care" (Breen et al., 2022, p. 427).

Providing psychoeducation to patients is essential in psychotherapy to increase the patient's understanding of their situation and stimulate their adherence to treatment (Groen et al., 2022). Providing information supports shared decision making, the use of patient expertise, and co-creation during treatment. In addition, psychoeducation contributes to normalizing people's reactions and countering fears and worries about the bearability and controllability of one's grief reactions. Indeed, many treatment approaches with documented effectiveness include psychoeducation (Boelen et al., 2007; Bryant et al., 2024; Rosner et al., 2024; Shear et al., 2016). While psychoeducation about grief may be incorporated into individual, family, and group therapy, the focus of this chapter will be on psychoeducation for individuals engaging in psychotherapy for prolonged and traumatic grief. Examples of psychoeducational content are provided below, primarily based on cognitive-behavioral conceptualizations of prolonged and traumatic grief and BEPPTG (Boelen & Eisma, 2022; Boelen & Van den Bout, 2011; Smid et al., 2015).

Psychoeducation is provided at the start of psychotherapy. Mental healthcare often involves an initial phase of diagnostic assessment preceding the actual start of psychotherapy. Depending on the healthcare setting, the assessment phase may be carried out by clinicians other than the therapist. In the latter situation, if it is the first time the patient and therapist meet, the

DOI: 10.4324/9781003429777-8

therapist may first need to summarize the conclusions from the assessment phase, explain the diagnosis, and elicit the patient's feedback.

During psychoeducation, empathic listening, validating, and providing information facilitate the working relationship. The relationship also benefits from the therapist familiarizing themselves with the life circumstances of the patient and their culture. During the entire therapy, the therapist may use the ***name of the deceased*** regularly to encourage the patient to understand the reality of the loss.

Patients are encouraged to bring a partner, family member, or friend to the psychoeducation session. If needed, a second psychoeducation session may be planned to enable the significant other to participate. Psychoeducation of supporters of bereaved individuals has been shown to have beneficial effects. Specifically, symptoms of PGD were lower in bereaved individuals with supporters who received psychoeducation compared with those who did not (Nam, 2016). Involving a significant other serves several aims. First, to increase the significant other's grief literacy and enhance social support. Second, to facilitate the development of trust in the therapist. Third, to prevent drop-out during the exposure phase of the therapy, as this may be associated with a temporary increase in emotional distress, and significant others may play a supportive role in keeping patients motivated (Nijdam et al., 2022). Fourth, to increase the therapist's understanding of the patient's sociocultural background.

Practical aspects are explained: The frequency of the sessions (initially weekly, later often more spaced), one-hour duration (doubles sessions may be scheduled for exposure), and average number of sessions, depending on the specific protocol being used (e.g., 16 (Shear et al., 2005) to 25 (Rosner et al., 2011)). The therapist may also provide a basic explanation of cognitive-behavioral therapy.

Explaining reactions to loss

Models of "normal" grief attempt to summarize aspects of the way the bereaved person experiences and attributes meaning to the loss of a loved one. Various professional models have been developed over the past century, many of which are commonly known, that will be briefly discussed below. Complementing professional models, cultural communities often share distinct perspectives on bereavement and the afterlife. Both cultural and professional models of grief vary according to the emphasis that is placed on ***detachment from*** vs. ***continuing bonds with*** the deceased, "letting go" or "holding on." Exploration of cultural ways of dealing with bereavement and grief is described later in this chapter. Therapists can use a flexible theoretical approach to grief, guided by the patient's cultural perspective, to foster shared understanding. This common ground strengthens the patient's motivation for therapy.

Models emphasizing detachment from the deceased

Earlier professional models emphasized detachment from the deceased. Freud's *grief work* model describes grief as an active process of detachment of the memories and expectations related to the "object" of the deceased: "Each single one of the memories and expectations in which the libido is bound to the object is brought up and hyper-cathected, and detachment of the libido is accomplished in respect of it" (Freud, 1975, p. 245). The process of detachment in grief involves physical distress, a *syndrome* of normal grief: "sensations of somatic distress occurring in waves lasting from twenty minutes to an hour at a time, a feeling of tightness in the throat, choking with shortness of breath, need for sighing, an empty feeling in the abdomen, lack of muscular power, and an intense subjective distress described as tension or mental pain" (Lindemann, 1994, p. 141). From the 1960s, grief was modeled as a progression through distinct *phases or stages* ultimately leading to detachment, reorganization, or acceptance. The phase model of grief initially described by Bowlby comprised three phases: Protest, despair, and detachment (Bowlby, 1961). Bowlby (1980) later described four phases, specifically, numbing, yearning and searching, disorganization and despair, and reorganization. Broadening the scope of grief reactions to losses beyond the loss of loved ones, Parkes (1971) described grief as a process that involves a psychosocial *transition*, a change in identity in response to major changes in life that take place over a relatively short period of time. Kübler-Ross (1973) described a five-stage response of terminally ill patients confronting their impending death: denial and isolation, anger, bargaining, depression, and acceptance, and these stages have been used for the bereaved as well. Importantly, stage models of grief have been critiqued because of their normative implications (Avis et al., 2021).

Models emphasizing continuing bonds with the deceased

Subsequent professional models of grief increasingly emphasized the continuing bonds between the bereaved and the deceased person. The *two-track model* of bereavement (Rubin, 1981) consists of a track of biopsychosocial functioning and a track representing the ongoing relationship with the deceased. Incorporating these tracks, Worden's (1991/2008) grief *task model* consists of four tasks: To accept the reality of the loss, to process the pain of grief, to adjust to a world without the deceased, and to find an enduring connection with the deceased in the midst of embarking on a new life (Worden, 2008). The *dual process model* of grief (Stroebe & Schut, 1999) posits an oscillation between loss-oriented processes and recovery-oriented processes in coping with bereavement. The loss-oriented processes include breaking as well as relocating bonds with the deceased. The dual process model has been supported empirically (e.g., Fiore, 2019). *Continuing bonds* with the deceased have been described as inter-subjective, central in constructing meaning, raising questions about the ontological status of interactions with the dead, but best understood within their cultural setting (Klass et al., 1996).

A *phenomenology* of grief (Fuchs, 2018) describes how bereaved people experience the persistent relationship with the deceased. The bereaved person experiences a fundamentally ambiguous presence in the absence of the deceased. A shared world with shared habits has been lost, and the smallest details in the remaining world indicate the absence of the deceased. Two strands of time increasingly become asynchronous: A still-going past and an alienated present. The grieving person may feel and sometimes perceive an "as-if presence" of the deceased. A transforming adjustment to the loss eventually enables integration of the conflicting reality. This transformation involves identification with the deceased as well as representation of the deceased through commemoration, symbolization, and narration.

Explaining the development of prolonged and traumatic grief

Factors influencing the development of prolonged and traumatic grief are elaborated in Chapter 4. The therapist may explain the role of attachment and a self-concept that is merged with the deceased (Maccallum & Bryant, 2013), negative cognitions related to both the loss and one's grief reactions, and anxious and depressive avoidance in maintaining symptoms of prolonged grief (Boelen et al., 2006). Following traumatic loss, the therapist may explain sensitization to traumatic loss-related stimuli, other relevant aspects of coping and appraisal following exposure to trauma, and consequences such as social withdrawal or reduced physical health.

Explaining symptoms of prolonged and traumatic grief

Symptoms of prolonged grief can be explained as follows: *When faced with the loss of a loved one, one is often forced to remain active and not dwell on feelings. Feelings about the loss may be so intense that they cause anxiety. One does not want to and cannot let go; it is unbearable to be alone, and missing someone hurts all the time. One may interpret these emotional reactions as unbearable or signs of impending insanity or loss of control. Such negative appraisals may contribute to persistent separation and traumatic distress and may fuel tendencies to minimize confrontation with loss-related stimuli. But keeping the feelings under control takes a lot of energy. One becomes exhausted and forgetful. It is necessary to allow the feelings of sadness to take hold and to learn what it means that the loss has taken place.* The information needs to be matched to the symptoms primarily present in the individual patient as identified during the diagnostic phase.

Following traumatic loss, symptoms of PTSD can be explained in the following way (Ehlers & Clark, 2000): *In the face of danger, being on edge is a useful and necessary reaction. Subsequently, if the environment is safe again, intrusive memories of the traumatic circumstances of the loss may maintain a sense of threat that no longer provides accurate information.*

Exploring reactions to the loss

Besides providing information, the therapist may further explore the patient's and their social environment's reactions to the loss as well as their (cultural) interpretations. This enables the therapist to tailor the information to meet the needs of patients in different care contexts as well as from different cultural backgrounds. Stigmatization and self-stigmatization may occur, particularly following violent loss, such as homicide and violent suicide (e.g., Hanschmidt et al., 2016), and the therapist may need to identify and explain this (see also the paragraph below about exploring cultural ways of dealing with bereavement and grief).

Explaining the rationale and course of treatment

The rationale of grief-focused treatment can be summarized in the following way: *During the treatment, facing the reality of the loss and the associated emotions allows you to fully understand what the loss means to you and to learn what it takes for you to engage with a changed world and a changed future – in a way that is meaningful to you.*

The conversation about avoidance can be introduced as follows: *People with grief problems seek to avoid emotions associated with the loss in various ways. First, they may suppress memories of certain events because they experience intense fear or grief. Second, they may suppress feelings and thoughts about the loss because they feel it is too painful. Third, people may avoid specific places, such as the grave of the deceased, or objects, such as photographs of the deceased. Another thing that may happen is that people try to "keep the deceased alive" by always being with the deceased in their thoughts and cherishing objects related to the deceased to maintain proximity with the deceased.* The therapist then explores the patient's avoidance tendencies as shown in Box 5.1. A form to identify types of avoidance can be obtained from the supplementary files of Komischke-Konnerup et al. (2023).

The therapist explains that in the upcoming sessions, the patient will gradually confront what they are avoiding. Actively engaging with memories of the death and associated emotions aims to gradually process the loss

Box 5.1 What do I avoid?

People experiencing prolonged or traumatic grief tend to avoid painful emotions related to their loss. Please indicate below which thoughts, feelings, or behaviors related to your loss you tend to avoid.

Feelings about the loss: What are the precise consequences of the loss that you would rather not think about? What are the feelings you would rather avoid (e.g., anger, sadness, guilt)?

Specific objects or places: Which specific situations or objects do you prefer to avoid since he or she died, because it is (too) painful to confront them?

Memories of specific events: Are there specific events in relation to the loss that you would rather not think about because they are too painful? Are there certain memories that frighten you and that you would rather forget?

The reality of the loss: One may try to "keep the deceased alive" and maintain proximity with the deceased by always being with the deceased in one's thoughts and cherishing objects related to the deceased. What are the things you do to keep your deceased loved one close – to honor them – and/or to not have to think about the fact that they will not come back?

and to enable the patient to experience that they are more capable of confronting the feelings, thoughts, concrete places, and memories related to the loss than they may fear.

The therapist explains that the patient will be encouraged to engage in symbolic interactions with the deceased, e.g., by writing a letter, conducting an imaginary conversation, or planning a ritual. Finally, the sessions will focus on the meanings the patient attributes to the loss. What does the loss mean for the way the patient looks at themselves, the relationship with the deceased, their view toward the world and toward others, and the future? Meaning attribution may support further processing, reengaging, and activation toward the end of the therapy.

From a cognitive behavioral viewpoint, reducing PGD and related issues involves completing three key tasks: (1) Confronting the loss and the emotional pain it brings; (2) Maintaining trust in oneself, others, life, and the future; and (3) Participating in constructive activities that support adaptation to the new reality. While accomplishing these tasks is a primary objective, individuals also establish additional personal goals (Boelen & Eisma, 2022).

Exploring cultural ways of dealing with bereavement and grief

Culturally appropriate death rituals may play an important role in attributing meaning to the loss of loved ones. Death rituals provide structured ways to mourn and express grief, and can perform important social, cultural, and psychological functions that promote adaptation to loss. Rituals may establish specific time frames for initial mourning and designate actions to be performed at particular intervals thereafter, such as holding a wake or conducting annual commemorations. They also prescribe the appropriate methods for handling and disposing of the deceased's body, and dictate when and how it is suitable for individuals to talk about the deceased (Cacciatore & DeFrain, 2015; Smid et al., 2018). Encounters with the deceased that may occur in dreams or when bereaved persons see, feel, smell, or talk to the deceased may have cultural explanations and involve concerns about the spiritual status of the deceased (Hinton et al., 2013). Following such encounters, a person may feel the urge to perform rituals. Sensory or quasi-sensory experiences of the dead, including dreams, may be interpreted within a cultural continuing bonds model of bereavement (Kamp et al., 2020). However, some cultural traditions suggest that spirits of the deceased may bring harm during a period following the death. According to Mexican tradition, a bad death is characterized by its suddenness and violence, occurring when the spirit is unprepared for death. The spirit subsequently remains bound to the location of its death, where it wanders with anger and resentment, potentially causing harm to others. A ritual performed by a healer intends to reunite the spirit with the body. Following reunion with the body, the spirit may protect family members and friends (Esteinou, 2015). Within several religions, the mode of death, e.g., suicide, is thought of as having implications for the afterlife. Exploring these implications may be helpful to identify unhelpful cognitions and support adaptive coping, e.g., identifying sources of support within or outside the religious community.

Many bereaved individuals engage in practices related to spiritual, religious, or moral traditions to cope with the loss of a loved one, including prayer and meditation. In addition, they may participate in worships or religious gatherings, speak with other people in their religious group, and with religious or spiritual leaders (Smid et al., 2018). Other kinds of help may have been suggested by family, friends, or others. Not having the opportunity to perform or participate in farewell rituals, e.g., due to migration, may impair grief reprocessing (Lechner-Meichsner & Comtesse, 2022). For clinicians, it is essential to explore the kinds of help the patient thinks would be most useful at this time to deal with the loss of loved ones.

The questions in Box 5.2 comprise a shortened version of the Bereavement and Grief Cultural Formulation Interview (BG-CFI) (Smid et al., 2018) that aims to validate a diagnosis of PGD, support treatment negotiation (i.e., matching the patient's expectations about treatment to the provider's treatment recommendations), increase rapport between patient and clinician, facilitate sharing of emotionally sensitive information, enhance the patient's ability to find meaningful ways of dealing with the loss, and help the therapist to integrate meaningful rituals in grief treatment (Smid et al., 2025). The feasibility, acceptability, and clinical utility of the BG-CFI has been demonstrated using a step-by-step procedure, in which clinicians and/or researchers conducted the BG-CFI with participants and debriefing interviews were conducted separately with clinicians and with bereaved participants (Killikelly et al., 2025). Further research exploring the context and the perspective of patients on loss, bereavement and grief symptoms using the BG-CFI is ongoing (Groen et al., 2022). The full BG-CFI as well as translations into several languages can be downloaded for free (Smid et al., 2024). The therapist explains: *Sometimes peoples' background affects how they deal with the loss of loved ones. In order to better help you, I would like to learn to understand the way you, your family, friends, and others in your community deal with the loss of loved ones.*

The therapist asks open-ended, gentle, Socratic questions to further explore the associated beliefs, values, traditions, and meanings. The therapist integrates all the information in order to explain maintaining factors to the patient that will be addressed during psychotherapy.

Box 5.2 Questions from the BG-CFI

The following questions aim to clarify key aspects of loss of loved ones, bereavement, and grief from the point of view of you and your family, friends, or others from your network.

If someone from your family, friends, or others in your community dies, how would people usually arrange the funeral?

Are there other rituals after people have passed away?

Is there a prescribed period of mourning or expressing grief?

When and how do people talk about the deceased?

When bereaved people have dreams or other types of encounters with the deceased, what may this mean?

What do your family, friends, and others in your community believe happens after death?

Do you engage in spiritual or religious practices to help you cope with the loss of a loved one?

Concluding remarks

In psychotherapy, providing information about reactions to loss and the symptoms of prolonged and traumatic grief is crucial for enhancing patients' understanding of their experience. This information should be tailored to address the needs of patients across diverse cultural backgrounds. Research has shown that psychoeducation for close others can benefit bereaved individuals, leading to lower symptoms of PGD. Involving a significant other has several purposes: Enhancing their understanding of grief, strengthening social support, building trust in the therapist, preventing therapy drop-out during emotionally intense phases, and helping the therapist better understand the patient's sociocultural background. As part of this process, the therapist can also explore the patient's reactions to their loss, along with the responses from their social environment and any cultural interpretations they may hold. By tailoring their approach to incorporate the patient's cultural beliefs about grief, therapists can create a common framework, enhancing the patient's engagement and commitment to the therapeutic process.

References

Avis, K. A., Stroebe, M., & Schut, H. (2021). Stages of grief portrayed on the internet: A systematic analysis and critical appraisal. *Frontiers in Psychology*, *12*, 772696. https://doi.org/10.3389/fpsyg.2021.772696

Boelen, P. A., de Keijser, J., Van den Hout, M. A., & Van den Bout, J. (2007). Treatment of complicated grief: A comparison between cognitive-behavioral therapy and supportive counseling. *Journal of Consulting and Clinical Psychology*, *75*(2), 277–284. https://doi.org/10.1037/0022-006X.75.2.277

Boelen, P. A., & Eisma, M. C. (2022). Cognitive behavior therapy for grief. In E. M. Steffen, E. Milman, & R. A. Neimeyer (Eds.), *The handbook of grief therapies* (pp. 111–120). Sage Publications.

Boelen, P. A., & Van den Bout, J. (2011). Protocollaire behandeling van gecompliceerde rouw. In G. Keijsers, A. van Minnen, & K. A. L. Hoogduin (Eds.), *Protocollaire behandelingen van volwassenen met psychische klachten* (pp. 341–377). Boom.

Boelen, P. A., Van den Hout, M. A., & Van den Bout, J. (2006). A cognitive-behavioral conceptualization of complicated grief. *Clinical Psychology: Science and Practice*, *13*(2), 109–128. https://doi.org/10.1111/j.1468-2850.2006.00013.x

Bowlby, J. (1961). Processes of mourning. *The International Journal of Psycho-Analysis*, *42*, 317–339.

Bowlby, J. (1980). *Attachment and loss: Loss, sadness and depression (vol. 3)*. Basic.

Breen, L. J., Kawashima, D., Joy, K., Cadell, S., Roth, D., Chow, A., & Macdonald, M. E. (2022). Grief literacy: A call to action for compassionate communities. *Death Studies*, *46*(2), 425–433. https://doi.org/10.1080/07481187.2020.1739780

Bryant, R. A., Azevedo, S., Yadav, S., Cahill, C., Kenny, L., Maccallum, F., Tran, J., Choi-Christou, J., Rawson, N., Tockar, J., Garber, B., Keyan, D., & Dawson, K. S. (2024). Cognitive behavior therapy vs mindfulness in treatment of prolonged grief disorder: A randomized clinical trial. *JAMA Psychiatry*, *81*(7), 646–654. https://doi.org/10.1001/jamapsychiatry.2024.0432

Cacciatore, J., & DeFrain, J. (2015). *The world of bereavement: Cultural perspectives on death in families*. Springer International Publishing.

Ehlers, A., & Clark, D. M. (2000). A cognitive model of posttraumatic stress disorder. *Behaviour Research and Therapy*, *38*(4), 319–345.

Esteinou, R. (2015). Death and grief in Mexican families. In J. Cacciatore & J. DeFrain (Eds.), *The world of bereavement: Cultural perspectives on death in families* (pp. 131–145). Springer International Publishing. https://doi.org/10.1007/978-3-319-13945-6_8

Fiore, J. (2019). A systematic review of the dual process model of coping with bereavement (1999–2016). *OMEGA - Journal of Death and Dying*, *84*(2), 414–458. https://doi.org/10.1177/0030222819893139

Freud, S. (1975). Mourning and melancholia. In J. Strachey, A. Freud, A. Strachey, & A. Tyson (Eds.), *The standard edition of the complete psychological works of Sigmund Freud, volume XIV (1914-1916): On the history of the psycho-analytic movement, papers on metapsychology and other works* (pp. 237–258). Vintage. (Original work published 1917)

Fuchs, T. (2018). Presence in absence. The ambiguous phenomenology of grief. *Phenomenology and the Cognitive Sciences*, *17*(1), 43–63. https://doi.org/10.1007/s11097-017-9506-2

Groen, S. P. N., Menninga, M. C., Cath, D. C., & Smid, G. E. (2022). Let's talk about grief: Protocol of a study on the recognition and psychoeducation of prolonged grief disorder in outpatients with common mental disorders. *Frontiers in Psychiatry*, *13*, 944233. https://doi.org/10.3389/fpsyt.2022.944233

Hanschmidt, F., Lehnig, F., Riedel-Heller, S. G., & Kersting, A. (2016). The stigma of suicide survivorship and related consequences—A systematic review. *PLOS ONE*, *11*(9), e0162688. https://doi.org/10.1371/journal.pone.0162688

Hinton, D. E., Peou, S., Joshi, S., Nickerson, A., & Simon, N. (2013). Normal grief and complicated bereavement among traumatized Cambodian refugees: Cultural context and the Central role of dreams of the dead. *Culture, Medicine, and Psychiatry*, *37*(3), 427–464. https://doi.org/10.1007/s11013-013-9324-0

Kamp, K. S., Steffen, E. M., Alderson-Day, B., Allen, P., Austad, A., Hayes, J., Larøi, F., Ratcliffe, M., & Sabucedo, P. (2020). Sensory and quasi-sensory experiences of the deceased in bereavement: An interdisciplinary and integrative review. *Schizophrenia Bulletin*, *46*(6), 1367–1381. https://doi.org/10.1093/schbul/sbaa113

Klass, D., Silverman, P. R., & Nickman, S. L. (1996). *Continuing bonds: New understandings of grief* (p. 384). Taylor & Francis.

Killikelly, C., Christen, L.-M., Groen, S., Ogrodniczuk, J. S., Maercker, A., Smid, G. E., & Heim, E. (2025). Feasibility, acceptability and clinical utility of the bereavement and grief cultural formulation interview for prolonged grief disorder. *Culture, Medicine, and Psychiatry*, 1–18. https://doi.org/10.1007/s11013-025-09927-2

Komischke-Konnerup, K. B., O'Connor, M., Hoijtink, H., & Boelen, P. A. (2023). Cognitive-behavioral therapy for complicated grief reactions: Treatment protocol and preliminary findings from a naturalistic setting. *Cognitive and Behavioral Practice*. https://doi.org/10.1016/j.cbpra.2023.11.001

Kübler-Ross, E. (1973). *On death and dying*. Routledge. https://doi.org/10.4324/9780203010495

Lechner-Meichsner, F., & Comtesse, H. (2022). Beliefs about causes and cures of prolonged grief disorder among Arab and sub-Saharan African refugees. *Frontiers in Psychiatry*, *13*. https://doi.org/10.3389/fpsyt.2022.852714

Lindemann, E. (1994). Symptomatology and management of acute grief. *American Journal of Psychiatry*, *151*(6), 155–160. (Original work published 1944)

Maccallum, F., & Bryant, R. A. (2013). A cognitive attachment model of prolonged grief: Integrating attachments, memory, and identity. *Clinical Psychology Review*, *33*(6), 713–727. https://doi.org/10.1016/j.cpr.2013.05.001

Nam, I. S. (2016). Effects of psychoeducation on helpful support for complicated grief: A preliminary randomized controlled single-blind study. *Psychological Medicine*, *46*(1), 189–195. https://doi.org/10.1017/S0033291715001658

Nijdam, M. J., Meewisse, M.-L., Smid, G. E., & Gersons, B. P. R. (2022). Brief eclectic psychotherapy for PTSD. In U. Schnyder & M. Cloitre (Eds.), *Evidence based treatments for trauma-related psychological disorders: A practical guide for clinicians* (pp. 281–306). Springer International Publishing. https://doi.org/10.1007/978-3-030-97802-0_13

Parkes, C. M. (1971). Psycho-social transitions: A field for study. *Social Science & Medicine (1967)*, *5*(2), 101–115. https://doi.org/10.1016/0037-7856(71)90091-6

Rosner, R., Pfoh, G., & Kotoučová, M. (2011). Treatment of complicated grief. *European Journal of Psychotraumatology*, *2*, 7995. https://doi.org/10.3402/ejpt.v2i0.7995

Rosner, R., Rau, J., Kersting, A., Rief, W., Steil, R., Rummel, A.-M., Vogel, A., & Comtesse, H. (2024). Grief-specific cognitive behavioral therapy vs present-centered therapy: A randomized clinical trial. *JAMA Psychiatry*. https://doi.org/10.1001/jamapsychiatry.2024.3409

Rubin, S. (1981). A two-track model of bereavement: Theory and application in research. *American Journal of Orthopsychiatry*, *51*(1), 101–109. https://doi.org/10.1111/j.1939-0025.1981.tb01352.x

Shear, M. K., Frank, E., Houck, P. R., & Reynolds, C. F. (2005). Treatment of complicated grief: A randomized controlled trial. *JAMA: The Journal of the American Medical Association*, *293*(21), 2601–2608. https://doi.org/10.1001/jama.293.21.2601

Shear, M. K., Reynolds, C. F. III, Simon, N. M., Zisook, S., Wang, Y., Mauro, C., Duan, N., Lebowitz, B., & Skritskaya, N. (2016). Optimizing treatment of complicated grief: A randomized clinical trial. *JAMA Psychiatry*, *73*(7), 685–694. https://doi.org/10.1001/jamapsychiatry.2016.0892

Smid, G. E., Groen, S., De la Rie, S. M., Kooper, S., & Boelen, P. A. (2018). Toward cultural assessment of grief and grief-related psychopathology. *Psychiatric Services*, *69*(10), 1050–1052. https://doi.org/10.1176/appi.ps.201700422

Smid, G. E., Killikelly, C., & Groen, S. (2024). *Bereavement and Grief—Cultural Formulation Interview (BG-CFI)*. https://doi.org/10.17605/OSF.IO/W7SVH

Smid, G. E., Kleber, R. J., De la Rie, S. M., Bos, J. B. A., Gersons, B. P. R., & Boelen, P. A. (2015). Brief eclectic psychotherapy for traumatic grief (BEP-TG): Toward integrated treatment of symptoms related to traumatic loss. *European Journal of Psychotraumatology*, *6*(1), 27324. https://doi.org/10.3402/ejpt.v6.27324

Smid, G. E., Texier, J., Özer, H., & Groen, S. (2025). Cultuursensitieve zorg bij persisterende en traumatische rouw [Culturally sensitive care for prolonged and traumatic grief]. In J. W. Knipscheer & S. M. De la Rie (Eds.), *Handboek Migratie & psychotrauma*. Boom Psychologie & Psychiatrie.

Stroebe, M. S., & Schut, H. A. W. (1999). The dual process model of coping with bereavement: Rationale and description. *Death Studies*, *23*(3), 197–224. https://doi.org/10.1080/074811899201046

Worden, J. W. (2008). *Grief counseling and grief therapy, fourth edition: A handbook for the mental health practitioner*. Springer Publishing Company. (Original work published 1991)

Chapter 6

Exposure in the treatment of prolonged grief and traumatic grief

An associative memory network perspective

Paul A. Boelen, Muriel A. Hagenaars, and Franziska Lechner-Meichsner

Exposure-based interventions are those in which individuals confront feared or otherwise emotionally charged situations and stimuli that they prefer to avoid. The rationale behind exposure therapy can best be understood from a (classical) conditioning perspective. One key concept is an unconditioned stimulus (US), which, loosely speaking, refers to any stimulus or event that naturally and reflexively triggers an (emotional and behavioral) unconditioned response (UR). In the context of mental disorder, an aversive US may refer to, e.g., physical, social, or moral threat. Through classical conditioning, a US may get paired with a neutral stimulus that (because of its association with the US) becomes a conditioned stimulus (CS). On confrontation with this CS, memory information about the US and the UR (also termed US-UR-representation) is activated. This elicits a conditioned response (CR) that is similar to the UR connected with the US. In the context of grief, the CS could be a picture of a deceased child evoking intense separation distress (CR), through its connection with, e.g., thoughts that the child will truly never come back and images of the funeral, and associated pain (US-UR-presentation). Or the CS could be the street where a close person was fatally hit by a car, evoking intrusive images and horror (CR), through its link with one's knowledge about what happened in the accident and associated emotions (US-UR-representation).

Exposure refers to therapeutic procedures focused on decreasing the CR (e.g., separation distress, anxiety) by making changes in the relationship between the CS and the US. There are different accounts of what happens during exposure and why it is effective, which we will outline here in broad terms (Craske et al., 2022; Knowles & Tolin, 2022). The first refers to *extinction*: by confronting a CS in the absence of a US, the association of the CS with the US-UR-representation is weakened (or overruled by a new memory trace CS-*no* US-UR), yielding a gradual decrement in the

DOI: 10.4324/9781003429777-9

CR on confrontation with the CS. The second is about *habituation*: by repeatedly confronting a CS, a natural reduction of the CR associated with activation of the US-UR-representation occurs. In treatment, patients with prolonged grief disorder (PGD) may experience that confronting a picture of the lost person initially evokes intense pain, which decreases as they acclimate. The third is *cognitive change*. From this perspective, changes in US-UR-expectancy or the meaning implicated in the US-UR-representation may occur during exposure to a CS. For instance, when a CS (e.g., a picture of the lost person, images of the accident) is expected to announce a mental catastrophe (e.g., losing control), exposure to the CS may help to falsify and correct this expectation ("When I look at the picture, I don't go crazy").

Some PGD reactions clearly reflect such expectancy-based anxiety responses (e.g., the lost person's picture evoking fear of one's own emotions). And similar to posttraumatic stress disorder (PTSD), PGD may be accompanied by frequent reliving of traumatic moments related to the death (e.g., images of the lost person being fatally hit by a car, reliving the moment one first heard about the death). However, not all symptoms of PGD and prolonged and traumatic grief (PTG) can be traced back to expectancy learning or re-experiencing circumstances of the death. Instead, PGD and PTG may manifest in a broad array of emotional responses which may relate to a wide range of experiences and events connected with the loss. For example, PGD may coincide with disbelief, defeat, and dissociation, as if loss acutely strikes a deep, unbridgeable chasm in ordinary life. PGD may also come with extreme guilt and shame, as if the loss signals that one has violated important standards of morality, or anger, when others transgressed these standards. In addition, PGD may be associated with existential loneliness, caused by the loss creating an acute gap in one's social state and status. These emotional experiences often involve anguish and distress but also unbidden thoughts and images of real or imagined events, and they can be retrieved in a controlled manner, but can also impose themselves involuntarily, as severe pangs of pain.

To understand these symptoms, we need a comprehensive perspective on the linkage between the different pivotal experiences and threats that may be implicated in a loss, on the one hand, and the broad array of symptoms that may occur in PGD and PTG, on the other hand. In this chapter, we introduce a memory network perspective on PGD, that can provide such a framework and offers leads for the application of exposure-based interventions to mitigate PGD and associated emotional problems following loss. This perspective draws heavily from cognitive theories of posttraumatic stress, including Foa and Kozak's (1986) network account and Ehlers and Clark's (2000) cognitive model of PTSD, as well as other multi-representational theories of PTSD (Dalgleish, 2004), and Neuner's (2023) transdiagnostic perspective on psychological trauma. It aims to complement extant cognitive behavioral theories of grief (Boddez, 2018; Boelen et al., 2006; Maccallum & Bryant, 2013; also see Chapter 4).

A key starting point of this perspective is that (i) the loss of a close person may be associated with different consequential and emotional experiences and threats, including threats to safety, moral integrity, and social connection, (ii) that information about these experiences and associated responses are represented in associative memory networks (or US-UR-representations) carrying maladaptive elements, and (iii) that symptoms of PGD, PTG, and associated symptoms (at least to some extent) reflect the activation of these networks, by the perception of stimuli (CSs) that resemble items from the associative network. In what follows, we will sketch this perspective. In the second part of this chapter, we discuss its implications for the application of exposure-based interventions for PGD and PTG.

An associative memory network perspective on PGD and PTG

In PTSD, events that are most likely to cause long-term psychopathology through memory processes are events that posed a threat to the safety and integrity of oneself or important others (e.g., physical or sexual assault). As explained in trauma theories referenced above, while taking place, such threats evoke a cascade of defensive reactions which become encoded in associative memory networks or "threat structures". Later, these can be reactivated on confrontation with stimuli resembling items from those networks. Such an uncontrolled reactivation of the threat structure through a reminder cue can cause intrusive images, thoughts, emotions, and behavioral tendencies, mirroring experiences during the moment the threat was initially experienced.

Loss-related emotional problems are often not solely associated with a single momentous event, such as the moment the loved one died. Instead, the death of a close person can involve confrontation with multiple consequential and emotional events and experiences. Accordingly, there may be multiple events and experiences connected with the death that may be encoded in associative memory networks and shape a person's experience of disruptive images, thoughts, and emotions. A central notion of the perspective introduced here is that such memory networks are at the core of PGD and PTG. These networks are made up of sensory information about the experience/events and cognitive, behavioral, and physiological reactions to it. They can be activated when internal or external stimuli resembling elements of the network are encountered, leading the person to experience unbidden, disruptive emotional episodes, and pangs of pain.

What, then, are experiences and events that are liable to lead to PGD and PTG? We argue that pivotal experiences and events are those that involve a threat to a person's fundamental needs and those that carry information that is strongly discrepant with preexisting mental representations and which, therefore, generate intense negative emotion (cf. Dalgleish, 2004; Neuner, 2023). In this nascent formulation, we propose that experiences posing such threats are those that undermine (i) attachment security, (ii) predictability, controllability, and comprehensibility, (iii) self-identity, (iv) safety, (v) moral integrity—both of the self and (vi) others, and (vii) social connectedness.

Threats to attachment security and separation distress

The experience most pertinent to PGD is the *irreversible separation* from a close person. Separation from an attachment figure (or other close person) poses immediate threats to the achievement of shared goals and to one's need for a safe haven (e.g., for an adult losing a partner or child losing a parent) or the need to nurture (e.g., for a parent losing a child). The threats associated with separation may evoke a cascade of defensive reactions (including distress, resistance, and proximity seeking behavior) that may be encoded in an associative memory network or (akin to fear networks in PTSD) a "separation network". Later, the network can be reactivated on confrontation with loss-related cues. This happens frequently due to the ubiquity of these cues (cf. Boddez, 2018). Reactivation of the "separation network" evokes psychological responses, similar to those occurring when the irreversibility of the separation was first felt in full force. Thus, some of the hallmark symptoms of PGD, including separation distress and intense emotional pain, may be understood as originating from activation of the associative memory network in which the separation is encoded.

Threats to comprehensibility, controllability, and predictability and disbelief

In some bereaved people, separation distress is overshadowed by a pervasive state of disbelief and "unrealness". Hypothetically, this experience results from an acute disconnection or mismatch between preexisting schematic knowledge (about one's internal world in which the lost person is present) and external reality (from which the lost person is suddenly absent). This poses an immediate threat to the need for comprehensibility, controllability, and predictability. An exemplar is the loss of multiple loved ones in a serious accident or war, which can profoundly disrupt emotional, social, and practical aspects of life. Stimulus and response information related to such an experience and threats contained therein may be encoded in a memory record in the form of sensory experiences (derealization, depersonalization), cognitions/appraisals (e.g., "I am lost"), and physiological and behavioral responses (e.g., numbing, deactivation). This memory record may be activated by various cues resembling elements within it, leading to recurrent waves of dissociation, disorganization, and lostness. For instance, certain verbal triggers may activate feelings of disorientation, specific locations may trigger a sense of confusion, and images of the lost person may elicit pervasive disbelief.

Threats to self-identity

In many cases where individuals suffer from PGD or PTG, the loss represents a significant threat to their self-identity. When a person's roles, plans, and views of self and life are strongly intertwined with and dependent on the close person, their death may significantly jeopardize one's self-identity (Maccallum & Bryant, 2013). An example is when parents unexpectedly lose their only underaged child. This may cause an acute mismatch between self-identity (strongly defined by the child's existence) and external reality (from which the child has disappeared), posing an immediate threat to one's view of self in the past, present, and future. The memory record of this threat may encompass images of oneself as inferior, failed, or devoid of identity, negative cognitions about the future, an urge to dwell on all that has been lost, and inhibition of restoration-oriented coping—which may be activated during waves of pain when triggered by relevant external and internal cues.

Threats to safety and traumatic distress

The death of a close person may be related to threats to one's own safety or that of close individuals. Exemplar situations are those in which patients were themselves exposed to the dangerous circumstances that eventually took their close person's life (e.g., during war, a motor vehicle accident, natural disaster). Other examples include violent deaths where there are substantial indications that the loved one endured significant suffering, even though the patient was not directly involved in the event (such as in cases of homicide or certain accidents and suicides). Further examples are cases in which a period of uncertainty about the condition of close persons preceded their eventual death (as in the case of a life-threatening medical condition). Such situations characterized by significant threats to the safety of close others (and oneself) may be encoded in memory networks resembling fear networks in anxiety-based PTSD; accordingly, these networks include sensory information (e.g., images of the close person's suffering) and response information (e.g., fear, powerlessness, tonic immobility) that reflect what one perceived and how one responded, when the threat was actually experienced. Activation of the network may subsequently be experienced in the form of PTSD-like re-experiencing symptoms and associated avoidant coping behaviors, characteristic of PGD and PTG following traumatic loss.

Threats to moral integrity, guilt, and shame

One further category of events is those in which bereaved individuals hold themselves responsible for not having prevented or having caused the death (cf. Bottomley et al., 2025). Examples are cases where a close person died in a car accident in which the bereaved person was involved as a driver or, more common, when bereaved individuals believe that the ultimate cause of death (e.g., illness, suicide) was foreseeable and "thus" preventable. In these cases, the death may be perceived as a situation of negligence and failure, that is discrepant from one's internalized ideal self. For instance, the suicide of a child can be highly discrepant with the representation of the self as a responsible, caring person. In such cases, the loss may also threaten the need to protect attachment figures or the need for moral congruency (i.e., doing what is morally right). When the loss is perceived as reflecting moral wrongdoing, this may cause acute responses of self-depreciation, self-punishment, and attempts to compensate for the negligence. It may cause social withdrawal, when the bereaved person believes that others also attribute the death to their (in)action. Similar to other types of threats and discrepancies that losses may bring, these reactions may be encoded in memory structures, that may be reactivated on confrontation with particular cues, leading to painful waves of guilt and self-reproach.

Losses can be perceived as events that one was co-responsible for (causing guilt), but these may also be perceived as proving someone's worthlessness as a person (causing shame). This can happen in cases of disenfranchised loss, such as losing a secret lover, where the loss may lead one to feel unworthy or bad because the relationship is viewed as inappropriate by others. Shame can also occur following losses that are deemed foreseeable and preventable (e.g., accidents, suicides, homicides). In these situations, guilt would be the dominant emotion if the death was seen as an act of omission ("I did a bad thing"), and shame would be more prominent when the loss was considered as a proof of one's worthlessness or inferiority as a person (Cunningham, 2020). Thus, in some cases, the distress caused by a loss is strongly fueled by the perceived threat the loss poses to fundamental moral values and one's sense of self-worth. Again, when first vividly realized, this threat may be encoded in the form of different stimulus- and response-elements, including, e.g., images of condemnation by others, thoughts of inferiority, severe mortification, and the urge to hide. As with other psychological experiences following loss, the nature of guilt and shame and their linkages with bereavement outcome are likely moderated by culture—with, e.g., guilt being more negatively valued in Western compared to Eastern culture (cf. Shi et al., 2021).

Threats to moral integrity of others and anger

Bereavement can also be associated with other people violating moral boundaries. This may occur when someone else is responsible for the death, such as a drunk driver causing a fatal accident. It can also happen when individuals, organizations, or institutions that a person relies on for survival fail to prevent death—for example, governments unable to prevent casualties in war or medical professionals unable to save a loved one's life. Such situations may be perceived as threats to the need for assurance that people and parties that a person depends on for survival are trustworthy and predictable, and act morally right. The realization that these needs were violated (and consequences thereof) can lead to an urge to fight, which may be encoded in memory in the form of images about retaliation, intense anger, and behavioral urges to undo the injustice, compensate for it, or seek revenge. These reactions may flare up whenever one is confronted with stimuli reminding one of the parties held accountable for the loss. It may also develop into a chronic state of anger and endless legal proceedings to seek justice and obtain some form of compensation for the loss.

Threats to social state and emotional loneliness

Losses may cause immediate social threats, including threats to affiliation with a social group or system, or threats to social inclusion, belongingness, and embeddedness (cf. Maciejewski et al., 2022). An example is a woman losing her only child. This can cause an acute rupture between social life before the death (in which her role as mother brought various social structures and contacts) and after the loss (in which there is an acute void in her social state). Other examples are elderly people losing their spouse after decades of marriage and situations where losses go hand in hand with profound changes in one's social situation, such as with refugees fleeing to a safe country after having lost loved ones in war. When losses pose serious social threats, this may fuel disbelief about the permanence of the separation and an urge to cling onto the lost person, as well as a social stress response (cf. Neuner, 2023). The memory record of this response may include imagery of abandonment and loneliness, a sense of dislocated identity, self-pejorative thoughts, and withdrawal from social contexts to prevent further distress. Conversely, it may also involve excessive social engagement, people-pleasing, or validation-seeking as compensatory behaviors (e.g., becoming hyperfocused on others' needs or attending every social event to avoid being alone). These responses may become embedded in associative memory networks as conditioned reactions and, until the person establishes a new social equilibrium, may be triggered by social cues.

Associative memory structures in healthy and unhealthy grief

A memory perspective on grief can account for the intrusive and unbidden character of different symptoms that may accompany PGD and PTG. That is, we postulate that momentous, consequential, emotional experiences and events connected with the death of a close person (deriving their importance from threatening key needs or conflicting with preexisting knowledge) are stored in associative memory networks (or US-UR representations). These networks may encompass stimulus information in all sensory modalities (visual, auditory, olfactory), cognitive appraisals connected with the event/experiences, and behavioral and physiological response tendencies to defend against the event and threats contained therein.

In the case of a traumatic loss, when circumstances threatening a person's safety surrounded the death, these memory representations include images of the danger (e.g., of life-threatening situations during war or natural disasters), threat appraisals (e.g., "I am in danger", "My child will die"), and fear-based fight, flight, or freeze reactions; these representations may all be activated on confrontation with reminders of the loss, resulting in the combination of separation distress and traumatic distress, typical of PTG. However, as argued above, responses to loss may also reflect the activation of memory traces from other pivotal experiences and threats, unrelated to the circumstances of the death. Thus, as outlined, especially when untimely and unforeseen, losses can bring an acute threat to attachment security, which may be encoded and subsequently relived in the form of images of the loss's circumstances (e.g., the policy bringing the news of death), flash-forward (of a bleak future), desperate thoughts ("I can't manage alone"), and tendencies to deny the loss or compulsive actions to maintain unadjusted ties with the lost person. When the loss is perceived as foreseeable and preventable by oneself, it may be encoded as an event that threatens one's moral integrity (or proves one's moral failure), giving rise to pervasive pangs of guilt, combined with negative prospective images (of other people's condemnation), intrusive cognitions ("I am a bad person"), and tendencies to self-punish. When the loss brings an acute threat to social state and status, PGD may coincide with images reflecting the void left by the deceased, plus negative thoughts about the self ("I don't belong anywhere"), loneliness, and behavioral demobilization and physiological deactivation.

Thus, in this understanding, some phenomena in PGD and PTG, particularly those that present themselves as intrusive, involuntary images, thoughts, feelings, and action tendencies, arise from the activation of associative memory networks, more than from deliberate, reflective cognitive processes. This, then, raises the question what characterizes the differences between associative memory networks underpinning unhealthy vs. healthy grief reactions? Again drawing from associative network theories of PTSD (e.g., Dalgleish, 2004; Foa & Kozak, 1986; Neuner, 2023), there are several answers to this question.

First, in unhealthy grief, associative networks with information about pivotal experiences and threats are proposed to be *larger*. That is, akin to PTSD being associated with a larger memory of the traumatic event (containing more representations), the "separation network" that emerged when the reality of the separation was felt in full force in people with PGD includes more elements (e.g., more sensory information, more appraisals/cognitions, and more, and *more diverse* response elements). As a result, activation of the network may elicit an overwhelming combination of visual but also tactile, auditory, and olfactory experiences (e.g., announcing the presence or return of the deceased), appraisals/cognitions ("I will never be able to bear this"), and ambiguous action tendencies (e.g., hiding and searching). And this activation can easily be triggered by numerous external or internal cues that resemble an element within the network. Similarly, in someone who perceives the death of a close person as caused by gross own negligence, the associated "guilt network" may encompass information about a whole series of situations in which one believes one has fallen short in the relationship with the lost person, which can cause debilitating guilt, self-depreciating thoughts, and self-punishment.

Second, within the associative networks underlying unhealthy grief reactions, *interconnections between the elements of the networks* are assumed to be *very strong*. In their cognitive model of PTSD, Ehlers and Clark (2000) postulate that traumatic memories are internally cohesive such that representations of both stimulus and response elements encoded during the event are very strongly related; as a result of these strong stimulus-stimulus (S-S) and stimulus-response (S-R) connections, the traumatic memory can be triggered very easily, even by the most tangential triggers. In people with PGD, memory records of acute threats to, e.g., attachment security, safety, or moral integrity, similarly include strong S-S and S-R associations. Therefore, any cue, be it external (e.g., an object, a person asking about the loss, a place) or internal (e.g., a stream of thoughts or feelings) may activate the full stimulus and response configuration of the memory records.

A third feature of memory networks in unhealthy grief is that these *networks often relate to multiple momentous, consequential, emotional experiences*. That is, the death of a close person mostly involves the confrontation with multiple events/experiences threatening key needs or contradicting preexisting knowledge. For instance, the violent death of a partner to homicide may bring an immediate threat to attachment security, a threat to safety, and a threat to social state and status. Akin to the threat networks of repetitive, multiple traumatization (Neuner, 2023), these events are represented in interwoven associate memory networks. These networks are likely to encompass overlapping stimulus-elements (e.g., images of the lost person suffering), meaning-based ("My life is ruined"), emotional (e.g., defeat, fear), and behavioral (e.g., deactivation) response-elements. As a result, encountering a stimulus resembling an element from one of the networks may rapidly activate the interconnected memory records of different events, leading to various unbidden images, feelings, and thoughts being experienced simultaneously or sequentially.

Maladaptive control strategies

Consistent with multi-representational theories of PTSD (e.g., Ehlers & Clark, 2000; Neuner, 2023), we hypothesize that uncontrolled activation of associative memory networks accounts for the *occurrence* of grief-related symptomatology, and that maladaptive control strategies account, at least partly, for the *maintenance* of this symptomatology. In our cognitive behavioral model, we proposed that anxious and depressive avoidance are key dysfunctional strategies in PGD (Boelen et al., 2006). Anxious avoidance entails deliberate or habitual strategies to avoid internal and external cues connected with the reality of the loss, driven by the fear that confronting this reality will cause some "mental catastrophe" (e.g., going mad, losing control). Depressive avoidance refers to withdrawal from activities that could foster adjustment, driven by the belief that engaging in these activities is impossible without the deceased, will not lead to emotional improvement, or signifies a betrayal of the lost person. Both anxious and depressive avoidance may reflect attempts to inhibit activation of, and thereby prevent changes in, associative memory networks underpinning unhealthy grief reactions. For instance, anxiously avoiding places associated with the loss may serve to prevent activation of the "separation network" and associated pangs of pain. Additionally, depressive avoidance of social situations may serve to prevent the activation of memory records of social threats caused by the loss, as well as, e.g., existential loneliness elicited by this activation.

The distinction between anxious and depressive avoidance provides a clinically useful typology of maladaptive avoidance behaviors in PGD and PTG. However, apart from maladaptive behaviors linked with threatening expectations (as with anxious avoidance) or pessimistic predictions (as with depressive avoidance), patients may engage in many other dysfunctional, deliberate or more habitual control strategies that are intended to prevent unwanted memories, thoughts, feelings and urges, but, in fact, perpetuate memory structures underlying these experiences. These strategies include *situational* (or overt) *avoidance of external cues.* For example, PGD patients may avoid looking at pictures of the deceased, because doing so evokes intense separation distress. Or they may avoid the scene of the death, as it serves as a powerful reminder of their guilt-ridden realization that the loss could have been prevented.

These behaviors can also include *cognitive avoidance and control strategies*. For instance, PGD patients may actively suppress thoughts, feelings, and memories connected with the loss to prevent emotional information about the loss to reach awareness. They may also engage in ruminative thinking about past positive experiences with the lost person, events leading up to the death, or one's own grief reactions to inhibit activation of the "separation network" or memory records underlying guilt, anger, or other key feelings. Some engage in other forms of cognitive avoidance such as denial and minimization of the meaning of the loss (e.g., a youngster insisting that nothing changed since the death of a sibling), excessive fantasy or wishful thinking (e.g., envisioning scenarios where a loved one lives on in a different form and stays near), or avoidant problem solving (e.g., neglecting the financial impact of partner loss).

Further strategies include *experiential avoidance strategies*, such as using substances or getting absorbed in distracting activities to alleviate emotional pain—and *compulsive proximity seeking behaviors*, such as spending hours at the deceased's grave to prevent confrontation with unwanted feelings, thoughts, and images connected with the irreversibility of the loss (cf. Shear et al., 2007). All these behaviors alleviate distress in the short term but, over time, inhibit the activation and modification of associative memory networks underlying emotional difficulties.

Implications for exposure therapy

Cognitive-behavioral theories of grief suggest that emotional responses such as fear, separation distress, and guilt are primarily driven by conscious cognitions and appraisals, which can be readily identified and are open to change through collaborative reflection and discussion (cf. Boelen et al., 2006; Maccallum & Bryant, 2013). The associative memory network perspective introduced here adds to that, that these responses are also driven by associative memory networks containing representational information about momentous and emotive events and experiences, and responses thereto, that threaten fundamental needs (for, e.g., safety, attachment, moral integrity of self and others) or contradict preexisting schematic knowledge about the self and the world. As such, these responses are "automatic", CRs, emerging on confrontation with cues connected with elements of the memory representation rather than appraisal-driven responses arising from deliberate evaluation of stimuli or situations. These responses are subsequently maintained by a host of deliberate or habitual control strategies.

This perspective bears clinical implications. For instance, targeting appraisals, cognitions, and maladaptive control strategies is still considered a key element of PGD treatment. However, the memory perspective implies that directly targeting associative memory records using exposure-based interventions, as described below, are complementary and sometimes even more appropriate methods to mitigate PGD and associated symptoms. This encompasses carefully reviewing and narrating memories, as well as thoughts and images connected with possible aversive situations in the future, underpinning the patient's emotional experiences and symptoms. The role of the therapist is to guide patients in engaging in the memories and images and enhancing the emotional experience by, e.g., having patients close their eyes, speak in the present tense, zoom in on the most meaningful and emotive elements, and give words to evoked action tendencies (cf. Dancu & Foa, 1993).

Exposure is assumed to cause a reduction of symptoms via several interrelated mechanisms. As noted, within a classical conditioning model, *extinction* is thought to underlie the impact of exposure. Consider a griever for whom certain social situations (CSs) following the suicide of a child are associated with shame, and other people making anger-inducing judgmental comments (US-UR representation) leading to fear and avoidance of these situations (CR). From the perspective of extinction, exposure to the CSs without receiving negative responses would lead to a reduction of the CR. However, exposure is not only focused on breaking a CS US-UR association. It also entails directly targeting associative memory networks. In those instances, other mechanisms account for its impact. One mechanism is *habituation*, referring to a decrease in responsiveness to a stimulus, with repeated exposure to that stimulus.

As mentioned above, perhaps the strongest account for the effectiveness of exposure is that it facilitates cognitive changes. That is, experiences of the patient during exposure to emotional stimuli provide feedback to the patient that is integrated in the memory network in the form of new meaning elements, facilitating adaptive network modification. This may take different forms. For instance, confronting avoided stimuli during exposure may increase patient's confidence in their ability to cope with their emotional experiences, *increasing self-efficacy*. In addition, exposure can reveal information that immediately *disconfirms predictions*. For instance, exposure to stimuli connected with the irreversibility of the loss may help the person to realize that the associated pain is bearable, challenging the prediction that the pain will spiral out of control. Exposure may also foster cognitive change by facilitating *access to detailed information* about a meaningful event. For instance, exposure to the circumstances of the death may lead someone to realize that it was inevitable, refuting the previously held belief that they were responsible and guilty. Similarly, when a loss is seen as caused by other people's negligence (e.g., medical doctors after an accident), repeated exposure to the event's context may provide new information (e.g., doctors acted quickly, the accident was fatal) that can be integrated into the memory records. Cognitive change can also occur through temporal and contextual information accessed during exposure. This *contextualization and differentiation* of specific memory records may help link an emotional experience to a particular event and time, counteracting its activation by unrelated cues not connected to the original threat (Neuner, 2023). For example, exposure to moments of loneliness and alienation may help individuals realize that the threat to social connectedness is primarily associated with social contexts where the lost person was typically present, while one's social state and status remain unaffected in other settings. As proposed by Ehlers and Clark (2000) in cognitive therapy for PTSD, new, adaptive cognitions and meanings may also be actively incorporated during subsequent rounds of imagining a particular past or future event.

These theoretical mechanisms are not mutually exclusive but overlapping and complementary. Each may apply to a given PGD patient, helping to motivate engagement in exposure and understanding its effects. In what follows, we will consider how exposure-based interventions may be used in the treatment of PGD and PTG. In so doing, we distinguish between "non-specific" or general exposure and "targeted", individualized exposure, the first including a standard step-by-step procedure potentially useful for any PGD patient, the latter encompassing a more personalized approach.

"Non-specific" (general) exposure

The "non-specific" approach follows a similar procedure across different patients. The first step entails *exposure to the story of the loss*. In this step, patients are encouraged to articulate a chronological narrative, starting with the moments they first knew that their close person would die or, in the case of sudden deaths, had died. This is followed by a detailed account of the moments immediately after the death, the funeral, and the first period thereafter. During this procedure, the therapist formulates hypotheses about the most painful and meaningful memories within the narrative, similar to the hot spots in prolonged exposure for PTSD. In doing so, the therapist tries to lead patients toward these moments and spend some time dwelling on the images, thoughts, and feelings associated with them.

This step is followed by *exposure to the irreversibility of the loss*. During this exposure, patients are encouraged to review the relationship with the deceased, zooming in on what is missed most now that they are gone. They are also instructed to give words to the implications of their loved one's death for their view of themselves, of life, and of their future. One key task of therapists is to slowly but surely force their patients to face head-on, with full awareness, the fact that the separation is irreversible and permanent—now, a year from now, and all the time that follows. Exposure to the story and irreversibility of the loss are primarily imaginary activities. However, it is useful to also use external and tangible stimuli to boost exposure, e.g., looking at photos, watching video material, visiting places, using memorabilia, and talking to people connected with the lost person or death's circumstances.

From an associative memory perspective, exposure to the story and reality of the loss is particularly powerful to mitigate symptoms of separation distress because they contribute to functional restoration of the "separation network" driving these symptoms. For instance, this exposure accelerates confrontation with the implications of the loss which, in turn, helps to "update" information about the separation, changing it from an event that just occurred to one that already left indelible marks. Moreover, confrontation with the loss's reality boosts adaptation of schematic knowledge about oneself and the relationship with the lost person, helps to disconfirm catastrophic predictions about the consequences of confronting reality, and counters anxious avoidance.

"Targeted" (individualized) exposure

Non-specific exposure may be complemented by "targeted" exposure, specifically tailored to the patient's problems. Such exposure may be applied through a series of overlapping steps. A first step is to select targets for exposure. In PGD and PTG, separation distress is often (if not always) a key problem and, hence, a key target for exposure. However, other emotional experiences may be starting points for exposure too, including disbelief and unrealness, fear, guilt, shame, anger, and emotional loneliness. The content of emotional episodes and recurring pangs of pain shed light on candidate starting points for exposure.

A second step involves formulating hypotheses about the pivotal experiences, events, and threats underpinning the patient's problems. Key emotions patients present with provide valuable information about such events with, e.g., fear originating from a threat to safety, guilt and shame reflecting threat to moral integrity of self, anger indicating confrontation with other people transgressing moral boundaries, and emotional loneliness reflecting threats to social connectedness (cf. Grey et al., 2001). In addition, hypotheses are formulated regarding the nature of sensory, meaning-based, and response-related information stored in the memory records of relevant threats. To help guide this process, the therapist seeks to obtain a clearer understanding of the images, feelings, and thoughts the patient experiences during emotional episodes. Critically, intrusive memories carry a lot of information. For example, a person may experience unbidden images of an indifferent doctor who treated a loved one who later died, evoking anger. Alternatively, a person may have an image intertwined with a sense of personal failure that evokes guilt—for instance, an image of the deceased just before their suicide, accompanied by the thought, "I should have been there for her/him". Recurring future images may also reveal important information about emotional/consequential events and threats the current problems can be traced back to. For instance, if a patient is troubled by images of being alone amidst people having fun, this might indicate that the loss posed a profound sense of social threat and disconnection.

Meaning-based information underlying the presenting problems can often be derived from recurring negative thoughts. Such thoughts may reflect the perception that basic needs have been threatened or violated (e.g., "My grip on life is jeopardized and I can no longer make plans", "My view of others is undermined, and no one can be trusted"). Recurring thoughts may also reflect discrepancies between the current reality and preexisting beliefs about, e.g., the self, other people, life. The sudden accidental death of a partner may be discrepant from beliefs that the world is safe and predictable ("I used to be safe, now there is danger everywhere"). Behavioral responses, urges, and actions can also reveal much about the momentous events/experiences and threats that the current problems can be traced back to. Dissociative reactions upon confrontation with loss-related cues may signal that the loss relates to a threat to comprehensibility, controllability, and predictability. Withdrawal from social situations (but also excessive approval-seeking) could signal that the loss is tied to a threat to social connection.

During the steps of identifying key emotional episodes and experiences and gathering information about elements of the associative memory network driving these experiences, exposure is already taking place. In the third step, exposure continues more purposefully to restore associative networks to mitigate emotional distress. The form of exposure and the triggers involved depend largely on the issues with which patients present.

Threats to comprehensibility, controllability, and predictability and disbelief

When the loss causes intense sense of *unrealness and disbelief* because it threatened predictability, controllability, and comprehensibility, exposure can be focused on reliving memories representing the reality of the death (e.g., memories of the deceased person lying in their coffin), supplemented by reliving moments of saying goodbye or imagining such moments when they could not occur in reality (e.g., because the body was too damaged). This may help to integrate factual knowledge that the separation is permanent into the memory network, that was so far dominated by experiences of confusion, thereby "unblocking" disbelief and boosting the grief process. The emotional pain that may subsequently be experienced may be mitigated by reviewing the loss' implications and confront associated emotions for the patient to experience that these are painful but bearable. Gradually, more space can be made for visualizing moments in the future without the deceased, to counter disbelief and regain a sense of control over the future.

Threats to self-identity

Threats to self-identity can be profound following loss, particularly when the lost person played a central role in shaping one's self-concept, roles, goals, and future plans. For some individuals, these threats to self-identity are primarily an individual experience, while for others, they are more socially oriented. In the first case, the experience may be more closely linked to anxiety, whereas in the second case, shame may be more predominant. When anxiety is the primary response, the underlying memory record may include images of being lost, cognitions reflecting impaired self-clarity (e.g., "I don't know who I am"), a sense of confusion about one's role in the world, and difficulty to engage in restoration-oriented activities. When shame is more central, the memory record may include images of social disconnection, concerns about being perceived as unworthy without the lost person, and a tendency to withdraw from others. As with other psychological threats, exposure initially focuses on exploring these emotional experiences and the various elements within the memory records that sustain them, followed by the repeated verbalization of images, cognitions, and behavioral tendencies that comprise this information.

Threats to safety and traumatic stress

Traumatic losses often involve threats to safety and security, resulting in separation and traumatic distress typical of PGD and PTG. Examples include sudden deaths in the context of danger, suffering, and violence. The circumstances of traumatic loss may backfire in the form of unbidden images of the fears and suffering that the deceased person (or oneself) endured, a sense of ongoing threat, and entrenched avoidance of external and internal cues reminding of the death. In this situation, exposure focuses on repeatedly recounting details of the events leading up to the death, as is typically done in prolonged exposure in PTSD treatment. When the death was the result of a violent or mutilating attack, the patient should be helped to verbalize images and feelings associated with the terror and helplessness that their close person likely experienced. The realization that one's close person suffered, was lonely in their struggle, or engendered humiliation can evoke feelings of powerlessness, anger, and guilt. It is crucial to provide patients with the opportunity to reflect on these feelings.

Threats to moral integrity, guilt, and shame

In the case of threats to moral integrity causing guilt, exposure may be focused on verbalizing all that one has done "wrong" and everything in which one has failed to fulfill responsibilities toward the lost person. With cognitive restructuring, therapists would attempt to translate this into refutable cognitions (e.g., "That I didn't prevent the death, means I am co-responsible and must pay for my wrongdoing"). During exposure, the focus is on giving detailed words to the situations in which patients believe that they were negligent, to dwell on cognitions about the foreseeability and preventability of the death, to feel through self-blame, and verbalize action tendencies (e.g., excessive apologizing or other compensatory behaviors).

With patients experiencing pervasive shame, it is similarly helpful to narrate all memories and images associated with having crossed moral boundaries. This could be extended by detailed reflection on the consequences thereof for one's worthiness as a person, perceived condemnation from the social environment, and action urges (e.g., self-punishment, isolation). Shame may be linked to severe suffering, including feelings of being flawed, self-hatred, self-punishment, and suicidality. Therapists should provide a supportive environment where patients can experience and articulate these experiences.

Exposure to guilt and shame inducing experiences can have different restorative effects (Paul et al., 2014). It may habituate tension and may provide emotional relief to share self-agonizing feelings and thoughts. Moreover, reviewing memories and thoughts associated with guilt and shame may provide access to information that can alter the memory record underlying these feelings. Voicing chronological details about the circumstances of the death can correct cognitions about preventability; experiencing therapeutic support and acceptance may counteract negative self-pejorative appraisals and induce self-compassion. Narrating details of one's alleged failures can also reconnect emotional experiences to specific events and times—counteracting generalization of guilt and shame to unrelated contexts.

Threats to moral integrity of others and anger

When the loss involves others failing to fulfill responsibilities or violating moral boundaries, leading to persistent anger, exposure should focus on processing the narratives of the events that triggered this anger. Therapists should help patients recount the events that led to their anger, identify the agents (individuals, institutions, or higher powers) who intentionally or negligently obstructed their goals, focus on the most provocative aspects of these narratives, and provide space for aggressive and vengeful thoughts and impulses. Encouraging clients to verbalize the urges associated with their anger and to imaginatively engage with their aggression can help to alleviate these feelings. Thus, through exposure, distress and experiential avoidance may be reduced, distress tolerance may increase, and individuals may gain awareness of new interpretations and meanings, potentially resolving anger or fostering constructive actions. Additionally, processing memory records related to anger may help correct faulty beliefs about the intentionality of others' omissions, the effectiveness of aggressive outbursts, and the view that not expressing anger is cowardly or dishonorable. During exposure, patients may also become aware that their anger has generalized to stimuli and situations unrelated to the original injustice. Like in PTSD (Clifton et al., 2017) anger and guilt in PGD and PTG may serve to disengage from more painful and vulnerable experiences, such as separation distress. When this is the case, exposure may successfully mitigate anger and guilt but simultaneously increase separation distress that subsequently needs to be targeted in treatment.

Threats to social state and emotional loneliness

Exposure may also be used when threats to social state and status cause the person to experience emotional or existential loneliness. As a starting point, it is beneficial to encourage patients to articulate the most profound changes in their social status, roles, connections, and needs resulting from their loss—taking time to contemplate thoroughly about memories, future images, thoughts, and feelings associated with these changes. They are also encouraged to explore any behavioral tendencies linked to their loneliness, such as social withdrawal, neglect of self-care— or, conversely approval- and attention-seeking behaviors, which may fuel desperation and resentment when unsuccessful. By giving careful thought to all these pieces of information connected with the threat to connectedness, the objective is to mitigate emotional loneliness and guide individuals past the point where everything seems altered. Reframing profound loneliness as a result of the abrupt disruption in social status following the loss, rather than as a permanent change in social connectedness, can interrupt the automatic activation of these emotions triggered by everyday reminders. This shift can also help the individual take steps toward adopting adaptive social behaviors.

Reducing maladaptive control strategies

Differences between healthy grief and PGD and PTG lie in both the nature, size, and interconnectedness of associative memory networks as well as in the ability to regulate the activation of these networks. Those with healthy grief allow corrective information to integrate, or modulate activation through distraction. In contrast, individuals with PGD/PTG engage in maladaptive control strategies, preventing changes in memory networks and sustaining symptoms. As such, the impact of exposure interventions is increased when applied in combination with interventions targeting these control strategies.

Therapists can employ different strategies to address maladaptive control and avoidance behaviors. A key initial step is to psycho-educate patients about these behaviors and how they perpetuate the problems. In so doing, it is useful to distinguish between avoidance of external cues—which patients are often aware of—and cognitive avoidance strategies, that patients may recognize less easily. Another important distinction is between strategies that involve inaction (where individuals refrain from certain behaviors to control distressing emotions) and those involving active efforts to keep unwanted psychological experiences out of awareness. Examples of the former include withdrawing from social situations that remind the bereaved person of the irreversibility of the separation or the threat to their social status. Examples of the latter include excessive fantasizing about alternative realities in which the deceased person is still alive and compulsive proximity-seeking behavior.

After having identified the patient's engagement in control strategies, cognitions underlying these control strategies may be identified and discussed. The validity and effectiveness of the patient's rationale for employing specific strategies are critically assessed. Then, steps are taken to systematically reduce the use of unhelpful strategies. For instance, gradual exposure to reminders of the death may be used with patients who avoid such reminders to control their separation distress. Maladaptive proximity-seeking behaviors (e.g., visiting the graveyard every day) could be gradually reduced in patients who engage in them compulsively to avoid confronting the irreversibility of the loss or other painful realizations. Reducing compensatory behaviors or self-punishment may be used with patients who associate the loss with their own perceived moral transgressions. Grounding techniques can be taught to patients who tend to dissociate when reminded of the threat to comprehensibility, controllability, and predictability brought about by the loss, along with feelings of "unrealness" and disbelief. Graded activation may be applied with patients using excessive social withdrawal to cope with the threat to social status brought about by the loss.

Conclusion and discussion

In our earlier cognitive behavioral conceptualization, we proposed that PGD was driven by insufficient elaboration and integration of the loss with other autobiographical knowledge, negative appraisals about, e.g., oneself, life, and one's reactions to the loss, and depressive and anxious avoidance (Boelen et al., 2006). Other models have emphasized the importance of a merged self-identity (i.e., maladaptive dependence on the lost person; Maccallum & Bryant, 2013) and disrupted emotion regulation blocking memory information about the relationship with the lost person from being updated (Shear & Shair, 2005).

The memory perspective introduced here complements this theorizing. Earlier theories have more or less explicitly posited that acute grief (and its persistence in people with PGD) is associated with threats to attachment security brought about the loss, causing hallmark symptoms of separation distress. The perspective in this chapter expands this claim, postulating that beyond threats to attachment security, the death of a close person may carry a range of threats and information contradicting existing schematic knowledge causing significant fear, guilt, shame, anger, and other emotional experiences. Pivotal experiences and threats are those undermining (i) attachment security, (ii) predictability, controllability, comprehensibility, (iii) self-identity, (iv) safety, (v) moral integrity of self and (vi) others, and (vii) social connectedness.

Apart from providing a framework for understanding why loss may precipitate a range of emotional experiences, the perspective presented in this chapter also offers an account for the involuntary and intrusive nature of these emotional experiences and why they manifest across different modalities, including images, thoughts, feelings, and action tendencies. From this framework, this is because these responses mirror affective states that are encoded in associative memory networks at the time the threats (or experiences contradicting existing schematic knowledge) were first felt in full force. As such, this framework complements existing theories, by suggesting associative memory networks as a critical driving mechanism of emotional experiences in PGD and PTG.

Exposure-based interventions have long been a key ingredient of effective therapies for unhealthy grief. From the earliest (e.g., Ramsay, 1977) to the most recent (e.g., Rosner et al., 2025) writings in which exposure was applied, it was mostly focused on alleviating separation distress by revisiting the story of the loss. The current chapter argues for a broader application for exposure-based techniques, by asserting that identifying, articulating, verbalizing, experiencing, deeply feeling, and processing all the meaningful experiences and threats associated with the death of a close person can have powerful therapeutic effects. This aligns with recent theorizing in PTSD, suggesting that exposure is indicated not only to reduce fear resulting from events of physical threat, but may also be applied to curb shame, mental defeat, and other emotions connected with broader social trauma (Neuner, 2023).

Throughout this book, we advocate that treatments for PGD and PTG include various interventions, tailored to the problems, goals, and possibilities of the patients. Accordingly, exposure could be amended and applied in written format, in cases where there are no options for face-to-face therapy or when talking about the threats and pain associated with loss is too difficult. Exposure could be expended with imagery rescripting when providing a corrective or supplementary emotional experience may be needed to reduce distress. For example, when significant childhood loss is linked to pervasive loneliness due to the absence of supportive adults, visualizing receiving support while grieving as a child can have a powerful effect (Lechner-Meichsner et al., 2024). In addition, exposure may be paired with physical relaxation or other responses counteracting arousal, in case exposure itself is deemed invasive, or too disruptive. Training patients to generate positive future images may be useful when symptoms coincide with negative flashforwards of, e.g., persistent social alienation, failure, or other catastrophes.

We clarified that the effectiveness of exposure is likely strengthened by targeting maladaptive control and avoidance strategies. It remains useful to reduce anxious avoidance of loss cues and depressive avoidance of activities that could foster adjustment. However, therapists should be aware that there may be many other dysfunctional, deliberate, or more habitual control strategies that are intended to prevent unwanted memories, thoughts, feelings, and urges, but, in fact, block changes in associative memory structures underlying pervasive pangs of emotional pain.

Our plea to use exposure-based interventions to foster emotional processing of the many different threats connected with loss leaves room for the application of cognitive restructuring techniques to address maladaptive cognitions and support the attribution of helpful meanings. Multimodal and multirepresentational theories propose that memory network activation can be controlled by reflective processes (Dalgleish, 2004; Neuner, 2023). Accordingly, identifying and challenging negative cognitions, to correct negative meanings connected with threats to attachment security ("I cannot cope"), self-identity ("I am broken beyond repair"), safety ("Nowhere is safe"), or other threats, remains an important element of treatment. The availability of nuanced appraisals that can help to counteract negative meanings, may help to update associative memory networks, inhibit their activation, and fuel functional coping. Exposure and cognitive restructuring can also be combined by explicitly reflecting on the insights gained during exposure; this may include evaluating the non-occurrence of a predicted outcome (e.g., when confronting the irreversibility of the loss was anticipated to lead to a mental catastrophe) or bringing threats into proper proportion (e.g., when the negligence of specific individuals accountable for the death was generalized to hatred toward humanity) (cf. Craske et al., 2022).

Empirical research is needed to test hypotheses implicated in the perspective explained in this chapter. If we extend the reasoning presented in this chapter, PGD is often the result of confrontation with specific momentous experiences that involve a threat to fundamental needs and carry information that is discrepant with preexisting knowledge that typically occurs early in the development of the disorder. That is, early violations of attachment security, comprehensibility, self-identity, safety, moral integrity, and social connection act as forms of trauma, keeping the individual trapped in a state of acute grief. This accords with the notion of PGD as a disorder of non-recovery and preliminary findings that early response to loss strongly predict later responses (cf. Boelen & Lenferink, 2022). Future research is needed to examine to what extent pervasive and unbidden symptoms of PGD and PTG can indeed be traced back to specific momentous experiences that involve a threat to fundamental needs and carry information that mismatches with preexisting knowledge. Research should also clarify whether the experiences and threats discussed in this chapter are indeed the most pivotal ones, and to identify other experiences and threats that may be implicated in loss. A related challenge would be to investigate to whether the encoding of these experiences is linked to the different modalities (images, thoughts, feelings) in which symptoms may be experienced. Research should also expand knowledge on the role of maladaptive control and avoidance strategies; research confirms the role of anxious and depressive avoidance, and rumination (cf. Boelen & Eisma, 2015; Eisma & Stroebe, 2021). However, the notion that any strategy individuals with PGD use to prevent the activation of memory information linked to threats to safety, attachment, morality, and affiliation can contribute to the persistence of PGD symptoms, deserves further examination. Therapy research is needed to better understand the effects of exposure-based interventions as stand-alone treatment.

It is a promising prospect that further refinement of exposure-based interventions and their wider applications to different emotional problems in PGD and PTG could potentially enhance the efficacy of these interventions. Eventually, this may benefit a subset of patients who currently derive limited benefit from existing treatments.

Acknowledgment

The authors used ChatGPT (OpenAI, Version 4.0) to improve the grammar and fluency of the English language in the manuscript. No content was generated by the tool; all ideas, interpretations, and conclusions are the authors' own.

References

Boddez, Y. (2018). The presence of your absence: A conditioning theory of grief. *Behaviour Research and Therapy*, *106*, 18–27. https://doi.org/10.1016/j.brat.2018.04.006

Boelen, P. A., & Eisma, M. C. (2015). Anxious and depressive avoidance behavior in post-loss psychopathology: A longitudinal study. *Anxiety, Stress, and Coping*, *28*(5), 587–600. https://doi.org/10.1080/10615806.2015.1004054

Boelen, P. A., & Lenferink, L. I. (2022). Prolonged grief disorder in DSM-5-TR: Early predictors and longitudinal measurement invariance. *The Australian and New Zealand Journal of Psychiatry*, *56*(6), 667–674. https://doi.org/10.1177/00048674211025728

Boelen, P. A., van den Hout, M. A., & van den Bout, J. (2006). A cognitive-behavioral conceptualization of complicated grief. *Clinical Psychology: Science and Practice*, *13*(2), 109–128. https://doi.org/10.1111/j.1468-2850.2006.00013.x

Bottomley, J. S., Campbell, K. W., Feigelman, W., Schamber, E. L., & Rheingold, A. A. (2025). Prospective relations between stigma, guilt, shame, posttraumatic stress and prolonged grief symptoms among overdose and suicide loss survivors. *Journal of Affective Disorders*, *379*, 223–231. https://doi.org/10.1016/j.jad.2025.02.102

Clifton, E. G., Feeny, N. C., & Zoellner, L. A. (2017). Anger and guilt in treatment for chronic posttraumatic stress disorder. *Journal of Behavior Therapy and Experimental Psychiatry*, *54*, 9–16. https://doi.org/10.1016/j.jbtep.2016.05.003

Craske, M. G., Treanor, M., Zbozinek, T. D., & Vervliet, B. (2022). Optimizing exposure therapy with an inhibitory retrieval approach and the OptEx nexus. *Behaviour Research and Therapy*, *152*, 104069. https://doi.org/10.1016/j.brat.2022.104069

Cunningham, K. C. (2020). Shame and guilt in PTSD. In M. T. Tull & N. A. Kimbrel (Eds.), *Emotion in posttraumatic stress disorder: Etiology, assessment, neurobiology, and treatment* (pp. 145–171). Elsevier Academic Press. https://doi.org/10.1016/B978-0-12-816022-0.00006-5

Dalgleish, T. (2004). Cognitive approaches to posttraumatic stress disorder: the evolution of multirepresentational theorizing. *Psychological Bulletin*, *130*(2), 228–260. https://doi.org/10.1037/0033-2909.130.2.228

Dancu, C. V., & Foa, E. B. (1993). Cognitive-behavior therapy with post-traumatic stress disorder. In A. Freeman & F.M. Dattilio (Eds.), *Casebook in cognitive behavior therapy*. Plenum.

Ehlers, A., & Clark, D. M. (2000). A cognitive model of posttraumatic stress disorder. *Behaviour Research and Therapy*, *38*(4), 319–345. https://doi.org/10.1016/s0005-7967(99)00123-0

Eisma, M. C., & Stroebe, M. S. (2021). Emotion regulatory strategies in complicated grief: A systematic review. *Behavior Therapy*, *52*(1), 234–249. https://doi.org/10.1016/j.beth.2020.04.004

Foa, E. B., & Kozak, M. J. (1986). Emotional processing of fear: Exposure to corrective information. *Psychological Bulletin*, *99*(1), 20–35. https://doi.org/10.1037/0033-2909.99.1.20

Grey, N., Holmes, E., & Brewin, C. R. (2001). Peritraumatic emotional "hot spots" in memory. *Behavioural and Cognitive Psychotherapy*, *29*(3), 367–372. https://doi.org/10.1017/S1352465801003095

Knowles, K. A., & Tolin, D. F. (2022). Mechanisms of action in exposure therapy. *Current Psychiatry Reports*, *24*(12), 861–869. https://doi.org/10.1007/s11920-022-01391-8

Lechner-Meichsner, F., Boelen, P. A., & Hagenaars, M. A. (2024). Imagery rescripting in the treatment of prolonged grief disorder: Insights, examples, and future directions. *European Journal of Trauma & Dissociation*, *8*(3), 100435. https://doi.org/10.1016/j.ejtd.2024.100435

Maccallum, F., & Bryant, R. A. (2013). A cognitive attachment model of prolonged grief: integrating attachments, memory, and identity. *Clinical Psychology Review*, *33*(6), 713–727. https://doi.org/10.1016/j.cpr.2013.05.001

Maciejewski, P. K., Falzarano, F. B., She, W. J., Lichtenthal, W. G., & Prigerson, H. G. (2022). A micro-sociological theory of adjustment to loss. *Current Opinion in Psychology*, 43, 96–101. https://doi.org/10.1016/j.copsyc.2021.06.016

Neuner F. (2023). Physical and social trauma: Towards an integrative transdiagnostic perspective on psychological trauma that involves threats to status and belonging. *Clinical Psychology Review*, *99*, 102219. https://doi.org/10.1016/j.cpr.2022.102219

Paul, L. A., Gros, D. F., Strachan, M., Worsham, G., Foa, E. B., & Acierno, R. (2014). Prolonged exposure for guilt and shame in a veteran of Operation Iraqi Freedom. *American Journal of Psychotherapy*, 68(3), 277–286. https://doi.org/10.1176/appi.psychotherapy.2014.68.3.277

Ramsay, R. W. (1977). Behavioural approaches to bereavement. *Behaviour Research and Therapy*, *15*(2), 131–135. https://doi.org/10.1016/0005-7967(77)90097-3

Rosner, R., Rau, J., Kersting, A., Rief, W., Steil, R., Rummel, A. M., Vogel, A., & Comtesse, H. (2025). Grief-specific cognitive behavioral therapy vs present-centered therapy: A randomized clinical trial. *JAMA Psychiatry*, *82*(2), 109–117. https://doi.org/10.1001/jamapsychiatry.2024.3409

Shear, K., Monk, T., Houck, P., Melhem, N., Frank, E., Reynolds, C., & Sillowash, R. (2007). An attachment-based model of complicated grief including the role of avoidance. *European Archives of Psychiatry and Clinical Neuroscience*, *257*(8), 453–461. https://doi.org/10.1007/s00406-007-0745-z

Shear, K., & Shair, H. (2005). Attachment, loss, and complicated grief. *Developmental Psychobiology*, *47*(3), 253–267. https://doi.org/10.1002/dev.20091

Shi, C., Ren, Z., Zhao, C., Zhang, T., & Chan, S. H. (2021). Shame, guilt, and posttraumatic stress symptoms: A three-level meta-analysis. *Journal of Anxiety Disorders*, *82*, 102443. https://doi.org/10.1016/j.janxdis.2021.102443

Chapter 7

Attribution of meaning, reengaging, and activation

Geert E. Smid and Robert A. Neimeyer

Attribution of meaning can be conceptualized as a multifaceted process, an outcome, and a key component in psychotherapy for prolonged and traumatic grief. As a cognitive, emotional, and spiritual process, it encompasses sense-making, evaluating the broader implications of the loss, and reappraisal or reframing through both intra-individual and interpersonal negotiation. As an outcome, it facilitates the integration of the loss, enhancing the individual's capacity to adapt to a changed life within their sociocultural context. Therapeutic interventions include cognitive restructuring and narrative meaning reconstruction in the domains of self, identity, and the relationship with the deceased. Additionally, reengagement and activation are addressed in relation to the individual's perception of the world, others, and the future. Experiential interventions using symbolic interactions, described in the next chapter, may be applied in parallel.

Within psychotherapy for prolonged and traumatic grief, attribution of meaning, alongside reengaging and activation, typically occurs following psychoeducation and is closely related to the narrative of the loss and the bereaved person's relationship with the deceased, as explored through trauma- and grief-focused exposure. The effectiveness of a sequential approach to psychotherapy for prolonged and traumatic grief is supported by research and practice. In a randomized, controlled trial (Boelen et al., 2007), patients with prolonged grief disorder (PGD) were allocated to either a condition of six sessions of exposure therapy and six sessions of cognitive therapy or a condition in which these interventions were applied in reverse order. Outcomes showed that exposure therapy followed by cognitive therapy was more efficacious than cognitive therapy followed by exposure therapy (Boelen et al., 2007). A similar sequential approach takes brief eclectic psychotherapy for posttraumatic stress disorder (BEPP), an evidence-based, grief-informed, manualized treatment. In BEPP, trauma-focused exposure is followed by a domain of meaning stage that focuses on the patient's changes in views on the self and the world (Nijdam et al., 2022). Restorative retelling, a meaning-focused approach

DOI: 10.4324/9781003429777-10

to grief therapy (Neimeyer, 2022), alternates trauma and grief focused exposure with attribution of meaning. Restorative retelling focuses on three stories: the "facts-based" story, the emotion-focused story, and the meaning-oriented story. Following the first two strands of the story often leads the patient to encounter a need to make sense of events or of themselves in terms of the third. In psychotherapy for prolonged and traumatic grief, the "facts-based" and emotion-focused stories emerge during imaginal and general exposure, respectively, and are followed by the meaning-oriented story during attribution of meaning. It should be noted that not all treatments for PGD with demonstrated effectiveness apply this sequence (e.g., Rosner et al., 2024). However, if traumatic circumstances of the loss contribute to severe symptoms of posttraumatic stress disorder (PTSD) besides PGD, exposure may be necessary before the patient can reflect on what happened without being overwhelmed by extreme emotions.

Before further exploring the territory of meaning, a brief note on terminology. Because meanings are determined by numerous circumstances and aspects of the loss, "attribution of" meaning may be preferred as a term over "making" or "constructing" meaning; "finding" meaning in a loss may not always be feasible. However, "attribution" may feel too intellectual or unfamiliar to some users, whereas "making" or "constructing" meaning suggests the active role of the person or group in framing or creating meaning in the context of loss and its aftermath. "Finding" meaning, for many, implies acts of grace, or the outcome of an active search. Here, for simplicity, we adopt "attribution" as a general term intended to encompass all of these activities.

Exploring the territory: Mapping meaning

The loss of a loved one confronts bereaved individuals with fundamental questions of meaning. Attribution of meaning to the loss is related to many circumstances and aspects of the loss. Efforts to attribute meaning are reported by most individuals facing highly stressful events (Park, 2010). Attribution of meaning initially focuses on making sense of what happened, attributing causes, and understanding the immediate implications, specifically if the death of a loved one was unexpected (Janoff-Bulman & Frantz, 1997). If the unanticipated death occurred under violent or accidental, "meaningless" circumstances, questions of meaning often present themselves in complex, urgent, and distressing ways. As this chapter will elaborate, attribution of meaning involves connecting events and circumstances with the individual's needs, beliefs, desires, plans, and goals. It happens mostly automatically and develops through dialogue, negotiation, and narration.

Why do people attribute meanings? The loss of loved ones confronts people with uncertainties inherent in life, suffering, and death. The psychological effects of the unknown have been described from antiquity. As the Roman philosopher Seneca wrote: "we shrink from the unknown" (Seneca, 1920, p. 251). The Danish philosopher Kierkegaard pointed out that the unknown is something people do not understand but that nevertheless evokes many possibilities and therefore constitutes the source of human anxiety. Incomprehensible possibilities are linked to guilt, prohibition, and punishment, as in the story of the tree of knowledge of good and evil described in the biblical book of Genesis (Kierkegaard, 1957/1844). Research evidence has confirmed that fear of the unknown is one of people's most fundamental fears (Carleton, 2016). In line with this, fear of the unknown and intolerance of uncertainty have been found to be key concepts in explaining the development of prolonged grief (Boelen et al., 2016). Attribution of meaning reduces uncertainty and uncontrollability by attempting to fill the void of meaninglessness left by the loss. It is therefore an adaptive process that helps people to survive as meaning-attributing beings.

Helpful meanings contribute to restoring a sense of meaning-in-life. As elaborated in the Introduction, meaning-in-life operates on multiple levels – existential, cognitive, affective, motivational, social, and somatic. On these levels, meanings may contribute to transcendence, coherence, significance, purpose, connectedness, and well-being (see Introduction).

Situational, global, and narrative meaning

To better understand how we attribute meanings to events and episodes, it is helpful to distinguish between situational and global meanings. *Situational meaning* refers to meaning in the context of a particular environmental encounter (Park, 2010). In the context of bereavement, situational meaning begins with the (impending) death of the loved one and describes an ongoing set of processes and outcomes, including initial assignment of meaning to the loss, and the subsequent events in the aftermath of the loss that may contribute to reappraisals of the event. *Global meaning* consists of beliefs, goals, and subjective feelings (Park, 2010). Each situation individuals experience is viewed through the lens of their global meaning system, shaping the individuals' initial understandings of the meaning of each situation (i.e., what the situation says about the world, oneself, etc.). Global beliefs comprise broad views regarding justice, control, predictability, and the self, and have also been termed core constructs (Kelly, 1955), core schemas (Beck, 2008), or fundamental beliefs that represent a person's *assumptive world* (Parkes, 1971). Global meaning provides a framework for individuals to make sense of the world around them and engage with important pursuits in their lives.

The loss of a loved one and its situational meanings may be discrepant with the individuals' global meaning system. Discrepancies between situational and global meanings induce distress (Park, 2010). Attribution of meaning consists of a process of negotiating conflicts between situational and global meanings. The individual negotiates the challenge that the death of a loved one poses to his or her manner of understanding and functioning in the world (Gillies et al., 2014). This negotiation is often understood using Piaget's and Baldwin's concepts of assimilation and accommodation (Hanfstingl et al., 2022). *Assimilation* refers to processes that lead to reframing the meaning of the event to cohere with one's global meaning system. *Accommodation* refers to processes that are designed to alter one's global meaning framework to fit with the meaning of the situation. Global meanings have been called schemas in cognitive processing theories; these are the processes targeted in Cognitive Processing Therapy for PTSD (Sobel et al., 2009), and changes in these processes are key mechanisms of change (Schumm et al., 2015). Successful assimilation or accommodation can occur through a variety of ways and result in specific outcomes, called *meanings made*. Examples of different forms of meanings made include: a sense of having "made sense," acceptance, reattributions and causal understanding, perceptions of growth or positive life changes, changed identity or integration of the stressful experience into identity, reappraised meaning of the stressor, changed global beliefs, changed global goals, and restored or changed sense of meaning-in-life (Park, 2010).

Whereas a global vs. situational formulation of meaning focuses on the match or discrepancy between general beliefs about the world and specific events, a narrative approach focuses on the inveterate need of human beings to weave stories that make sense of events and of themselves in light of them (Bruner, 1990). The essence of narrative is to give a coherent account of an experience, real or imagined, integrating elements of setting, characterization of protagonists and other actors, plot, theme, and fictional goal into an intelligible whole, whether the audience is oneself or relevant others (Neimeyer, 2000). Crucially, narrative recalls, relates, and projects the significance of events by organizing them *over time* – in contrast to the episodic focus on the moment when situational meanings clash with global beliefs. Traumatic narratives can be viewed as an attempt to integrate one or more episodic challenges to core life themes into an extended temporal account that captures and conveys their larger significance for the narrator and the listener. Indeed, the effectiveness of narrative reconstruction has been shown in evidence-based treatments for PTSD and depression, e.g., life review therapy (Jiang et al., 2024) and narrative exposure therapy (Lely et al., 2019). A brief example of meaning disruption in the context of traumatic loss can clarify the distinction between an event-based *episodic focus* on global vs. situational meanings and a person-based narrative approach to meaning reconstruction.

Julia, a young pediatrician, awoke one morning to every parent's nightmare, when she discovered her infant daughter lifeless in her crib, evidently a victim of Sudden Infant Death Syndrome or SIDS. Overwhelmed by a toxic amalgam of posttraumatic arousal and avoidance and prolonged grief, she sought therapy several months later to address her ongoing inability to function in her work and family roles. Viewed through the lens of episodic meaning disruption, Julia's tragic loss clearly assaulted her global beliefs in her sense of control over the illness and injury of someone under her care, an element of her assumptive world powerfully reinforced by her identity as a physician and central to her role as a new mother. It also violated her presumption of life's fairness, and specifically her belief in a loving and omnipotent God. The seismic impact of these disruptions to foundational elements of her meaning system was evident in her bitterness, disillusionment, and loss of purpose and direction in life, all of which became key themes in her therapy. Viewing her baby's death through a narrative lens, however, clarified the precise challenges she faced in trying to construct a story arc that made sense of this shattering experience, in a way that restored a measure of coherence to the micro-narrative of the death event and to the macro-narrative of her life (Neimeyer, 2000).

In this respect, an episodic focus on global and situational meanings and a narrative focus on the reconstruction of meaning in storied form represent complementary approaches to therapy for prolonged and traumatic grief.

Determinants of meaning attribution

What determines how people evaluate, interpret, narrate, and attribute meaning to the loss of loved ones? The meanings that people attribute to bereavement and grief depend on the *events* that led to the death of the loved one, the person's *cultural* background, *social* circumstances, *individual* factors, and the *relationship* with the loved one – both before and after the death (Smid, 2020). Event-related factors include non-natural or sudden causes of death and the person's immediate grief response. Cultural factors include beliefs, rituals, and care provision. Social factors include social support, juridical and political, economic and environmental factors, and media representation. Individual factors include gender and age, biological and somatic aspects, personality and attachment, and history of trauma and loss. Factors related to the relationship with the deceased include the type and quality of the relationship, involvement in the death, opportunities to say farewell or ambiguity (uncertainty) surrounding the loss, and (again) rituals that may need to be performed according to cultural traditions. Determinants of meaning attribution following loss are related to the risk of the development or maintenance of disordered grief as well as factors that contribute to resilience and recovery (Smid, 2020; Smid et al., 2021) that are elaborated in Chapter 3. Attribution of meaning to a loss can determine the extent to which a grieving process disrupts the bereaved survivor's functioning (Milman et al., 2019a). Meanings thus can have a favorable or unfavorable impact on the grieving process.

After listening to the patient's narration of the story of the loss during trauma and grief focused exposure, the therapist explores other contextual and psychological determinants of meaning. The therapist learns about factors that may influence the patient's appraisal of the traumatic loss of the loved one, such as concomitant losses of resources, judicial procedures, availability of social support, previous trauma or loss experiences, and history of mental health problems.

Assessing meanings and cognitions following loss

Assessment scales can serve as measures of either process or outcome in research on prolonged and traumatic grief, as well as being used as "conversation starters" with patients about domains in which therapeutic work is indicated.

In the context of cognitive behavioral theorizing, negative and maladaptive cognitions – some of which reflect disrupted meanings – are considered to play a key role in emotional difficulties following a loss. The *Grief Cognitions Questionnaire* or GCQ (Boelen & Lensvelt-Mulders, 2005) is a questionnaire that can be used to measure such cognitions in adults. It consists of 9 subscales: *Self* (e.g., "Since [–] is dead, I am of no importance to anybody anymore"), *Self-Blame* (e.g., "I will never be able to forgive myself for the things I did wrong in the relationship with [–]"), *Appropriateness of Grief* (e.g., "I don't mourn the way I should do"), *Cherish Grief* (e.g., "As long as I mourn, I do not really have to let [–] go"), *Threatening Interpretation of Grief* (e.g., "Once I start crying, I will lose control"), *Life* (e.g., "My life is meaningless since [–] died"), *World* (e.g., "Since [–] died, I realize that the world is a bad place"), *Others* (e.g., "Many people have let me down since [–]'s death"), and *Future* (e.g., "Since [–] is no longer here, I have a negative view on the future"). Changes in unhelpful grief cognitions have been shown to mediate PGD treatment effects (Lechner-Meichsner et al., 2022) and to play a key role in long-term treatment effects (Bryant et al., 2024; Rosner et al., 2024).

The following validated instruments help map both those domains in which meaning has been disrupted for the bereaved and those in which robust meaning-making can serve as a resource for integrating the loss and reaffirming life.

The *Integration of Stressful Life Experiences Scale* or ISLES (Holland et al., 2010, 2014) assesses *Comprehensibility* of the loss (e.g., I have difficulty integrating this loss into my understanding of the world) and *Footing in the World* (e.g., Since this event, the world seems like a more confusing and scary place). In both the original 16-item and abbreviated 6-item format, the ISLES has demonstrated strong reliability, factorial validity, and construct validity, and has been translated into several languages. Recent research has established the interpretability of the scale's bi-factor structure and a clinical cut score for determining levels of meaning disruption associated with clinically significant impairment of family, work, and social functioning (Lee et al., 2024; Lee et al., 2024).

The *Grief and Meaning Reconstruction Inventory* or GMRI (Gillies et al., 2015) consists of 29 items that assess five factors of meaning-making in loss: *Continuing Bonds* with the deceased, *Personal Growth* through grief, *Sense of Peace* about the significant other's dying process, *Valuing Life* in the wake of loss and *Emptiness and Meaninglessness*, a reverse-scored measure of a struggle to find significance in or after the event. The GMRI therefore provides a multidimensional assessment of potentially affirmative meaning-making in bereavement, as well as a global index of meaning disruption. Like the ISLES, it has been translated and validated in a growing number of languages, though with some reduction in the number of items. A large body of research using these measures documents the role of meaning as a mediator of prolonged grief (Neimeyer, 2019).

Attribution of meaning across four domains

Attribution of meaning following loss encompasses the domains of self, the relationship with the deceased, the world/others, and the future. These domains are described in detail below, along with the role of the therapist and illustrated using quotations from patients. Across these domains, cognitive restructuring is used preceding narrative meaning reconstruction. Cognitive restructuring is an evidence-based technique to address negative and maladaptive cognitions following loss (Boelen et al., 2007; Bryant et al., 2024; Rosner et al., 2024). Cognitive restructuring of loss- and grief-related negative appraisals referring to the self and future without the deceased and one's own grief reactions is an integral part of CBT-based treatments for PGD and has been effectively applied in adolescents (Boelen et al., 2021; Kaplow et al., 2023) along with and meaning-focused interventions for prolonged and traumatic grief (Kaplow et al., 2023).

To introduce cognitive restructuring, the therapist explains how situations evoke thoughts that in turn induce feelings and behaviors. This can be clarified as follows: *A situation is something that happens or something that is going on. A thought is an idea that comes up or something we tell ourselves. A feeling or emotion is a reaction to a thought that often can be felt in our body. A behavior is how we act or what we do, usually because of a feeling.* The therapist may assign homework to increase the patient's ability to distinguish and understand links between situations, thoughts, feelings, and behaviors. The therapist explains how thoughts may be helpful or hurtful and helps the patient to identify their own helpful or hurtful thoughts and ways to manage them.

Hurtful thoughts can be challenged by asking Socratic questions such as: Is the thought correct? Does the thought help me? Do I have evidence for this thought? The therapist encourages the patient to be their own "best friend" by thinking of more helpful thoughts. Homework may be assigned to practice identifying hurtful thoughts and replacing them with more helpful thoughts. Table 7.1 shows examples of hurtful and helpful thoughts across the four domains. Meanings made in the four domains that have been identified in research among bereaved individuals (Gillies et al., 2014) are also presented in Table 7.1.

During narrative attribution of meaning, therapist's main role is to listen, ask, validate, and accept the patient's meanings, feelings, and narratives while refraining from judging, advising, and filling in. Meaning domains emerge naturally during narration and the therapist can often just follow the process as it unfolds; indeed, "pushing" a patient toward premature meaning is contraindicated, as it can communicate intolerance of the patient's distressing emotion and elicit understandable resistance. Symbolic interactions (described in Chapter 8) can be integrated in all domains. There is no prescribed order to address the domains, as the domain to be addressed is the one with which a patient is contending at a given moment in the therapy. As a starting point, a suggested order is presented in Table 7.2.

Self and identity

Who am I without my loved one? This question, referring to the way people define themselves in a practical (not a theoretical or metaphysical) sense, is at the heart of the meaning attribution process following bereavement. *Practical identity* provides "a description under which you value yourself, a description under which you find your life to be worth living and your actions to be worth undertaking" (Korsgaard, 1996, p. 101). Besides identity, the domain encompasses the self and the way individuals deal with themselves. A benevolent and supportive attitude toward the self and self-compassion (Neff, 2023) is encouraged and modeled by the therapist. The *centrality* of a loss or traumatic event to an individual's identity, i.e., an individual's retrospective construal, present understandings, and anticipated future role of the loss or trauma as central to one's identity, is associated with greater symptomatology of PGD, PTSD, and depression (Boelen, 2012). By contrast, meaning made of a loss is associated with positive outcomes, and meaning made has been shown to moderate the impact of centrality on bereavement outcomes (Bellet et al., 2018).

Table 7.1 Examples of thoughts and meanings made across four domains of meaning

Hurtful and helpful thoughts[1]	*Meanings made*[2]
Self	
I can no longer save anything for anyone now that [...] is dead	live to the fullest
If I grieve, I will probably lose control	personal growth
I will never be able to cope with this loss properly	coping
It won't always hurt so bad	greater perspective
Whenever I think of him it's sad and painful, I miss him	identity as bereaved person
Waves of grief come and go, and I can get through them	survivor identity
Deceased	
I could have prevented his death and therefore should have prevented it	acceptance
I need to take revenge	decedent preparation for death
No one knew this was going to happen, including me	memories
I may feel regret about what happened, but I don't have to feel guilty for it; regret and guilt are two very different things	time together
If I hurt or kill someone, it won't bring [...] back	affirmation of deceased
My spiritual beliefs tell me that [...] is watching over me and will see me succeed if I try	release from suffering
	spirituality
Others	
Nobody cares how I really feel	impermanence
I still have other people in my life who care about me	family bonds
It's better to have loved and lost then to never love at all	valuing relationships
I don't have to give up trying just because I'm feeling discouraged	compassion
Future	
None of my plans for the future will ever be fulfilled	lifestyle changes
Life has nothing more to offer me	moving on
Even though my life will be very different, it can still be a good life	valuing life

[1] (Boelen & Van den Bout, 2011; Kaplow et al., 2023)
[2] (Gillies et al., 2014)

Role of the therapist

The role of the therapist is to listen, learn, validate, and normalize. The therapist may introduce or elaborate specific themes using Socratic questions, e.g., "What does the loss of your loved one mean for the way you look at yourself now?" Therapeutic goals in this domain include daring to

Table 7.2 Attribution of meaning, reengaging and activation: Possible order of sessions and possible combinations with other interventions

*Possible order of sessions**	*Meaning domain*	*Representative interventions*
1, 2	Self	Cultural exploration: dealing with bereavement and grief; imaginal conversations with aspects of self; values clarification
3, 4	Relationship with deceased	Imaginal conversation with deceased; legacy projects; correspondence with the deceased
5, 6	Engaging with others	Couples and family interventions; group work; discuss and plan shared ritual of remembrance
7, 8	Activation and future	Future self-dialogues; review ritual of remembrance; ritual of renewal

* Within the attribution of meaning, engaging and activation part of the therapy.

experience oneself as vulnerable and through this increase self-efficacy, self-compassion, and resilience. Unhelpful cognitions and assumptions can be identified and challenged, exploring ways to maintain a positive view of self while incorporating the painful loss. Actively continuing valued roles and activities that are not associated with the lost person may contribute to making the loss less central to identity and diminish PGD and PTSD symptoms. Helping to identify personal values and goals, and taking constructive action toward these goals may increase self-clarity and thereby reduce depression and bereavement-related PTSD (Boelen, 2017).

Reflecting on one's grief reactions

As therapy progresses, fluctuations in the intensity of grief may be noted, with anniversaries and other reminders often leading to intensified grieving. How do patients interpret their emotional reactions to the loss now? Thoughts about the closure of grief or the lack thereof may be discussed. As a father who lost his only son put it:

> I thought I would get a closure with the death of my son but in my experience closure is not possible. In the course of living, the pain, it got easier to carry it, but it's the same pain. It feels like a part of me has been cut off, but I still feel that missing part.

Cultural ways of dealing with bereavement and grief

Culture is represented in the form of intersubjective perceptions, i.e., beliefs and values that members of a culture perceive to be widespread in their group (Chi-Yue et al., 2010). Exploring cultural ways of dealing with bereavement and grief is supported by the Bereavement and Grief Cultural Formulation Interview (BG-CFI) (see also Chapters 5 and 15). Exploring cultural ways of dealing with bereavement and grief aims to enhance the patient's ability to find meaningful ways of dealing with the loss, using knowledge that has been passed through generations:

> This knowledge isn't really written down. It's something you absorb from the previous generation by observing their actions. Older people lead this process. As you watch them, you learn and internalize their practices, with the goal of passing this information on to the next generation.

Many bereaved individuals engage in practices related to spiritual, religious, or moral traditions to cope with the loss of a loved one, including prayer and meditation, participating in worship services or religious gatherings, or speaking with other people in their religious group and with religious or spiritual leaders. In a migrant setting this may be difficult or impossible, and alternative approaches may need to be found.

A life-span perspective

The therapist may apply a life-span perspective to help patients to better understand their reactions to the loss. Early losses and other adverse developmental experiences may foster negative attitudes and biases about the self (Beck, 2008). The impact of these experiences may be transformed into a durable attitude (e.g., helplessness, pervasive fear, anger, or guilt), which may be activated by the traumatic loss and increase its negative meaning. The attachment style of the individual and the nature of the attachment relation may shape the grief reaction, as research has demonstrated (Smigelsky et al., 2020).

Relationship with the deceased

Following the death, the relationships with deceased loved ones continue to develop and change (Pearce, 2019). Many bereaved experience an as-if presence of the deceased. Sensory and quasi-sensory experiences of the deceased are most often comforting and not generally associated with bereavement-related distress (Kamp et al., 2022). Rather, they should be viewed in the cultural, biographical, and situational context of the individual.

Role of the therapist

The therapist explores ***"unfinished business,"*** matters that could no longer be settled due to the death of the loved one, which have been found to predict more intense and preoccupying grief responses (Holland et al., 2020; Klingspon et al., 2015). The therapist may then apply relational problem-solving interventions such as imaginal conversations with the deceased (see Chapter 8). Self-blame may be especially prominent if the death is felt as a failure of caregiving, such as following the death of a child (Lichtenthal et al., 2020). Therapists may explore the validity of cognitions about responsibility and guilt and help the bereaved individual to assimilate the inability to prevent the death into a friendly and compassionate view on the self. Strong feelings of guilt can be addressed using cognitive techniques that may help discriminating between real and perceived (exaggerated) guilt, such as the "responsibility pie" (Greenberger & Padesky, 1995), in which the contribution of the self and others to the traumatic loss can be visualized. Feelings of guilt often stem from imagined scenarios in which the loved one would not have died. Such alternative scenarios, often termed ***"counterfactual" or "if-only" thinking***, distract from the ***reality of the loss*** of the loved one, and call for subtle clinical intervention (Neimeyer et al., 2021). Repetitive thinking after loss, also called grief ***rumination***, may negatively affect adaptation to bereavement (Eisma & Stroebe, 2017; Milman et al., 2019b). Exposure to the reality of the loss and allowing the associated feelings may be needed before guilt feelings can be addressed directly. In cases of "objective" guilt (e.g., when the patient was driving under the influence of a substance in a car accident that killed their loved one), the goal of meaning-focused interventions may be to learn and live with guilt and to plan potentially meaningful compensatory actions.

Suicide grief

In people bereaved due to suicide, the idea that one somehow contributed to the death is common. In a longitudinal study (Kõlves et al., 2020), suicide bereaved people had higher feelings of responsibility for the suicide, as well as higher guilt, stigmatization, and feelings of rejection than people bereaved after other sudden deaths, up to 2 years after the death. Other common grief experiences in suicide bereaved people include search for explanation, shame, and somatic reactions. A violent suicide strongly impacts grief experiences compared with other ways of a self-chosen death and physician-assisted dying (Snijdewind et al., 2022). The less the loved one's suicide was expected, the more the bereaved seek explanations and meaning after the death (Wojtkowiak et al., 2012). Importantly, of all the needs voiced by survivors of tragic loss (e.g., by suicide and overdose), such as practical, informational, emotional, and relational needs, unmet needs to find meaning in the experience have been found to be most strongly predictive of prolonged and preoccupying grief symptomatology (Bottomley et al., 2024).

Survivor guilt

Survivor guilt and shame are often associated with surviving mass traumatic events, notably among refugees (Eisenbruch, 1990), related to the realization of having failed in situations with irrevocable consequences, such as the death of loved ones. There is an inherent injustice in the fact that, unlike the survivor, loved ones have been denied the opportunity to live on. A sense of injustice and guilt may maintain grief as well as PTSD symptoms (Tay et al., 2017). A society that represses, denies, or obscures its past has every chance of losing sight of its war victims. For the therapist, it is essential to recognize one's own feelings of shame and guilt for a genuine encounter with those affected by war and to enable an empathic response to survivor guilt and survivor shame (Wepster, 2003).

Rituals that could not take place

Concepts of guilt may be linked to broader cultural concepts of fairness and fate that may involve the afterlife. For example, the Buddhist concept of karma consists of the consequences of the good and evil deeds committed in all one's previous existences; suffering, therefore, is the karmic consequence of one's past sins, and one can only hope for a better existence in the next rebirth by performing numerous acts of merit (Boehnlein, 1987). While some rituals may be thought of as having implications for the afterlife, performing prescribed rituals may be more generally necessary for proper role fulfillment. Not performing rituals creates guilt or more intense and problematic grief, as research on the suspension of funerals in the course of the COVID-19 pandemic has documented (Neimeyer & Lee, 2022). The therapy fragment below of a patient who had fled a war-torn country illustrates this (Smid, 2020).

Patient: *For 4 years I couldn't cry about my father. You remember the last time we spoke about the loss. Two days later, after I heard a Turkish song, I cried for one and a half hours. I was alone in my room. So I cried and cried so much.*

Therapist: *How was it?*

P: *It was very comforting. Because I cried and I cried long and I spoke to my father at the same moment.*

T: *You talked to your father.*

P: *Yes, I spoke to him.*
T: *What did you say?*
P: *I asked him to forgive me, because I left him alone, I had not been with him. I asked if he was OK, if he was in a good situation in heaven. All the time I asked him to forgive me. Yes, it was difficult. It was as if he died at that moment. So I cried so much. That comforted me a lot.*
T: *What happened to your guilt feeling?*
P: *The guilt feeling is less now. Even if I had been in Syria he would have been dead. There is nothing else. But what made me feel guilty is because I left him alone and he died. We must be beside him. That's it. That's what made me guilty.*
T: *You feel that still?*
P: *Yes of course, yes. Because I left him alone and we couldn't visit him at his grave. So he is alone now. I wish if I just could visit him at the grave. But there is no way. If I could go now, I would be beside him.*
T: *You actually want to keep him company.*
P: *Yeah, I want to. Because no one from our family is in Syria. All of us are out of Syria. No one visits his grave. No one speaks with him. No one stays with him. [Silence]*

Engaging with others

The loss of a loved one may impact a person's sense of safety and trust and may evoke questions about intimacy, esteem, and power (McCann et al., 1988). Experiencing a traumatic loss confronts people with vulnerability, helplessness, and extreme and frightening aspects of human behavior that may undermine a positive view of the world and other people. The "illusion of safety" disappears and fundamental questions arise concerning the extent to which confidence in others or in technology is possible again.

Role of the therapist

Sample questions to address these themes include: How safe do you feel in this world? To what extent can people close to you, the government, or higher powers, still be trusted? Can you start loving others again? To what extent do you dare to be – emotionally – intimate with others? How positive or negative is your perception of others? How is everyone in the family doing? In what ways do you talk about the deceased or the death? Therapeutic goals in this domain include developing a more relative and realistic sense of safety, exploring how to trust others again, overcoming emotional barriers to being intimate again with others, mitigating the effects of guilt or shame on self-esteem, and regaining sufficient sense of control despite vulnerability, anger, or feelings of revenge (Smid et al., 2015).

Thresholds to reengaging with others

There may be various obstacles to reengaging with others that can be discussed during the sessions. First, cultural traditions may prescribe how to interact with others during the period of mourning, as illustrated below.

During the first six months, you must be home before sunset. So, during that period, I always had to rush home before it got dark. In my experience, it's crucial to be mindful of what has happened. You can't just go to a partying immediately after the loss of your love one; you need to take the time to sit with it and reflect.

Second, engaging with others may confront the bereaved with emotional pain, as illustrated below.

When I'm with people and they ask if I have children, it tears me up inside. I try to conceal my pain because I often don't want to burden them with the story of what happened to my son.

Third, ***stigmatization*** occurs when the social environment reacts negatively to a person's grief. Stigma related to the circumstances of the death are widespread and may take a variety of shapes. Following ***physician-assisted suicide***, grief reactions in the relatives may be more severe if they expect social disapproval (Wagner et al., 2011). ***Suicide bereaved*** are likely to experience high levels of rejection, stigmatization, shame, and (indirect) blaming for the death (Kõlves et al., 2020). Fourth, in some situations, cultural norms can prevent the loss of a loved one from being openly acknowledged, publicly mourned, or socially supported. The term ***disenfranchised grief*** denotes these situations (Doka, 2002). Cultural norms may condemn the person of the deceased (e.g., a person on the wrong side during the war), the relationship with the deceased (e.g., an extramarital relationship), or the circumstances of the death (e.g., drug-related death).

Anger, bitterness, or thoughts of revenge

Bereaved people may experience strong dissatisfaction with the medical or other authorities to effectively manage, prevent, and make sense of the death (Pearce, 2019). Violent deaths and deaths due to homicide are often connected with anger and revenge thoughts (Van Denderen et al., 2014). The therapist can help by normalizing anger and encouraging the expression of anger in ways that do not harm others, e.g., writing an angry letter (see Chapter 8). Following violent death, moral injury may co-occur with prolonged and traumatic grief. Potentially morally injurious events have been described (Litz et al., 2009, p. 195) as "perpetrating, failing to prevent, or bearing witness to acts that transgress deeply held moral beliefs and expectations." Revenge feelings due to moral transgressions may need to be addressed using cognitive interventions, as in the following example of a patient who lost his sister Alma during the war in former Yugoslavia.

Therapist: *You're carrying thoughts of revenge. This man took your sister Alma's life, so naturally you're thinking about taking his. What is it that you want most strongly: do you feel the strongest urge to see this man dead, or is it that you want to be free of the need to act on this thought?*
Patient: *That's difficult. Really tough. I want revenge, but I also want peace. Hard to say.*
T: *What makes you want to be free from this thought of killing this man?*
P: *A lot of time has passed since then.*
T: *Are there other reasons as well?*
P: *Maybe because I don't want to be like him. I still carry the pain, but I'd like to believe I'm better than he is.*

Activation and future

What makes life worth living now that my loved one is no longer alive? Bereavement often necessitates a new future orientation, as illustrated below by a patient who lost his only child.

Patient: *The saddest thing for me is growing up with the constant message that our children are the living messengers for a future we cannot see. It's painful to say, but I no longer have that messenger. It feels like a dead end street for me, and that weighs heavily on my heart because it feels like my future ends with me.*
Therapist: *I can feel your pain very well. I think we are at the core of your pain and I can imagine so well how painful this must be. Exactly the things you just said.*

Psychotherapy enables the patient to experience the gradual subsiding of sadness, leaving room for new meanings that allow them to reinvest in other people and activities.

Role of the therapist

Reduced participation in habitual or potentially satisfying activities, and problems engaging with friends, pursuing interests, or planning for the future are characteristic of prolonged grief. Behavioral activation can enhance a patient's sense of identity by engaging in personal interests, artistic endeavors, or the pursuit of values shared with the deceased, e.g., preserving a tradition. Unhelpful cognitions in activation may stem from predicting disasters in the future and may be addressed by identifying and changing unhelpful cognitions.

Behavioral activation can be introduced as follows: *The loss of a loved one makes everyday life come to a standstill. It can be difficult to continue activities for several reasons: feeling incapable or thinking that activities will not provide any pleasure. To support recovery, it is important to continue doing the things you always did. The loss can only find a place in everyday life if you keep it going. Even if you don't feel like doing something you planned to do, you often notice afterwards that it was good you did it.*

The therapist explains the procedure of this part of the treatment: discussing activities the patient is doing in daily life and how much satisfaction these activities can give, identifying personal values, setting positive, social, recreational, or educational goals, formulating steps toward the goal, strengthening personal resources needed to achieve the goal, and planning of specific actions. The therapist encourages the patient to formulate positive goals rather than situations they want to avoid. To help set goals for the future, the therapist can ask: "Imagine that one year later, you have managed to get back to your life and are able to engage in enjoyable and satisfying activities. What would your life be like then? What would you do? What activities would you engage in?"

Concluding remarks

Attribution of meaning to the loss of a loved one and the circumstances surrounding it helps the bereaved reconnect with their personal needs, beliefs, desires, plans, and goals. Loss often triggers feelings of vulnerability, helplessness, and existential uncertainty. The therapist plays a key role in normalizing these feelings, identifying and challenging unhelpful thoughts, and promoting transformation. Meaning can be explored in four key areas: self, relationship with the deceased, world/others, and future. Moving away from negative cognitions, adaptive meanings help patients reorient themselves toward personal values. Attribution of meaning supports existential and spiritual growth, enhancing the ability to cope with the loss within a sociocultural context.

Further research is essential to enhance our understanding of attribution of meaning in psychotherapy for prolonged and traumatic grief, as existing evidence for the value of meaning making in grief therapy is promising. For example, a recent open trial of a multifaceted meaning-focused protocol for PGD documented substantial improvement over the course of treatment, and further found that session-to-session increases in meaning predicted reduction in PGD symptomatology in the week that followed (Batista et al., 2024). Additional studies could shed light on the relationship between adaptive meanings and negative cognitions across various domains of meaning, both cross-sectionally and longitudinally. Investigating the long-term impact of meaning attribution in therapy for prolonged and traumatic grief, its influence on spiritual and existential dimensions, and its relevance within diverse cultural contexts could provide crucial insights. Additionally, evaluating multidisciplinary approaches to attribution of meaning may contribute to developing evidence-based strategies to support coping, healing, and resilience in diverse populations. These insights can inform therapeutic techniques and broaden our understanding of prolonged and traumatic grief.

References

Batista, J., Alves, D., Pires, N., Silva, J. R., Mendes, I., Magalhães, C., Rosa, C., Oliveira, J. T., Gonçalves, M. M., & Neimeyer, R. A. (2024). The meaning in loss protocol: A clinical trial of online grief therapy. *Death Studies*, *49*(1), 8–20. https://doi.org/10.1080/07481187.2024.2370633

Beck, A. T. (2008). The evolution of the cognitive model of depression and its neurobiological correlates. *American Journal of Psychiatry*, *165*(8), 969–977.

Bellet, B. W., Neimeyer, R. A., & Berman, J. S. (2018). Event centrality and bereavement symptomatology: The moderating role of meaning made. *OMEGA - Journal of Death and Dying*, *78*(1), 3–23. https://doi.org/10.1177/0030222816679659

Boehnlein, J. K. (1987). Clinical relevance of grief and mourning among Cambodian refugees. *Social Science & Medicine*, *25*(7), 765–772. https://doi.org/10.1016/0277-9536(87)90034-7

Boelen, P. A. (2012). A prospective examination of the association between the centrality of a loss and post-loss psychopathology. *Journal of Affective Disorders*, *137*(1), 117–124. https://doi.org/10.1016/j.jad.2011.12.004

Boelen, P. A. (2017). Self-identity after bereavement: Reduced self-clarity and loss-centrality in emotional problems after the death of a loved one. *Journal of Nervous & Mental Disease*, *205*(5), 405–408. https://doi.org/10.1097/NMD.0000000000000660

Boelen, P. A., de Keijser, J., Van den Hout, M. A., & Van den Bout, J. (2007). Treatment of complicated grief: A comparison between cognitive-behavioral therapy and supportive counseling. *Journal of Consulting and Clinical Psychology*, *75*(2), 277–284. https://doi.org/10.1037/0022-006X.75.2.277

Boelen, P. A., Lenferink, L. I. M., & Spuij, M. (2021). CBT for prolonged grief in children and adolescents: A randomized clinical trial. *American Journal of Psychiatry*, *178*(4), 294–304. https://doi.org/10.1176/appi.ajp.2020.20050548

Boelen, P. A., & Lensvelt-Mulders, G. J. L. M. (2005). Psychometric properties of the Grief Cognitions Questionnaire (GCQ). *Journal of Psychopathology and Behavioral Assessment*, *27*(4), 291–303. https://doi.org/10.1007/s10862-005-2409-5

Boelen, P. A., Reijntjes, A., & Smid, G. (2016). Concurrent and prospective associations of intolerance of uncertainty with symptoms of prolonged grief, posttraumatic stress, and depression after bereavement. *Journal of Anxiety Disorders*, *41*, 65–72. https://doi.org/10.1016/j.janxdis.2016.03.004

Boelen, P. A., & Van den Bout, J. (2011). Protocollaire behandeling van gecompliceerde rouw. In G. Keijsers, A. van Minnen, & K. A. L. Hoogduin (Eds.), *Protocollaire behandelingen van volwassenen met psychische klachten* (pp. 341–377). Boom.

Bottomley, J. S., Smigelsky, M. A., Campbell, K. W., Neimeyer, R. A., & Rheingold, A. A. (2024). Bereavement-related needs and their relation to mental health symptoms among adults bereaved by suicide and fatal overdose. *Journal of Loss and Trauma*, *30*(2), 145–166. https://doi.org/10.1080/15325024.2024.2357776

Bruner, J. (1990). *Acts of meaning: Four lectures on mind and culture*. Harvard University Press.

Bryant, R. A., Azevedo, S., Yadav, S., Cahill, C., Kenny, L., Maccallum, F., Tran, J., Choi-Christou, J., Rawson, N., Tockar, J., Garber, B., Keyan, D., & Dawson, K. S. (2024). Cognitive behavior therapy vs mindfulness in treatment of prolonged grief disorder: A randomized clinical trial. *JAMA Psychiatry*, *81*(7), 646–654. https://doi.org/10.1001/jamapsychiatry.2024.0432

Carleton, R. N. (2016). Fear of the unknown: One fear to rule them all? *Journal of Anxiety Disorders*, *41*, 5–21. https://doi.org/10.1016/j.janxdis.2016.03.011

Chi-Yue, C., Michele, J. G., Toshio, Y., Garriy, S., & Ching, W. (2010). Intersubjective culture: The role of intersubjective perceptions in cross-cultural research. *Perspectives on Psychological Science*, *5*(4), 482–493. https://doi.org/10.1177/1745691610375562

Doka, K. J. (2002). *Disenfranchised grief: New directions, challenges, and strategies for practice*. Research Press.

Eisenbruch, M. (1990). The cultural bereavement interview: A new clinical research approach for refugees. *Psychiatric Clinics of North America*, *13*(4), 715–735. https://doi.org/10.1016/S0193-953X(18)30345-9

Eisma, M. C., & Stroebe, M. S. (2017). Rumination following bereavement: An overview. *Bereavement Care*, *36*(2), 58–64. https://doi.org/10.1080/02682621.2017.1349291

Gillies, J. M., Neimeyer, R. A., & Milman, E. (2014). The meaning of loss codebook: Construction of a system for analyzing meanings made in bereavement. *Death Studies*, *38*(4), 207–216. https://doi.org/10.1080/07481187.2013.829367

Gillies, J. M., Neimeyer, R. A., & Milman, E. (2015). The grief and meaning reconstruction inventory (GMRI): Initial validation of a new measure. *Death Studies*, *39*(2), 61–74. https://doi.org/10.1080/07481187.2014.907089

Greenberger, D., & Padesky, C. A. (1995). *Mind over mood: Change how you feel by changing the way you think*. Guilford Press.

Hanfstingl, B., Arzenšek, A., Apschner, J., & Gölly, K. I. (2022). Assimilation and accommodation. *European Psychologist*, *27*(4), 320–337. https://doi.org/10.1027/1016-9040/a000463

Holland, J. M., Currier, J. M., Coleman, R. A., & Neimeyer, R. A. (2010). The integration of stressful life experiences scale (ISLES): Development and initial validation of a new measure. *International Journal of Stress Management*, *17*(4), 325–352. https://doi.org/10.1037/a0020892

Holland, J. M., Currier, J. M., & Neimeyer, R. A. (2014). Validation of the integration of stressful life experiences Scale–Short form in a bereaved sample. *Death Studies*, *38*(4), 234–238. https://doi.org/10.1080/07481187.2013.829369

Holland, J. M., Plant, C. P., Klingspon, K. L., & Neimeyer, R. A. (2020). Bereavement-related regrets and unfinished business with the deceased. *Death Studies*, *44*(1), 42–47. https://doi.org/10.1080/07481187.2018.1521106

Janoff-Bulman, R., & Frantz, C. M. (1997). The impact of trauma on meaning: From meaningless world to meaningful life. In M. J. Power & C. R. Brewin (Eds.), *The transformation of meaning in psychological therapies: Integrating theory and practice* (pp. 91–106). John Wiley & Sons Inc.

Jiang, V., Galin, A., & Lea, X. (2024). Life review for older adults: An integrative review. *Psychogeriatrics*, *24*(6), 1402–1417. https://doi.org/10.1111/psyg.13194

Kamp, K. S., Moskowitz, A., Due, H., & Spindler, H. (2022). Are sensory experiences of one's deceased spouse associated with bereavement-related distress? *Omega*, *89*(3). https://doi.org/10.1177/00302228221078686

Kaplow, J. B., Layne, C. M., Pynoos, R. S., & Saltzman, W. (2023). *Multidimensional grief therapy: A flexible approach to assessing and supporting bereaved youth.* Cambridge University Press. https://doi.org/10.1017/9781316422359

Kelly, G. A. (1955). *The psychology of personal constructs. Vol. 1. A theory of personality. Vol. 2. Clinical diagnosis and psychotherapy* (pp. xxviii, 1218). W. W. Norton.

Kierkegaard, S. (1957). *The concept of dread* (W. Lowrie, Trans.). Princeton University Press.

Klingspon, K. L., Holland, J. M., Neimeyer, R. A., & Lichtenthal, W. G. (2015). Unfinished business in bereavement. *Death Studies*, *39*(7), 387–398. https://doi.org/10.1080/07481187.2015.1029143

Kõlves, K., Zhao, Q., Ross, V., Hawgood, J., Spence, S. H., & de Leo, D. (2020). Suicide and sudden death bereavement in Australia: A longitudinal study of family members over 2 years after death. *Australian & New Zealand Journal of Psychiatry*, *54*(1), 89–98. https://doi.org/10.1177/0004867419882490

Korsgaard, C. M. (1996). *The sources of normativity.* Cambridge University Press.

Lechner-Meichsner, F., Mauro, C., Skritskaya, N. A., & Shear, M. K. (2022). Change in avoidance and negative grief-related cognitions mediates treatment outcome in older adults with prolonged grief disorder. *Psychotherapy Research*, *32*(1), 78–90. https://doi.org/10.1080/10503307.2021.1909769

Lee, S. A., Caycho-Rodríguez, T., Vilca, L. W., & Neimeyer, R. A. (2024). Can a global score be derived from the Integration of Stressful Life Experiences Scale-Short Form (ISLES-SF)? Empirical support for a bi-factor model. *Death Studies*, *49*(1), 31–39. https://doi.org/10.1080/07481187.2024.2368330

Lee, S. A., Neimeyer, R. A., Ng, C., Veglahn, L., & Tucci, A. S. (2024). When does disruption of meaning in bereavement become debilitating? Screening for deleterious outcomes with the ISLES-SF. *Death Studies*, *49*(1), 1–7. https://doi.org/10. 1080/07481187.2024.2364495

Lely, J. C. G., Smid, G. E., Jongedijk, R. A., Knipscheer, W., & Kleber, R. J. (2019). The effectiveness of narrative exposure therapy: A review, meta-analysis and meta-regression analysis. *European Journal of Psychotraumatology*, *10*(1), 1550344. https://doi.org/10.1080/20008198.2018.1550344

Lichtenthal, W. G., Roberts, K. E., Catarozoli, C., Schofield, E., Holland, J. M., Fogarty, J. J., Coats, T. C., Barakat, L. P., Baker, J. N., Brinkman, T. M., Neimeyer, R. A., Prigerson, H. G., Zaider, T., Breitbart, W., & Wiener, L. (2020). Regret and unfinished business in parents bereaved by cancer: A mixed methods study. *Palliative Medicine*, *34*(3), 367–377. https://doi.org/10.1177/0269216319900301

Litz, B. T., Stein, N., Delaney, E., Lebowitz, L., Nash, W. P., Silva, C., & Maguen, S. (2009). Moral injury and moral repair in war veterans: A preliminary model and intervention strategy. *Clinical Psychology Review*, *29*(8), 695–706. https://doi.org/10.1016/j.cpr.2009.07.003

McCann, I. L., Sakheim, D. K., & Abrahamson, D. J. (1988). Trauma and victimization: A model of psychological adaptation. *The Counseling Psychologist*, *16*(4), 531–594. https://doi.org/10.1177/0011000088164002

Milman, E., Neimeyer, R. A., Fitzpatrick, M., MacKinnon, C. J., Muis, K. R., & Cohen, S. R. (2019a). Prolonged grief and the disruption of meaning: Establishing a mediation model. *Journal of Counseling Psychology*, *66*(6), 714–725. https://doi.org/10.1037/cou0000370

Milman, E., Neimeyer, R. A., Fitzpatrick, M., MacKinnon, C. J., Muis, K. R., & Cohen, S. R. (2019b). Rumination moderates the role of meaning in the development of prolonged grief symptomatology. *Journal of Clinical Psychology*, *75*(6), 1047–1065. https://doi.org/10.1002/jclp.22751

Neff, K. D. (2023). Self-compassion: Theory, method, research, and intervention. *Annual Review of Psychology*, *74*(1), 193–218. https://doi.org/10.1146/annurev-psych-032420-031047

Neimeyer, R. A. (2000). Narrative disruptions in the construction of the self. In R. A. Neimeyer & J. Raskin (Eds.), *Constructions of disorder: Meaning-making frameworks for psychotherapy* (pp. 207–242). American Psychological Association. https://doi.org/10.1037/10368-009

Neimeyer, R. A. (2019). Meaning reconstruction in bereavement: Development of a research program. *Death Studies*, *43*(2), 79–91. https://doi.org/10.1080/07481187.2018.1456620

Neimeyer, R. A. (2022). Grief therapy as a quest for meaning. In E. M. Steffen, E. Milman, & R. A. Neimeyer (Eds.), *The handbook of grief therapies* (pp. 53–67). SAGE Publications.

Neimeyer, R. A., & Lee, S. A. (2022). Circumstances of the death and associated risk factors for severity and impairment of COVID-19 grief. *Death Studies*, *46*(1), 34–42. https://doi.org/10.1080/07481187.2021.1896459

Neimeyer, R. A., Pitcho-Prelorentzos, S., & Mahat-Shamir, M. (2021). "If only…": Counterfactual thinking in bereavement. *Death Studies*, *45*(9), 692–701. https://doi.org/10.1080/07481187.2019.1679959

Nijdam, M. J., Meewisse, M.-L., Smid, G. E., & Gersons, B. P. R. (2022). Brief eclectic psychotherapy for PTSD. In U. Schnyder & M. Cloitre (Eds.), *Evidence based treatments for trauma-related psychological disorders: A practical guide for clinicians* (pp. 281–306). Springer International Publishing. https://doi.org/10.1007/978-3-030-97802-0_13

Park, C. L. (2010). Making sense of the meaning literature: An integrative review of meaning making and its effects on adjustment to stressful life events. *Psychological Bulletin*, *136*(2), 257–301. https://doi.org/10.1037/a0018301

Parkes, C. M. (1971). Psycho-social transitions: A field for study. *Social Science & Medicine (1967)*, *5*(2), 101–115. https://doi.org/10.1016/0037-7856(71)90091-6

Pearce, C. (2019). *The public and private management of grief: Recovering normal.* Springer International Publishing. https://doi.org/10.1007/978-3-030-17662-4

Rosner, R., Rau, J., Kersting, A., Rief, W., Steil, R., Rummel, A.-M., Vogel, A., & Comtesse, H. (2024). Grief-specific cognitive behavioral therapy vs present-centered therapy: A randomized clinical trial. *JAMA Psychiatry*. https://doi.org/10.1001/jamapsychiatry.2024.3409

Schumm, J. A., Dickstein, B. D., Walter, K. H., Owens, G. P., & Chard, K. M. (2015). Changes in posttraumatic cognitions predict changes in posttraumatic stress disorder symptoms during cognitive processing therapy. *Journal of Consulting and Clinical Psychology*, *83*(6), 1161–1166. https://doi.org/10.1037/ccp0000040

Seneca, L. A. (1920). *Epistles, volume II: Epistles 66-92* (R. M. Gummere, Trans.). Harvard University Press. https://www.loebclassics.com/view/seneca_younger-epistles/1917/pb_LCL076.251.xml

Smid, G. E. (2020). A framework of meaning attribution following loss. *European Journal of Psychotraumatology*, *11*(1), 1776563. https://doi.org/10.1080/20008198.2020.1776563

Smid, G. E., Killikelly, C., & Wagner, B. (2021). Editorial: Grief disorders: Clinical, cultural, and epidemiological aspects. *Frontiers in Psychiatry*, *12*, 681523. https://doi.org/10.3389/fpsyt.2021.681523

Smid, G. E., Kleber, R. J., De la Rie, S. M., Bos, J. B. A., Gersons, B. P. R., & Boelen, P. A. (2015). Brief eclectic psychotherapy for traumatic grief (BEP-TG): Toward integrated treatment of symptoms related to traumatic loss. *European Journal of Psychotraumatology*, *6*(1), 27324. https://doi.org/10.3402/ejpt.v6.27324

Smigelsky, M. A., Bottomley, J. S., Relyea, G., & Neimeyer, R. A. (2020). Investigating risk for grief severity: Attachment to the deceased and relationship quality. *Death Studies*, *44*(7), 402–411. https://doi.org/10.1080/07481187.2018.1548539

Snijdewind, M. C., de Keijser, J., Casteelen, G., Boelen, P. A., & Smid, G. E. (2022). "I lost so much more than my partner" – Bereaved partners' grief experiences following suicide or physician-assisted dying in case of a mental disorder. *BMC Psychiatry*, *22*(1), 454. https://doi.org/10.1186/s12888-022-04098-5

Sobel, A. A., Resick, P. A., & Rabalais, A. E. (2009). The effect of cognitive processing therapy on cognitions: Impact statement coding. *Journal of Traumatic Stress*, *22*(3), 205–211. https://doi.org/10.1002/jts.20408

Tay, A. K., Rees, S., Steel, Z., Liddell, B., Nickerson, A., Tam, N., & Silove, D. (2017). The role of grief symptoms and a sense of injustice in the pathways to post-traumatic stress symptoms in post-conflict Timor-Leste. *Epidemiology and Psychiatric Sciences*, *26*(4), 403–413. https://doi.org/10.1017/S2045796016000317

Van Denderen, M., de Keijser, J., Gerlsma, C., Huisman, M., & Boelen, P. A. (2014). Revenge and psychological adjustment after homicidal loss. *Aggressive Behavior*, *40*(6), 504–511. https://doi.org/10.1002/ab.21543

Wagner, B., Keller, V., Knaevelsrud, C., & Maercker, A. (2011). Social acknowledgement as a predictor of post-traumatic stress and complicated grief after witnessing assisted suicide. *International Journal of Social Psychiatry*, *58*(4), 381–385. https://doi.org/10.1177/0020764011400791

Wepster, D. (2003). Over tegenoverdracht en empathie bij overlevingsschuld en overlevingsschaamte. *Tijdschrift voor Psychotherapie*, *29*(2), 69. https://doi.org/10.1007/BF03062003

Wojtkowiak, J., Wild, V., & Egger, J. (2012). Grief experiences and expectance of suicide. *Suicide and Life-Threatening Behavior*, *42*(1), 56–66. https://doi.org/10.1111/j.1943-278X.2011.00070.x

Chapter 8

Symbolic interactions

Writing assignments, imagery rescripting, imaginary conversations, and rituals

Robert A. Neimeyer, Hannah Comtesse, and Geert E. Smid

The present chapter integrates cognitive behavioral interventions for prolonged and traumatic grief with techniques that cohere with a *constructivist* theory of knowledge, one that emphasizes the active, socially embedded, meaning-making processes that impart coherence, significance, and purpose to lived experience (Kelly, 1955; Martela & Steger, 2016; Neimeyer, 2009). Viewed in a constructivist perspective, a central process in grieving entails *the attempt to reaffirm or reconstruct a world of meaning that has been challenged by loss* (Neimeyer, 2016). Across a wide range of causes of death, both natural and violent, the capacity of bereaved individuals to find or reconstruct sense and significance in the death and in their own lives in its aftermath prospectively predicts reduced prolonged grief symptomatology (Milman et al., 2019; see Neimeyer, 2019, for review). In this chapter we will focus on four broad types of symbolic interactions: writing assignments aimed at tolerating intense emotions and ambivalence, including creative work that enhances perspective taking, imagery rescripting aimed at fulfilling unmet needs, dialogical interactions with imagined others that may help reduce guilt, anger and longing, and ritual validation of the mourner's transition in a form that carries both deeply personal and broadly cultural meaning. A common feature of most of these techniques is their recruitment of the *power of the imagination*, a constructive process required to integrate the often-harsh realities associated with bereavement, including traumatic circumstances of the loss and painful memories of the deceased. By enacting alternative symbolic possibilities for events related to the loved one's death and by reaffirming or reconstructing the continuing bond with the deceased, the goal of symbolic interactions is typically to realign the relationship with the deceased rather than relinquish it (Neimeyer & Hooghe, 2017). From a cognitive-behavioral perspective, mental imagery has been recognized as a powerful means to change affective experiences, behavior, and cognitions (Pearson et al., 2015). Table 8.1 provides an overview of different forms of symbolic interactions that will be discussed in this chapter.

DOI: 10.4324/9781003429777-11

Symbolic interactions are an effective means of addressing unresolved relational issues with the deceased, also known as unfinished business (UB), that has been presumed for decades to complicate bereavement. A growing body of research has documented the role of distress over UB and related self-evaluative emotions in predicting prolonged grief symptomatology (Holland et al., 2020; Klingspon et al., 2015; Lichtenthal et al., 2020). For example, UB has been reported by over 40% of bereaved adults suffering a variety of losses and was especially prevalent among close family members and in cases of violent, sudden death (Holland et al., 2020). In the pandemic era, when healthcare policies commonly limited or prohibited contact with loved ones who died unattended in the hospital, literally 100% of the over 200 bereaved participants in one study reported guilt, shame, regret, or UB, and most of them reported complex composites of these symptoms (Lee et al., 2022). Both Unfulfilled Wishes and Unresolved Conflict regarding the deceased, as measured by the Unfinished Business in Bereavement Scale or UBBS (Holland et al., 2020), were strongly associated with high levels of prolonged grief, with a history of relational conflict being a particularly strong predictor (Lee et al., 2022). Importantly, symbolic interactions may also involve the self or others, as shown in Table 8.1 elaborated in this chapter.

Table 8.1 Overview of symbolic interactions

Mode of interaction	*Interaction with...*		
	Deceased	*Self*	*Others*
Writing assignments	Correspondence with the deceased Poetry	Letter to a friend Chapters of our lives Directed journaling Other assignments	Letter writing to express anger Letters to love, time, and death
Imagery rescripting	UB, troubled minds, and regrets Unsatisfactory goodbyes	Unfulfilled responsibilities, self-blame, and guilt Shattered self-identity, reduced self-clarity	Emotional loneliness Third-party failures, other-blame, and anger
Imaginary dialogues	With the deceased "Walk to the Grave"	Imaginary dialogue with a future self	Imaginary dialogue with a moral authority
Rituals	Honoring deceased	Mark transition	Letting go of traumatic experience

Writing assignments

A robust empirical literature attests to the therapeutic value of expressive writing in promoting both psychological and physical health benefits following stressful and traumatic life events. The best-established forms of writing for wellbeing entail journaling for 15–20 minutes regarding a distressing life event on 3–5 occasions, usually over a short period of time, such as one week, with a focus on emotional expression (Pennebaker, 2010). Meta-analyses of the use of expressive writing for posttraumatic stress disorder (PTSD) (van Emmerik et al., 2012) and depression (Reinhold et al., 2018) largely support the efficacy of these methods, as does the growing number of studies that have used various forms of therapeutic journaling in the context of cognitive behavioral telehealth interventions for prolonged and traumatic grief (Wagner et al., 2020; see also Chapter 9). Below we will discuss different forms of writing assignments that have been developed to facilitate symbolic interactions with the deceased, the self, or others (see also Table 8.1).

Correspondence with the deceased

In correspondence with the deceased (Neimeyer, 2012b), the patient writes with the intent not to "say goodbye," so much as to "say hello again" (Hedtke, 2012). The crucial goal of these letters is not so much to express endless love and lamentation, but rather to (a) affirm constructive continuing bonds when these are earnestly desired, (b) process UB when this complicates grief, and (c) draw on the relationship to support relevant behavioral engagement with the changed world. Seeking the reopening of a dialogue prematurely closed by death, the patient might draw upon a "conversation starter" offered by the therapist that addresses a growing edge of the patient's need in relation to the deceased. For example, to express affirmation, the patient might begin with, *I want to keep you in my life by ...* or to self-disclose, could open with, *What you never understood was ....* A letter seeking to resolve ambivalence might start with, *The most confusing thing about our relationship was ...*, whereas conflict might be addressed by commencing with, *I am working to forgive you for ....* Ambivalent feelings toward the deceased can also be expressed in *three letters*: the patient writes a letter expressing their anger or dissatisfaction toward the deceased, then writes a second letter expressing their love and what they miss most, and finally writes a third letter in which positive and negative feelings are integrated (Hoogduin, 1980). Recruiting the deceased as an ally in the therapy and in ongoing life, the patient could also share lessons learned in the course of grieving, beginning the letter, *What I now realize is ...*, or drawing inspiration for change from the relation to the deceased, could choose the prompt, *The step I promise you I will take is ....*

Then *Response letters*, written as if from the deceased, can complete the dialogical cycle. Ultimately, the goal of such work is to reaffirm a constructive attachment bond, problem-solve a difficult or disappointing one, and use the reconstructed relationship to support valued behavior change going forward. The patient's need may be based on the attachment rupture or UB. This intervention will usually be assigned after some form of emotional processing (e.g., via exposure to the worst moment) has taken place. Similar "hello again" letters have been incorporated as a key intervention in the *Meaning In Loss* therapy format, an open trial of which suggests impressive effectiveness in reducing a broad range of prolonged grief disorder (PGD) and trauma symptomatology (Batista et al., 2024).

Poetry

Poetry therapy offers a diverse set of practices amenable to both individual and group therapy applications, with no requirement that patients have any special talent for creative writing. As noted expressive arts theorist Stephen Levine (2014, p. 15) explains, "it is not only the work of art that is effective but the very experience of art making … that restores people to their authentic existence as human beings [so that they] can take the capacities that have been awakened and bring them back into their daily experience." Among these are the capacities to articulate inchoate emotion, take perspective on troubling losses, imagine how they might be viewed differently, and ultimately make fuller meaning of them. As such, a variety of poetic practices could be appropriate at various stages of treatment, as metaphoric means of articulating what is otherwise unspeakable, reframing its significance, or symbolically consolidating new perspectives. Poetry therapy in its considerable variety is useful for clients struggling to articulate in literal language the impact or meaning of a loss that seems to go beyond words, attempting to memorialize a beloved other, or take perspective on the broader significance of the loss or the other in their lives. Moreover, virtually every culture has a rich poetic tradition, offering inspiration in a patient's own language for modeling and conveying the expression of grief. Collective spoken word poems integrating the expressions of participants in a writing group for bereaved fathers have also been used as a qualitative research method (Lehmann et al., 2024).

Viewed through the lens of Mazza's (2003) model, poetic practices can be clustered into three groups. The first includes *Receptive/prescriptive* techniques, such as the use of published poetry or other literature to help patients identify and validate particular feelings, promote self-disclosure, or foster group discussion. The second consists of *Expressive/creative* procedures, featuring patient-generated poetry to facilitate safe forms of self-expression and self-exploration or to foster greater cohesion and sharing in a group context. And the third involves a *Symbolic/ceremonial* component in which figurative language, movement, and rituals can be used to attribute meaning to grief and loss (see Chapter 7). An example of a hybrid form of *receptive and expressive poetry* is the *scaffolded verse* used by the Pongo Poetry Project (https://pongopoetryproject.org/) for children and teens in juvenile detention, whose lives are characteristically littered with sudden and traumatic losses of all kinds.

Letter to a friend

Hypothetical letters to a grieving friend or someone else experiencing a similar loss, e.g., a fellow bereaved parent (Lehmann et al., 2025), can be prompted by an open instruction to write compassionately to another about the loss or to address the hypothetical other's unrealistic guilt, dysfunctional thinking and behaviors, potential resources and consoling memories (Wagner & Maercker, 2015). This has also been called writing to an imaginal companion in misfortune (Smid et al., 2015). Randomized controlled trials of internet-based interventions incorporating this technique support its efficacy in the treatment of prolonged grief disorder (Litz et al., 2014; Wagner et al., 2006). The aim of these writing assignments is to help participants regain a sense of control over their lives and define a new role for themselves. Instructions are to write a supportive letter to a hypothetical friend now facing similar difficulties, encouraging the friend to activate resources and to find rituals to express their grief. The letter should reflect and acknowledge burdensome feelings such as guilt, shame, or anger, while correcting unrealistic assumptions (Kersting et al., 2013; Treml et al., 2021; Wagner et al., 2006).

Chapters of our lives

Viewed in narrative terms, the coherence of our life stories can be shaped, shaken, or shattered by traumatic loss (Neimeyer, 2000). It can be a healing practice, then, to step back from anguished immersion in the story of our grief to a self-distancing vantage point, viewing our life from a meta-perspective that allows us to name and claim our significant losses and transitions, and to better grasp their meaning and direction. In a sense, the shift from being merely a hapless victim of our life story to becoming its author or narrator allows us to hold our loss, rather than have it hold us. The *Chapters of Our Lives* exercise was introduced as a form of creative writing to encourage just this sort of reflection (Neimeyer, 2014). In the context of working with bereaved adolescents or adults, patients are asked to imagine writing their autobiography—the story of what they've been through or experienced. But rather than face the overwhelming task of drafting a 500-page tome, they are asked to imagine their life as a book, and then simply to compile its Table of Contents, consisting of the titles of each chapter. Although any structure or titles are acceptable—as it is the author's life story, after all—patients are gently encouraged to engage their imagination, using figurative language that goes beyond a merely factual chronology: *Birth, Infancy, Childhood, School Years, University, Work Life, Marriage*, etc. Instead, they might craft something richly descriptive of how they experienced each chapter: *A Star is Born, One Too Many, Weathering the Storm, A Tragic Turn, Darkness Visible, Seeking the Light.* The number of chapters is left to the author. Upon completion of the Table of Contents, the patient can be invited to select a few facilitative questions to address in therapeutic journaling to further explore, challenge, and potentially advance the story in new directions. Alternatively, similar questions might be explored directly with the therapist or with members of a therapeutic group. In the context of bereavement, *Chapters of Our Lives* is best situated in the later stages of therapy, after anguishing symptoms have been addressed (see Chapters 6 and 7), ability to function has been restored, and patients are ready to explore the longer range meaning that their loss(es) might come to have in a lifespan perspective. In this form, it has been integrated into a research-based protocol of therapeutic writing for bereaved parents (Lehmann et al., 2022, 2024). In the treatment of depression and PTSD in older adults, *life review* therapy has been found effective, in which patients are encouraged to actively recall, analyze, and integrate important life events throughout the life span, both negative and positive. Life review has been adapted into different, e.g., written, modalities (Jiang et al., 2024).

Directed journaling

Because commonly practiced forms of emotion-focused journaling have been found to be inconsistent in their efficacy for bereavement (Neimeyer et al., 2009), more directed, meaning-oriented prompts for journaling have been devised for use in grief therapy. For example, Lichtenthal and Neimeyer (2012) have suggested several questions to promote *sense-making* (e.g., *How did you make sense of the death or loss at the time? How do you interpret the loss now? What philosophical or spiritual beliefs contributed to your adjustment to this loss? How were they affected by it, in turn?*) and to enhance *benefit-finding* or life-lessons in bereavement (e.g., *In your view, have you found any unsought gifts in grief? If so, what? How has this experience affected your sense of priorities? Your sense of yourself?*). A randomized controlled trial of both forms of directed journaling and conventional emotional disclosure journaling documented the significant and durable effects on PGD symptoms of all treatment conditions compared to a neutral writing condition upon 3-month follow-up and suggested the particular impact of the benefit-finding condition (Lichtenthal & Cruess, 2010).

Directed journaling can also be used to promote activation, e.g., using a 7-day activity diary, in which patients indicate how pleasurable and important they found the activities they undertook during these days. In the subsequent homework assignments, patients are encouraged to continue keeping a diary, identify their core values, and to develop new meaningful and pleasurable activities based on these values and making plans to achieve valued goals (Eisma et al., 2015; Lenferink et al., 2020).

Other assignments

Writing assignments constitute a central part of online therapeutic interventions for people with prolonged and traumatic grief (Eisma et al., 2015; Kersting et al., 2013; Lenferink et al., 2020; Treml et al., 2021; Wagner et al., 2006). These are described in more detail in Chapter 9. Online trauma- and grief-focused exposure involves *self-confrontation* (Kersting et al., 2013), i.e., assignments where patients are asked to write a detailed account of the loss and its circumstances, express all their fears and thoughts about the event and to focus on sensory perceptions in as much detail as possible, while writing in the present tense, in the first person (Kersting et al., 2013; Treml et al., 2021; Wagner et al., 2006); and also write what they missed most now that their loved one was gone (Lenferink et al., 2023). Especially when the relationship with loss was traumatic or the deceased was abusive, the patient might write a final goodbye letter to take symbolic leave from the event or person, or to someone who witnessed the loss, or to the client's previous self (Kersting et al., 2013).

As brief, scaffolded fiction written to include elements provided by the therapist, *Virtual Dreams* (Neimeyer & Young-Eisendrath, 2015) are short stories that deliberately include prompts for fantasy or magical realism that have been included in a 14-session *Meaning In Loss* online intervention for PGD (Batista et al., 2024), which showed large reductions in grief-related symptoms.

As minimally constrained and brief forms of therapeutic writing, *free writes* are frequently used to access thoughts and feelings without conscious "editing" of self-expression, prompted by a topic (e.g., sensation, experience) or phrase, such as *I remember …* or *If I'm really honest …* Free writes can be used to explore a particular emotion relevant to grief, such as guilt or anger, and in this form have been incorporated into research-based programs of therapeutic writing for bereaved parents (Lehmann et al., 2025).

Letter writing to express anger

The *angry letter* is intended to express feelings of anger toward the people/agencies held responsible for the death (e.g., perpetrator of murder, negligent bystanders, government) in an uncensored way. Expressing anger in writing and reading it aloud may provide relief and support acceptance of understandable emotions without causing harm to the self or others. The angry letter may later be burned as part of a ritual (Smid et al., 2015). Angry letter writing is part of brief eclectic psychotherapy, an evidence-based treatment for PTSD (Nijdam et al., 2022).

Letters to love, time, and death

In this novel procedure, patients are encouraged to write a letter to a relevant personified abstraction, such as Love, Death, Security or Justice, in the wake of a traumatizing loss (Neimeyer, 2022) that violated their assumptive world bearing on their sense of predictability, fairness, control, identity and meaning in life, as well as their spiritual beliefs. Such symbolic letters speak to the disruption of core beliefs and meanings that have been found to powerfully explain the impact of pandemic losses, for example, in both North American and European populations (Milman et al., 2020; Negri et al., 2023).

Imagery rescripting

Imagery rescripting is an effective symbolic interaction technique in the treatment of PTSD (Kip et al., 2023; Kroener et al., 2023) that has also been suggested for the treatment of PGD (Lechner-Meichsner et al., 2024). Traumatic bereavements leave individuals with emotions, cognitions, and action tendencies that make them appear “stuck” and unable to accept and move on. Imagery rescripting contributes to identifying unmet needs and fulfilling them in a symbolic way, promoting a sense of mastery and self-efficacy. Imagery rescripting can be used to address several common themes in patients with prolonged and traumatic grief. Imagery rescripting techniques related to these themes have been described in detail elsewhere (Lechner-Meichsner et al., 2024) and will be described briefly below.

Firstly, themes related to the deceased include unsatisfactory goodbyes and UB, troubled minds, and regrets. Unsatisfactory goodbyes represent the unmet need to say goodbye to the deceased in an appropriate way. Imagery rescripting related to this theme involves more satisfactory final moments with their loved one. UB, troubled minds, and regrets may be addressed by rescripting an imaginary encounter that allows the patient to resolve unfinished themes.

Secondly, themes related to the self include unfulfilled responsibilities, self-blame, and guilt, and shattered self-identity and reduced self-clarity. Unfulfilled responsibilities represent an unmet need to fulfill important responsibilities toward the loved one. Rescripting may involve redirecting the blame or stepping into the image as his present self and providing comfort and support to his past self. Third-party failures, other-blame, and anger involve situations where patients hold other people accountable for (not having prevented) the death and represent an unfulfilled need to punish those responsible for the death. Rescripting may involve confronting the responsible other.

Thirdly, themes related to others and the world include emotional loneliness and third-party failures, other-blame, and anger. Emotional loneliness represents an unmet need of being seen, loved, and taken care of. Imagery rescripting involves filling the gap left behind by the deceased with love from others. Shattered self-identity and reduced self-clarity occur when a person's sense of self-identity has been disrupted by the loss, leading to confusion about roles, values, characteristics, and goals, and problems envisioning and creating a meaningful future without the deceased. Imagery rescripting involves developing a metaphorical image and transforming this image in a way that makes the patient feel more secure about who they are, as well as creating positive images about future goals and plans.

Imaginary dialogues

Imaginary dialogue with the deceased

Given the prominence of these relational issues in bereavement, it is not surprising that some form of "chair work" or imaginal encounter with the deceased to address these lingering concerns is a common prescription in grief therapy. But too often the facilitation of this dialogue is simply intuitive on the part of therapists, who instruct the patient to imagine the deceased in an empty chair across from them, and to begin a conversation with them, periodically shifting the patient to the empty chair to voice the deceased person's response. In our experience, however, these sorts of performative techniques require great skill on the part of the therapist to safely address UB that may have persisted for decades, maintained rather than resolved by avoidance coping (Keisari et al., 2023). Here we briefly summarize guidelines for the use of this procedure and illustrate its use with a patient, deferring to more comprehensive coverage of this technique and its variations for detailed training (Neimeyer, 2012a).

Table 8.2 summarizes the primary steps in the use of chair work or other forms of imaginal dialogues, such as the conversational visualization of the deceased without the use of chairs that forms part of evidence-based

Table 8.2 Simplified guidelines for use of imaginal dialogues in grief therapy

Sequence	*Guideline*
Ensure safety	Deeply experiential work in therapy requires the secure base provided by a strong therapeutic alliance.
Read the need	Listen for cues that the patient feels a definite need to express something to, hear something from, or resolve something with the deceased; if offered at other moments, imaginal dialogue can be ill-timed, irrelevant, and understandably resisted.
Recognize the readiness	Ensure that the patient feels ready for an emotionally evocative encounter; if not, build the setting for the work, postpone it or pursue it in another format, such as written correspondence with the deceased (see above).
Check acceptance	Secure the patient's permission to pursue the work; avoid coercion or persuasion.
Stage the encounter	Function as a director rather than an instructor, prompting the patient toward greater depth and honesty from both positions (self and deceased).
Keep it real	Avoid lapses into talking *about* the relationship in third-person language; instead, reorient the conversation to first and second person (I-you) speech, stated directly to the deceased.
Direct the dialogue	Suggest timely changes in role (e.g., from self to deceased and back), briefly summarizing the key phrases of each if needed at points of transition.
Invite processing	Seek a propitious moment to return the patient to the original chair and share observations and insights regarding the interaction.
Consider action steps	Prompt the patient toward useful behavioral activation by considering one relevant and feasible step that can be taken that extends or applies what was learned in the dialogue.

cognitive-behavioral therapies for PGD (Shear et al., 2022), or meaning-focused imaginal dialogues adapted to an online format (Neimeyer, 2022).

Although some of these guidelines may be self-evident, others merit brief elaboration. As is true with any other form of responsive psychotherapy, we presume that offering this intervention to patients is predicated on their evidenced *need* in the moment for such work, as well as their *readiness* to pursue it, rather than routine prescription of the method on the part of the therapist (Neimeyer & Rynearson, 2022). Once this is established, and the patient consents to the therapist's suggestion, the therapist shifts smoothly to the largely extemporaneous facilitation of the dialogue, taking care to avoid therapist or patient-initiated interpretations, commentaries, or side issues until the dialogue reaches a natural conclusion for the moment (commonly 10–15 minutes). At that point choreographing a shift of the patient back to the original chair (or a witnessing position in advanced versions of the technique; see Neimeyer, 2012a) initiates the processing phase, with the patient taking the lead in sharing relevant emotional reactions and cognitive insights engendered by the work (which frequently requires another 10–15 minutes). Care should be taken to ensure that the patient is fully present and grounded following the typically moving encounter. At this point the therapeutic team can consider whether the work suggests a further action step of a concrete sort following the session (e.g., journaling to reflect more about the experience, writing a letter to the deceased, engaging in a previously avoided activity that would make the deceased proud, talking more candidly with a trusted family member about troubling aspects of the relation to the deceased), thereby fostering useful behavioral activation. The following 15-minute encounter of a patient with her deceased father illustrates the impact of this procedure.

Bobbie, a working-class woman in her early 30s, sought therapy "to process the feelings" that seemed relatively unchanging in the two years after her father's death. He had long been her "rock," she explained, a secure base in an otherwise stormy home environment dominated by her alcoholic mother. Now, she noted, the house felt empty, and she found herself withdrawing from friends, family, and most worryingly, from the young husband she had recently married. Touchingly, she described the household "memorials" to her father—a framed photo and candles on the fireplace near the urn holding his ashes, his unwashed robe hanging on his familiar chair—all efforts to "hold onto his essence," as she explained ... though it was not enough. At times, she confessed, "I wanted to be with him, to the point that I was having some dark thoughts" of suicide, though she "didn't feel that was the right way to go about things." In short, she continued to feel "really lost without him," and only the day before, "getting emotional ... [she] really wanted to talk with [her] dad."

Alerted to this need, which was keenly evident in this first session, I (RAN) noted, "But I'm struck by that .... Part of your processing of your dad's death feels like, intuitively for you, it has to do with ... having a conversation with him?" Bobbie confirmed this, even if it were about the events of the day, joking, or more seriously, having a conversation about her mother. Clearly sensing her readiness for such an encounter, I offered:

I wonder ... in counselling, you can kind of bend the rules of usual social life and you can make things happen and make them real and substantial ... (Patient: Mm hmm.) that you wouldn't ordinarily do ... (P: Right.) and one thing that I sometimes find quite helpful is to help people find a way of conversing again with those they have loved and lost ... And sometimes I offer them the opportunity to symbolically place their loved one in an empty chair and then have a conversation with that person, just as they were present, sometimes even taking the other person's chair and responding back to what they've said.

"Kind of like role play," Bobbie responded, slightly anxious, but clearly intrigued. I agreed, and then asked:

Therapist (T): *Does that idea appeal to you? Would that be something interesting to try here?*
Patient (P): *(nodding) Possibly.*
T: *Is that a conversation that you'd like to begin now?*
P: *(giggling) We could try!*
T: *Let's give it a try. (Standing up) What I'd do is to bring in a chair off to the side here … (shifting another chair over) and I'd offer … your dad maybe my chair. And I just wonder what you would find kind of in your heart and in just these few minutes of beginning a conversation, one that we can continue in the future … beginning a conversation with him about what is happening with you now. What would you want dad to know about that? What do you call him? Do you call him dad or do you call him …?*
P: *Dad … Daddio!*
T: *Daddio (smiling). So what would Bobbie have to say to Daddio about what her life is like now and what she wants him to know?*
P: *I'd say, Dad … I really miss you and … life changed immensely since you've been gone … and it's scary … and it's uncertain … and there have been a lot of changes and I don't know how to deal with them … and … (5 secs of silence)*
T: *Tell him more about what scares you now … in this uncertain life that you now face.*
P: *It scares me not to have his assurance even … him being here physically.*
T: *Say that to him. Dad, what scares me is not having …*
P: *Dad, what scares me is … not having you around to reassure me that everything is going to be ok. Hearing your voice, seeing your smile … laughing things off in a joking way … having a hug … saying goodnight … even sitting quietly watching TV with you … at the kitchen table … (4 secs of silence) looking up at your urn knowing that whatever is left of you is in there and I have no physical access to you.*
T: *(ventriloquizing for patient) And I really want that access to you, dad … I really miss that.*
P: *I really want that access … it drives me crazy (giggling) … (T: Yeah … yeah …) I wish I could just pick up the phone and call you … (T: Yes.) whenever I needed to … (T: Yes.) just hear your voice … just hear your little stories about the corn on sale at the farm … or your little trip to the grocery … or … your trip to the doctor, hearing your concerns about how you're feeling … sharing*

my concerns about how you're feeling ... being able to go out on a boat with you ... just ... joke around.

T: *Mm ... just all those daily things, all of the jokes, all of that ... which was you. (P nodding: Right.) To really have that again.*

P: *Having coffee with you, going out to dinner, spending birthdays, Father's Day, Christmas ... none of it is the same.*

Falling silent for 6 seconds, Bobbie looked to me, as if for guidance. I responded:

T: *I wonder, Bobbie, if you can come over here (pointing the opposite chair) and ... (P switches chairs) just kind of ... in a way, loan your father your own voice and speak as if from who he is to this daughter (pointing P's chair) who is saying, "You know, dad, I just feel such uncertainty in the world now, it doesn't feel safe in the same way and ... I really miss all of those conversations with you, your humuor, your physical hugs, your presence in my life, the chance to talk with you." How would you respond to this daughter who is saying this to you?*

P: *(giggling) What, are you nuts?*

T: *(laughing with patient) Go ahead, tell her, You're nuts!*

P: *(growing serious, with 3 seconds of silence). You know I'm still here for you ... you know I love you ... I know you can feel me ...*

T: *Tell her more about that. Tell her how she can feel you.*

P: *(4 seconds of silence) You can feel me ... at the beach ... around the places that we shared our memories ... at the house ... when I pop little things in your head ... that you know I'd say at certain times, like What, are you nuts? (giggling) ... when I'd tell you, The bus is leaving! Or ... gosh, I'm thinking some of the little things that he'd say right in this moment ... I'm overwhelmed (tearing up) ...*

T: *(7 secs of silence) Tell her what you need from her now.*

P: *(8 secs of silence) I need you to try and go on ... do the best you can ... (4 secs of silence) make decisions based on what we learned together ... and what I tried to teach you ... (6 secs of silence) values ... be as honest as you can ... (4 secs of silence) and be loving ... and just remember, she's still your mom.*

Bobbie then sat in silence for a full 8 seconds, almost imperceptibly nodding her head, and staring into the space before her. Sensing that the conversation had come to its natural conclusion for the time being, I then invited her back into her original chair, removed the third chair and resumed my own, asking, "How was it for you to ... in this small way, to try to reopen that conversation with him a little bit? What did that feel like?" Pointing to her chest, she said that usually, since his death, her chest had been tight (making a fist), as she "couldn't talk to anyone really honestly about how I feel ... how much I miss him" (sounding teary). "So," she said, "I kind of felt ... a little looser." She continued, "Because I know ... in my heart (wiping a tear), that this would be what he wanted me to do. But to say it as if he were to say it, kind of made it a little more real." Summing up a meaningful first session and a reopened dialogue with a father Bobbie still very much needed, I expressed my hope that, just as she had repaired a previous decade-long rift with her father brought about in her teen years by her mother, she could "not only heal those rifts as [she] did, but that [she] would also be able to heal some of those rifts or tears of this loss as well ... (P nodding). And even tonight to feel like there's a little more loosening in that tightness, that closing down, it feels like a very good thing to me." "To me too," she added, smiling broadly and peacefully, as she reached forward to shake my hand in anticipation of the partnership to come.

Virtual reality (VR) interventions on grief employ virtual representations of the deceased to augment symbolic, dialogical interactions with the deceased. VR applications in mental health have been studied most extensively in the context of anxiety disorders, supporting their effectiveness (Powers & Emmelkamp, 2008). Studies are needed to carefully assess the possible psychological risks and benefits related to VR-augmented symbolic interactions in prolonged and traumatic grief (Pizzoli et al., 2023).

"Walk to the Grave"

A specific type of imaginal conversation is the "Walk to the Grave" exercise to achieve acceptance of the loss and open oneself up for a new life without the deceased (Rosner et al., 2018). The grave is understood here symbolically and can be replaced by other places or things such as a lake or tree. After describing the grave and laying out its actual dimensions on the floor, the patient is asked to describe the grave as seen from objects such as a candle (e.g., "I am a candle and give light to the deceased in the night. I see people come and go during the day, some cry, some don't ..."). Then, the patient is asked to speak to the deceased person: things that had been left unsaid or requests that were never made can be formulated here for the last time (e.g., "What I always wanted to tell you ..."). Finally, the patient changes roles and speaks from the standpoint of the deceased. This allows patients to receive answers or the permission to continue with their lives (e.g., "For the rest of your life, I wish you ...").

Imaginary dialogues with a future self

Patients struggling to envision a hopeful future in the aftermath of traumatic loss can benefit from a performed or written dialogue with themselves as they will be 5 years in the future, offering a glimpse of what living beyond loss might look and feel like, and advice on the concrete behavioral steps they can take to make it so (Den Elzen et al., 2023).

Imaginary dialogue with a moral authority

Traumatic loss of a loved one may be morally injurious, due to moral transgressions by perpetrators of violence or moral confusions related to a patient's own actions. The literature on psychotherapy for moral injury suggests the use of imaginary dialogues with a moral authority to support processing of moral dilemmas (Litz et al., 2017).

Rituals

Across countries and communities, rituals have been crucial in dealing with grief and loss. Death rituals, such as funerals and memorials, help mourners transition into their new inner states and social statuses, e.g., from "wife/husband/child" to "widow(er)/orphan," and to symbolically keep a bond with the deceased (Romanoff & Terenzio, 1998). Guilt feelings may stem from prescribed rituals that could not be performed, e.g., due to migration or traumatic circumstances of the death (see also Chapter 7).

Rituals in therapeutic interventions may be defined as *sensory, attentive, and intentional acts that are performed in a structured, imaginative, or aesthetic way and make use of symbols, symbolic language, and symbolic action* (Wojtkowiak et al., 2021). Rituals create a symbolic, alternative reality that enables meaningful actions—the symbolic, imagined world and the real world become one. As they have a clear beginning and end, rituals create a safe environment to express emotions. As elaborated in Chapter 5, questions from the bereavement and grief cultural formulation interview (BG-CFI) support integration of culturally appropriate rituals in therapy, taking the patient's personal relation with their cultural traditions into account.

From interviews with 10 therapists with expertise in both grief therapy and grief rituals, three types of rituals were identified (Sas & Coman, 2016): (1) rituals to honor the deceased loved one and to maintain a symbolic bond, e.g., creating a symbol or place of remembrance; (2) rituals to let go of the traumatic experience, e.g., renouncing things related to the traumatic circumstances of the death; and (3) rituals to mark an inner transition, e.g., visiting a special place or performing a culturally appropriate ritual. Thus, when planning a ritual, the patient in collaboration with the therapist needs to determine whether the ritual will support holding on or letting go, and whether holding on or letting go refers to the deceased, others, or aspects of the self.

In a scoping review of rituals in evidence-informed grief interventions (Wojtkowiak et al., 2021), different ritual elements were identified, ranging from meditation, symbolic communication with the deceased or an imaginary friend, to metaphorization and other types of symbolic expression (e.g. silence at the beginning or end of a session, writing assignments, the use of religious texts or poems). Some interventions consist of one specific ritual element (e.g., metaphorization of loss), while others have more or even include a complete ceremony at the end of the treatment (e.g., having a commemorative ceremony). The degree of ritual use thus differs in the different grief interventions. Some interventions make use of specific body techniques, such as sitting or meditation, while others use specific objects, such as memorial objects that are linked to the deceased or the loss that are used in a commemorative presentation or ceremony. Some interventions include a farewell ritual that the patient can conduct privately, such as with family or other significant people. In some individual ritual interventions or home assignments, patients are asked to conduct the ritual privately, e.g., to read mindfulness exercise instructions online or follow them in audio form. The reviewed studies revealed significant treatment effects on symptom reduction, but the reported effects mostly concerned the entire treatment and not specifically the ritual elements.

The following case vignette below illustrates the use of ritual in psychotherapy for prolonged and traumatic grief (Gersons et al., 2020).

Mr. M is a 55-year-old Dutch military veteran who lost one of his closest comrades due to an accident during a mission abroad at age 17. Many years later, during psychotherapy, he talked about his comrade. Mr. M had never visited his comrade's grave and started preparing for this. He also wrote a letter to his comrade. In the final phase of the treatment, Mr. M arranged a farewell ritual at his comrade's grave, where he invited some close others and read his letter out loud. Then he placed a small keepsake at the grave. He now felt as if the loss of his comrade had become a part of his life that he could accept.

Concluding remarks

Symbolic interactions represent a wide range of experiential interventions that can be used to support the attribution of adaptive meanings and to work through painful emotions, cognitions, and action tendencies in psychotherapy for prolonged and traumatic grief. They are characterized by a symbolic, as-if quality and the use of creative imagination while interacting with the deceased person, oneself, or others and the world. A recent meta-analysis of cognitive behavioral interventions for grief (Komischke-Konnerup et al., 2024), mostly involving exposure, cognitive therapy, and activation, concludes that these appeared to yield a smaller pooled effect on PGD symptoms in studies of individuals who lost a loved one due to unnatural causes compared to natural causes. Symbolic interactions can additionally meet the needs of traumatically bereaved individuals by fostering mental imagery as a powerful means to change affective experiences, behavior, and cognitions and by involving the power of interactions within dyads, groups, communities, and societies to create and co-construct meanings that may inspire personal growth and contribute to restoring a sense of meaning-in-life.

References

Batista, J., Alves, D., Pires, N., Silva, J. R., Mendes, I., Magalhães, C., Rosa, C., Oliveira, J. T., Gonçalves, M. M., & Neimeyer, R. A. (2024). The meaning in loss protocol: A clinical trial of online grief therapy. *Death Studies*, *49*(1), 8–20. https://doi.org/10.1080/07481187.2024.2370633

Den Elzen, K., Breen, L. J., & Neimeyer, R. A. (2023). Rewriting grief following bereavement and non-death loss: A pilot writing-for-wellbeing study. *British Journal of Guidance & Counselling*, *51*(3), 425–443. https://doi.org/10.1080/03069885.2022.2160967

Eisma, M. C., Boelen, P. A., van den Bout, J., Stroebe, W., Schut, H. A. W., Lancee, J., & Stroebe, M. S. (2015). Internet-based exposure and behavioral activation for complicated grief and rumination: A randomized controlled trial. *Behavior Therapy*, *46*(6), 729–748. https://doi.org/10.1016/j.beth.2015.05.007

Gersons, B. P. R., Nijdam, M. J., Smid, G. E., & Meewisse, M. L. (2020). Brief eclectic psychotherapy for PTSD. In L. F. Bufka, C. V. Wright, & R. Halfond (Eds.), *Casebook to the APA clinical practice guideline for the treatment of PTSD* (pp. 139–161). American Psychological Association. https://doi.org/10.1037/0000196-007

Hedtke, L. (2012). Introducing the deceased. In R. A. Neimeyer (Ed.), *Techniques of grief therapy: Creative practices for counseling the bereaved* (pp. 253–255). Routledge.

Holland, J. M., Klingspon, K. L., Lichtenthal, W. G., & Neimeyer, R. A. (2020). The unfinished business in bereavement scale (UBBS): Development and psychometric evaluation. *Death Studies*, *44*(2), 65–77. https://doi.org/10.1080/07481187.2018.1521101

Holland, J. M., Plant, C. P., Klingspon, K. L., & Neimeyer, R. A. (2020). Bereavement-related regrets and unfinished business with the deceased. *Death Studies*, *44*(1), 42–47. https://doi.org/10.1080/07481187.2018.1521106

Hoogduin, C. (1980). De drie brieven [the three letters]. In K. Van der Velden (Ed.), *Directieve therapie* (Vol. 2, pp. 257–266). Van Loghem Slaterus.

Jiang, V., Galin, A., & Lea, X. (2024). Life review for older adults: An integrative review. *Psychogeriatrics*, *24*(6), 1402–1417. https://doi.org/10.1111/psyg.13194

Keisari, S., Yaniv, D., Gesser-Edelsburg, A., Palgi, Y., & Neimeyer, R. A. (2023). Meaning reconstruction 70 years later: Processing older adults' unfinished business in a drama therapy group. *Psychotherapy*, *60*(4), 573–586. https://doi.org/10.1037/pst0000497

Kelly, G. A. (1955). *The psychology of personal constructs. Vol. 1. A theory of personality. Vol. 2. Clinical diagnosis and psychotherapy* (pp. xxviii, 1218). W. W. Norton.

Kersting, A., Dölemeyer, R., Steinig, J., Walter, F., Kroker, K., Baust, K., & Wagner, B. (2013). Brief internet-based intervention reduces posttraumatic stress and prolonged grief in parents after the loss of a child during pregnancy: A randomized controlled trial. *Psychotherapy and Psychosomatics*, *82*(6), 372–381. https://doi.org/10.1159/000348713

Kip, A., Schoppe, L., Arntz, A., & Morina, N. (2023). Efficacy of imagery rescripting in treating mental disorders associated with aversive memories – An updated meta-analysis. *Journal of Anxiety Disorders*, *99*, 102772. https://doi.org/10.1016/j.janxdis.2023.102772

Klingspon, K. L., Holland, J. M., Neimeyer, R. A., & Lichtenthal, W. G. (2015). Unfinished business in bereavement. *Death Studies*, *39*(7), 387–398. https://doi.org/10.1080/07481187.2015.1029143

Komischke-Konnerup, K. B., Zachariae, R., Boelen, P. A., Marello, M. M., & O'Connor, M. (2024). Grief-focused cognitive behavioral therapies for prolonged grief symptoms: A systematic review and meta-analysis. *Journal of Consulting and Clinical Psychology*, *92*(4), 236–248. https://doi.org/10.1037/ccp0000884

Kroener, J., Hack, L., Mayer, B., & Sosic-Vasic, Z. (2023). Imagery rescripting as a short intervention for symptoms associated with mental images in clinical disorders: A systematic review and meta-analysis. *Journal of Psychiatric Research*, *166*, 49–60. https://doi.org/10.1016/j.jpsychires.2023.09.010

Lechner-Meichsner, F., Boelen, P. A., & Hagenaars, M. A. (2024). Imagery rescripting in the treatment of prolonged grief disorder: Insights, examples, and future directions. *European Journal of Trauma & Dissociation*, *8*(3), 100435. https://doi.org/10.1016/j.ejtd.2024.100435

Lee, S. A., Neimeyer, R. A., Mancini, V. O., & Breen, L. J. (2022). Unfinished business and self-blaming emotions among those bereaved by a COVID-19 death. *Death Studies*, *46*(6), 1297–1306. https://doi.org/10.1080/07481187.2022.2067640

Lehmann, O. V., Kalstad, T. G., & Neimeyer, R. A. (2024). Experiences of fathers in Norway attending an online course on therapeutic writing after the death of a child. *Qualitative Health Research*, *34*(5), 458–472. https://doi.org/10.1177/10497323231216099

Lehmann, O. V., Neimeyer, R. A., & Kalstad, T. G. (2025). *Writing through bereavement: A therapeutic workbook for grieving parents.* Routledge & CRC Press. https://www.routledge.com/Writing-Through-Bereavement-A-Therapeutic-Workbook-for-Grieving-Parents/Lehmann-Neimeyer-GivingKalstad/p/book/9781032714592

Lehmann, O. V., Neimeyer, R. A., Thimm, J., Hjeltnes, A., Lengelle, R., & Kalstad, T. G. (2022). Experiences of Norwegian mothers attending an online course of therapeutic writing following the unexpected death of a child. *Frontiers in Psychology*, *12*. https://doi.org/10.3389/fpsyg.2021.809848

Lenferink, L. I. M., de Keijser, J., Eisma, M., Smid, G., & Boelen, P. (2020). Online cognitive-behavioural therapy for traumatically bereaved people: Study protocol for a randomised waitlist-controlled trial. *BMJ Open*, *10*(9), e035050. https://doi.org/10.1136/bmjopen-2019-035050

Lenferink, L. I. M., Eisma, M. C., Buiter, M. Y., de Keijser, J., & Boelen, P. A. (2023). Online cognitive behavioral therapy for prolonged grief after traumatic loss: A randomized waitlist-controlled trial. *Cognitive Behaviour Therapy*, *52*(5), 508–522. https://doi.org/10.1080/16506073.2023.2225744

Levine, S. K. (2014). Poiesis, praise and lament: Celebration, mourning and the "architecture" of expressive arts therapy. In B. E. Thompson & R. A. Neimeyer (Eds.), *Grief and the expressive arts*. Routledge.

Lichtenthal, W. G., & Cruess, D. G. (2010). Effects of directed written disclosure on grief and distress symptoms among bereaved individuals. *Death Studies*, *34*(6), 475–499. https://doi.org/10.1080/07481187.2010.483332

Lichtenthal, W. G., & Neimeyer, R. A. (2012). Directed journaling to facilitate meaning-making. In R. A. Neimeyer (Ed.), *Techniques of grief therapy: Creative practices for counseling the bereaved* (pp. 165–168). Routledge/Taylor & Francis Group. https://doi.org/10.4324/9780203152683

Lichtenthal, W. G., Roberts, K. E., Catarozoli, C., Schofield, E., Holland, J. M., Fogarty, J. J., Coats, T. C., Barakat, L. P., Baker, J. N., Brinkman, T. M., Neimeyer, R. A., Prigerson, H. G., Zaider, T., Breitbart, W., & Wiener, L. (2020). Regret and unfinished business in parents bereaved by cancer: A mixed methods study. *Palliative Medicine*, *34*(3), 367–377. https://doi.org/10.1177/0269216319900301

Litz, B. T., Lebowitz, L., Gray, M. J., & Nash, W. P. (2017). *Adaptive disclosure: A new treatment for military trauma, loss, and moral injury*. Guilford Publications.

Litz, B. T., Schorr, Y., Delaney, E., Au, T., Papa, A., Fox, A. B., Morris, S., Nickerson, A., Block, S., & Prigerson, H. G. (2014). A randomized controlled trial of an internet-based therapist-assisted indicated preventive intervention for prolonged grief disorder. *Behaviour Research and Therapy*, *61*(0), 23–34.

Martela, F., & Steger, M. F. (2016). The three meanings of meaning in life: Distinguishing coherence, purpose, and significance. *The Journal of Positive Psychology*, *11*(5), 531–545. https://doi.org/10.1080/17439760.2015.1137623

Mazza, N. (2003). *Poetry therapy: Theory and practice*. Routledge. https://doi.org/10.4324/9780203954706

Milman, E., Lee, S. A., Neimeyer, R. A., Mathis, A. A., & Jobe, M. C. (2020). Modeling pandemic depression and anxiety: The mediational role of core beliefs and meaning making. *Journal of Affective Disorders Reports*, *2*, 100023. https://doi.org/10.1016/j.jadr.2020.100023

Milman, E., Neimeyer, R. A., Fitzpatrick, M., MacKinnon, C. J., Muis, K. R., & Cohen, S. R. (2019). Prolonged grief and the disruption of meaning: Establishing a mediation model. *Journal of Counseling Psychology*, *66*(6), 714–725. https://doi.org/10.1037/cou0000370

Negri, A., Conte, F., Caldiroli, C. L., Neimeyer, R. A., & Castiglioni, M. (2023). Psychological factors explaining the COVID-19 pandemic impact on mental health: The role of meaning, beliefs and perceptions of vulnerability and mortality. *Behavioral Sciences*, *13*(2), Article 2. https://doi.org/10.3390/bs13020162

Neimeyer, R. A. (2000). Narrative disruptions in the construction of the self. In R. A. Neimeyer & J. D. Raskin (Eds.), *Constructions of disorder: Meaning-making frameworks for psychotherapy* (pp. 207–242). American Psychological Association. https://doi.org/10.1037/10368-009

Neimeyer, R. A. (2009). *Constructivist psychotherapy*. Routledge.

Neimeyer, R. A. (2012a). Chair work. In R. A. Neimeyer (Ed.), *Techniques of grief therapy: Creative practices for counseling the bereaved* (Vol. 1, pp. 266–273). Routledge.

Neimeyer, R. A. (2012b). Correspondence with the deceased. In R. A. Neimeyer (Ed.), *Techniques of grief therapy: Creative practices for counseling the bereaved* (Vol. 1, pp. 259–261). Routledge.

Neimeyer, R. A. (2014). Chapters of our lives. In B. E. Thompson & R. A. Neimeyer (Eds.), *Grief and the expressive arts* (pp. 80–84). Routledge.

Neimeyer, R. A. (Ed.). (2016). *Techniques of grief therapy: Assessment and intervention*. Routledge/Taylor & Francis Group.

Neimeyer, R. A. (2019). Meaning reconstruction in bereavement: Development of a research program. *Death Studies, 43*(2), 79–91. https://doi.org/10.1080/07481187.2018.1456620

Neimeyer, R. A. (2022). Grief therapy as a quest for meaning. In E. M. Steffen, E. Milman, & R. A. Neimeyer (Eds.), *The handbook of grief therapies* (pp. 53–67). SAGE Publications.

Neimeyer, R. A., & Hooghe, A. (2017). Reconstructing the continuing bond: A case study in grief therapy. In D. Klass & E. M. Steffen (Eds.), *Continuing bonds in bereavement*. Routledge.

Neimeyer, R. A., & Rynearson, E. (2022). From retelling to reintegration: Narrative fixation and the reconstruction of meaning. In L. A. Burke & E. K. Rynearson (Eds.), *The restorative nature of ongoing connections with the deceased* (pp. 95–110). Routledge.

Neimeyer, R. A., Van Dyke, J. G., & Pennebaker, J. W. (2009). Narrative medicine: Writing through bereavement. In H. M. Chochinov & W. Breitbart (Eds.), *Handbook of psychiatry in palliative medicine*. Oxford University Press.

Neimeyer, R. A., & Young-Eisendrath, P. (2015). Assessing a Buddhist treatment for bereavement and loss: The mustard seed project. *Death Studies, 39*(5), 263–273. https://doi.org/10.1080/07481187.2014.937973

Nijdam, M. J., Meewisse, M.-L., Smid, G. E., & Gersons, B. P. R. (2022). Brief eclectic psychotherapy for PTSD. In U. Schnyder & M. Cloitre (Eds.), *Evidence based treatments for trauma-related psychological disorders: A practical guide for clinicians* (pp. 281–306). Springer International Publishing. https://doi.org/10.1007/978-3-030-97802-0_13

Pearson, J., Naselaris, T., Holmes, E. A., & Kosslyn, S. M. (2015). Mental imagery: Functional mechanisms and clinical applications. *Trends in Cognitive Sciences, 19*(10), 590–602. https://doi.org/10.1016/j.tics.2015.08.003

Pennebaker, J. W. (2010). *Writing to heal: A guided journal for recovering from trauma and emotional upheaval*. New Harbinger Publications.

Pizzoli, S. F. M., Monzani, D., Vergani, L., Sanchini, V., & Mazzocco, K. (2023). From virtual to real healing: A critical overview of the therapeutic use of virtual reality to cope with mourning. *Current Psychology, 42*(11), 8697–8704. https://doi.org/10.1007/s12144-021-02158-9

Powers, M. B., & Emmelkamp, P. M. G. (2008). Virtual reality exposure therapy for anxiety disorders: A meta-analysis. *Journal of Anxiety Disorders, 22*(3), 561–569. https://doi.org/10.1016/j.janxdis.2007.04.006

Reinhold, M., Bürkner, P., & Holling, H. (2018). Effects of expressive writing on depressive symptoms—A meta-analysis. *Clinical Psychology: Science and Practice, 25*(1). https://doi.org/10.1037/h0101749

Romanoff, B. D., & Terenzio, M. (1998). Rituals and the grieving process. *Death Studies, 22*(8), 697–711. https://doi.org/10.1080/074811898201227

Rosner, R., Pfoh, G., Kotoučova, M., & Comtesse, H. (2018). Integrative cognitive-behavioral therapy for prolonged grief disorder: Introduction of a treatment manual. *Verhaltenstherapie, 29*(1), 40–48. https://doi.org/10.1159/000489509

Sas, C., & Coman, A. (2016). Designing personal grief rituals: An analysis of symbolic objects and actions. *Death Studies, 40*(9), 558–569. https://doi.org/10.1080/07481187.2016.1188868

Shear, M. K., Skritskaya, N., & Bloom, C. (2022). Prolonged grief disorder therapy (PGDT). In U. Schnyder & M. Cloitre (Eds.), *Evidence based treatments for trauma-related psychological disorders: A practical guide for clinicians* (pp. 329–344). Springer International Publishing. https://doi.org/10.1007/978-3-030-97802-0_15

Smid, G. E., Kleber, R. J., De la Rie, S. M., Bos, J. B. A., Gersons, B. P. R., & Boelen, P. A. (2015). Brief eclectic psychotherapy for traumatic grief (BEP-TG): Toward integrated treatment of symptoms related to traumatic loss. *European Journal of Psychotraumatology*, *6*(1), 27324. https://doi.org/10.3402/ejpt.v6.27324

Treml, J., Nagl, M., Linde, K., Kündiger, C., Peterhänsel, C., & Kersting, A. (2021). Efficacy of an Internet-based cognitive-behavioural grief therapy for people bereaved by suicide: A randomized controlled trial. *European Journal of Psychotraumatology*, *12*(1), 1926650. https://doi.org/10.1080/20008198.2021.1926650

van Emmerik, A. A. P., Reijntjes, A., & Kamphuis, J. H. (2012). Writing therapy for posttraumatic stress: A meta-analysis. *Psychotherapy and Psychosomatics*, *82*(2), 82–88. https://doi.org/10.1159/000343131

Wagner, B., Knaevelsrud, C., & Maercker, A. (2006). Internet-based cognitive-behavioral therapy for complicated grief: A randomized controlled trial. *Death Studies*, *30*(5), 429–453. https://doi.org/10.1080/07481180600614385

Wagner, B., & Maercker, A. (2015). Internet-based writing. In R. A. Neimeyer (Ed.), *Techniques of grief therapy* (pp. 201–204). Routledge.

Wagner, B., Rosenberg, N., Hofmann, L., & Maass, U. (2020). Web-based bereavement care: A systematic review and meta-analysis. *Frontiers in Psychiatry*, *11*, 525. https://doi.org/10.3389/fpsyt.2020.00525

Wojtkowiak, J., Lind, J., & Smid, G. E. (2021). Ritual in therapy for prolonged grief: A scoping review of ritual elements in evidence-informed grief interventions. *Frontiers in Psychiatry*, *11*, 1655. https://doi.org/10.3389/fpsyt.2020.623835

Chapter 9

Internet- and mobile-based interventions for prolonged and traumatic grief

Anaïs Aeschlimann, Lyanne Reitsma, and Clare Killikelly

The term internet-based intervention (IBI) covers a broad variety of psychological interventions delivered at least partly via the internet, for instance on a computer or smartphone (Andersson & Titov, 2014). IBIs have been a field of interest since the first studies on the topic were published in the mid-1990s (Lange et al., 2000; Ruwaard et al., 2011). The first IBIs primarily involved simple writing tasks with additional email support, which was partly due to early internet access being slow and broadband access still rather limited among the general population (Andersson et al., 2008; Marks et al., 1998). However, with technological advancements and the advent of smartphones, IBIs have consistently gained importance in research and practice over the past three decades and have evolved, becoming more sophisticated (Andersson, 2018b). These advancements include the integration of various multimedia components, such as videos, audios, interactive features, gamification elements, virtual reality experiences, chatbots, and as the latest development, artificial intelligence (AI) (Andersson, 2018a; Carlbring et al., 2023; Geraets et al., 2021).

There is a large treatment gap for bereavement care with many affected individuals wanting or needing support but not receiving it (Breen & Moullin, 2022; Lichtenthal et al., 2015). A study by Lichtenthal et al. (2015) showed for instance, that 40% of cancer-bereaved individuals who wanted or needed support did not receive any. In another study, Lenferink et al. (2020) reported that 19% of people bereaved through road traffic accidents with care needs or pathological grief did not receive adequate care.

Recently, the field has embraced the public health approach to bereavement care. A three-tiered model of care (i.e., identifying individuals with high, medium, and low need for support) may help define the right type of intervention at the right time for those who need it (Aoun et al., 2012, 2015). The application of this tiered approach to online interventions has not yet been explored. In this chapter, we present examples of foundational IBIs in the field of grief and bereavement and explore how IBIs may provide

DOI: 10.4324/9781003429777-12

support across the different tiers of the three-tiered model of bereavement care (Aoun et al., 2012).

Current state of the field

The introduction of IBIs has opened up new possibilities for bereavement support as it may overcome traditional barriers to care such as fear of stigmatization (especially in suicide-bereaved individuals), thinking that it may be too difficult to find help, and worrying that it may be too painful to speak about the grief experience (Andriessen et al., 2019; Lichtenthal et al., 2015; Pitman et al., 2016; Wagner et al., 2013). Apart from IBIs being an affordable alternative for individuals seeking support, they are also cost-effective on a structural level due to their scalability (Tur et al., 2022). At the same time, IBIs can be easily personalized and tailored to individual needs (Taylor et al., 2021). To decrease therapists' workload and reduce expenses, there is a growing trend toward integrating online components into traditional face-to-face therapy. These additions may occur before or during in-person sessions, as supplementary modules to bridge the waiting time prior to starting therapy, alongside face-to-face therapy, or as posttreatment support to prevent relapse (Békés et al., 2020). However, it is also important to note that IBIs face several limitations, including difficulties in detecting and responding to elevated suicide risk, ensuring the accuracy of self-reported data, legal and ethical challenges, the need for adequate therapist support to prevent high dropout rates and ensure patient safety, and issues related to digital literacy and access to technology (Andersson & Titov, 2014).

IBIs come in many different formats. Traditionally, a way to classify them is according to the phase of psychosocial care (prevention, treatment, aftercare, relapse-prevention), as well as the amount and type of therapist contact (Berger, 2015). IBIs may range from completely self-guided (e.g., self-help apps) to fully therapist-guided (e.g., email- or videoconference-therapy), where the internet is purely used as communication tool. Furthermore, various blended formats exist, such as for instance guided self-help, where users are regularly in contact with a therapist while using a self-help intervention (Berger, 2015). One can further differentiate between synchronous (e.g., live chat) and asynchronous (e.g., email) guidance (Berger, 2015). Finally, IBIs may vary in structure, ranging from less structured formats like self-help apps to more structured ones such as internet-based cognitive behavioral therapy, with distinct modules that users progress through sequentially (Tur et al., 2022).

Many studies have investigated the efficacy of IBIs specifically for bereavement care, with the majority of IBIs investigated being guided self-help interventions and a large part of these consisting in writing assignments, a form of IBI borrowed from treatment for posttraumatic stress disorder

(PTSD; Lange et al., 2001). The meta-analyses of Wagner et al. (2020) and Zuelke et al. (2021) show that IBIs for bereaved individuals show moderate (Hedge's $g = .54$) to high (Hedge's $g = .86$) effects for grief and PTSD symptoms, which remain stable over time. Wagner et al. (2020) further highlighted that these effects are moderated by factors such as the number of sessions, with higher session counts generally associated with greater efficacy. The latter review equally reports high user satisfaction for IBIs across included studies. IBIs are thus a promising, low-threshold approach to bereavement care.

IBIs and the tiered model of bereavement care

After a loss individuals may fluctuate between acute or severe symptoms of grief and typical natural resolving responses. It is therefore important to provide the right support at the right time. In grouping exemplar IBIs in terms of low, medium, and high risk groups we aim to offer clinicians and researchers more tailored guidance (Aoun et al., 2012, 2015).

Universal bereavement support (low need)

Universal bereavement support generally includes information (psychoeducation, practical tools) about bereavement, support is provided by family friends or the local community, and it is targeted to support the needs of all bereaved people experiencing typical grief (Aoun et al., 2012). Below we provide three examples of IBIs providing universal bereavement support (online support groups, GriefCoach, GriefCOVID). Please refer to Table 9.1 for a more comprehensive overview.

Online support groups for the bereaved are increasingly popular (Wagner et al., 2013). Typically, users can post messages (e.g., the story of their loss) and read and comment others' posts. Some groups are monitored by facilitators, others are between peers only (Robinson & Pond, 2019). Although many online support groups for bereavement exist, only little research has been conducted on the topic so far. A systematic review by Robinson and Pond (2019) found that there is not enough high-quality evidence to conclude whether online support groups are effective in reducing psychological distress. Nevertheless, their qualitative results showed that users appreciated this format because it fostered a sense of belonging within a supportive community, provided emotional support, and facilitated information exchange. However, findings also included negative experiences such as the potential for evoking distressing emotions due to triggering stories of other users.

Grief Coach is a text-based IBI developed by the company Help Texts providing grief support to help hospices support bereaved family members (Levesque et al., 2023). The IBI sends text messages twice a week containing

Table 9.1 Tier 1 studies: Non-clinical, general sample

Author, date Study location	*Type of loss*	*Intervention type (guided or unguided)*	*Primary outcome measure/ grief measure/diagnostic inclusion criteria*	*Study design/ strength of evidence*	*Study conclusions/ recommendation*
Dominguez-Rodriguez etal.(2023), Mexico N = 114	Loss of loved one, COVID	Web-based, "Grief COVID", unguided CBT, mindfulness and positive psychology: 12 sessions in video or text format	Inventory of complicated grief, no cut-off score for inclusion	Efficacy and Usability, RCT	The results indicated that the treatment significantly reduced baseline clinical symptoms in the intervention group for all variables including grief. **Strong support**
Dominick et al. (2009),USA N = 86	Loss of parent, older relative	Internet-based, The Internet Tool: Making Sense of Grief, unguided Social cognitive theory, interactive exercises supplemented by video testimonial	Attitude, Self-efficacy, state anxiety (STAI)	RCT, efficacy, and usability	Significant program effects were obtained on all three outcome measures: attitude (η^2 = .177), self-efficacy (η^2 quare = .106), and state anxiety (η^2 = .083). **Requires further testing, on grief measure**
Levesque et al. (2023),USA N = 350	Loss of family member (hospice patients)	Text-message-based grief Coach, unguided CBT and ACT: twice-weekly text support	Helpfulness, supportiveness	Satisfaction with program	Seventy-three percent of respondents rated the program as "Very helpful", 13-month program retention rate was high (86%). **Requires further testing in RCT format**

(*Continued*)

Table 9.1 (Continued)

Author, date Study location	*Type of loss*	*Intervention type (guided or unguided)*	*Primary outcome measure/ grief measure/diagnostic inclusion criteria*	*Study design/ strength of evidence*	*Study conclusions/ recommendation*
Van der Houwen et al. (2010) USA (and UK) *N* = 460	Close person	Web-based writing exercises, unguidedCBT: email-based writing assignments	Nine items based on the criteria for complicated grief and rumination, threatening grief interpretations, and deliberate grief avoidance	RCT	Results showed that writing decreased feelings of emotional loneliness and increased positive mood, in part through its effect on rumination. However, writing did not affect grief or depressive symptoms. **Requires further testing**

Note: Studies investigating the same IBI were combined into the same row.

support, education, tips, and reminders to individuals experiencing grief, as well as to their supportive friends and family. Program subscribers and their supporters can contact the Help Texts team through various channels, with mental health professionals reviewing incoming messages daily to address inquiries and identify individuals at risk, providing assistance and conducting risk assessments when necessary. A survey study by Levesque et al. (2023) found that Grief Coach was perceived as helpful, supportive and that retention rates were high (86%), while efficacy remains to be investigated.

Grief COVID is a website-based 12-module self-help IBI developed by Dominguez-Rodriguez et al. (2023). It was developed using a user experience design to target the needs of individuals bereaved by or during COVID and incorporates techniques from CBT, mindfulness, behavioral activation therapy and positive psychology. Each session was delivered video and text (user could choose) and ended with a short quiz. Users were encouraged to complete two modules per week. The session topics included: psychoeducation (grief in general and particular impact of pandemic), recognizing and coping with emotions alternative parting rituals, behavioral activation, connecting with support network, self-care, repositioning deceased, goal setting, and relapse prevention. In an RCT, the authors found high usability rates and medium effect sizes (Hedges $g = 0.7$) for grief symptom reduction compared to a waitlist control group with further decrease in grief symptoms at 3-month follow-up (Dominguez-Rodriguez et al., 2023).

Selective or targeted groups (medium need)

Selected or targeted interventions are developed for individuals with a medium level of need who are at risk of developing more chronic symptoms. For example, individuals from at-risk groups (e.g., child loss, sudden violent loss) but present with sub-clinical symptoms would be the target group. Please see Table 9.2 for an overview.

The following interventions would be well-suited to specific groups that have a medium to high risk of developing more severe PGD symptoms.

Eklund et al. (2024) developed a smartphone app called My Grief, based on CBT and the structure of an existing app called PTSD Coach (Hallenbeck et al., 2022). It is an unguided IBI for parents dealing with the loss of a child with elevated prolonged grief disorder (PGD) symptoms comprising four sections, which users can access in any order according to their needs and interests: (1) Learning – psychoeducation on grief and PGD, (2) symptom monitoring, (3) exercises – mindfulness exercises (audios) and exposure through writing prompts, and (4) get support – contact details for various support functions. In an RCT, the IBI was considered to be helpful, easy to navigate, and a small but significant reduction in grief ($d = -0.26$) was found (Eklund et al., 2024; Sveen et al., 2024). However, 22% of participants also

Table 9.2 Tier 2 studies: Developed for specific at-risk groups and may be helpful for a sub-clinical sample

Author, Date Study Location	*Type of loss*	*Intervention type (guided or unguided)*	*Primary outcome measure/grief measure/diagnostic inclusion criteria*	*Study design/ strength of evidence*	*Study conclusions/ recommendation*
Aeschlimann et al. (2025) Switzerland N=30	Not specified (app for Syrian refugees)	Mobile application (module in SUI app) unguided in-app psychoeducation, exercises, and mood monitoring, using a mixture of written and audio exercises	A minimum score of 3 on at least one item of the IPGDS	RCT: pilot	High treatment satisfaction, a low dropout rate, and adherence of 40 % were found. Qualitative interviews indicated the intervention was relevant and beneficial, further adaptations were suggested. No significant group differences were found on bereavement or secondary outcomes. While trends are promising, a larger RCT is needed to investigate efficacy. **Requires further testing**
Brodbeck et al. (2019), (German version) *N* = 110 Efinger et al. (2022) (French version) *N* = 24 Switzerland	Loss of partner, older adults	Internet-based self-help intervention: "LIVIA" semi guided CBT; Text-based modules including writing assignments	Texas Revised Inventory of Grief; ¾ of sample non clinical, and about a quarter of the participants (24.5%) reached the B, C, and D criteria of a Persistent Complex Bereavement Disorder in the DSM-5.	RCT	Brodbeck: Findings indicate that an internet intervention based on models for coping with grief after bereavement was not only beneficial for widowed but also separated or divorced participants. Efinger: Clinical benefits were observed on grief symptoms and avoidance strategies. No other improvement was noted on depressive symptomatology, anxiety, well-being, life satisfaction, or loneliness. **Strong support**

(*Continued*)

Table 9.2 (Continued)

Author, Date Study Location	*Type of loss*	*Intervention type (guided or unguided)*	*Primary outcome measure/grief measure/diagnostic inclusion criteria*	*Study design/ strength of evidence*	*Study conclusions/ recommendation*
Eklund et al. (2022, 2024) Sveen et al. (2024) Sweden *N* = 67	Loss of child (health-related)	Mobile application, "My Grief", unguided CBT: in-app psychoeducation, exercises, mood monitoring, and signposting	PG-13, (inclusion >16)	Satisfaction, usability study	The app was experienced as easy to navigate and around half of the parents used the app more than one day a week. Almost all parents were satisfied with the app and would recommend it to other parents in similar situations. **Also recommended tier 3** **Requires further testing of intervention effect**
Lehmann et al. (2022) Norway *N* = 35	Child	Group-based via Zoom, guided Pluralistic psychotherapy approaches: Therapeutic writing course	Qualitative Data Inventory of Complicated Grief filled out at inclusion	Qualitative design (existential phenomenological)	Online writing courses could be of benefit for bereaved parents who are grieving the unexpected death of a child, but do not replace other interventions such as psychotherapy. **Requires further testing, small sample size**

(*Continued*)

Table 9.2 (Continued)

Author, Date Study Location	*Type of loss*	*Intervention type (guided or unguided)*	*Primary outcome measure/grief measure/diagnostic inclusion criteria*	*Study design/ strength of evidence*	*Study conclusions/ recommendation*
Sveen et al. (2021) Sweden *N* = 21	Loss of child (cancer)	Web-based, "iCBT-I" semi-guided CBT: internet-delivered writing assignments for insomnia, with active support from therapists	PG-13 (no cut-off) Insomnia Severity Index as primary outcome and inclusion criteria	RCT	The intervention group improved significantly from pre- to posttreatment and had a significantly larger reduction of insomnia when analyzed over all four time points. **Requires further testing, small sample size**
Tur et al. (2022) Spain *N* = 6	Close person	Web-based and mobile application, "GROw program", semi-guided CBT: eight modules, with weekly support calls	Inclusion: meeting criteria for PGD according to ICD-11, measured Structured Clinical Interview for Complicated Grief and Inventory of Complicated Grief App items were adapted from Inventory of Complicated Grief and PG-13	A single-case multiple-baseline AB design, where A refers to the baseline phase and B corresponds to the treatment phase, was used in the study to evaluate the treatment outcomes.	(…) the present study clearly shows strong potential for this intervention as an alternative to face-to-face therapy for PGD. Patients reported high usability and satisfaction with the intervention. **Also recommended for tier 3. Requires further testing, small sample size**

reported experiencing negative consequences from the app (e.g., painful reminders of the loss).

A guided self-help IBI called LIVIA was developed for older adults who have lost their spouse due to death or separation/divorce (Brodbeck et al., 2019). The text-based IBI is grounded in CBT principles as well as the task model of mourning (Worden, 2018) and the dual-process model of bereavement (Schut & Stroebe, 1999). The ten sessions include (a) psychoeducation about interpersonal loss and assessment of own situation, (b) loss-oriented interventions (e.g., exposure) to address painful memories and unfinished business, and (c) restoration-oriented interventions to foster resources, self-care, positive emotions, social relationships, and a new life without the partner. Users receive weekly support regarding questions about the intervention and technical problems, as well as motivational support via email from master's level Psychology students (supervised by a fully trained Psychotherapist). In an RCT, large effect sizes for grief symptom reduction were found for both widowed (d = 0.81) and separated/divorced (d = 0.94) individuals compared to a waitlist control group (Brodbeck et al., 2019).

An 8-week online group course for therapeutic writing for bereaved parents 2 or 3 months since loss was developed by Lehmann et al. (2022). The program includes writing tasks based on a given prompt (e.g., piece of music, poem, etc.) – see also Chapter 8 – with discussion of writing experience in small group and in plenary. The session topics included: psychoeducation around grief, meaning-making, self-compassion, introducing the loved one, existential meaning and purpose (e.g., life chapters exercise). Qualitative results showed that mothers and fathers attending the course found it a valuable experience, no studies testing efficacy have been conducted so far (Lehmann et al., 2022, 2024).

A culturally sensitive unguided self-help app for grieving Syrian refugees in Switzerland was developed by Aeschlimann et al. (2025) with the Swiss Red Cross. To ensure that the app and its content were culturally relevant, acceptable, and feasible, the IBI was developed bottom-up and refined in several iterations based on qualitative findings from interviews with bereaved Syrian refugees and experts working with grieving Syrians. The app contains five interactive chapters, which users work though sequentially at their own pace: (1) Introduction, grief reactions and dealing with emotions (e.g., psychoeducation, video testimonials, mindful breathing audio); (2) Resources, strengths and activities (e.g., resource lifeline, planning positive activities); (3.1) Space for grief and the loved one (e.g., writing tasks, planning rituals, digital altar); (3.2) Social activities; (4) Negative thoughts and being a good friend to yourself (e.g., reflecting negative thoughts, self-compassion exercise); and (5) Future and growth (e.g., imaginary conversation, planning for difficult dates, letter to a friend reflecting on what was learnt). A pilot feasibility RCT confirmed low dropout rate and high treatment satisfaction (Aeschlimann et al., 2025).

Indicated groups (high need)

Indicated interventions aim to support individuals with a high level of need, for example, meeting diagnostic criteria for PGD. IBIs should be evidence-based interventions that are tested with a randomized controlled trial in a clinical sample.

A guided, asynchronous IBI based on an intervention initially created for PTSD (Interapy; Lange et al., 2001) was developed by Wagner et al. (2006) and is considered to be the first IBI for pathological grief. Users received two weekly 45-minute structured writing tasks via email from a therapist over 5 weeks and received weekly feedback on their assignments. The IBI is structured around three phases: (1) exposure – describing the loss circumstances, (2) cognitive reappraisal – supportive letter to a friend, identification of rituals to remember the deceased, activation of social resources and competencies, and (3) integration and restoration – take symbolic leave of the traumatic event by writing a letter to a significant person or themselves. An RCT for this IBI found significant reductions in probable PGD symptoms and overall psychopathology immediately after treatment, as well as at 1.5-year follow-up (Wagner & Maercker, 2007; Wagner et al., 2006).

Treml et al. (2021) adapted the IBI developed by Wagner et al. (2006) for individuals bereaved by suicide. Over 5 weeks, users were sent 10 writing tasks of each 45 minutes duration, and received asynchronous, written feedback from therapists. The program starts with psychoeducation around suicide and suicide bereavement. The IBI is structured around three phases: (1) self-confrontation (describing most painful experience related to the loss), (2) cognitive reappraisal (writing letter to hypothetical friend focusing on feelings of guilt or shame and correcting unrealistic assumptions), and (3) social sharing (writing letter to significant other or themselves taking symbolic leave of the event). An RCT revealed large effect sizes for grief symptom reduction compared to a waitlist control group (Treml et al., 2021).

Since this foundational study from Wagner et al. (2006), there has been a surge of IBIs developed for PGD. Many use CBT-based techniques and are tailored to different at risk groups for example loss of a spouse (Eisma et al., 2015; Litz et al., 2014), pregnancy loss (Kersting et al., 2013), suicide loss (Treml et al., 2021; Wager et al., 2022b), traffic accidents (Lenferink et al., 2023), cancer loss (Kaiser et al., 2022) and COVID loss (Reitsma et al., 2023). The evidence base for the effectiveness and feasibility of these IBIs in reducing symptoms of PGD is strong. Please see Table 9.3 for more details on each study.

Table 9.3 Tier 3 studies: RCT with clinical sample with a diagnosis or probable diagnosis of PGD

Author, Date Study Location	*Type of loss*	*Intervention type (guided or unguided)*	*Primary outcome measure/grief measure/diagnostic inclusion criteria*	*Study design/ strength of evidence*	*Study conclusions/ recommendation*
Eisma et al. (2015) Netherlands *N* = 47	Loss of spouse	Web-based exposure and behavioral activation, semi-guided CBT: email-based homework assignments	Inventory of Complicated Grief -R (inclusion >25) and Utrecht Grief Rumination Scale (>40)	RCT effectiveness and feasibility	Results supported potential applicability of online exposure but not behavioral activation to decrease complicated grief and rumination. **Strong recommendation for the exposure condition, more assessment for behavioral activation needed**
Kaiser et al. (2022) Germany *N* = 87	Cancer	Web-based, "Online-Trauertherapie" (Online Grief Therapy), semi-guided CBT: internet-based writing tasks.	Inventory of Complicated Grief (>25 for inclusion)	RCT: randomized waitlist-controlled trial	The intervention reduced symptoms of prolonged grief (intention-to-treat: $P < .001$; $\eta^2 = 0.34$; Cohen's $d = 0.80$) to a clinically significant extent. **Strong support**

(*Continued*)

Table 9.3 (Continued)

Author, Date Study Location	*Type of loss*	*Intervention type (guided or unguided)*	*Primary outcome measure/grief measure/diagnostic inclusion criteria*	*Study design/ strength of evidence*	*Study conclusions/ recommendation*
Kersting et al. (2011, 2013) Germany (German-speaking European country) $N = 228$	Pregnancy loss	Web-based, semi-guided CBT: email-based writing assignments	Inventory of Complicated Grief (> 36 as PGD however not relevant for in-/exclusion)	RCT	Significant improvement in all symptoms of PTSD and prolonged grief was found from the posttreatment evaluation to the 12-month follow-up. The attrition rate of 14% was relatively low. **Strong support**
Lenferink et al. (2023) Netherlands $N = 40$	People bereaved through traffic accidents	Web-based, semi-guided CBT: eight sessions	Traumatic Grief Inventory-Self Report plus (TGI-SR+) Inclusion of DSM-5 criteria for probable persistent complex bereavement disorder, PTSD, and/or depression, based on self-report questionnaires	RCT: A two-arm (online CBT vs. waiting list) multicenter open-label parallel RCT was conducted	strongly reduced prolonged grief, posttraumatic stress, and depression symptoms relative to the control condition at posttreatment and follow-up. **Strong support**

(Continued)

Table 9.3 (Continued)

Author, Date Study Location	*Type of loss*	*Intervention type (guided or unguided)*	*Primary outcome measure/grief measure/diagnostic inclusion criteria*	*Study design/ strength of evidence*	*Study conclusions/ recommendation*
Litz et al. (2014) USA *N* = 84	Partner, relative, close person	Web-based "HEAL intervention", semi-guided CBT: Internet-based psychoeducation (18 sessions)	PG-13 (inclusion > 23)	RCT, Intention to treat analysis	HEAL was associated with large reductions in prolonged grief (d = 1.10), depression (d =.71), anxiety (d =.51), and posttraumatic stress (d =.91). **Strong support**
Reitsma et al. (2023) Netherlands *N* = 65	People bereaved during the COVID-19 pandemic	Web-based, unguided CBT: eight sessions	Traumatic Grief Inventory-Clinician Administered (TGI-CA) Inclusion of DSM-5 criteria for probable persistent complex bereavement disorder, PTSD, and/or depression, based on telephone interviews	RCT: A two-arm (online CBT vs. waiting list) monocenter open-label parallel RCT was conducted	Strongly reduced prolonged grief, posttraumatic stress, and depression symptoms relative to the control condition at posttreatment. **Strong support**

(*Continued*)

Table 9.3 (Continued)

Author, Date Study Location	*Type of loss*	*Intervention type (guided or unguided)*	*Primary outcome measure/grief measure/diagnostic inclusion criteria*	*Study design/ strength of evidence*	*Study conclusions/ recommendation*
Treml et al. (2021) (adapted the IBI developed by Wagner et al., 2006) Germany *N* = 58	Loved one (suicide)	Web-based, semi-guided CBT: writing assignments	Inventory of Complicated Grief and Grief Experience Questionnaire PG-13 to verify PGD criteria at inclusion	RCT	ICBGT effectively treats PGD symptoms after suicide bereavement, offering a stable, efficient alternative to face-to-face grief interventions with small doses and short duration. **Strong support**
Wagner & Maercker (2007); Wagner et al. (2006) (older adults) (German-speaking participants) *N* = 55 Wagner et al. (2022a) (bereaved siblings) Germany *N* = 86	Close person	Web-based, semi-guided CBT: email-based writing assignments	5 items from the revised symptom list for complicated grief measured by the Impact of Events scale	RCT, intention to treat design	Participants in the treatment group (n.26) improved significantly relative to participants in the waiting condition on symptoms of intrusion, avoidance, maladaptive behavior, and general psychopathology. **Strong support**

(*Continued*)

Table 9.3 (Continued)

Author, Date Study Location	*Type of loss*	*Intervention type (guided or unguided)*	*Primary outcome measure/grief measure/diagnostic inclusion criteria*	*Study design/ strength of evidence*	*Study conclusions/ recommendation*
Wagner et al. (2022b) Germany *N* = 140	Suicide	Group, web-based, guided CBT: 12 weekly modules as webinars in a group format	Inventory of complicated grief and Grief experience questionnaire. Primary outcomes (not grief): BDI-II, BSSI, ACSS-FAD	RCT: randomized controlled trial with two conditions: a treatment group and a waitlist control group	The results of this study indicate that completing an online group intervention for the suicide bereaved could reduce trauma-related outcomes. However, the waiting control group also improved significantly from pre- to post-measurement in all other outcomes. **Strong support**

Discussion

This chapter provides an overview of the range and scope of IBIs developed specifically following grief and bereavement. In this chapter, we provide an overview of the current state of the field in terms of different intervention structures and user experiences that may be recommended for bereaved individuals across the three-tiered public health model of bereavement. We aim to provide recommendations for future use and development. Although not comprehensive, a brief literature search, building on the existing meta-analyses of Wagner et al. (2020) and Zuelke et al. (2021), confirms the existence of approximately 20 IBIs focused on grief and bereavement. These interventions vary in terms of modality, targeted service user, intervention components, and the strength of evidence base. Several IBI are developed in the pilot form and for reasons of funding, or technological updates these interventions are not tested following the gold standard randomized controlled methodology. All in all, the strength of the evidence base for IBI for grief and bereavement is limited to a handful of well-designed studies. We recommend that clinicians and researchers consider the following recommendations as a preliminary guide to navigating the recent surgencies of IBIs for grief and bereavement and when planning to use such an intervention for individuals with clinically relevant symptoms (Klein et al., 2018). Firstly, consider the strength of the research support by asking the following questions; was an RCT conducted? Did the results confirm a significant decrease in PGD symptoms? Were these effects maintained at follow-up? What was the retention, adherence or dropout rate? Secondly, consider the target group for which the intervention was developed, does the intervention include specific modules that may provide a more tailored and supportive experience? For example, was the app developed and tested with a sample meeting criteria for PGD or with subclinical symptoms? Would it be suitable to acute, early bereavement or/and for typical bereavement? Thirdly, consider the level of therapist guidance. Research from other areas of mental health suggests the importance of clinician and research support throughout the intervention (Mohr et al., 2011). Fourthly, consider the accessibility and long-term sustainability of the intervention. Is it free for participants? Are there secure data storage methods?

Despite the proliferation of IBIs, researchers and clinicians are increasingly aware of short- and long-term challenges with the acceptability and implementation of this therapeutic modality. In the short term, one of the biggest considerations is the high dropout rate and low adherence to IBIs (Karyotaki et al., 2015). For example, researchers and clinicians need to consider a more tailored approach beyond "one size fits all". IBIs may be particularly suitable and effective for a group of patients who would benefit from this modality (e.g., accessibility, privacy, affordability) but other patients may find this modality off-putting or unapproachable. Consideration of internet and technological literacy is also paramount (Kim et al., 2024). In some cases of suicidality and high risk, an IBI intervention could be counter-indicated (Parrish et al., 2022).

In terms of long-term challenges changes in the new AI landscape and advancing technologies mean that existing and new applications may not adhere to the recent requirements for data security and safety at a national and global level (Bennett et al., 2010). Additionally, many existing apps may become outdated and redundant requiring technological expertise and programming skills beyond the original research team's ability. Research financing often cannot cover the updates needed and the app is discontinued.

The sustainability of IBI across different areas of mental health has led to questions about the long-term usability and the direction of the field. Although IBI are a promising modality for scalability, accessibility, and adaptability, the long-term use of these interventions is constrained by funding limitations (i.e., limited grant money) and the need for technological expertise (i.e., programming skills) often beyond the scope of a clinicians training. Researchers and clinicians working with IBIs will need to tackle to the above challenges for the field to move in a meaningful, sustainable direction.

Future directions

The landscape of IBI is evolving and moving in exciting new directions. With recent advances in AI, virtual reality, avatars, and the use of ChatGPT or deathbots for mental health purposes, the horizon of possibilities seems ever-expanding (Dergaa et al., 2024; Kothgassner et al., 2023). However, this should be tempered with considerable ethical questions about the true benefit of these developments for bereaved and grieving individuals (Allen et al., 2021; Borgueta et al., 2018). Consideration of the high dropout rates to existing IBIs and the lack of high-quality studies suggests the need for more research to determine which type of interventions are both acceptable and effective for bereaved individuals. Future research should consider dismantling or mechanistic studies to determine which components of IBIs may be essential for intervention effects beyond a modest improvement for PGD (e.g., Kersting et al., 2013; Litz et al., 2014) and which components improve the usage and acceptance of this modality.

Acknowledgments

The authors thank Ayala Licht for her assistance with the tables.

References

Aeschlimann, A., Heim, E., Killikelly, C., Mahmoud, N., Haji, F., Stoeckli, R. T., Aebersold, M., Thoma, M., & Maercker, A. (2025). Cultural adaptation of a self-help app for grieving Syrian refugees in Switzerland. A feasibility and acceptability pilot-RCT. *Internet Interventions*, *39*, 100800. https://doi.org/10.1016/j.invent.2025.100800

Allen, S., Hammett, R., & Schweizer, M. (2021). Global Governance Toolkit for Digital Mental Health | World Economic Forum. Retrieved June 18, 2024, from https://www.weforum.org/publications/global-governance-toolkit-for-digital-mental-health/

Andersson, G. (2018a). Internet interventions. In Erin Martz (Eds.), *Promoting self-management of chronic health conditions: Theories and practice* (pp. 482–495). Oxford University Press.

Andersson, G. (2018b). Internet interventions: Past, present and future. *Internet Interventions*, *12*, 181–188. https://doi.org/10.1016/j.invent.2018.03.008

Andersson, G., Bergström, J., Buhrman, M., Carlbring, P., Holländare, F., Kaldo, V., Nilsson-Ihrfelt, E., Paxling, B., Ström, L., & Waara, J. (2008). Development of a new approach to guided self-help via the internet: The Swedish experience. *Journal of Technology in Human Services*, *26*(2–4), 161–181. https://doi.org/10.1080/15228830802094627

Andersson, G., & Titov, N. (2014). Advantages and limitations of internet-based interventions for common mental disorders. *World Psychiatry*, *13*(1), 4–11. https://doi.org/10.1002/wps.20083

Andriessen, K., Lobb, E., Mowll, J., Dudley, M., Draper, B., & Mitchell, P. B. (2019). Help-seeking experiences of bereaved adolescents: A qualitative study. *Death Studies*, *43*(1), 1–8. https://doi.org/10.1080/07481187.2018.1426657

Aoun, S. M., Breen, L. J., Howting, D. A., Rumbold, B., McNamara, B., & Hegney, D. (2015). Who needs bereavement support? A population based survey of bereavement risk and support need. *PloS One*, *10*(3), e0121101. https://doi.org/10.1371/journal.pone.0121101

Aoun, S. M., Breen, L. J., O'Connor, M., Rumbold, B., & Nordstrom, C. (2012). A public health approach to bereavement support services in palliative care. *Australian and New Zealand Journal of Public Health*, *36*(1), 14–16. https://doi.org/10.1111/j.1753-6405.2012.00825.x

Békés, V., Grondin, F., & Bouchard, S. (2020). Barriers and facilitators to the integration of web-based interventions into routine care. *Clinical Psychology: Science and Practice*, *27*(2), e12335. https://doi.org/10.1111/cpsp.12335

Bennett, K., Bennett, A. J., & Griffiths, K. M. (2010). Security considerations for e-mental health interventions. *Journal of Medical Internet Research*, *12*(5), e61. https://doi.org/10.2196/jmir.1468

Berger, T. (2015). *Internetbasierte Interventionen bei psychischen Störungen*. Hogrefe.

Borgueta, A. M., Purvis, C. K., & Newman, M. G. (2018). Navigating the ethics of internet-guided self-help interventions. *Clinical Psychology: A Publication of the Division of Clinical Psychology of the American Psychological Association*, *25*(2), e12235. https://doi.org/10.1111/cpsp.12235

Breen, L. J., & Moullin, J. C. (2022). The value of implementation science in bridging the evidence gap in bereavement care. *Death Studies*, *46*(3), 639–647. https://doi.org/10.1080/07481187.2020.1747572

Brodbeck, J., Berger, T., Biesold, N., Rockstroh, F., & Znoj, H. J. (2019). Evaluation of a guided internet-based self-help intervention for older adults after spousal bereavement or separation/divorce: A randomised controlled trial. *Journal of Affective Disorders*, *252*, 440–449. https://doi.org/10.1016/j.jad.2019.04.008

Carlbring, P., Hadjistavropoulos, H., Kleiboer, A., & Andersson, G. (2023). A new era in internet interventions: The advent of Chat-GPT and AI-assisted therapist guidance. *Internet Interventions*, *32*, 100621. https://doi.org/10.1016/j.invent.2023.100621

Dergaa, I., Fekih-Romdhane, F., Hallit, S., Loch, A. A., Glenn, J. M., Fessi, M. S., Ben Aissa, M., Souissi, N., Guelmami, N., Swed, S., El Omri, A., Bragazzi, N. L., & Ben Saad, H. (2024). ChatGPT is not ready yet for use in providing mental health assessment and interventions. *Frontiers in Psychiatry*, *14*, 1277756. https://doi.org/10.3389/fpsyt.2023.1277756

Dominguez-Rodriguez, A., Sanz-Gomez, S., Ramírez, L. P. G., Herdoiza-Arroyo, P. E., Garcia, L. E. T., Rosa-Gómez, A., de la, González-Cantero, J. O., Macias-Aguinaga, V., & Miaja, M. (2023). The efficacy and usability of an unguided web-based grief intervention for adults who lost a loved one during the COVID-19 pandemic: Randomized controlled trial. *Journal of Medical Internet Research*, *25*(1), e43839. https://doi.org/10.2196/43839

Dominick, S. A., Irvine, A. B., Beauchamp, N., Seeley, J. R., Nolen-Hoeksema, S., Doka, K. J., & Bonanno, G. A. (2009). An internet tool to normalize grief. *Omega*, *60*(1), 71–87. https://doi.org/10.2190/om.60.1.d

Finger, L., Debrot, A., & Pomini, V. (2022, December). LIVIA-FR: Implémentation et évaluation d'une intervention par Internet pour des personnes francophones peinant à surmonter la perte de leur partenaire. In *Annales Médico-psychologiques, revue psychiatrique* (Vol. 180, No. 10, pp. 1000–1007). Elsevier Masson.

Eisma, M. C., Boelen, P. A., van den Bout, J., Stroebe, W., Schut, H. A., Lancee, J., & Stroebe, M. S. (2015). Internet-based exposure and behavioral activation for complicated grief and rumination: A randomized controlled trial. *Behavior Therapy*, *46*(6), 729–748. https://doi.org/10.1016/j.beth.2015.05.007

Eklund, R., Eisma, M. C., Boelen, P. A., Arnberg, F. K., & Sveen, J. (2022). My grief app for prolonged grief in bereaved parents: A pilot study. *Frontiers in Psychiatry*, *13*, 872314. https://doi.org/10.3389/fpsyt.2022.872314

Eklund, R., Eisma, M. C., Boelen, P. A., Arnberg, F. K., & Sveen, J. (2024). The self-help app my grief: Bereaved parents' experiences of helpfulness, satisfaction and usability. *Internet Interventions*, *35*, 100712. https://doi.org/10.1016/j.invent.2024.100712

Geraets, C. N. W., van der Stouwe, E. C. D., Pot-Kolder, R., & Veling, W. (2021). Advances in immersive virtual reality interventions for mental disorders: A new reality? *Current Opinion in Psychology*, *41*, 40–45. https://doi.org/10.1016/j.copsyc.2021.02.004

Hallenbeck, H. W., Jaworski, B. K., Wielgosz, J., Kuhn, E., Ramsey, K. M., Taylor, K., Juhasz, K., McGee-Vincent, P., Mackintosh, M.-A., & Owen, J. E. (2022). PTSD coach version 3.1: A closer look at the reach, use, and potential impact of this updated mobile health app in the general public. *JMIR Mental Health*, *9*(3), e34744. https://doi.org/10.2196/34744

Kaiser, J., Nagl, M., Hoffmann, R., Linde, K., & Kersting, A. (2022). Therapist-assisted web-based intervention for prolonged grief disorder after cancer bereavement: Randomized controlled trial. *JMIR Mental Health*, *9*(2), e27642. https://doi.org/10.2196/27642

Karyotaki, E., Kleiboer, A., Smit, F., Turner, D. T., Pastor, A. M., Andersson, G., Berger, T., Botella, C., Breton, J. M., Carlbring, P., Christensen, H., de Graaf, E., Griffiths, K., Donker, T., Farrer, L., Huibers, M. J., Lenndin, J., Mackinnon,

A., Meyer, B., Moritz, S., & Cuijpers, P. (2015). Predictors of treatment dropout in self-guided web-based interventions for depression: An 'individual patient data' meta-analysis. *Psychological Medicine*, *45*(13), 2717–2726. https://doi.org/10.1017/S0033291715000665

Kersting, A., Kroker, K., Schlicht, S. et al. (2011). Efficacy of cognitive behavioral internet-based therapy in parents after the loss of a child during pregnancy: Pilot data from a randomized controlled trial. *Archives of Women's Mental Health*, *14*, 465–477. https://doi.org/10.1007/s00737-011-0240-4

Kersting, A., Dölemeyer, R., Steinig, J., Walter, F., Kroker, K., Baust, K., & Wagner, B. (2013). Brief internet-based intervention reduces posttraumatic stress and prolonged grief in parents after the loss of a child during pregnancy: A randomized controlled trial. *Psychotherapy and Psychosomatics*, *82*(6), 372–381. https://doi.org/10.1159/000348713

Kim, J., Livingston, M. A., Jin, B., Watts, M., & Hwang, J. (2024). Fundamentals of digital health literacy: A scoping review of identifying core competencies to use in practice. *Adult Learning*, *35*(3), 131–142. https://doi.org/10.1177/10451595231178298

Klein, J. P., Knaevelsrud, C., Bohus, M., Ebert, D. D., Gerlinger, G., Günther, K., Jacobi, C., Löbner, M., Riedel-Heller, S. G., Sander, J., Sprick, U., & Hauth, I. (2018). Internetbasierte Selbstmanagementinterventionen: Qualitätskriterien für ihren Einsatz in Prävention und Behandlung psychischer Störungen [Internet-based self-management interventions: Quality criteria for their use in prevention and treatment of mental disorders]. *Der Nervenarzt*, *89*(11), 1277–1286. https://doi.org/10.1007/s00115-018-0591-4

Kothgassner, O. D., Reichmann, A., & Bock, M. M. (2023). Virtual reality interventions for mental health. *Current Topics in Behavioral Neurosciences*, *65*, 371–387. https://doi.org/10.1007/7854_2023_419

Lange, A., van de Ven, J. P., Schrieken, B. A., Bredeweg, B., & Emmelkamp, P. M. (2000). Internet-mediated, protocol-driven treatment of psychological dysfunction. *Journal of Telemedicine and Telecare*, *6*(1), 15–21. https://doi.org/10.1258/1357633001933880

Lange, A., van de Ven, J.-P., Schrieken, B., & Emmelkamp, P. M. G. (2001). Interapy. Treatment of posttraumatic stress through the internet: A controlled trial. *Journal of Behavior Therapy and Experimental Psychiatry*, *32*(2), 73–90. https://doi.org/10.1016/S0005-7916(01)00023-4

Lehmann, O. V., Kalstad, T. G., & Neimeyer, R. A. (2024). Experiences of fathers in Norway attending an online course on therapeutic writing after the death of a child. *Qualitative Health Research*, *34*(5), 458–472. https://doi.org/10.1177/10497323231216099

Lehmann, O. V., Neimeyer, R. A., Thimm, J., Hjeltnes, A., Lengelle, R., & Kalstad, T. G. (2022). Experiences of Norwegian mothers attending an online course of therapeutic writing following the unexpected death of a child. *Frontiers in Psychology*, *12*. https://doi.org/10.3389/fpsyg.2021.809848

Lenferink, L. I. M., de Keijser, J., Eisma, M. C., Smid, G. E., & Boelen, P. A. (2020). Treatment gap in bereavement care: (Online) bereavement support needs and use after traumatic loss. *Clinical Psychology and Psychotherapy*, *28*(4), 907–916. https://doi.org/10.1002/cpp.2544

Lenferink, L. I. M., Eisma, M. C., Buiter, M. Y., de Keijser, J., & Boelen, P. A. (2023). Online cognitive behavioral therapy for prolonged grief after traumatic loss: A randomized waitlist-controlled trial. *Cognitive Behaviour Therapy*, *52*(5), 508–522. https://doi.org/10.1080/16506073.2023.2225744

Levesque, D. A., Lunardini, M. M., Payne, E. L., & Callison-Burch, V. (2023). Grief coach, a text-based grief support intervention: Acceptability among hospice family members. *OMEGA - Journal of Death and Dying*, 00302228231159450. https://doi.org/10.1177/00302228231159450

Lichtenthal, W. G., Corner, G. W., Sweeney, C. R., Wiener, L., Roberts, K. E., Baser, R. E., Li, Y., Breitbart, W., Kissane, D. W., & Prigerson, H. G. (2015). Mental health services for parents who lost a child to cancer: If we build them, will they come? *Journal of Clinical Oncology*, *33*(20), 2246–2253. https://doi.org/10.1200/JCO.2014.59.0406

Litz, B. T., Schorr, Y., Delaney, E., Au, T., Papa, A., Fox, A. B., Morris, S., Nickerson, A., Block, S., & Prigerson, H. G. (2014). A randomized controlled trial of an internet-based therapist-assisted indicated preventive intervention for prolonged grief disorder. *Behaviour Research and Therapy*, *61*, 23–34. https://doi.org/10.1016/j.brat.2014.07.005

Marks, I., Shaw, S., & Parkin, R. (1998). Computer-aided treatments of mental health problems. *Clinical Psychology: Science and Practice*, *5*(2), 151–170. https://doi.org/10.1111/j.1468-2850.1998.tb00141.x

Mohr, D. C., Cuijpers, P., & Lehman, K. (2011). Supportive accountability: A model for providing human support to enhance adherence to eHealth interventions. *Journal of Medical Internet Research*, *13*(1), e30. https://doi.org/10.2196/jmir.1602

Parrish, E. M., Filip, T. F., Torous, J., Nebeker, C., Moore, R. C., & Depp, C. A. (2022). Are mental health apps adequately equipped to handle users in crisis? *Crisis*, *43*(4), 289–298. https://doi.org/10.1027/0227-5910/a000785

Pitman, A. L., Osborn, D. P. J., Rantell, K., & King, M. B. (2016). The stigma perceived by people bereaved by suicide and other sudden deaths: A cross-sectional UK study of 3432 bereaved adults. *Journal of Psychosomatic Research*, *87*, 22–29. https://doi.org/10.1016/j.jpsychores.2016.05.009

Reitsma, L., Boelen, P. A., de Keijser, J., & Lenferink, L. I. M. (2023). Self-guided online treatment of disturbed grief, posttraumatic stress, and depression in adults bereaved during the COVID-19 pandemic: A randomized controlled trial. *Behaviour Research and Therapy*, *163*, 104286. https://doi.org/10.1016/j.brat.2023.104286

Robinson, C., & Pond, D. R. (2019). Do online support groups for grief benefit the bereaved? Systematic review of the quantitative and qualitative literature. *Computers in Human Behavior*, *100*, 48–59. https://doi.org/10.1016/j.chb.2019.06.011

Ruwaard, J., Lange, A., Schrieken, B., & Emmelkamp, P. (2011). Efficacy and effectiveness of online cognitive behavioral treatment: A decade of interapy research. *Studies in Health Technology and Informatics*, *167*, 9–14. https://doi.org/10.3233/978-1-60750-766-6-9

Schut, M., & Stroebe, H. (1999). The dual process model of coping with bereavement: Rationale and description. *Death Studies*, *23*(3), 197–224. https://doi.org/10.1080/074811899201046

Sveen, J., Jernelöv, S., Pohlkamp, L., Kreicbergs, U., & Kaldo, V. (2021). Feasibility and preliminary efficacy of guided internet-delivered cognitive behavioral therapy for insomnia after the loss of a child to cancer: Randomized controlled trial. *Internet Interventions*, *25*, 100409.

Sveen, J., Eisma, M. C., Boelen, P. A., Arnberg, F. K., & Eklund, R. (2024). My grief app for prolonged grief in bereaved parents: A randomised waitlist-controlled trial. *Cognitive Behaviour Therapy*, 1–17. https://doi.org/10.1080/16506073.2024.2429068

Taylor, C. B., Graham, A. K., Flatt, R. E., Waldherr, K., & Fitzsimmons-Craft, E. E. (2021). Current state of scientific evidence on Internet-based interventions for the treatment of depression, anxiety, eating disorders and substance abuse: An overview of systematic reviews and meta-analyses. *European Journal of Public Health*, *31*(Suppl 1), i3–i10. https://doi.org/10.1093/eurpub/ckz208

Treml, J., Nagl, M., Linde, K., Kündiger, C., Peterhänsel, C., & Kersting, A. (2021). Efficacy of an Internet-based cognitive-behavioural grief therapy for people bereaved by suicide: A randomized controlled trial. *European Journal of Psychotraumatology*, *12*(1), 1926650. https://doi.org/10.1080/20008198.2021.1926650

Tur, C., Campos, D., Suso-Ribera, C., Kazlauskas, E., Castilla, D., Zaragoza, I., García-Palacios, A., & Quero, S. (2022). An internet-delivered cognitive-behavioral therapy (iCBT) for prolonged grief disorder (PGD) in adults: A multiple-baseline single-case experimental design study. *Internet Interventions*, *29*, 100558. https://doi.org/10.1016/j.invent.2022.100558

Van der Houwen, K., Schut, H., van den Bout, J., Stroebe, M., & Stroebe, W. (2010). The efficacy of a brief internet-based self-help intervention for the bereaved. *Behaviour Research and Therapy*, *48*(5), 359–367. https://doi.org/10.1016/j.brat.2009.12.009

Wagner, B., Grafiadeli, R., Schäfer, T., & Hofmann, L. (2022b). Efficacy of an online-group intervention after suicide bereavement: A randomized controlled trial. *Internet Interventions*, *28*, 100542. https://doi.org/10.1016/j.invent.2022.100542

Wagner, B., Hofmann, L., & Maaß, U. (2022a). A therapist-supported internet-based intervention for bereaved siblings: A randomized controlled trial. *Palliative Medicine*, *36*(10), 1532–1543. https://doi.org/10.1177/02692163221122344

Wagner, B., Knaevelsrud, C., & Maercker, A. (2006). Internet-based cognitive-behavioral therapy for complicated grief: A randomized controlled trial. *Death Studies*, *30*(5), 429–453. https://doi.org/10.1080/07481180600614385

Wagner, B., & Maercker, A. (2007). A 1.5-year follow-up of an internet-based intervention for complicated grief. *Journal of Traumatic Stress*, *20*(4), 625–629. https://doi.org/10.1002/jts.20230

Wagner, B., Rosenberg, N., Hofmann, L., & Maass, U. (2020). Web-based bereavement care: A systematic review and meta-analysis. *Frontiers in Psychiatry*, *11*. https://doi.org/10.3389/fpsyt.2020.00525

Wagner, B., (2013). 17 internet-based bereavement interventions and support. An overview. In M. Stroebe, H. Schut, & J. van den Bout (Eds.), *Complicated grief: Scientific foundations for health care professionals*. Routledge.

Worden, J. W. (2018). *Grief counseling and grief therapy: A handbook for the mental health practitioner*. Springer Publishing Company.

World Health Organization. (2018). *Digital health: Seventy-first World Health Assembly*. https://iris.who.int/bitstream/handle/10665/279505/A71_R7-en.pdf?sequence=1

Zuelke, A. E., Luppa, M., Löbner, M., Pabst, A., Schlapke, C., Stein, J., & Riedel-Heller, S. G. (2021). Effectiveness and feasibility of internet-based interventions for grief after bereavement: Systematic review and meta-analysis. *JMIR Mental Health*, *8*(12), e29661. https://doi.org/10.2196/29661

Chapter 10

Pharmacotherapy in prolonged and traumatic grief

Charles Tesnières, Geert E. Smid, and Eric Bui

Responses to bereavement (i.e., the death of a loved one), are highly individualized and range on a spectrum from normal and adaptive, to pathological and maladaptive. Although most individuals will adapt in the months following the death, some will fail to adapt, and go on experiencing prolonged, enduring symptoms. This distressing and impairing psychiatric condition resulting from the death of a loved one has been recently included in the 11th edition of the WHO International Classification of Diseases and in the Text Revision of the Fifth Edition Diagnostic and Statistical Manual (American Psychiatric Association, 2022) as prolonged grief disorder (PGD). While psychotherapeutic treatments for PGD no longer have to prove their efficacy (Bryant et al., 2024; Komischke-Konnerup et al., 2024; Rosner et al., 2025; Simon & Shear, 2024; Shear et al., 2016), they may take some time to achieve symptom relief, require a great deal of health care resources, and can only be widely disseminated through training and supervision. Further more, PGD is often comorbid with other psychiatric conditions that may contribute to maintaining it over time. Thus, targeting such conditions with pharmacotherapy that can be prescribed by primary care physicians, might play a role in the management of PGD, by successfully targeting related and comorbid conditions. The present chapter will review the existing literature on the pharmacotherapy of PGD and other bereavement-related conditions, as well as current research perspectives.

Pharmacotherapy of prolonged grief disorder

The specific diagnostic criteria sets for PGD have only been formalized recently (i.e., 2018 in ICD-11 and 2022 in DSM-5TR), and the vast majority of available research had thus not relied on those. In fact, prior research has either focused on complicated grief, or traumatic grief or former definitions of prolonged grief (Prigerson et al., 2009) that have diagnostic criteria sets differing from PGD, or on bereavement-related

DOI: 10.4324/9781003429777-13

depression, also conceptualized at the time as a loss-related condition. For this section, we will use the term PGD, assuming that these terms (PGD, complicated grief, traumatic grief, bereavement-related depression) are basically referring to a single phenomenon of maladaptive prolonged grieving. For the sake of accuracy and to help interpret data, specific measures of grief symptom severity are reported each time.

Limited data, mostly uncontrolled, is available on the efficacy of pharmacotherapy for PGD.

Antidepressants

Studies of the effectiveness of antidepressants in PGD focused on both tricyclic antidepressants and serotonin/noradrenaline reuptake inhibitors.

Tricyclic antidepressants

To date, only two open trials and a small randomized trial have been conducted examining the efficacy of a tricyclic antidepressant (TCA) on PGD. Historically, the first molecule studied in the treatment of pathological reactions to bereavement was a tricyclic antidepressant. Jacobs et al. (1987) studied the efficacy of desipramine on bereavement-related depression, and associated PGD symptoms. Their open trial of 10 patients who had experienced the death of their spouse (80% women, age between 26 and 65) found that, after 4 weeks of desipramine (75 to 150 mg/day, depending on the patient), all patients who showed improvement showed a significant reduction in depressive symptoms. Of the 10 patients, one dropped out due to adverse effects, and 7 patients were rated as responders. However, the efficacy on grief symptoms was more limited, with only three of the participants reporting a significant reduction in grief symptom severity.

Pasternak et al. (1991) studied the effects of nortriptyline on 13 older bereaved spouses (61.5% women), presenting with bereavement-related depression. Patients showed a significant reduction in depressive symptoms (67.9% reduction on the Hamilton Depression Rating Scale), after a mean dose of nortriptyline of 49.2mg/day, over a median period of 6.4 weeks. However, again, the effects on PGD symptom severity were negligible (9.3% on the Texas Revised Inventory of Grief).

Finally, Reynolds et al. (Reynolds et al., 1999) conducted a 18-week randomized trial among n = 80 older adults (72.5% women) with spousal bereavement-related depression, who were randomized to either nortriptyline alone (n = 25), placebo alone (n = 22), nortriptyline plus interpersonal therapy (IPT) (n = 16), or placebo plus interpersonal therapy (n = 17). As in the two previous studies, nortriptyline was not efficacious on PGD symptom severity (Texas Revised Inventory of Grief, Inventory of Complicated Grief). Nortriptyline was found to have a significant effect on bereavement-related depressive symptoms compared to placebo: 69% remission of depression in the nortriptyline + IPT group, 56% in the nortriptyline group, compared with 45% in the placebo group and 29% in the placebo + IPT group. Although IPT was not found to be effective, it was noted that the lowest attrition rate was in the nortriptyline + IPT group.

Serotonin/Noradrenaline reuptake inhibitors

To date, only one case series, three open trials, and one randomized trial of a selective serotonin reuptake inhibitor (SSRI) for PGD have been conducted. A first open-label trial among 15 adults suffering from PGD (mean age = 57 years; 73.3% women) found that paroxetine (30 mg/day) lead to 53% reduction in PGD symptom severity (Inventory of Complicated Grief) and a 54% reduction in depression symptom severity at 16 weeks (Zygmont et al., 1998).

In a case series of four women with PGD (mean age 41.8 years) of whom three also endorsed comorbid posttraumatic stress disorder (PTSD), and two comorbid major depressive disorder (MDD), Simon et al. (Simon et al., 2007) found that 10 week of escitalopram 20 mg/day was associated with a significant mean reduction in PGD symptom severity (Inventory of Complicated Grief from 34.5 [SD = 6.0] to 8.25 [SD = 8.97], $p = 0.001$). In addition, there was a significant reduction in depressive symptoms (Hamilton Depression Rating Scale), with all four participants responding "much improved" on an overall symptom improvement scale. Also, a 16-week open-label trial of flexible dose (10–20 mg/day) escitalopram on 17 adults with PGD (Shear et al., 2006) found a 38% reduction in PGD symptom severity among study completers, and a 24% reduction in the intent-to-treat sample. Further more, a trial of 12-week flexible-dose (10–20 mg/day) escitalopram for bereavement-related MDD failed to show a significant effect of the drug on PGD symptom severity (the Texas Revised Inventory of Grief, and the Inventory of Complicated Grief) among a subgroup of patients with comorbid PGD (N = 14) (Hensley et al., 2009). However, at endpoint, two-thirds of patients were responders for the MDD, and over half were in remission of their MDD at endpoint.

Shear et al. (2016) conducted a large 4-site 20-week randomized controlled trial of citalopram vs. placebo, with or without a bereavement-focused 16-session individual therapy called Prolonged Grief Disorder Therapy (PGDT; formerly Complicated Grief Treatment) for PGD. Adult participants with PGD (n = 395; mean age = 53 years; 78.0% females) were thus randomized to either citalopram alone (median dose = 40mg/day;

n = 101), placebo alone (n = 99), citalopram with PGDT (n = 99) and placebo with PGDT (n = 96). This well-powered study failed to show the efficacy of citalopram vs. placebo on PGD symptoms (measured by the Inventory of Complicated Grief), nor an adjunctive/facilitating effect of citalopram on the PGDT intervention. However, compared to placebo, citalopram was associated with greater reductions in depressive symptoms when added to PGDT. Further, secondary outcome analyses failed to show the efficacy of citalopram vs. placebo on comorbid PTSD symptoms either with or without the PGDT intervention (Na et al., 2021).

In a 8-week open trial of flexible dose (50 to 300 mg/day) extended-release bupropion, a selective inhibitor of catecholamines (noradrenaline and dopamine) among 22 spousal bereaved adults (mean age = 63.5 years, 77.3% women) Zisook et al. (2001) reported a large effect on depressive symptoms (59% responders and 54% reduction in depressive symptom severity) and a much smaller effect on PGD symptoms (5% on the Texas Revised Inventory of Grief, and 18% on the Inventory of Complicated Grief).

There are currently no published studies on serotonin and noradrenalin reuptake inhibitors (SNRIs). However, one study (Cymbalta for Depression as a Complication of Bereavement, ClinicalTrials.gov ID NCT00658931) reported as starting in 2008, currently unpublished, is investigating the efficacy of the SNRI duloxetine on depression associated with bereavement (17-item Hamilton Rating Scale for Depression (HRSD-17)), as well as the PGD (after eight weeks of treatment compared to baseline).

Taken together, these empirical data available suggest that antidepressant medications, across classes (e.g., TCAs, SSRIs), may be efficacious to treat comorbid depressive symptoms in individuals with PGD, but not the core symptoms of PGD.

Benzodiazepines

Benzodiazepines have been studied (Warner et al., 2001) in a single randomized controlled trial, that failed to demonstrate the efficacy of diazepam in the immediate aftermath of the loss of a loved one, on symptomatology over the following 6 months, and therefore on the onset of PGD. The methodology of the study consisted in studying the effect on grief symptoms using the Bereavement Phenomenology Questionnaire (BPQ) by comparing two groups of randomized patients presenting the loss of a spouse or partner 2 weeks before: a diazepam group (n = 14, 20 tablets of 2 mg diazepam to be taken over 6 weeks, maximum 3 times a day) and a placebo group (n = 16). There was no evidence of a clinically significant positive or negative effect of benzodiazepines on the course of bereavement.

Recommendations for the pharmacological management of PGD

To date, no practice guidelines for the pharmacological management of PGD with or without MDD and/or PTSD are available. Based on the available literature, we propose here a few recommendations, depending on the timeframe since the loss.

Pharmacotherapy in the first months post loss

Given the frequent anxiety and associated symptoms such as insomnia, this phase may be associated with, or even correspond to, the diagnostic criteria for acute stress disorder (ASD). But these symptoms are not specific. There is an overlap with the symptoms of acute grief like insomnia, concentration problems (Simon et al., 2020).

Although prescription trends have recently changed worldwide, clinicians still frequently prescribe benzodiazepines to the elderly, including for anxiety (Gerlach et al., 2018). However, the only study carried out on this subject did not identify any indications in the immediate aftermath of death. Taken together with the fact that benzodiazepines are not recommended in the immediate aftermath of trauma exposure, these data suggest that great caution should be exercised when prescribing them after a loss (Cook et al., 2007). Other anxiolytic compounds, including buspirone or hydroxyzine, that have not been found to impair extinction learning, and that are less addictive, might therefore be considered.

Since the introduction of DSM-5, there is no longer a bereavement exclusion for depression, and for patients diagnosed with MDD during the first weeks following bereavement, pharmacological treatments may be warranted. These treatment options are outlined below.

Pharmacological management of pathological reactions in the first 6–12 months post-loss

In the sub-acute phase, during the timeframe that does not qualify for PGD (i.e., within 6 months for ICD-11, 12 months for DSM-5-TR after the loss) patients may meet diagnostic criteria for PTSD, MDD, and/or simply an adjustment disorder.

Specific pharmacological recommendations exist for both PTSD and MDD (Table 10.1). To date, there is no evidence that bereavement-related PTSD or MDD respond differently to these agents than their non-bereavement-related counterparts. Thus, these conditions when precipitated by bereavement should be treated pharmacologically according to the official drug labels.

If the patient presents with PTSD and/or MDD in the first weeks or months after the death, it would be important to successfully address them, both to alleviate the associated distress, as well as potentially help

Table 10.1 Pharmacological recommendations for the treatment of PTSD and MDD (daily dose)

Antidepressant		*PTSD*		*MDD*	
SSRIS	Sertraline	FDA/EMA	25–200 mg	FDA/EMA	50–200 mg
	Paroxetine	FDA/EMA	20–50 mg	FDA/EMA	20–50 mg
	Citalopram			FDA/EMA	20–40 mg
	Escitalopram			FDA/EMA	10–20 mg
	Fluoxetine	EB	20–60 mg	FDA/EMA	20–80 mg
	Fluvoxamine			EMA	100–300 mg
SNRIs	Venlafaxine	EB	75–300 mg	FDA/EMA	75–375 mg
	Desvenlafaxine			FDA	50 mg
	Duloxetine			FDA/EMA	40–120 mg
	Milnacipran			FDA/EMA	100–200 mg
	Levomilnacipran			FDA	40–120 mg
NASSAs	Mianserine			EMA	30–90 mg
	Mirtazapine			FDA/EMA	15–45 mg
Tricyclic	Imipramine			FDA/EMA	75–200 mg (300 mg if hospitalized)
	Clomipramine			FDA/EMA	100–250 mg
Others	Bupropion			FDA/EMA	150–300 mg

Note: FDA = US Food and Drug Administration; EMA = European Medicines Agency; EB = evidence-based (at least two large randomized controlled trials); SSRIs = Selective serotonin reuptake inhibitor; SNRIs = Serotonin and norepinephrine reuptake inhibitors; NaSSAs = Noradrenergic and specific serotonergic antidepressants; NRD = No recommended doses.

the patients to cope more easily with their grief. In fact, some patients have described the reduction of depressive symptoms (Zisook et al., 2001), as a facilitator in their grieving process, reducing their avoidance of anxiety-provoking situations.

Here again, it may be helpful to stay away from benzodiazepines that may initially alleviate the anxiety but that can serve as an avoidance mechanism preventing successful cognitive and emotional adaptation to the loss.

Pharmacological management of PGD (more than 6–12 months post loss)

In the absence of evidence-based pharmacological treatment for the core symptoms of PGD, addressing comorbid conditions here again is warranted. The first-line treatment of PGD should rely mainly on evidence-based grief-focused psychotherapies (Bryant et al., 2024; Komischke-Konnerup et al., 2024; Rosner et al., 2025; Simon & Shear, 2024). However, a body of research has confirmed that the patient often meets diagnostic criteria for comorbid conditions such as MDD (Sung et al., 2011), PTSD (e.g., Djelantik et al., 2020), or an anxiety disorder (Komischke-Konnerup et al., 2021; Marques et al., 2013). Although these comorbid conditions may be targeted by psychotherapy, they may also interfere with successful psychotherapy sometimes and/or require urgent pharmacological treatment. In such cases, pharmacological management may be applied either sequentially – i.e., prior to initiating psychotherapy – or in parallel to psychotherapy. In practice, because of the lack of trained therapists in the community, the health care system, or the cost of psychotherapy; patients with PGD and a comorbid condition often receive first-line pharmacological treatment prior to starting therapy.

Emerging evidence suggests that antidepressants may be efficacious in treating comorbid MDD among individuals with PGD (Shear et al., 2016); however, this is not the case for comorbid PTSD, though the data are more scarce. The choice of treatment and dosage should therefore be guided by the patient, his or her history, and other drug treatments, which often increase with age. However, given the high rate of anxiety and anxiety disorder comorbidity among those with PGD (Bui et al., 2015; Marques et al., 2013; Robinaugh et al., 2014) general guidelines for prescribing antidepressants for anxiety disorders should be followed including a low initiation dose, and a slow ramp-up.

Future developments

Despite its recent inclusion in international classifications, there are no approved medications the treatment of PGD. However, recent advances in our understanding of the neurobiological pathways involved in PGD suggest potential targets for pharmacological interventions. Here, we are reviewing the available evidence for treatment development efforts.

The reward pathway

A main symptom of PGD is yearning for the deceased, with over 95% of treatment-seeking adults with PGD presenting with this symptom (Bui et al., 2015). In fact, PGD can be conceptualized as a craving disorder, with social attachment described as a trigger for reward pathways similar to those involved in addiction (Insel, 2003; Kakarala et al., 2020). Patients suffering from PGD have thus shown greater activity on functional Magnetic Resonance Imaging (fMRI) in the nucleus accumbens, a brain structure involved in craving, than bereaved subjects without PGD (O'Connor et al., 2008). Further, a relationship has been reported between opioid receptor dysregulation and depression (Jelen et al., 2022).

Opioid receptors regulate mood-related processes including reward, motivation, and social behaviors.

Naltrexone, an opioid receptors antagonist and has been successfully used to treat alcohol addiction, suggesting a potential effect on yearning, a core symptom of PGD. A pilot study (ClinicalTrials.gov NCT04547985) of naltrexone for PGD began in 2021 (Gang et al., 2021), but was halted prematurely in 2023 due to insufficient enrolment; however, a placebo-controlled trial (ClinicalTrials.gov NCT06140420) testing the efficacy of 8 weeks of Naltrexone for PGDR is currently underway (as of July 2024).

Relatedly, the efficacy of dopamine antagonists (antipsychotics) for PGD has not been examined. Antipsychotics, however, have been studied in the context of cravings. To date, data on the effectiveness of antipsychotics in addiction are mixed (Hamilton et al., 2009; Kampman et al., 2007). Furthermore, the often-advanced age of patients suffering from PGD will likely limit their use in real life.

The oxytocin pathway

Oxytocin has been studied for its action on attachment and social interactions, based on the mother-child model. The model of bereavement can be compared to that of attachment disorder: as a disorder of separation and lack of the other. A study reported that individuals with PGD had higher levels of circulating oxytocin compared to bereaved controls and bereaved adults with MDD. According to this study, in PGD, in addition to hyperactivity of the nucleus accumbens, there may be a dysfunctional cerebral oxytocinergic signaling which persists throughout all the phases of bereavement (Bottemanne et al., 2024).

A study (ClinicalTrials.gov NCT04505904) on this subject has been completed but not yet published. A randomized double-blind trial from the University of Arizona is exploring the role of oxytocin in the development of prolonged grief responses. Thirty-nine widowed elderly adults (n = 17 with PGD, n = 22 without PGD) each received one session of intranasal oxytocin and one session of intranasal placebo. After each session, participants' reaction time to visual stimuli was measured in a behavioral task, in order to identify behavioral differences, depending on the type of stimulus, in PGD and to study the interactive effects of PGD, type of stimulus, and oxytocin.

The hypothalamic-pituitary-adrenal (HPA) pathway

Some have proposed that PGD might be a post-loss stress disorder (Simon, 2012). Several human studies point to the involvement of the hypothalamic-pituitary-adrenal (HPA) axis in PGD, by several hormones involved in stress.

Studies on bereavement have demonstrated an early increase in catecholamines and cortisol in the early stages of bereavement, without differing from other stress responses (O'Connor, 2012). In fact, individuals with PGD show a significantly flatter slope over the course of the day than bereaved adults without PGD: lower cortisol levels in the morning (45 minutes after waking), and higher levels in the evening (O'Connor et al., 2012). In addition, the same team identified that participants with high levels of epinephrine before treatment had a significantly higher intensity of grief after treatment (O'Connor et al., 2013), suggesting that dysfunction of this pathway could interfere with the grieving process, and with resistance to grief-focused psychotherapies. Pharmacological targeting of this pathway could therefore prove promising for alleviating the symptoms of PGD.

The pain pathway

Pain is defined by the International Association for the Study of Pain (IASP) as "an unpleasant sensory and emotional experience associated with, or resembling that associated with, actual or potential tissue damage". Emotional pain is therefore an integral part of pain.

Early models of bereavement emphasized the central role of emotional pain (Parkes, 1972). This central role has been confirmed by more recent studies: emotional pain related to the loss of a loved one is a characteristic feature of the grief reaction (Eisenberger, 2011), and a network analysis confirmed the central role of emotional pain in PGD (Robinaugh et al., 2014). Thus, some authors have suggested targeting this pain pathway with analgesics to reduce emotional pain induced by bereavement (DeWall et al., 2010), though this has not been studied to date.

Psychedelics and psychedelic-assisted psychotherapy

Preliminary and emerging evidence suggests a likely future role of psychedelics, such as ketamine, MDMA, psilocybin, LSD, cannabis, and ayahuasca, and psychedelic-assisted psychotherapy in prolonged and traumatic grief. Psychedelics often produce subjective effects, such as transcendence, mystical experiences, and a sense of oneness, that may be uniquely relevant to the existential distress experienced in PGD (Ehrenkranz et al., 2024). Applications in older adults should also be considered, although safety in the presence of somatic comorbidity has yet to be demonstrated in this population (Johnston et al., 2023). The potential effectiveness of ayahuasca was investigated in a naturalistic, uncontrolled study among people seeking help for grief during a retreat in a temple in Peru under the guidance of traditional healers (González et al., 2020). Application of ayahuasca in combination with restorative retelling has been described in a case with PGD (González et al., 2022). However, the ability to draw definitive conclusions from the existing research about the effectiveness of psychedelics and psychedelic-assisted psychotherapy in the treatment of prolonged and traumatic grief is constrained by the small size of study samples and the absence of control conditions (Ehrenkranz et al., 2024).

Conclusions

Scientific data on the specific pharmacological treatment of PGD are currently limited, with grief-focused psychotherapy being the first-line treatment for PGD. However, pharmacological treatment, and more specifically SSRIs or tricyclics, does have a place in the treatment of the psychiatric complications of bereavement, and conditions frequently comorbid with PGD, including PTSD and MDD.

New pharmacological avenues targeting new pharmacological pathways are currently being studied or have yet to be investigated. These could lead to a better understanding of the pathophysiological mechanisms implicated in PGD, and therefore to improved pharmacological action.

References

American Psychiatric Association (2022). *Diagnostic and Statistical Manual of Mental Disorders, Fifth Edition, Text Revision (DSM-5-TR)*. APA. https://doi.org/10.1176/appi.books.9780890425787

Bottemanne, H., English, I., Bottemanne, L., Torres, P., Beauquier, B., & Joly, L. (2024). From love to pain: Is oxytocin the key to grief complications? *L'Encéphale*, *50*(1), 85–90.

Bryant, R. A., Azevedo, S., Yadav, S., Cahill, C., Kenny, L., Maccallum, F., Tran, J., Choi-Christou, J., Rawson, N., Tockar, J., Garber, B., Keyan, D., & Dawson, K. S. (2024). Cognitive behavior therapy vs mindfulness in treatment of prolonged grief disorder: A randomized clinical trial. *JAMA Psychiatry*, *81*(7), 646–654. https://doi.org/10.1001/jamapsychiatry.2024.0432

Bui, E., Horenstein, A., Shah, R., Skritskaya, N. A., Mauro, C. M., Wang, Y., Duan, N., Reynolds, C. F., Zisook, S., Shear, M. K., & Simon, N. M. (2015). Grief-related panic symptoms in complicated grief. *Journal of Affective Disorders*, *170*, 213–216. https://doi.org/10.1016/j.jad.2014.08.028

Bui, E., Mauro, C. M., Robinaugh, D. J., Skritskaya, N. A., Wang, Y., Gribbin, C., Ghesquiere, A., Horenstein, A., Duan, N., Reynolds, C. F., Zisook, S., Simon, N. M., & Shear, M. K. (2015). The structured clinical interview for complicated grief: Reliability, validity, and exploratory factor analysis. *Depression and Anxiety*, *32*(7), 485–492. https://doi.org/10.1002/da.22385

Cook, J. M., Biyanova, T., & Marshall, R. (2007). Medicating grief with benzodiazepines: Physician and patient perspectives. *Archives of Internal Medicine*, *167*(18), 2006. https://doi.org/10.1001/archinte.167.18.2006

DeWall, C. N., MacDonald, G., Webster, G. D., Masten, C. L., Baumeister, R. F., Powell, C., Combs, D., Schurtz, D. R., Stillman, T. F., Tice, D. M., & Eisenberger, N. I. (2010). Acetaminophen reduces social pain: Behavioral and neural evidence. *Psychological Science*, *21*(7), 931–937. https://doi.org/10.1177/0956797610374741

Djelantik, A. A. A. M. J., Robinaugh, D. J., Kleber, R. J., Smid, G. E., & Boelen, P. A. (2020). Symptomatology following loss and trauma: Latent class and network analyses of prolonged grief disorder, posttraumatic stress disorder, and depression in a treatment-seeking trauma-exposed sample. *Depression and Anxiety*, *37*, 26–34. https://doi.org/10.1002/da.22880

Ehrenkranz, R., Agrawal, M., Penberthy, J. K., & Yaden, D. B. (2024). Narrative review of the potential for psychedelics to treat prolonged grief disorder. *International Review of Psychiatry*, 1–12. https://doi.org/10.1080/09540261.2024.2357668

Eisenberger, N. I. (2011). The neural basis of social pain: Findings and implications. In G. MacDonald & L. A. Jensen-Campbell (Eds.), *Social pain: Neuropsychological and health implications of loss and exclusion* (pp. 53–78). American Psychological Association. https://doi.org/10.1037/12351-002

Gang, J., Kocsis, J., Avery, J., Maciejewski, P. K., & Prigerson, H. G. (2021). Naltrexone treatment for prolonged grief disorder: Study protocol for a randomized, triple-blinded, placebo-controlled trial. *Trials*, *22*(1), 110. https://doi.org/10.1186/s13063-021-05044-8

Gerlach, L. B., Wiechers, I. R., & Maust, D. T. (2018). Prescription benzodiazepine use among older adults: A critical review. *Harvard Review of Psychiatry*, *26*(5), 264–273. https://doi.org/10.1097/HRP.0000000000000190

González, D., Aixalà, M. B., Neimeyer, R. A., Cantillo, J., Nicolson, D., & Farré, M. (2022). Restorative retelling for processing psychedelic experiences: Rationale and case study of complicated grief. *Frontiers in Psychology*, *13*, 832879. https://doi.org/10.3389/fpsyg.2022.832879

González, D., Cantillo, J., Pérez, I., Farré, M., Feilding, A., Obiols, J. E., & Bouso, J. C. (2020). Therapeutic potential of ayahuasca in grief: A prospective, observational study. *Psychopharmacology*, *237*(4), 1171–1182. https://doi.org/10.1007/s00213-019-05446-2

Hamilton, J. D., Nguyen, Q. X., Gerber, R. M., & Rubio, N. B. (2009). Olanzapine in cocaine dependence: A double-blind, placebo-controlled trial. *The American Journal on Addictions*, *18*(1), 48–52. https://doi.org/10.1080/10550490802544318

Hensley, P. L., Slonimski, C. K., Uhlenhuth, E. H., & Clayton, P. J. (2009). Escitalopram: An open-label study of bereavement-related depression and grief. *Journal of Affective Disorders*, *113*(1–2), 142–149. https://doi.org/10.1016/j.jad.2008.05.016

Insel, T. R. (2003). Is social attachment an addictive disorder? *Physiology & Behavior*, *79*(3), 351–357. https://doi.org/10.1016/S0031-9384(03)00148-3

Jacobs, S. C., Nelson, J. C., & Zisook, S. (1987). Treating depressions of bereavement with antidepressants. A pilot study. *Psychiatric Clinics of North America*, *10*(3), 501–510.

Jelen, L. A., Stone, J. M., Young, A. H., & Mehta, M. A. (2022). The opioid system in depression. *Neuroscience & Biobehavioral Reviews*, *140*. https://doi.org/10.1016/j.neubiorev.2022.104800

Johnston, C. B., Mangini, M., Grob, C., & Anderson, B. (2023). The safety and efficacy of psychedelic-assisted therapies for older adults: Knowns and unknowns.

The American Journal of Geriatric Psychiatry, *31*(1), 44–53. https://doi.org/10.1016/j.jagp.2022.08.007

Kakarala, S. E., Roberts, K. E., Rogers, M., Coats, T., Falzarano, F., Gang, J., Chilov, M., Avery, J., Maciejewski, P. K., Lichtenthal, W. G., & Prigerson, H. G. (2020). The neurobiological reward system in prolonged grief disorder (PGD): A systematic review. *Psychiatry Research: Neuroimaging*, *303*, 111135. https://doi.org/10.1016/j.pscychresns.2020.111135

Kampman, K. M., Pettinati, H. M., Lynch, K. G., Whittingham, T., Macfadden, W., Dackis, C., Tirado, C., Oslin, D. W., Sparkman, T., & O'Brien, C. P. (2007). A double-blind, placebo-controlled pilot trial of quetiapine for the treatment of Type A and Type B alcoholism. *Journal of Clinical Psychopharmacology*, *27*(4), 344–351. https://doi.org/10.1097/JCP.0b013e3180ca86e5

Komischke-Konnerup, K. B., Zachariae, R., Boelen, P. A., Marello, M. M., & O'Connor, M. (2024). Grief-focused cognitive behavioral therapies for prolonged grief symptoms: A systematic review and meta-analysis. *Journal of Consulting and Clinical Psychology*, *92*(4), 236–248. https://doi.org/10.1037/ccp0000884

Komischke-Konnerup, K. B., Zachariae, R., Johannsen, M., Nielsen, L. D., & O'Connor, M. (2021). Co-occurrence of prolonged grief symptoms and symptoms of depression, anxiety, and posttraumatic stress in bereaved adults: A systematic review and meta-analysis. *Journal of Affective Disorders Reports*, *4*, 100140. https://doi.org/10.1016/j.jadr.2021.100140

Marques, L., Bui, E., LeBlanc, N., Porter, E., Robinaugh, D. J., Dryman, M. T., Nadal-Vicens, M., Worthington, J., & Simon, N. M. (2013). Complicated grief symptoms in anxiety disorders: Prevalence and associated impairment. *Depression and Anxiety*, *30*(12), 1211–1216. https://doi.org/10.1002/da.22093

Na, P. J., Adhikari, S., Szuhany, K. L., Chen, A. Z., Suzuki, R. R., Malgaroli, M., Robinaugh, D. J., Bui, E., Mauro, C. M., Skritskaya, N. A., Lebowitz, B. D., Zisook, S., Reynolds, C. F. 3rd, Shear, M. K., & Simon, N. M. (2021). Posttraumatic distress symptoms and their response to treatment in adults with prolonged grief disorder. *The Journal of Clinical Psychiatry*, *82*(3). https://doi.org/10.4088/JCP.20m13576

O'Connor, M.-F. (2012). Immunological and neuroimaging biomarkers of complicated grief. *Dialogues in Clinical Neuroscience*, *14*(2), 141–148. https://doi.org/10.31887/DCNS.2012.14.2/mfoconnor

O'Connor, M.-F., Shear, M. K., Fox, R., Skritskaya, N. A., Campbell, B., Ghesquiere, A., & Glickman, K. (2013). Catecholamine predictors of complicated grief treatment outcomes. *International Journal of Psychophysiology*, *88*(3), 349–352. https://doi.org/10.1016/j.ijpsycho.2012.09.014

O'Connor, M.-F., Wellisch, D. K., Stanton, A. L., Eisenberger, N. I., Irwin, M. R., & Lieberman, M. D. (2008). Craving love? Enduring grief activates brain's reward center. *NeuroImage*, *42*(2), 969–972. https://doi.org/10.1016/j.neuroimage.2008.04.256

O'Connor, M.-F., Wellisch, D. K., Stanton, A. L., Olmstead, R., & Irwin, M. R. (2012). Diurnal cortisol in complicated and non-complicated grief: Slope differences across the day. *Psychoneuroendocrinology*, *37*(5), 725–728. https://doi.org/10.1016/j.psyneuen.2011.08.009

Parkes, C. (1972). *Bereavement : Studies of grief in later life*. International Universities Press.

Pasternak, R. E., Reynolds 3rd, C. F., Schlernitzauer, M., Hoch, C. C., Buysse, D. J., Houck, P. R., & Perel, J. M. (1991). Acute open-trial nortriptyline therapy of bereavement-related depression in late life. *The Journal of Clinical Psychiatry*, *52*(7), 307–310.

Prigerson, H. G., Horowitz, M. J., Jacobs, S. C., Parkes, C. M., Aslan, M., Goodkin, K., Raphael, B., Marwit, S. J., Wortman, C., Neimeyer, R. A., Bonanno, G., Block, S. D., Kissane, D., Boelen, P., Maercker, A., Litz, B. T., Johnson, J. G., First, M. B., & Maciejewski, P. K. (2009). Prolonged grief disorder: Psychometric validation of criteria proposed for DSM-V and ICD-11. *PLoS Medicine*, *6*(8), e1000121. https://doi.org/10.1371/journal.pmed.1000121

Reynolds, C. F., Frank, E., & Mazumdar, S. (1999). Treatment of bereavement-related major depressive episodes in later life: A controlled study of acute and continuation treatment with nortriptyline and interpersonal psychotherapy. *The American Journal of Psychiatry*, *156*(2), 202–208.

Robinaugh, D. J., LeBlanc, N. J., Vuletich, H. A., & McNally, R. J. (2014). Network analysis of persistent complex bereavement disorder in conjugally bereaved adults. *Journal of Abnormal Psychology*, *123*(3), 510–522. https://doi.org/10.1037/abn0000002

Robinaugh, D. J., McNally, R. J., LeBlanc, N. J., Pentel, K. Z., Schwarz, N. R., Shah, R. M., Nadal-Vicens, M. F., Moore, C. W., Marques, L., Bui, E., & Simon, N. M. (2014). Anxiety sensitivity in bereaved adults with and without complicated grief. *Journal of Nervous & Mental Disease*, *202*(8), 620–622. https://doi.org/10.1097/NMD.0000000000000171

Rosner, R., Rau, J., Kersting, A., Rief, W., Steil, R., Rummel, A.-M., Vogel, A., & Comtesse, H. (2025). Grief-specific cognitive behavioral therapy vs present-centered therapy: A randomized clinical trial. *JAMA Psychiatry*, *82*(2), 109–117. https://doi.org/10.1001/jamapsychiatry.2024.3409

Shear, M. K., Fagiolini, A., & Houck, P. (2006). Escitalopram for complicated grief: A pilot study. *NCDEU 46th Annual Meeting Abstracts*, Boca Raton.

Shear, M. K., Reynolds, C. F., Simon, N. M., Zisook, S., Wang, Y., Mauro, C. M., Duan, N., Lebowitz, B. D., & Skritskaya, N. A. (2016). Optimizing treatment of complicated grief: A randomized clinical trial. *JAMA Psychiatry*, *73*(7), 685. https://doi.org/10.1001/jamapsychiatry.2016.0892

Simon, N. M. (2012). Is complicated grief a post-loss stress disorder? *Depression and Anxiety*, *29*(7), 541–544. https://doi.org/10.1002/da.21979

Simon, N. M., & Shear, M. K. (2024). Prolonged grief disorder. *New England Journal of Medicine*, *391*(13), 1227–1236. https://doi.org/10.1056/NEJMcp2308707

Simon, N. M., Shear, M. K., Reynolds, C. F., Cozza, S. J., Mauro, C., Zisook, S., Skritskaya, N., Robinaugh, D. J., Malgaroli, M., Spandorfer, J., & Lebowitz, B. (2020). Commentary on evidence in support of a grief-related condition as a DSM diagnosis. *Depression and Anxiety*, *37*(1), 9–16. https://doi.org/10.1002/da.22985

Simon, N. M., Thompson, E. H., Pollack, M. H., & Shear, M. K. (2007). Complicated grief : A case series using escitalopram. *American Journal of Psychiatry*, *164*(11), 1760–1761. https://doi.org/10.1176/appi.ajp.2007.07050800

Sung, S. C., Dryman, M. T., Marks, E., Shear, M. K., Ghesquiere, A., Fava, M., & Simon, N. M. (2011). Complicated grief among individuals with major depression : Prevalence, comorbidity, and associated features. *Journal of Affective Disorders*, *134*(1–3), 453–458. https://doi.org/10.1016/j.jad.2011.05.017

Warner, J., Metcalfe, C., & King, M. (2001). Evaluating the use of benzodiazepines following recent bereavement. *British Journal of Psychiatry*, *178*(1), 36–41. https://doi.org/10.1192/bjp.178.1.36

Zisook, S., Shuchter, S. R., Pedrelli, P., Sable, J., & Deaciuc, S. C. (2001). Bupropion sustained release for bereavement: Results of an open trial. *The Journal of Clinical Psychiatry*, *62*(4), 227–230. https://doi.org/10.4088/jcp.v62n0403

Zygmont, M., Prigerson, H. G., Houck, P. R., Miller, M. D., Shear, M. K., Jacobs, S., & Reynolds, C. F. (1998). A post hoc comparison of paroxetine and nortriptyline for symptoms of traumatic grief. *The Journal of Clinical Psychiatry*, *59*(5), 241–245. https://doi.org/10.4088/jcp.v59n0507

Part III

Special Populations

Chapter 11

Ambiguous loss

Assessment and intervention after the disappearance of a loved one

Hannah Comtesse and Geert E. Smid

An ambiguous loss occurs when there is uncertainty about the fate and the whereabouts of a loved one or when a loved one no longer behaves and acts like the familiar person. Thus, there are two types of ambiguous loss (Boss, 2004): When a person is physically absent but is kept psychologically present, and when a person is physically present but seems mentally absent. Both types are often characterized by persistent ambiguity and problems in the grief process for the affected family members and friends (Boss, 2016).

A common example of ambiguous loss due to psychological absence occurs when a loved one has advanced dementia and the familiar personality is no longer present due to the progressive illness. Other causes of this type of ambiguous loss are long-standing coma, severe brain injury, and chronic mental illness such as addiction.

Ambiguous loss due to physical absence can occur when people disappear. People often go missing in the context of natural disasters (e.g., tsunamis), mass trauma events such as terrorist attacks, armed conflicts, displacement (Boss, 2016), or forced disappearance, meaning the forced abductions by state agents or by persons or groups of persons acting with the authorization, support or acquiescence of the State (United Nations, 2007).

Multilevel effects of ambiguous loss

The theory of ambiguous loss (Boss, 2004, 2016) emphases the impacts not only on the individual, but also on the family system and community. An ambiguous loss leads to the perception of boundary ambiguity, meaning not knowing who is a member of a particular system. High boundary ambiguity is supposed to compromise coping capacities and, on the individual level, reduce processing capabilities, evoke negative feelings, and thus increase the risk for poor mental health outcomes, including problematic grief reactions. On the systemic level, family conflicts are likely to result as there may be an incongruence of perceptions of family membership and role confusion. In case of low boundary ambiguity, systemic boundaries

DOI: 10.4324/9781003429777-15

are perceived as clear. Cultural, historical, socioeconomic, or psychosocial context variables can influence the perception of boundaries and available coping resources. In addition, ambiguous loss is supposed to be the most stressful type of loss because it makes closure impossible. The focus of the next paragraphs will be on a specific type of ambiguous loss due to physical absence, namely disappearances. In this context, associations of specific factors proposed by the theory of ambiguous loss with mental health outcomes will be described.

Occurrence of disappearances

Tens of thousands of people go missing worldwide every year (International Commission on Missing Persons, 2023). Although this occurs particularly frequently in countries affected by armed conflicts (International Commission on Missing Persons, 2023), people also go missing in countries not affected by conflict or large-scale disasters, but the numbers of disappearances are supposed to be comparatively lower (Lenferink et al., 2019). Yet for every disappeared person, it has been estimated that up to 12 other people are affected by the loss (Henderson & Henderson, 1998). For example, about 100,000 persons have been estimated to be missing due to the conflict in Syria (Syrian Network for Human Rights, 2020). The fall of the Syrian dictatorship and the opening of prisons in December 2024 have made visible the immense and long-lasting pain and desperate search activities of the relatives of missing persons for clues to the fate of their loved ones for a global audience (Lennon, 2025). Yet, reliable statistics on the exact number of long-term missing persons are scarce. In the United States, for example, more than 600,000 persons are reported missing every year (National Crime Information Center, 2022). The vast majority of persons is located in a short time, but a significant minority of persons remain missing (e.g., about 24,000 persons in the United States in 2023; National Institute of Justice, 2024). Refugees are a particularly vulnerable group to be affected by the disappearance of a loved one. In Australia, for example, 19% of a representative sample of refugees stated the disappearance or violent death of at least one family member (Bryant et al., 2020). Explicitly referring to disappeared persons only, 33% of a sample of asylum seekers living in collective accommodations in Germany (Comtesse & Rosner, 2019) reported at least one missing loved one. Other contexts with likely high numbers of missing persons are ongoing conflicts. In Ukraine, 28,000 persons have been registered as missing by the end of 2023 (International Commission of Missing Persons, 2024). This means that for clinicians who are working with patients who have reported a disappearance as a traumatic event or with refugees or conflict-affected patients that they should ask about missing loved ones and the associated reactions (see Box 11.1).

Box 11.1 Questions for exploring about a disappeared person

- Is a loved person missing? Who is the person?
- When did the person disappear? Under which circumstances?
- Do you often think about the person and his/her whereabouts?
- Are you searching for him/her?
- How are you dealing with the uncertainty of not knowing?

Prolonged and traumatic grief in persons with a disappeared loved one

Persons with a disappeared loved one can develop problems adjusting to the loss that is complicated by the persistent uncertainty about the fate of the disappeared person. The rates of different psychological symptoms and mental disorders are high in persons with a disappeared loved one. Reviews have reported elevated symptoms of anxiety, depression, posttraumatic stress disorder (PTSD), and prolonged grief disorder (PGD) for relatives of missing persons, across different types of disappearances (e.g., forced, leaving without goodbye) and also in comparison to bereaved persons (Kennedy et al., 2019; Lenferink et al., 2019b). The rates of these symptoms found in refugees with disappeared loved ones seem to exceed even those found in conflict-affected and other samples with ambiguous loss (Comtesse et al., 2022; Renner et al., 2021; see also Chapter 15). Studies have identified several factors that are related to high rates of mental health problems, in particular an intolerance for uncertainty (Kennedy et al., 2021b) and moderate levels of hope for return (Heeke et al., 2015). Also, a higher prevalence is more likely in parents or partners of the missing person and those with a high exposure to other traumatic events (Lenferink et al., 2019b). Especially with regard to grief, affected persons with elevated prolonged grief symptoms are more likely to engage in counterfactual thinking (e.g., imaging how things could have been better; Kennedy et al., 2021a), catastrophizing of one's own reactions (Lenferink et al., 2018), ruminating about the loss and its consequences, and withdrawal from activities and other people (Lenferink et al., 2018).

With regard to the assumption that ambiguous loss is the most stressful loss, thus even more stressful than bereavement (Boss, 2004, 2016), there is no evidence for consistent differences in psychopathology between persons with disappeared or deceased loved ones (Lenferink et al., 2019b). For example, a study with relatives of missing persons in the Netherlands found lower PGD levels compared to homicidally bereaved persons (Lenferink et al., 2017). First evidence suggests that psychological symptoms related to a disappearance may also be present in persons not personally acquainted with a missing person in the context of highly publicized mass trauma events (e.g., terror attack, natural disaster). A study in the general public in Israel examined reactions to hostage-taking in the context of a terror attack in late 2023 (Yehene et al., 2024). It showed that levels of separation distress related to a disappeared person did not differ between persons who were familiar with a hostage and those who were not. This means that different types of loss can lead to difficulties in adjusting to the new reality without the person and impairing grief reactions. However, it should be noted that the available studies are mostly of rather small sample sizes and often lack appropriate control groups, indicating the need for more research on the specific mental health consequences of disappearances.

Beyond the mental health impact, the disappearance of a loved one can also evoke specific emotional responses and facilitate certain coping strategies in the affected persons. A review of psychological responses to a disappearance showed that persons with a disappeared loved one often experience negative feelings that seem to be related to the circumstances of the disappearance (Kennedy et al., 2019). For example, anger tends to be directed to the responsible agent (e.g., the government) under forced disappearance but toward the missing person or the authorities in charge for the search under unclear circumstances. The affected persons use a variety of different coping strategies to deal with their loss. Proximity-seeking (e.g., dwelling on pictures or belonging of the disappeared), cognitive avoidance (e.g., denial of the possible death), and seeking mental health support have been identified as particularly frequent strategies (Kennedy et al., 2019). Seeking support from people with a shared experience (e.g., abductions) in the form of support groups or activism is also a prominent strategy (Kennedy et al., 2019). In addition, many affected persons see the loss as a legal problem and thus seek help from humanitarian networks or legal counselling and engage in extensive search activities (Smid et al., 2020). The perceived stigma of receiving mental health care for the loss is a barrier to help-seeking (Smid et al., 2020). The strategies often used by persons with a missing loved one underscore the importance of a sensitive way in talking about the disappearance, and accounting for the specific context of the disappearance. Box 11.2 summarizes recommendations for working with these patients.

Assessment of specific mental health and other psychological consequences of the disappearance of a loved one

In research and practice, we need valid instruments to assess the specific psychological effects of disappearances. This is particularly important as many possible consequences of increased distress are intertwined with

Box 11.2 Recommendations for working with patients with a disappeared loved one

- Explore and reflect on expectations about and fears of seeking professional help
- Validate and normalize negative feelings and coping strategies
- Respect ongoing search activities and the hope for return and/or survival
- Provide recommendations for humanitarian and/or legal support
- Assist in prioritizing activities that need to be undertaken (self-care, family support, searching)
- Prepare to work with multiple losses and traumas
- Prepare to work from a systemic perspective

the specific effects of an ambiguous loss that do not necessarily apply to bereavement (e.g., not being able to perform farewell rituals). For the assessment of psychological symptoms, established measures can be used (e.g., for depressive or anxiety symptoms). These can even be referenced to a disappeared person. For example, PGD symptom measures (see also Chapter 2) have been referenced to a missing instead of deceased person while answering the questions (e.g., Comtesse et al., 2022; Heeke et al., 2015). With regard to specific psychological responses to disappearances, such as preoccupation, distress due to a lack of rituals, or hope for return (Smid et al., 2020), researchers often employ ad hoc questions (e.g., Heeke et al., 2015), interviews (Testoni et al., 2020), or questionnaires for related concepts (e.g., intolerance of uncertainty; Kennedy et al., 2021). In addition, they use specific measures for persons with a disappeared loved one that can be easily employed in practice and are available in different languages.

Boundary Ambiguity Scales

The *Boundary Ambiguity Scales* (BAS; Boss et al., 1990) are the most commonly used instrument (Carroll et al., 2007). The BAS capture the concept of boundary ambiguity in the context of an ambiguous loss based on the theory by Boss (2004, 2016). The concept refers to perceptions of the missing person as part of the family system and the systems' capacities to cope with the unresolved status. High boundary ambiguity, meaning high levels of confusion regarding belonging to and relationships within the system, is supposed to increase the risk for psychological symptoms in individual family members (Boss, 2004, 2016). Strong associations of adapted versions of the BAS with PGD and other psychological symptoms have been shown in treatment-seeking Syrian refugees (Renner et al., 2021) and Israeli citizens after a terror attack (Yehene et al., 2024). There are a number of different scales adapted to the specific type of loss (e.g., families of husbands/fathers missing in action, children after divorce), with the number of items ranging from 9-25, all rated on a 5-point scale (never/strongly disagree to almost always/strongly agree; Boss et al., 1990). As the concept of boundary ambiguity is defined as a perceptional variable, all items refer to the perceptions of the affected persons (e.g., "I continue to keep alive my hope that __ will return home to live", "I feel it will be difficult, if not impossible, to carve out a new life for myself without my husband", "I still feel disturbed about my parents' divorce"). The scales have been validated in research with families, with good psychometric qualities (see Carroll et al., 2007).

Ambiguous Loss Inventory-Plus

The *Ambiguous Loss Inventory-Plus* (ALI+; Comtesse et al., 2023) is an alternative measure that was developed for two reasons. First, several cognitive, emotional, and behavioral reactions to an ambiguous loss beyond boundary ambiguity (Boss, 2004, 2016) have been identified in studies with persons with a disappeared loved (e.g., distress due to a lack of mourning rituals, an urge to help the missing person and engaging search activities; Smid et al., 2021) but were not included in a questionnaire yet. Second, prior research has provided relatively consistent evidence for elevated PGD symptoms in persons with missing loved ones, across different circumstances of the disappearance including forced and voluntary disappearances (e.g., Heeke et al., 2015; Lenferink et al., 2018). Therefore, a direct assessment of the described reactions and symptoms with one instrument appeared efficient. The ALI+ consists of a 17-item scale on grief-like responses (e.g., "longing or yearning for the person who disappeared", which was adapted from a validated PGD measure, namely, the Traumatic Grief Inventory-Self Report Plus (Lenferink et al., 2022; see also Chapter 2), and a 15-item scale on general reactions to the disappearance on the basis of the BAS, current literature, and expert consensus (e.g., "distress because of the absence of proper ceremonies or rituals, e.g., funeral", "lack of emotional and/or practical support in dealing with his/her disappearance"). All items are rated on a 5-point scale (not at all to always). The items of the ALI+ showed promising content validity on the basis of feedback from relatives of missing persons and international experts (Comtesse et al., 2023). However, the instrument has not yet undergone a proper psychometric evaluation. Different language versions of the ALI+ are freely available (https://osf.io/ydj7w/).

Interventions for persons with a disappeared loved one

The situation after the disappearance of a loved one differs from other loss events as there is no possibility for closure. Yet, there is a new reality without the missing person to which their loved one has to adapt, including to update working models that include internalized attachment relationships (see Chapter 4). In addition, affected persons often see the disappearance and their associated reactions as a legal rather than a mental health problem, which may become salient in expectations about therapy. These key aspects need to be considered when providing psychotherapy for persons with a disappeared loved one.

Systemic interventions

Focusing on a systemic perspective and work with families with different types of ambiguous loss, Boss (2016) proposed six guidelines for family meetings after ambiguous loss. These are more general strategies, which do not suggest specific techniques and are not proscribed to be included at all or in a specific order. The strategies are (1) finding meaning, (2) adjusting mastery, (3) reconstructing identity, (4) normalizing ambivalence, (5) revising attachment, and (6) discovering new hope. These strategies are currently employed in support groups in conflict and humanitarian contexts, such as Ukraine (Kuryka, 2024), with the goal that those affected can better accept their fate and the uncertainty and develop a new perspective to life.

Cognitive-behavioral therapy approaches

With regard to the individual level, cognitive-behavioral therapy (CBT) interventions with the core elements of cognitive restructuring of dysfunctional beliefs and exposure to the loss or its circumstances should be the first choice for grief-related psychopathology (see also Chapter 6). In the case of bereavement, this is often combined with experiential methods, such as empty-chair work (e.g., talking to the deceased person; see also Chapter 8), to target unfinished business or help to achieve closure and open up for a new life without the deceased person. However, this needs to be adapted to the specificities of an ambiguous loss. Although emotional processing of the loss is intended, closure cannot be achieved. This is illustrated by a qualitative study on support needs of relatives of missing persons in Mexico showing that the perceived pressure for closure may constitute a barrier to psychosocial care despite high needs for mental health support (Smid et al., 2020). On this basis, the three-stage model of interventions for ambiguous loss was derived (Smid et al., 2020). It suggests to focus interventions on (1) psychoeducation on the consequences of a disappearance and effects of uncertainty and mobilization of support by significant others, (2) exposure to memories of the disappearance and the relationship with the missing person and meaning attribution, and (3) future orientation by setting goals and priorities for a life without the person. In addition, strategies to help to cope with the unresolvable ambiguity should be included in any intervention with persons with disappeared loved ones (e.g., Boss, 2004).

Two controlled studies investigated CBT-informed treatments for relatives of disappeared persons (Hagl et al., 2015; Lenferink et al., 2019). In a study with women whose husbands went missing or were killed during the war in Bosnia-Herzegovina, dialogical exposure was investigated (Hagl et al., 2015). This intervention consisted of seven group sessions and was based on empty-chair work, encouraging the women to enter direct dialogues with or talk about their husbands and to express painful feelings and thoughts. It was combined with psychoeducation, strengthening mutual support, practicing relaxation strategies, and reinforcing active coping. A total of 119 women (48% with missing husbands) were quasi-randomized (based on loss type and date of birth) to dialogical exposure or a supportive control condition. The complete analysis showed a superiority of dialogical exposure in terms of improving PGD and PTSD symptoms and general health with small to moderate effect sizes. The effects were maintained at the 1-year follow-up. Only 6% of participants dropped out during treatment, and 34% to follow-up.

Lenferink et al. (2019a) examined CBT enriched by mindfulness in Dutch relatives of missing persons who disappeared in the context of crimes, accidents, or left voluntarily. The 17 relatives had clinically relevant levels of depressive, PGD, and PTSD symptoms and were randomized to either CBT+ Mindfulness (CBT+M) or a waiting list condition. CBT+M consisted of eight sessions that focused on psychoeducation, strengthening social support, exposure-based writing assignments, and mindfulness exercises in order to facilitate tolerance of the ambiguity. The drop-out rate was high (47%). Due to the low number of completers, differences in symptom reduction between the two groups could not be statistically investigated, although CBT+M coincided with changes on measures of psychological symptoms for completers, indicating a potential for effectiveness.

Case description

The disappearance of a loved one is often incremental to traumatic experiences and bereavement in conflict survivors and refugees (e.g., Comtesse et al., 2022; Heeke et al., 2015), thus adding to overall psychopathology (de Heus et al., 2017). Therefore, we employed an add-on intervention for persons with disappeared loved ones undergoing a trauma- or grief-focused treatment at the ARQ National Psychotrauma Centre (Comtesse & Smid, 2021). The intervention, the CBT-based Support for Ambiguous Loss

(CBT-AL; Comtesse & Smid, 2021), is based on the three-stage model (Smid et al., 2020) and aims to increase the tolerance for the ambiguity and pain due to the situation and balance the care for family or daily functioning with search activities. It adapts elements of other interventions (Boss, 2016; Lenferink et al., 2019a) and consists of four 90-min sessions: (1) psychoeducation and social support, (2) exposure, (3) adjusting mastery and behavioral activation, (4) meaning attribution and future orientation. The CBT-AL protocol has been used in practice at the ARQ National Psychotrauma Centre, but has not been evaluated in terms of efficacy. The case description in Box 11.3 illustrates the course of the intervention with a fictitious patient treated at the ARQ National Psychotrauma Centre.

Box 11.3 Case description

The 30-year-old Mazaa is from Western Africa and now lives in Europe. Her 5-year-old son was taken from her while she was in captivity in the context of a war in her home country. She does not know whether he is alive or dead or where he might be now, almost ten years later. She thinks about her son every day, longing for him and feeling powerless but a strong need to find him. She was treated with trauma-focused CBT for over a year. Now she comes to a short add-on intervention to focus on her ambiguous loss. During psychoeducation, she learns that her emotional and behavioral reactions are effects of the ambiguity, which is normal for relatives of missing persons. This makes her curious, but also critical. She is very worried that the inner closeness she feels to her missing son vanishes. On the other hand, she is aware that she has become socially isolated because she spends so much time with thinking of her son and conducting online searches. In the exposure phase, she writes about her long search history and reflects on her feelings of restlessness but also extortion. It becomes clear to her that the function of the online searches is to give her relief. Mazaa also writes about her missing son and the circumstances of the disappearance. With this she could see that she had tried to protect her son but that she was simply not able to do so as she was held captive during the war. She learns a body scan to temper the sense that she has to have control over everything because she often experienced an inability to solve problems and despair. She attributes the meaning that she still experiences herself as a mother who has both feelings of acceptance and hope for her son. She plans to finish her studies in the future. At the end of the intervention, she still experiences distress but is clearly calmer and more optimistic and indicates more acceptance of her loss.

Conclusions

The disappearance of a loved one has often severe psychological consequences for the persons left behind. This loss experience is likely to increase worldwide due to increasing extreme weather events and ongoing wars that can lead to mass disappearances and difficulties in locating the victims. More systematic research on the development and evaluation of specific measures and interventions is urgently needed. This includes research on the effects of disappearance contexts (e.g., forced vs. voluntarily) and other risk factors, further conceptual clarification, possible differences between disappearance and other forms of ambiguous loss (e.g., psychological ambiguous loss such as a chronic illness), collective and cultural aspects, and controlled intervention studies.

References

Boss, P. (2004). Ambiguous loss research, theory, and practice: Reflections after 9/11. *Journal of Marriage and Family*, *66*, 551–566. https://doi.org/10.1111/j.0022-2445.2004.00037.x

Boss, P. (2016). The context and process of theory development: The story of ambiguous loss. *Journal of Family Theory & Review*, *8*, 269–286. https://doi.org/10.1111/jftr.12152

Boss, P., Greenberg, J., & Pearce-McCall, D. (1990). Measurement of boundary ambiguity in families. In: *Station bulletin* (pp. 593–1990). University of Minnesota.

Bryant, R. A., Edwards, B., Creamer, M., O'Donnell, M., Forbes, D., Felmingham, K. L., Silove, D., Steel, Z., McFarlane, A. C., van Hooff, M., Nickerson, A., & Hadzi-Pavlovic, D. (2020). A population study of prolonged grief in refugees. *Epidemiology and Psychiatric Sciences*, *29*, e44. https://doi.org/10.1017/S2045796019000386

Carroll, J. S., Olson, C. D., & Buckmiller, N. (2007). Family boundary ambiguity: A 30-year review of theory, research, and measurement. *Family Relations*, *56*(2), 210–230.

Comtesse, H., Lechner-Meichsner, F., Haneveld, J., Vogel, A., & Rosner, R. (2022). Prolonged grief in refugees living in Germany confronted with ambiguous or confirmed loss. *Anxiety, Stress, & Coping*, *35*(3), 259–269. https://doi.org/10.1080/10615806.2021.1967936

Comtesse, H., & Rosner, R. (2019). Prolonged grief disorder among asylum seekers in Germany: The influence of losses and residence status. *European Journal of Psychotraumatology*, *10*, 1591330. https://doi.org/10.1080/20008198

Comtesse, H., & Smid, G. E. (2021). *Cognitive-behavioral therapy-based support for ambiguous loss (TAL)*. Unpublished manuscript. ARQ National Psychotrauma Centre.

Comtesse, H., Killikelly, C., Hengst, S. M., Lenferink, L. I., de la Rie, S. M., Boelen, P. A., & Smid, G. E. (2023). The Ambiguous Loss Inventory Plus (ALI+): Introduction of a measure of psychological reactions to the disappearance of a loved one. *International Journal of Environmental Research and Public Health*, *20*(6), 5117. https://doi.org/10.3390/ijerph20065117

de Heus, A., Hengst, S. M., de la Rie, S. M., Djelantik, A. M. J., Boelen, P. A., & Smid, G. E. (2017). Day patient treatment for traumatic grief: Preliminary evaluation of a one-year treatment programme for patients with multiple and traumatic losses. *European Journal of Psychotraumatology*, *8*, 1375335. https://doi.org/10.1080/20008198.2017.1375335

Hagl, M., Powell, S., Rosner, R., & Butollo, W. (2015). Dialogical exposure with traumatically bereaved Bosnian women: Findings from a controlled trial. *Clinical Psychology & Psychotherapy*, *22*(6), 604–618. https://doi.org/10.1002/cpp.1921

Heeke, C., Stammel, N., & Knaevelsrud, C. (2015). When hope and grief intersect: Rates and risks of prolonged grief disorder among bereaved individuals and relatives of disappeared persons in Colombia. *Journal of Affective Disorders*, *173*, 59–64. https://doi.org/10.1016/j.jad.2014.10.038

Henderson, M., & Henderson, P. (1998). *Missing people: Issues for the Australian community*. Commonwealth of Australia.

International Commission on Missing Persons (2023). *Global report on missing persons*. ICMP.

International Commission of Missing Persons (2024). *ICMP annual report 2023*. https://icmp.int/?resources=icmp-annual-report-2023

Kennedy, C., Deane, F. P., & Chan, A. Y. (2019). In limbo: A systematic review of psychological responses and coping among people with a missing loved one. *Journal of Clinical Psychology*, *75*(9), 1544–1571. https://doi.org/10.1002/jclp.22799

Kennedy, C., Deane, F. P., & Chan, A. Y. (2021a). "What might have been...": Counterfactual thinking, psychological symptoms and posttraumatic growth when a loved one is missing. *Cognitive Therapy and Research*, *45*, 322–332. https://doi.org/10.1007/s10608-020-10156-7

Kennedy, C., Deane, F. P., & Chan, A. Y. (2021b). Intolerance of uncertainty and psychological symptoms among people with a missing loved one: Emotion regulation difficulties and psychological inflexibility as mediators. *Journal of Contextual Behavioral Science*, *21*, 48–56. https://doi.org/10.1016/j.jcbs.2021.05.006

Kuryka, V. (2024). We had to learn to help each other, not go through pain on repeat. *Network for Border Crossing Journalism*. Published online on January 25, 2025. https://n-ost.org/article/we-had-to-learn-to-help-each-other-not-go-through-pain-on-repeat

Lenferink, L. I., de Keijser, J., Wessel, I., & Boelen, P. A. (2018). Cognitive-behavioral correlates of psychological symptoms among relatives of missing persons. *International Journal of Cognitive Therapy*, *11*, 311–324. https://doi.org/10.1007/s41811-018-0024-y

Lenferink, L. I., de Keijser, J., Wessel, I., & Boelen, P. A. (2019a). Cognitive behavioural therapy and mindfulness for relatives of missing persons: A pilot study. *Pilot and Feasibility Studies*, *5*(1), 17. https://doi.org/10.1186/s40814-019-0472-z

Lenferink, L. I., de Keijser, J., Wessel, I., de Vries, D., & Boelen, P. A. (2019b). Toward a better understanding of psychological symptoms in people confronted with the disappearance of a loved one: A systematic review. *Trauma, Violence, & Abuse*, *20*(3), 287–302. https://doi.org/10.1177/1524838017699602

Lenferink, L. I., Wessel, I., & Boelen, P. A. (2018). Exploration of the associations between responses to affective states and psychopathology in two samples of people confronted with the loss of a loved one. *The Journal of Nervous and Mental Disease*, *206*(2), 108–115.

Lenferink, L. I. M., Eisma, M. C., Smid, G. E., de Keijser, J., & Boelen, P. A. (2022). Valid measurement of DSM-5 persistent complex bereavement disorder and DSM-5-TR and ICD-11 prolonged grief disorder: The Traumatic Grief Inventory-Self Report Plus (TGI-SR+). *Comprehensive Psychiatry*, *112*, 152281. https://doi.org/10.1016/j.comppsych.2021.152281

Lenferink, L. I. M., van Denderen, M. Y., de Keijser, J., Wessel, I., & Boelen, P. A. (2017). Prolonged grief and post-traumatic stress among relatives of missing persons and homicidally bereaved individuals: A comparative study. *Journal of Affective Disorders*, *209*, 1–2. https://doi.org/10.1016/j.jad.2016.11.012

Lennon, C. (2025). 'We all have someone missing': Families of the thousands of Syrians 'disappeared' by Assad regime share stories of loss. Available at: https://news.un.org/en/story/2025/02/1159956 (last accessed: February 13, 2025).

National Crime Information Center (2022). 2022 NCIC Missing person and unidentified person statistics. Retrieved from the Federal Bureau of Investigation website:https://www.fbi.gov/file-repository/cjis/2022-ncic-missing-person-and-unidentified-person-statistics.pdf/view

National Missing and Unidentified Persons System (2024). Unresolved missing person cases published in NamUs. Retrieved from the US Department of Justice website: https://namus.nij.ojp.gov/sites/g/files/xyckuh336/files/media/document/namus-bi-annual-report-january-2024.pdf

Renner, A., Jäckle, D., Nagl, M., Plexnies, A., Röhr, S., Löbner, M., & Kersting, A. (2021). Traumatized Syrian refugees with ambiguous loss: Predictors of mental distress. *International Journal of Environmental Research and Public Health*, *18*(8), 3865. https://doi.org/10.3390/ijerph18083865

Smid, G. E., Blaauw, M., & Lenferink, L. I. (2020). Relatives of enforced disappeared persons in Mexico: Identifying mental health and psychosocial support needs and exploring barriers to care. *Intervention Journal of Mental Health and Psychosocial Support in Conflict Affected Areas*, *18*(2), 139–149. https://doi.org/10.4103/INTV.INTV_55_19

Syrian Network for Human Rights (2020). The Ninth Annual Report on Enforced Disappearance in Syria on the International Day of the Victims of Enforced Disappearances; There Is No Political Solution without the Disappeared. Available at: https://bit.ly/3vPrBHC (last accessed: February 13, 2025).

Testoni, I., Franco, C., Palazzo, L., Iacona, E., Zamperini, A., & Wieser, M. A. (2020). The endless grief in waiting: A qualitative study of the relationship between ambiguous loss and anticipatory mourning amongst the relatives of missing persons in Italy. *Behavioral Sciences*, *10*(7), 110. https://doi.org/10.3390/bs10070110

United Nations (2007). *International convention for the protection of all persons from enforced disappearance*. United Nations.

Yehene, E., Ohayon, S., Yahav, A., & Levine, H. (2024). Collective ambiguous loss after mass hostage-taking in war: Exploring public mental health outcomes and resilience. *European Journal of Psychotraumatology*, *15*(1), 2434313. https://doi.org/10.1080/20008066.2024.2434313

Chapter 12

Diagnosing prolonged and traumatic grief in children and adolescents

Lauren Alvis, Oscar Widales-Benitez, Benjamin Oosterhoff, and Julie B. Kaplow

The death of a caregiver, sibling, or loved one is one of the most commonly reported (Pynoos et al., 2014) and most distressing forms of potentially traumatic events among youth (Kaplow et al., 2010). In the US general population, 6.6% of children (4.5 million) will experience parental death and 1.5% will experience a sibling death before age 18 (Burns et al., 2020). Similarly, in the UK, 4.7% of children will experience the death of a parent by age 16 (Parsons, 2011). The COVID-19 pandemic has further elevated rates of childhood bereavement, particularly among Black and Latino/a/x youth (Hillis et al., 2021). Refugees, who often face life-threatening experiences, are also at elevated risk for bereavement (Bryant et al., 2021); for example, 56% of West Papuan refugees reported traumatic losses such as witnessing violent deaths or disappearances of loved ones (Tay et al., 2016). In a significant minority of children, childhood bereavement is associated with the development of a host of mental and behavioral health problems, including depression (Cerel et al., 2006), posttraumatic stress reactions (Keyes et al., 2014), substance use (Kaplow et al., 2010), suicide-related behaviors (Hill et al., 2019), decreased academic performance (Oosterhoff et al., 2018), and impairments in developmental tasks (Brent et al., 2012).

A growing body of research indicates that prolonged and traumatic grief reactions (those that feel overwhelming and debilitating to the individual) are the most commonly occurring mental health complaint among bereaved youth (Boelen et al., 2017). Without intervention, prolonged grief reactions remain relatively stable (Melhem et al., 2011), emphasizing the need for early detection to prevent long-term psychosocial impacts in adulthood (Lytje & Dyregrov, 2019). Simultaneously, and unlike many other psychological issues, grief is a largely natural and universal aspect of life, generally reflecting the depth of one's love for the person who died. The potential for grief to be beneficial, normative, and adaptive in nature has important implications for efforts to conceptualize, assess, diagnose, and treat prolonged grief. This chapter will focus on how to conceptualize and assess prolonged and traumatic grief in children and adolescents to assist

DOI: 10.4324/9781003429777-16

clinicians in accurately identifying bereaved youth who need a higher level of care. Specially, we will (a) review the current DSM-5-TR and ICD-11 prolonged grief disorder (PGD) diagnostic criteria through a developmentally informed lens; (b) describe how grief reactions manifest in children and adolescents of different ages using Multidimensional Grief Theory as a conceptual framework; (c) review practice elements and measurement tools for assessing prolonged grief in children and adolescents; and (d) highlight key moderating factors that influence childhood grief.

Phenomenology and diagnostic criteria

Most youth undergo an emotionally painful yet natural grieving process, wherein the intensity of grief-related distress tends to naturally diminish over time. In the majority of cases, grief facilitates positive adaptation to a world in which the deceased person is no longer physically present, thus allowing bereaved youth to maintain "normal functioning" across various life domains (Kaplow et al., 2010; Keyes et al., 2014). However, a notable subset of children can experience persistent and severe symptoms of prolonged grief that result in functional impairment beyond cultural norms (Kaplow et al., 2018; Melhem et al., 2011). Historically, the signs and symptoms of prolonged grief have been inadequately captured by existing psychiatric categories, which led to the inclusion of a distinct diagnostic category called PGD in the 11th edition of the International Classification of Diseases (ICD-11) and the Diagnostic and Statistical Manual for Psychiatric Disorders, fifth edition, text revision (DSM-5-TR). PGD diagnostic criteria provide common language to describe grief reactions that are likely to become unhealthy or debilitating over time (see also Chapter 1).

In contrast to normative grieving processes in which the intensity of grief gradually diminishes with time, PGD involves distressing grief reactions that persist and/or grow over time. The prolonged duration of intense grief reactions that are otherwise normative in the first few months after the death, coupled with functional impairment, are the primary distinguishing features of maladjustment. According to the ICD-11, criteria for PGD include "persistent and pervasive longing for and/or persistent preoccupation with the deceased, accompanied by any of the 10 symptoms that indicate intense emotional pain (e.g., sadness, guilt, anger, denial, blame; difficulty accepting the death; feeling one has lost a part of one's self; an inability to experience positive mood; emotional numbness; difficulty in engaging with social or other activities) for at least six months following bereavement" (World Health Organization [WHO], 2022). The ICD-11 includes a cultural caveat that specifies that the duration and manifestation of grief reactions must clearly violate "expected social, cultural or religious norms for the individual's culture and context". In 2022, the ICD-11 added a text in which it is stated that intense grief reactions could be regarded as normal at various points during the child's development and that PGD should therefore be diagnosed with caution in children and adolescents (WHO, 2022).

According to the DSM-5-TR (American Psychological Association [APA], 2022), PGD can be diagnosed in children after at least 6 months have passed since the death of someone close (or after 12 months in adults; Criterion A). Additional criteria include intense yearning or preoccupation regarding the deceased person (Criterion B), accompanied by at least 3 of 8 symptoms of: identity disruption, disbelief about the death, avoidance (characterized by efforts to avoid reminders in children and adolescents), emotional pain related to the loss, difficulties moving on with life, emotional numbness, a sense that life is meaningless, and intense loneliness, nearly every day or more often, for at least one month (Criterion C), that cause distress or functional impairment (Criterion D), exceed cultural and contextual norms (Criterion E) and are not better explained by another mental disorder or substance (Criterion F; Prigerson et al., 2021).

The DSM-5-TR committee's decision to adopt a shorter duration (six months) as a criterion for bereaved youth was influenced by several developmental considerations. First, research indicates that children exhibiting severe pathological grief reactions typically do so within the initial months of the death (Melhem et al., 2007), emphasizing the importance of early and accurate detection. Second, a longitudinal study of adolescents bereaved by suicide found that prolonged grief reactions at six months predict the onset and course of depression and posttraumatic stress disorder (PTSD) (Melhem et al., 2004). The ability to identify early grief reactions predictive of severe maladjustment supports the clinical utility of a shorter time duration as opposed to requiring a full year to pass before diagnosis (Kaplow et al., 2012). Third, in line with the adage "children grow up fast", evidence in child development literature (Patterson, 2008) suggests that one year in a young child's life can encompass a major developmental period, which may limit opportunities for timely prevention and remediation.

Despite the growing body of research on PGD, studies of bereaved children have yet to systematically examine potential age-related manifestations or specific cultural considerations in DSM-5-TR or ICD-11 PGD symptom domains. PGD symptom presentations may be confounded by age due to the developing cognitive capacity of youth and their reliance on adults during the grieving process (Alvis et al., 2022; Kentor & Kaplow, 2020). For example, the DSM-5-TR recommends that one of the Criterion C symptoms—avoidance of reminders—should be developmentally modified to reflect a child's *wish* to avoid reminders of the deceased, even if behavioral avoidance may not be feasible. Further, both the ICD-11 and DSM-5-TR highlight the importance of ensuring that youths' grief reactions clearly do not exceed expected social, cultural, or religious norms. Thus, youths' cultural background must be considered in the diagnostic process. Literature on culturally driven grief reactions or mourning practices in youth is scarce, and available literature on the topic primarily focuses on the experience of white adults (Laurie & Neimeyer, 2008). Although the diagnostic criteria for PGD are instrumental in identifying grief reactions impeding youth functioning, further theoretical and empirical exploration is needed to understand the nuanced ways in which cultural practices are tied to children's grief reactions (see Section *Key Factors That May Alter Childhood Grief* below).

Multidimensional grief theory as a theoretical lens for childhood grief

Examining the criteria for PGD through the framework of multidimensional grief theory provides valuable clinical insights into the diverse manifestations of grief, encompassing both maladaptive and adaptive features, across different age groups of children. Multidimensional grief theory proposes that childhood grief reactions can be characterized by three broad dimensions: *Separation Distress*, *Existential/Identity Distress*, and *Circumstance-Related Distress* (Kaplow et al., 2013; Layne et al., 2017). This theory assumes that both maladjustment and positive adjustment can coexist within each dimension, emphasizing the need to consider the complexity of grief reactions. Below, we describe the three dimensions, elucidating the psychological and behavioral manifestations of grief at varying ages.

Separation Distress entails reactions to the ongoing physical absence of, and the inability to reunite with, the deceased individual. Manifestations of separation distress include missing the deceased, heartache over their non-return, and a deep yearning for reunion, often triggered by reminders of the deceased. Designated as a required Criteria B symptom in both DSM-5-TR and ICD-11 PGD (Layne & Kaplow, 2020), separation distress is thought to manifest universally across age groups, but may potentially exhibit greater intensity in younger children (Kaplow et al., 2012). Among young children, reactions to separation from the deceased loved one may manifest as temper tantrums, increased irritability, or language delays. Among adolescents, separation distress may present as suicidal ideation involving the persistent longing for reunion in an afterlife (Kaplow et al., 2012). Youth grappling with separation distress may also exhibit developmental slowing or regression, sometimes reflecting a desire to maintain a connection with the deceased by clinging to a previous developmental stage, life circumstances, or immature behavior patterns (Layne et al., 2017), representing a time that they felt most connected to the person. Conversely, adaptive responses to separation distress may involve finding healthy avenues to stay connected, such as engaging in activities the child and deceased shared or transforming the relationship into a more spiritual connection.

Existential Identity Distress centers on the altered sense of self and existential meaning following the death of a loved one (Layne et al., 2011b). Maladaptive existential/identity reactions may result in a severe disruption of one's identity, purpose, and life aspirations. Younger children, challenged by articulating or understanding existential concepts like the meaning of life or death, may manifest existential distress behaviorally in the form of lethargy, anhedonia, or social withdrawal (Kaplow et al., 2012). Fears and concerns related to daily life may also emerge (e.g., who is going to take me to school, brush my hair, help me with my homework, etc.). Both children and adolescents may express identity discontinuity as shame or self-consciousness (e.g., "I'm different from other kids because I don't have a mother anymore"), which may be particularly salient in older age groups due to increased peer prioritization and the critical task of identity development (Brown & Larson, 2009; Kroger, 2006). Existential identity distress may also manifest in adolescents as extreme risk-taking, indifference to one's safety or well-being ("I don't care if I live or die"), and feeling like life is meaningless ("nothing really matters anymore"; Kaplow et al., 2012, 2013; Layne et al., 2017). In contrast, adaptive existential/identity reactions may involve living the legacy of the deceased or pursuing activities that would have made the deceased person proud.

Circumstance-Related Distress involves troubling thoughts and emotional pain concerning the manner of death and is theorized to increase in response to deaths that have occurred under tragic and potentially traumatic conditions such as accidents, homicide, or suicide (i.e., traumatic loss; Kaplow & Layne, 2014). These reactions may include "traumatic grief" reactions whereby posttraumatic stress reactions accompany or interfere with the child's ability to process their grief (e.g., fear-inducing mental images of how the person died lead to the child's avoidance of *any* thoughts related to the deceased person). However, maladaptive circumstance-related distress reactions go beyond traumatic grief to encompass other intense negative emotions (anger, revulsion, shame) and distressing thoughts regarding blame, bewilderment, and retaliatory fantasies. Younger children may receive less information about the circumstances of the death due to adults' assumptions about their limited capacity to understand, which may leave them with questions regarding the cause of death as well as increase the likelihood of them receiving misinformation tied to its circumstances. Young children may re-enact distressing elements of the death through drawing or play, sometimes with alternate or counterfactual acts that depict what children feel they or others could have done to prevent the death (Kentor & Kaplow, 2020). Adolescents, with enhanced abstract thinking and perspective-taking abilities, may experience negative emotions rooted in empathy and concern when thinking about the circumstances of their loved one's death (e.g., sadness over the suffering their loved one may have experienced). In contrast, adaptive reactions to circumstance-related distress may involve transforming the circumstances into actions that prevent similar suffering, such as fundraising for related causes or entering professions that could have prevented the loss.

Taken together, the DSM-5-TR has integrated some developmental perspectives on grief, primarily in Criteria A and B. Multidimensional Grief Theory highlights the broad array of grief manifestations across children's development relative to adults. Further, the dearth of developmentally informed criteria for PGD poses challenges for clinicians in accurately identifying and diagnosing PGD in children and adolescents (Layne et al., 2020). Empirical research on developmental differences or changes in grief over time remains limited, necessitating continued exploration in this area.

Traumatic grief and differential diagnosis

Traumatically challenging situations surrounding a death, such as violence or sudden, unexpected accidents, may pose difficulties for the bereavement process in childhood (Layne et al., 2008; Pynoos, 1992). It is crucial to acknowledge that, even in the absence of overtly traumatic elements, the loss of a primary attachment figure can be perceived as inherently traumatic for young children because of their high dependence on the caregiver, and the profound destabilizing impact of the caregiver's physical absence on the child's ability to self-regulate and perform simple daily tasks (Lieberman et al., 2003). Posttraumatic stress related to the circumstances of the death, particularly among younger children, also manifests in situations involving anticipated or illness-related losses, such as terminal cancer (Kaplow et al., 2014).

Given the potentially traumatic nature of bereavement in childhood, it is important to consider common comorbidities when evaluating PGD, such as PTSD and major depressive disorder (Szuhany et al., 2021). Studies that have examined symptoms of PGD in children and adolescents offer support for the distinctiveness of PGD from other disorders. Symptoms of intense yearning, difficulties in accepting the loss, anger, and a sense that life is meaningless constitute a unique grief symptom cluster that can be distinguished from other common post-loss symptoms, including PTSD and depression (Spuij et al., 2012). Further, prolonged grief is significantly related to functional impairment in youth following the death of a loved one, even after accounting for PTSD and depression (Melhem et al., 2007; Spuij et al., 2012). Finally, grief can be further distinguished from most other psychiatric disorders that do not have an "adaptive" counterpart. For instance, unlike grief, PTSD and depression are NOT traditionally conceptualized as inherently beneficial and adaptive processes that, only in rare cases, involve functional impairment (Layne et al., 2017).

Although trauma reactions and grief reactions are distinct, research suggests they can and do co-occur and may mutually influence one another (Kaplow et al., 2012). Pynoos (1992) proposed that posttraumatic stress reactions can keep youths' minds focused on the circumstances of the death, detracting from their capacity to grieve and adjust to the loss. An early study of bereaved children and adolescents indicated that both posttraumatic stress and grief reactions may act as moderators of each other's clinical course, intensifying the severity and prolonging the duration when both are present (Nader et al., 1990). Children are notably susceptible to encountering challenges in managing the dual burdens of trauma and loss, as efforts to alleviate fear-based traumatic stress typically supersede mourning, which is loss-based (Layne et al., 2017).

Assessment of grief in childhood and adolescence

When assessing grief in children, certain elements must be considered to ensure an accurate and comprehensive evaluation. "Double-barreled" items, particularly those conflating different concepts or symptoms, can complicate and lengthen the assessment process, leading to potential errors and ambiguity (Kaplow et al., 2018; Layne et al., 2020). Additionally, children may struggle with negatively phrased items on positive ascending scales due to an increased cognitive burden that can affect children's capacity for decision-making (Van Dijk et al., 2023). Thus, using positively phrased items without conjunctions may enhance response reliability (Omrani et al., 2019). Children's emotional states are often fleeting, and their limited vocabularies hinder expressive capacity. Further, bereaved children may experience a constrained ability for self-reflection and insight, which can make it difficult for youth to evaluate how well they have been doing since the death or consider whether they are experiencing an identity crisis. Taken together, the challenges experienced by bereaved children and their broader developmental capacities underscore the importance of using age-appropriate responsive measures, assessing functioning across multiple developmental domains (e.g., school, family, peers), and including multiple informants when possible.

Several instruments have been developed to assess grief reactions in children and adolescents. Instruments like the Inventory of Prolonged Grief for Children and Adolescents (IPG-C and IPG-A; Spuij et al., 2012), the Traumatic Grief Inventory for Children (TGIC; Dyregrov et al., 2001), the

Adolescent Grief Inventory (Andriessen et al., 2018), and the Inventory for Complicated Grief-Revised for Children (ICG-RC; Melhem et al., 2013) have been developed based on prior conceptualizations of prolonged grief, which have changed and evolved with new scientific discoveries (for a review, see Zhang et al., 2023). Few measures have been developed based on PGD criteria as currently defined by the DSM-5-TR and ICD-11, with the exception of the Traumatic Grief Inventory – Kids – Clinician Administered (TGI-K-CA; Van Dijk et al., 2023) and the PGD Checklist (Layne et al., 2022). The TGI-K-CA is a 16-item clinician-administered interview for youths aged 8–17 years that measures symptoms of PGD according to DSM-5-TR and ICD-11 criteria (Van Dijk et al., 2023). Items were vetted with professional experts and a large sample of children through cognitive interviewing (Van Dijk et al., 2023), supporting high content validity. However, the TGI-K-CA is currently limited to reflect only the specific symptoms outlined in the DSM-5-TR and ICD-11 and may potentially omit developmental manifestations of grief not specified or explicated under these criteria. Additionally, to date, the TGI-K-CA has only been validated in Dutch, which limits the applicability of the measure to youth in other countries.

The PGD Checklist (Layne et al., 2022) is a theoretically derived and developmentally informed assessment tool rooted in multidimensional conceptualizations of grief. The PGD Checklist (formerly the Persistent Complex Bereavement Disorder [PCBD] checklist) encompasses screening items (Criterion A) related to the death's circumstances, gateway symptoms (Criterion B) measuring distress over circumstances, and the full PGD symptom constellation (Criterion C) assessing the frequency of grief reactions in the past month. Criterion D includes youth self-report and optional caregiver observational reports, evaluating functional impairment in various domains. The PGD checklist provides a DSM-5-TR PGD diagnosis and can be used to assess PGD symptoms according to ICD-11 criteria. In addition, its supplemental scoring system generates multidimensional grief theory conceptual domain subscale scores (separation distress, existential/identity distress, circumstance-related distress) for individual assessment profiles, which can be used to support case conceptualization and intervention planning and tailoring. Prior research has found that grief items adapted from adult measures were often difficult for children to understand (Kaplow et al., 2019). Thus, the PDG checklist was developed using a "bottom up" developmentally grounded approach, generating a child-friendly item pool and undergoing extensive refinement and testing with bereaved youth and clinicians (Layne et al., 2011a). Validation studies of the original (PCBD) version of the measure demonstrate that the measure has good content validity, inter-rater convergence, and discriminant-groups validity (Kaplow et al., 2018).

Key factors that may alter childhood grief

In assessing childhood grief, it is important to consider contextual factors that impact how children cope with the loss of a loved one over time. For instance, given that children and adolescents rely heavily on the adults in their environment to navigate and cope with the death of a loved one, the caregiving context is one of the most critical factors in facilitating adaptive grief among youth (Alvis et al., 2020; Alvis et al., 2022; Haine et al., 2006; Kaplow et al., 2012). Caregivers' own grief and mental health also significantly impact children's post-loss adjustment, as higher levels of caregiver distress are associated with poorer emotional outcomes in bereaved children, potentially due to the caregivers' reduced ability to provide consistent support (Bergman et al., 2017; Bryant et al., 2021). The passage of time since the loss also influences grief, with children typically demonstrating more intense negative emotions and behavioral changes immediately after a death. While most youth show diminishing intensity of grief reactions within 6–12 months, some may experience prolonged grief even years later (Maciejewski et al., 2007). Furthermore, individuals who experience the death of a parent during childhood or adolescence are significantly more likely to meet the diagnostic criteria for psychiatric disorders in adulthood compared to those who did not experience such a loss (McKay et al., 2021).

Additional aspects of the bereavement context—including the circumstances of the death and relationship to the deceased—may also influence how youth grieve. Consistent with perspectives on "traumatic grief", the circumstances surrounding the death, particularly in cases of violence like suicide or murder, can complicate children's grief reactions, with studies linking violent deaths to increased anxiety, depression, posttraumatic stress, and prolonged grief in adolescents (Layne et al., 2008). Other studies have highlighted that even anticipated deaths can lead to posttraumatic stress, prolonged grief, and depression in youth (Kaplow et al., 2014). However, some studies report non-significant associations between the cause of death and prolonged grief reactions in youth, suggesting that the nature of the death may not always be a significant predictor (Melhem et al., 2007). The relationship to the deceased is another key factor among bereaved youth, as the loss of a primary relationship, such as a parent or caregiver, results in more intense distress compared to more distant relationships (e.g., extended family; Kaplow et al., 2010,, 2020; Lobb et al., 2010). Among adolescents, those who experienced the death of a friend report higher prolonged grief reactions compared to those who experienced the death of a grandparent (Servaty-Seib & Pistole, 2007).

Research suggests that there may also be racial differences in youths' grief reactions, with studies showing that youth of color may be at higher risk for experiencing prolonged grief compared to white youth. For example, in a study of clinic-referred children and adolescents, Black youth reported more severe prolonged grief reactions compared to White youth, and this disparity was explained by an increased likelihood of experiencing the death of a loved one by homicide among Black youth in under-resourced communities (Douglas et al., 2021). When assessing grief among youth of color, it is important to consider the systems of oppression (e.g., racism) that intersect with and shape the contexts in which youth are exposed to bereavement (Alvis et al., 2022).

Grief reactions must also be explored within the context of cultural factors, such as religion, spiritual beliefs, and mourning traditions, all of which may influence youths' perceptions of death (i.e., what it means to die) as well as the experience of loss. For instance, various religious beliefs have been documented as potentially complicating grief tied to bereavement by suicide in adult populations (Čepulienė & Skruibis, 2022). Similarly, differences across cultures have been noted in the expected duration of grief reactions, with some Christian practices accepting a "mourning year" following a loss (Hays & Hendrix, 2008). Cultural differences have also been documented in caregiver practices surrounding grief and loss. For example, European-Americans generally seek to shield children from perceived difficult conversations related to death (Rosengren et al., 2014). In contrast, various Latin American communities, most notably Mexican families, openly honor and engage in discussions about death through celebrations like the annual *Dia de Los Muertos* (Gutiérrez et al., 2020). Ignoring cultural differences that may influence how youth grieve can lead to pathologizing a cultural norm or possibly denying access to care among those in need.

Given the complex interplay of culture, bereavement, and grief, it is recommended that providers adopt a stance of cultural humility when investigating grief practices and the influence of cultural factors on prolonged and traumatic grieving. This entails a willingness to learn from those they support and to strive to understand experiences from their client's perspective (Tervalon & Murray-Garcia, 1998, see also Smid et al., 2018). Overall, cultural humility principles provide a framework from which to explore experiences of loss and grief reactions when assessing PGD in youth and can be used to determine whether the severity of the youth's grief reactions exceeds those typically seen within their culture.

In summary, understanding factors that may alter youth's grief reactions is vital for providing effective support. Recognizing the individual, contextual, and cultural differences that influence childhood grief speaks to the need for a comprehensive and individualized approach to grief assessment with children and adolescents.

References

Alvis, L., Dodd, C. G., Oosterhoff, B., Hill, R. M., Rolon-Arroyo, B., Logsdon, T., Layne, C. M., & Kaplow, J. B. (2020). Caregiver behaviors and childhood maladaptive grief: Initial validation of the Grief Facilitation Inventory. *Death Studies*, 1–9. https://doi.org/10.1080/07481187.2020.1841849

Alvis, L., Zhang, N., Sandler, I. N., & Kaplow, J. B. (2022). Developmental manifestations of grief in children and adolescents: Caregivers as key grief facilitators. *Journal of Child & Adolescent Trauma*, *16*(2), 447–457. https://doi.org/10.1007/s40653-021-00435-0

American Psychiatric Association. (2022). *Diagnostic and Statistical Manual of Mental Disorders, Fifth Edition, Text Revision (DSM-5-TR)*. APA. https://doi.org/10.1176/appi.books.9780890425787

Andriessen, K., Hadzi-Pavlovic, D., Draper, B., Dudley, M., & Mitchell, P. B. (2018). The Adolescent Grief Inventory: Development of a novel grief measurement. *Journal of Affective Disorders*, *240*, 203–211. https://doi.org/10.1016/j.jad.2018.07.012

Bergman, A. S., Axberg, U., & Hanson, E. (2017). When a parent dies–a systematic review of the effects of support programs for parentally bereaved children and their caregivers. *BMC Palliative Care*, *16*(1), 15.

Boelen, P. A., Spuij, M., & Reijntjes, A. H. A. (2017). Prolonged grief and posttraumatic stress in bereaved children: A latent class analysis. *Psychiatry Research*, *258*, 518–524. https://doi.org/10.1016/j.psychres.2017.09.002

Brent, D. A., Melhem, N. M., Masten, A. S., Porta, G., & Payne, M. W. (2012). Longitudinal effects of parental bereavement on adolescent developmental competence. *Journal of Clinical Child & Adolescent Psychology*, *41*(6), 778–791. https://doi.org/10.1080/15374416.2012.717871

Brown, B. B., & Larson, J. (2009). Peer relationships in adolescence. In R. M. Lerner & L. Steinberg (Eds.), *Handbook of adolescent psychology* (pp. 74–103). John Wiley & Sons, Inc. https://doi.org/10.1002/9780470479193.adlpsy002004

Bryant, R. A., Edwards, B., Creamer, M., O'Donnell, M., Forbes, D., Felmingham, K. L., Silove, D., Steel, Z., McFarlane, A. C., Van Hooff, M., Nickerson, A., & Hadzi-Pavlovic, D. (2021). Prolonged grief in refugees, parenting behaviour and children's mental health. *Australian & New Zealand Journal of Psychiatry*, *55*(9), 863–873. https://doi.org/10.1177/0004867420967420

Burns, M., Griese, B., King, S., & Talmi, A. (2020). Childhood bereavement: Understanding prevalence and related adversity in the United States. *American Journal of Orthopsychiatry*, *90*(4), 391–405. https://doi.org/10.1037/ort0000442

Čepulienė, A. A., & Skruibis, P. (2022). The role of spirituality during suicide bereavement: A qualitative study. *International Journal of Environmental Research and Public Health*, *19*(14), 8740. https://doi.org/10.3390/ijerph19148740

Cerel, J., Fristad, M. A., Verducci, J., Weller, R. A., & Weller, E. B. (2006). Childhood bereavement: Psychopathology in the 2 years postparental death. *Journal of the American Academy of Child & Adolescent Psychiatry*, *45*(6), 681–690. https://doi.org/10.1097/01.chi.0000215327.58799.05

Douglas, R. D., Alvis, L. M., Rooney, E. E., Busby, D. R., & Kaplow, J. B. (2021). Racial, ethnic, and neighborhood income disparities in childhood posttraumatic stress and grief: Exploring indirect effects through trauma exposure and bereavement. *Journal of Traumatic Stress*, *34*(5), 929–942. https://doi.org/10.1002/jts.22732

Dyregrov, A., Yule, W., Smith, P., Perrin, S., Gjestad, R., & Prigerson, H. (2001). Traumatic Grief Inventory for Children (TGIC). Children and War Foundation.

Gutiérrez, I. T., Menendez, D., Jiang, M. J., Hernandez, I. G., Miller, P., & Rosengren, K. S. (2020). Embracing death: Mexican parent and child perspectives on death. *Child Development*, *91*(2), e491–e511. https://doi.org/10.1111/cdev.13263

Haine, R. A., Wolchik, S. A., Sandler, I. N., Millsap, R. E., & Ayers, T. S. (2006). Positive parenting as a protective resource for parentally bereaved children. *Death Studies*, *30*(1), 1–28. https://doi.org/10.1080/07481180500348639

Hays, J. C., & Hendrix, C. C. (2008). The role of religion in bereavement. In M. S. Stroebe, R. O. Hansson, H. Schut, & W. Stroebe (Eds.), *Handbook of bereavement research and practice: Advances in theory and intervention* (pp. 327–348). American Psychological Association. https://doi.org/10.1037/14498-016

Hill, R. M., Kaplow, J. B., Oosterhoff, B., & Layne, C. M. (2019). Understanding grief reactions, thwarted belongingness, and suicide ideation in bereaved adolescents: Toward a unifying theory. *Journal of Clinical Psychology*, *75*(4), 780–793. https://doi.org/10.1002/jclp.22731

Hillis, S. D., Blenkinsop, A., Villaveces, A., Annor, F. B., Liburd, L., Massetti, G. M., Demissie, Z., Mercy, J. A., Nelson, C. A. III, Cluver, L., Flaxman, S., Sherr, L., Donnelly, C. A., Ratmann, O., & Unwin, H. J. T. (2021). COVID-19–Associated orphanhood and caregiver death in the United States. *Pediatrics*, *148*(6), e2021053760. https://doi.org/10.1542/peds.2021-053760

Kaplow, J. B., Howell, K. H., & Layne, C. M. (2014). Do circumstances of the death matter? Identifying socioenvironmental risks for grief-related psychopathology in bereaved youth. *Journal of Traumatic Stress*, *27*(1), 42–49. https://doi.org/10.1002/jts.21877

Kaplow, J. B., & Layne, C. M. (2014). Sudden loss and psychiatric disorders across the life course: Toward a developmental lifespan theory of bereavement-related risk and resilience. *American Journal of Psychiatry*, *171*(8), 807–810. https://doi.org/10.1176/appi.ajp.2014.14050676

Kaplow, J. B., Layne, C. M., Oosterhoff, B., Goldenthal, H., Howell, K. H., Wamser-Nanney, R., Burnside, A., Calhoun, K., Marbury, D., Johnson-Hughes, L., Kriesel, M., Staine, M. B., Mankin, M., Porter-Howard, L., & Pynoos, R. (2018). Validation of the persistent complex bereavement disorder (PCBD) checklist: A developmentally informed assessment tool for bereaved youth. *Journal of Traumatic Stress*, *31*, 244–254. https://doi.org/10.1002/jts.22277

Kaplow, J. B., Layne, C. M., Pynoos, R. S., Cohen, J. A., & Lieberman, A. (2012). DSM-V diagnostic criteria for bereavement-related disorders in children and adolescents: Developmental considerations. *Psychiatry: Interpersonal and Biological Processes*, *75*(3), 243–266. https://doi.org/10.1521/psyc.2012.75.3.243

Kaplow, J. B., Layne, C. M., & Pynoos, R. S. (2019). Persistent complex bereavement disorder. In M. J. Prinstein, E. A. Youngstrom, E. J. Mash, & R. A. Barkley (Eds.), *Treatment of disorders in childhood and adolescence* (4th ed., pp. 560–590). The Guilford Press.

Kaplow, J. B., Layne, C. M., Saltzman, W. R., Cozza, S. J., & Pynoos, R. S. (2013). Using multidimensional grief theory to explore effects of deployment, reintegration, and death on military youth and families. *Clinical Child and Family Psychology Review*, *16*(3), 322–340. https://doi.org/10.1007/s10567-013-0143-1

Kaplow, J. B., Saunders, J., Angold, A., & Costello, E. J. (2010). Psychiatric symptoms in bereaved versus non-bereaved youth and young adults: A longitudinal epidemiological study. *Journal of the American Academy of Child and Adolescent Psychiatry*, *49*(11), 1145–1154. https://doi.org/10.1016/j.jaac.2010.08.004

Kaplow, J. B., Wamser-Nanney, R., Layne, C. M., Burnside, A., King, C., Li-Jung, L., Steinberg, A., Briggs, E., Suarez, L., & Pynoos, R. (2020). Identifying bereavement-related markers of mental and behavioral health problems among clinic-referred adolescents. *Psychiatric Research and Clinical Practice*. https://doi.org/10.1176/appi.prcp.20190021

Kentor, R. A., & Kaplow, J. B. (2020). Supporting children and adolescents following parental bereavement: Guidance for health-care professionals. *The Lancet Child & Adolescent Health*, *4*(12), 889–898. https://doi.org/10.1016/S2352-4642(20)30184-X

Keyes, K. M., Pratt, C., Galea, S., McLaughlin, K. A., Koenen, K. C., & Shear, M. K. (2014). The burden of loss: Unexpected death of a loved one and psychiatric disorders across the life course in a national study. *American Journal of Psychiatry*, *171*(8), 864–871. https://doi.org/10.1176/appi.ajp.2014.13081132

Kroger, J. (2006). *Identity development: Adolescence through adulthood*. Sage Publications.

Laurie, A., & Neimeyer, R. A. (2008). African Americans in bereavement: Grief as a function of ethnicity. *Omega: Journal of Death and Dying*, *57*(2), 173–193. https://doi.org/10.2190/OM.57.2.d

Layne, C. M., & Kaplow, J. B. (2020). Assessing bereavement and grief disorders. In M. J. Prinstein, E. J. Mash, & R. A. Barkley (Eds.), *Assessment of disorders in childhood and adolescence* (5th ed., pp. 471–508). The Guilford Press.

Layne, C. M., Kaplow, J. B., Oosterhoff, B., Hill, R., & Pynoos, R. (2017). The interplay between posttraumatic stress and grief reactions in traumatically bereaved adolescents: When trauma, bereavement, and adolescence converge. *Adolescent Psychiatry*, *7*(4), 266–285. https://doi.org/10.2174/2210676608666180306162544

Layne, C. M., Kaplow, J. B., & Pynoos, R. S. (2011). *Multidimensional grief reactions scale*. University of California.

Layne, C. M., Kaplow, J. B., & Pynoos, R. S. (2022). Prolonged grief disorder (PGD) checklist for bereaved children and adolescents: DSM-5-TR version. *Behavioral Health Innovations*. www.reactionindex.com

Layne, C. M., Kaplow, J. B., & Pynoos, R. S. (2011). *Multidimensional grief reactions scale*. University of California.

Layne, C. M., Olsen, J., Kaplow, J., & Pynoos, R. (2011). Do traumatic circumstances of the death matter? Predicting the longitudinal course of grief in adolescents. In C. M. Layne (Chair), *Developmental perspectives on proposed DSM-V bereavement criteria: Three longitudinal studies of bereaved children and adolescents*. Symposium presented at the 27th Annual Meeting of the International Society for Traumatic Stress Studies, Baltimore, MD.

Layne, C. M., Oosterhoff, B., Pynoos, R. S., & Kaplow, J. B. (2020). *Developmental analysis of draft DSM-5-TR criteria for prolonged grief disorder: Report from the child and adolescent bereavement subgroup*. American Psychiatric Association. www.researchgate.net/profile/Christopher-Layne-4

Layne, C. M., Saltzman, W. R., Poppleton, L., Burlingame, G. M., Pašalić, A., Duraković, E., Mušić, M., Ćampara, N., Dapo, N., Arslanagić, B., Steinberg, A. M., & Pynoos, R. S. (2008). Effectiveness of a school-based group psychotherapy program for war-exposed adolescents: A randomized controlled trial. *Journal of the American Academy of Child & Adolescent Psychiatry*, *47*(9), 1048–1062. https://doi.org/10.1097/CHI.0b013e31817eecae

Lieberman, A. F., Compton, N. C., Van Horn, P., & Ippen, C. G. (2003). *Losing a parent to death in the early years: Guidelines for the treatment of traumatic bereavement in infancy and early childhood*. ZERO TO THREE/National Center for Infants, Toddlers and Families.

Lobb, E. A., Kristjanson, L. J., Aoun, S. M., Monterosso, L., Halkett, G. K. B., & Davies, A. (2010). Predictors of complicated grief: A systematic review of empirical studies. *Death Studies*, *34*(8), 673–698. https://doi.org/10.1080/07481187.2010.496686

Lytje, M., & Dyregrov, A. (2019). The price of loss – A literature review of the psychosocial and health consequences of childhood bereavement. *Bereavement Care*, *38*(1), 13–22. https://doi.org/10.1080/02682621.2019.1580854

Maciejewski, P. K., Zhang, B., Block, S. D., & Prigerson, H. G. (2007). An empirical examination of the stage theory of grief. *JAMA*, *297*(7), 716–723.

McKay, M. T., Cannon, M., Healy, C., Syer, S., O'Donnell, L., & Clarke, M. C. (2021). A meta-analysis of the relationship between parental death in childhood and subsequent psychiatric disorder. *Acta Psychiatrica Scandinavica*, *143*(6), 472–486. https://doi.org/10.1111/acps.13289

Melhem, N. M., Day, N., Shear, M. K., Day, R., Reynolds, C. F., & Brent, D. (2004). Traumatic grief among adolescents exposed to a peer's suicide. *American Journal of Psychiatry*, *161*(8), 1411–1416. https://doi.org/10.1176/appi.ajp.161.8.1411

Melhem, N. M., Moritz, G., Walker, M., Shear, M. K., & Brent, D. (2007). Phenomenology and correlates of complicated grief in children and adolescents. *Journal of the American Academy of Child & Adolescent Psychiatry*, *46*(4), 493–499. https://doi.org/10.1097/chi.0b013e31803062a9

Melhem, N. M., Porta, G., Payne, M. W., & Brent, D. A. (2013). Identifying prolonged grief reactions in children: Dimensional and diagnostic approaches. *Journal of the American Academy of Child and Adolescent Psychiatry*, *52*(6), 599–607. https://doi.org/10.1016/j.jaac.2013.02.015

Melhem, N. M., Porta, G., Shamseddeen, W., Walker Payne, M., & Brent, D. A. (2011). Grief in children and adolescents bereaved by sudden parental death. *Archives of General Psychiatry*, *68*(9), 911. https://doi.org/10.1001/archgenpsychiatry.2011.101

Nader, K., Pynoos, R. S., Fairbank, J. A., & Frederick, C. (1990). Children's PTSD reactions one year after a sniper attack at their school. *American Journal of Psychiatry*, *147*(11), 1526–1530. https://doi.org/10.1176/ajp.147.11.1526

Omrani, A., Wakefield-Scurr, J., Smith, J., & Brown, N. (2019). Survey development for adolescents aged 11–16 years: A developmental science based guide. *Adolescent Research Review*, *4*(4), 329–340. https://doi.org/10.1007/s40894-018-0089-0

Oosterhoff, B., Kaplow, J. B., & Layne, C. M. (2018). Links between bereavement due to sudden death and academic functioning: Results from a nationally representative sample of adolescents. *School Psychology Quarterly*, *33*(3), 372–380. https://doi.org/10.1037/spq0000254

Patterson, C. (2008). *Child development*. McGraw-Hill.

Parsons, S (2011). *Long-term impact of childhood bereavement: Preliminary analysis of the 1970 British Cohort Study (BCS70)*. Child Well-being Research Centre.

Prigerson, H. G., Boelen, P. A., Xu, J., Smith, K. V., & Maciejewski, P. K. (2021). Validation of the new DSM-5-TR criteria for prolonged grief disorder and the PG-13-Revised (PG-13-R) scale. *World Psychiatry*, *20*(1), 96–106. https://doi.org/10.1002/wps.20823

Pynoos, R. S. (1992). Grief and trauma in children and adolescents. *Bereavement Care*, *11*(1), 2–10. https://doi.org/10.1080/02682629208657280

Pynoos, R. S., Steinberg, A., Layne, C., Liang, L.-J., Vivrette, R., Briggs, E., Kisiel, C., Habib, M., Belin, T., & Fairbank, J. (2014). Modeling constellations of trauma exposure in the National Child Traumatic Stress Network Core Data Set. *Psychological Trauma Theory Research Practice and Policy*, *6*(51), S9–S17. https://doi.org/10.1037/a0037767

Rosengren, K., Miller, P., Gutierrez, I. T., Chow, P., Schein, S., Anderson, K. N., & Callanan, M. (2014). Children's understanding of death: Toward a contextualized and integrated account. *Monographs of the Society for Research in Child Development*, *79*, 1–162.

Servaty-Seib, H. L., & Pistole, M. C. (2007). Adolescent grief: Relationship category and emotional closeness. *OMEGA - Journal of Death and Dying*, *54*(2), 147–167. https://doi.org/10.2190/M002-1541-JP28-4673

Smid, G. E., Groen, S., de la Rie, S. M., Kooper, S., & Boelen, P. A. (2018). Towards cultural assessment of grief and grief-related psychopathology. *Psychiatric Services*, *69*(10), 1050–1052. https://doi.org/10.1176/appi.ps.201700422

Spuij, M., Prinzie, P., Zijderlaan, J., Stikkelbroek, S., Dillen, L., De Roos, C., & Boelen, P. A. (2012). Psychometric properties of the Dutch Inventories of Prolonged Grief for Children and Adolescents (IPG-C and IPG-A). *Clinical Psychology & Psychotherapy*, 19, 540–551. https://doi.org/10.1002/cpp.765

Spuij, M., Reitz, E., Prinzie, P., Stikkelbroek, Y., de Roos, C., & Boelen, P. A. (2012). Distinctiveness of symptoms of prolonged grief, depression, and post-traumatic stress in bereaved children and adolescents. *European Child & Adolescent Psychiatry*, *21*(12), 673–679. https://doi.org/10.1007/s00787-012-0307-4

Szuhany, K. L., Malgaroli, M., Miron, C. D., & Simon, N. M. (2021). Prolonged grief disorder: Course, diagnosis, assessment, and treatment. *FOCUS*, *19*(2), 161–172. https://doi.org/10.1176/appi.focus.20200052

Tay, A. K., Rees, S., & Chen, J. et al (2016). Factorial structure of complicated grief: Associations with loss-related traumatic events and psychosocial impacts of mass conflict amongst West Papuan refugees. *Social Psychiatry and Psychiatric Epidemiology*, *51*, 395–406.

Tervalon, M., & Murray-García, J. (1998). Cultural humility versus cultural competence: a critical distinction in defining physician training outcomes in multicultural education. *Journal of health care for the poor and underserved*, *9*(2), 117–125. https://doi.org/10.1353/hpu.2010.0233

Van Dijk, I., Boelen, P. A., De Keijser, J., & Lenferink, L. I. M. (2023). Assessing DSM-5-TR and ICD-11 prolonged grief disorder in children and adolescents: Development of the Traumatic Grief Inventory – Kids – Clinician-Administered. *European Journal of Psychotraumatology*, *14*(2), 2197697. https://doi.org/10.1080/20008066.2023.2197697

World Health Organization [WHO] (2022). *International Classification of Diseases Eleventh Revision (ICD-11)*. WHO. https://icd.who.int/browse11/l-m/en

Zhang, T., Krysinska, K., Alisic, E., & Andriessen, K. (2023). Grief instruments in children and adolescents: A systematic review. *OMEGA - Journal of Death and Dying*. https://doi.org/10.1177/00302228231171188

Chapter 13

Psychotherapy for prolonged and traumatic grief in children and adolescents

Julie B. Kaplow and Paul A. Boelen

Despite the growing body of research on the deleterious effects of childhood *bereavement*, particularly traumatic bereavement, on youth mental health, the field of childhood *grief* is still relatively new. Specifically, few studies have rigorously examined the etiology, clinical presentation, developmental manifestations, and predictive utility of prolonged grief or traumatic grief above and beyond the effects of childhood bereavement. In other words, we are just beginning to understand the unique ways in which children and adolescents *react to* the death of a loved one (particularly under traumatic circumstances), how those reactions can influence long-term trajectories of mental health and well-being, and the effectiveness of interventions designed to ameliorate distressing grief reactions in youth. Drawing from the extant research in this area, the goal of this chapter is to provide an overview of existing treatments for children and adolescents experiencing prolonged or traumatic grief, the effectiveness of these interventions, and their common practice elements. We also provide suggestions for future research that can help to inform treatments for prolonged and traumatic grief in childhood and ensure the long-term health and well-being of bereaved youth.

Review of grief treatments for children and adolescents

Childhood bereavement is both the most common (Pynoos et al., 2014) and the most distressing form of trauma among youth (Kaplow et al., 2010). Although most bereaved youth will go on to lead healthy, happy, productive lives following the death of a loved one, a significant minority of bereaved youth will experience long term mental and behavioral health problems, including the intersection of posttraumatic stress and grief (i.e., traumatic grief) as well as prolonged grief disorder (PGD; see Chapter 12). Given that most grief reactions are considered "adaptive" and a natural reflection of the love the child has for the person who died, the critical role of assessment in determining which bereaved youth will actually require treatment cannot be

DOI: 10.4324/9781003429777-17

understated. A number of the treatments reviewed below are "assessment-driven" in that the assessment data help to determine (1) who is a good fit for treatment; (2) whether the treatment is working over time; and, in some cases, (3) which practice elements of the treatment would be most effective for that particular child.

Although several trauma-focused therapeutic interventions for children currently exist, comparatively few have been developed to assist bereavement-exposed youth who are experiencing prolonged grief and/or the complex interplay of grief and trauma. Below we provide a brief review of the primary existing evidence-based interventions for bereaved youth (see also Breen et al., 2023; Hanauer et al., 2024; and Kaplow et al., 2019 for comprehensive reviews).

Individual treatments for bereaved youth

CBT grief-help

Building on cognitive-behavioral approaches to adult PGD, CBT Griefhelp is based on the premise that healthy adjustment to loss in children with PGD is hindered by several processes. These include: (i) a tendency to avoid confronting the reality of the loss, (ii) recurrent negative thoughts about oneself, one's life, and the future, (iii) withdrawal from previously enjoyable activities, (iv) an inclination to assume excessive responsibility for the well-being of parents, siblings, or others affected by the loss, and (v) reduced availability and quality of care from parents/caregivers. Accordingly, treatment targets are (i) to slowly but surely face the permanence of the loss and the associated pain, (ii) rebuild self-confidence and foster a positive, adaptive outlook on life and the future, (iii) resume engagement in meaningful activities (e.g., sports, school, and social interactions), (iv) focus more on personal challenges rather than those of others, particularly when beyond the child's control, and (v) to support parents in supporting their children. Interventions to address these targets are (i) exposure to the story and reality of the loss, (ii) cognitive restructuring, (iii) graded activation, (iv) improving problem solving, and (v) improving positive parenting, including good communication between parents and children.

Interventions are embedded in a manualized treatment encompassing nine individual sessions for the child (or adolescent) plus five separate sessions for the parents (or caretakers; see Spuij et al., 2013). The children's manual centers around four parts. One part focuses on explaining that adjusting to loss involves working through four key tasks: (i) facing the reality and pain of the loss, (ii) regaining confidence in yourself, other people, life, and the future, (iii) focusing on your own problems and not only those of others, and (iv) continuing activities that you used to enjoy. In another part, attention is focused on "Who died?"; this is meant for the therapist to get to know the lost person and to facilitate confrontation with the fact that the loss is permanent and what this means to the child. In a further part, the child is helped to identify negative (unhelpful) cognitions and alter these into more positive (helpful) views of self, life, and the future, promoting positive feelings and adjustment. In the fourth part, attention is paid to reduce coping behavior that is unhelpful (e.g., avoidance of loss-related cues, depressive withdrawal, taking up too much responsibility for others) and increase coping that is helpful (e.g., engaging with situations, places, and people reminding of the loss, reengaging in activities, and focusing on personal problems, needs, and challenges). All information and assignments of the manual are presented with friendly, appealing materials that have a pleasant look and feel, designed to engage children. Materials facilitate a more creative and exploratory approach for younger children, while allowing for a more structured, rational, and language-based engagement for older children. Parent sessions are planned in parallel with the children's sessions. These are not meant to mitigate the parents' grief but to coach parents in supporting the child in their grief. Parents receive assignments focused on strengthening positive parenting (e.g., expressing warmth and support), improving communication, and increasing engagement in "quality time" activities.

In a randomized controlled trial (RCT), comparing CBT Griefhelp with supportive counseling (both including parenting sessions), CBT Griefhelp was found to yield significantly greater reductions in PGD-symptoms at the post-treatment and 3-, 6-, and 12-month follow-up assessments, and more successfully mitigated depression, PTSD, and internalizing problems 6- and 12-months following treatment (Boelen et al., 2021). Secondary analyses showed that PGD symptom reduction occurred gradually (with sudden gains being a rare event) and that no specific components seemed particularly responsible for symptom improvement (Lechner-Meichsner et al., 2025). Indeed, more research is needed to identify the most important therapy elements, including the added value of the parental sessions.

Multidimensional grief therapy

Multidimensional Grief Therapy (MGT; Kaplow et al., 2023) is a theoretically derived, assessment-driven intervention designed to reduce PGD, traumatic grief, and associated mental health issues (e.g., depression, suicide risk) while promoting adaptive grieving in bereaved children and adolescents, aged 7–18. This intervention is based on the notion that youth grieve in different ways and that "one-size-fits-all" grief treatments lack effectiveness (Kaplow et al., 2019). MGT is grounded in multidimensional grief theory (Kaplow et al., 2013; Layne et al., 2017) and is designed to target each dimension of grief including separation distress (yearning and longing for the person who died), existential/identity distress (feeling lost without the deceased), and circumstance-related distress (preoccupation with the way the person died) based upon each child's individual assessment profile as well as their developmental needs and strengths.

Given that not every child requires an intensive psychosocial treatment following a death, MGT is also designed to provide a continuum of care, spanning the needs of children who may be experiencing normative struggles after a death to those who meet full criteria for PGD. To do this, MGT uses a two-phased approach. The first phase (six sessions) is designed to provide general grief support and focuses primarily on psychoeducation, normalizing grief reactions, emotion regulation skills, recognizing personal loss and trauma reminders, and positive reminiscing activities. Although Phase I can be offered in clinical settings, it can also be provided by bereavement support centers, faith-based organizations, pediatric offices, schools, or other settings that are focused on tier one supports after a death. The second phase of MGT (ranging from four to eight sessions) is generally conducted by a trained clinician and is designed to address more maladaptive grief reactions through grief processing as well as identifying and replacing maladaptive thoughts such as "it was all my fault" or "I'm never going to be happy again." Practice elements for Phase II include guiding the child through a loss narrative by focusing on each grief domain, promoting adaptive grief reactions and meaning-making activities, creating alternative plans for a future without the deceased person, and finding comforting ways to carry on their legacy. Reflecting key intervention objectives of enhancing parent-child communication and strengthening caregivers' capacity to facilitate their child's grief, dyadic caregiver-child sessions are incorporated throughout Phases I and II, including coaching caregivers to help their child grieve in adaptive ways (Kaplow et al., 2023).

MGT can be implemented individually or in group settings. MGT and its core practice elements have been found to significantly reduce maladaptive grief reactions across all three domains of grief (including symptoms of PGD and traumatic grief), depression, and posttraumatic stress among diverse populations of youth across a wide range of bereavement-related circumstances including homicide, suicide, mass shootings and anticipated deaths due to illness (Grassetti et al., 2015; Hill et al., 2019).

Trauma-focused cognitive-behavioral therapy

Trauma-focused cognitive-behavioral therapy (TFCBT) is an evidence-based trauma-focused therapy for youth ages 6–17 years, originally encompassing 16 sessions (Cohen et al., 2017). Intervention objectives focus on reducing children's trauma- and grief-related symptoms and improving adaptive functioning. TF-CBT includes trauma-focused components summarized by the acronym PRACTICE: Parenting skills; Relaxation skills; Affect modulation skills and Cognitive coping skills; Trauma narration and processing; In vitro mastery of trauma reminders; Conjoint child-parent sessions; and Enhancing safety. Although TF-CBT was originally designed for traumatized youth (e.g., youth with PTSD resulting from sexual abuse), children experiencing "childhood traumatic grief" (CTG; defined as trauma symptoms that impinge upon the child's ability to navigate the normal grieving process) (Cohen et al., 2004) receive additional grief-focused components. These components include grief psychoeducation, grieving the loss, preserving positive memories, redefining the relationship, and treatment closure. Effectiveness studies of TF-CBT to treat CTG found significant improvements in CTG, PTSD, depressive symptoms, and behavior problems (Cohen et al., 2004; Cohen et al., 2006; O'Donnell et al., 2014). Group-based TF-CBT was recently found effective in reducing PGD and PTSD symptoms in children in Kenya and Tanzania who had experienced parental loss (Dorsey et al., 2020). Like the original protocol (Cohen et al., 2017), it incorporated psychoeducation, stress management skills, narrative recounting of the loss, and processing of maladaptive cognitions. To adapt the approach, the intervention was delivered through a combination of group and individual sessions and cultural modifications were introduced.

Group treatments for bereaved youth

The Family Bereavement Program (FBP) is among the most extensively studied interventions for bereaved youths. It is a 12-session group treatment for parentally bereaved children (ages 8–16) and their caregivers, aimed at improving both individual-level variables (e.g., self-esteem, adaptive thinking) and family-level variables (e.g., parent-child relationship quality) hypothesized to impact the mental health of bereaved children. Practice elements include teaching clients positive coping strategies, skills for adaptive emotional expression, positive parenting techniques, and ways of dealing with bereavement-related stressors. It was originally intended as a preventive intervention to reduce internalizing and externalizing symptoms (Sandler et al., 2003), rather than a treatment for reducing clinically significant prolonged or traumatic grief. However, several follow-up analyses published since the initial study indicate that the program has beneficial long-term effects on various outcomes, including symptoms of PGD. For instance, compared to youth in a control group (i.e., parents and children each received three books focused on dealing with grief), youth who participated in the FBP had lower levels of externalizing problems, reduced intrusive/disruptive grief-related thoughts, higher self-esteem, and improved academic performance at post-test and 6 years post-treatment (Sandler et al.,

2010). Youth in the FBT also demonstrated a lower prevalence of suicidal ideation or behaviors (Sandler et al., 2016).

Trauma and Grief Component Therapy for Adolescents (TGCTA) is an 8- to 20-session, modularized, assessment-driven treatment for adolescents, ages 11–18, whose histories of exposure to trauma, bereavement, and/or traumatic loss place them at high risk for severe persisting distress, functional impairment, and developmental disruption (Saltzman et al., 2017). Originally designed for use in group-based settings, TGCTA has also been adapted for, and used in, individual therapy settings (Alvis et al., 2024; Saltzman et al., 2017) and is tailored to the trauma- and grief-related needs of the clients based on their assessment profiles. TGCTA is comprised of four modules: (1) Foundational Knowledge and Skills; (2) Working through Traumatic Experiences; (3) Working through Grief Experiences; and (4) Refocusing on the Present and Looking to the Future. The Grief Module is comprised of six sessions, and practice elements include grief psychoeducation, cognitive coping (linking loss reminders, grief reactions, and consequences), processing difficult grief reactions (e.g., anger, guilt, remorse), legacy building/meaning making, memorializing/continuing bonds, and future planning/relapse prevention. TGCTA has been shown to reduce posttraumatic stress, depressive symptoms, maladaptive grief reactions, and violent behavior, while increasing rule compliance and connectedness across diverse settings and populations, including in schools following the Bosnian civil war, youth exposed to community violence, mass shootings (e.g., Santa Fe and Uvalde school shootings in Texas) and in juvenile justice settings across the United States (Alvis et al., 2024; Clow et al., 2019; Herres et al., 2017; Layne et al., 2001, 2008).

The Grief and Trauma Intervention (GTI) is a group-based intervention (10 group-based sessions, one individual session, one parent session) designed for children who have experienced trauma and/or "traumatic bereavement" (murder or violent death) (Salloum, 2008). Practice elements are derived from cognitive-behavioral therapy and narrative therapy and are structured around three treatment phases: resilience and safety, restorative retelling, and reconnecting (Herman, 1997; Rynearson, 2001). The resilience and safety phase is designed to strengthen positive coping skills, emotion regulation skills, and a sense of safety. The restorative retelling phase involves drawing images associated with the event and discussing them individually with the group facilitator. These individual sessions also address negative emotions such as guilt, shame, and specific trauma and loss reminders. The reconnecting phase involves reminiscing and memorializing activities, paired with actively engaging in meaningful relationships and interests that may have been thwarted by the death. At the end of the treatment, children are invited to share their stories outside of the group, preferably with a caring adult whom they have already identified. Effectiveness studies of GTI found significant improvements in posttraumatic stress symptoms, depression, traumatic grief, and global distress (Salloum & Overstreet, 2008; 2012) and maintained these improvements at a 12-month follow-up (Salloum & Overstreet, 2012).

Treatment effectiveness

In an earlier article reviewing available treatments for grief in childhood, Currier et al. (2007) found only 13 controlled studies of bereavement interventions with children that generally did not generate positive outcomes. They called for the development of well-validated and clinically relevant measures of childhood grief, as well as a theory capable of guiding interventions for bereaved youth. A little later, when some more effective treatments emerged in the literature, Rosner et al. (2010) drew more optimistic conclusions—with some findings suggesting interventions were more effective when they directly targeted grief and related psychological distress among bereaved children with more complaints. With the growing consensus on the symptomatology of prolonged grief in children and the evaluation of theory-based interventions such as TGCTA, TF-CBT, CBT Griefhelp, MGT, and others referenced above, the effects and availability of grief interventions for children are now viewed in a more favorable light. For instance, two systematic reviews and meta-analyses of studies among 14–24-year-olds (Breen et al., 2023) and children up to 18 years (Hanauer et al., 2024) showed that contemporary interventions, particularly those encompassing CBT-based common practice elements addressed below, effectively mitigate PGD as well as co-occurring depression, anxiety, and posttraumatic stress.

Common practice elements

A conceptual analysis of the interventions briefly reviewed above reveals a common set of shared intervention components. These components include (1) grief psychoeducation, (2) emotion identification and regulation, (3) grief- and trauma-focused exposure and processing, (4) cognitive coping, restructuring, and meaning making, (5) ongoing connection and symbolic interactions, (6) reengagement in valued activities, and (7) parental grief facilitation.

Grief psychoeducation

Several evidence-based interventions for bereaved youth begin by providing psychoeducation about grief and its various manifestations to both children and caregivers. This psychoeducation component typically emphasizes the fact that the range of grief responses varies from person to person, and that there is no single "best" way to grieve and no set timeline for grieving. Bereaved youth are often distressed by inappropriate expectations held by themselves or others about their own course of bereavement. For example, many youths believe that something may be wrong with them because of unrealistic expectations about how long their grief reactions should persist. Describing the wide range of potential grief responses helps youth to appreciate and understand their own reactions, as well as those of family and friends (Kaplow et al., 2023). In the CBT Griefhelp program, it is explained that there are four tasks in adjusting to loss, focused on (among others) acknowledging the permanence of the loved one's absence and restoring or maintaining self-trust. This information provides children with a framework of steps that need to be taken to come to terms with their loss and to establish a supportive and positive tone of the therapy. That is, the therapy does not primarily aim to alter supposedly "unhealthy processes underlying abnormal or pathological grief." Instead, it emphasizes that the child already possesses various strengths to navigate the grieving process, with the interventions designed to help them effectively utilize these capacities. Similarly, some treatments utilize a strength-based approach with regard to grief psychoeducation (e.g., MGT, TGCT), emphasizing the co-existence of both maladaptive grief reactions as well as adaptive grief reactions (Kaplow et al., 2023; Saltzman et al., 2017) and the ways in which certain grief reactions can foster positive growth. Discussion-based activities may also include information about trauma and loss reminders, including efforts to identify specific reminders that evoke the child's personal grief reactions (Kaplow et al., 2019, 2023; Salloum, 2008; Saltzman et al., 2017). Trauma reminders include people, places, objects, or situations that remind the child of the way the person died, often leading to symptoms of PTSD or circumstance-related distress. In contrast, loss reminders include people, places, objects, or situations that remind the child of the deceased person's ongoing absence (Layne et al., 2006), often leading to separation distress.

Emotion identification and regulation

Several evidence-based treatments for bereaved youth include an emotion identification and regulation component designed to enhance children's emotional vocabulary and emotion regulation skills (e.g., Cohen et al., 2004; Kaplow et al., 2023; Saltzman et al., 2017; Sandler et al., 2013). Although these exercises are not specific to grief per se, general emotion regulation strategies are often considered a necessary precursor to trauma/grief processing and cognitive coping, given that these latter components can temporarily increase emotional distress. Emotion regulation practice elements often include deep breathing exercises, meditation, progressive muscle relaxation, and guided imagery (Kaplow et al., 2019).

Grief-and trauma-focused exposure and processing

A key assumption underlying CBT therapies for childhood prolonged and traumatic grief is that these problems are, to some extent, maintained by tendencies to avoid elaborating on the permanence of the separation and processing the associated feelings of pain, sadness, despair, and emptiness. For children with persistent debilitating grief, confronting the reality and pain of the loss is often perceived as too distressing, unbearable, or linked to threatening predictions, such as that doing so will cause one to "go mad" or "become depressed forever." This fear may lead them to avoid thoughts, objects, places, situations, people, and other cues associated with the loss. In case of traumatic loss, when PGD symptoms are accompanied by intrusive images and a sense of threat related to the circumstances of the death, avoidant tendencies are likely to extend to thoughts, situations, and people that may trigger unbidden memories connected with the cause of the death. Exposure-based interventions aim to gradually encourage children to confront internal and external cues, situations, and stimuli associated with the loss and its cause. The goal is to reduce avoidance and to increase emotional awareness of the reality and implications of the loss. In CBT Griefhelp, exposure is addressed in the initial phase of treatment, during which attention is given to who has passed away, how the loss occurred, what has changed in the child's life since the loss, and all emotions associated with this. Additionally, attention is given to replacing "unhelpful behaviors" that hinder the child's adjustment to loss (e.g., avoiding the situation where the death took place, not talking to anyone about the loss) with "helpful behaviors" that facilitate this process (visiting the site of the loss with a confident, telling friends about the lost person and how they died). Exposure to internal and external cues can be supplemented with writing assignments in which the child is encouraged to express, in their own words, what has happened and how it feels to have experienced it (cf. Kalantari et al., 2012).

In various other therapeutic approaches, exposure and emotional processing are also incorporated, although they may be described using different terminology. For instance, in both TF-CBT and TGCT, one core element of treatment involves the creation of a "trauma narrative" to help them process the (presumably) traumatic circumstances of the death. The development of the trauma narrative usually progresses from a more restricted, factual account of "what happened" to an in-depth and highly personal "unpacking" of the experience, including the most difficult aspects or "worst moments" over multiple sessions. This process of constructing the trauma narrative in a supportive setting carries multiple therapeutic benefits. Specifically, the narrative (1) increases tolerance and lends coherence to painful memories that may have been avoided; (2) reduces reactivity to these memories; (3) provides insight into current trauma reminders, as well as unhelpful thoughts or beliefs; and (4) validates the child's experience through the act of sharing and having others bear witness to the event (including the therapist and/or peers if in a group setting) (Saltzman et al., 2017).

The trauma narrative construction in the context of bereavement necessarily involves an in-depth discussion of the circumstances of the death (i.e., "trauma processing"). Consequently, the narrative construction serves as a key treatment component in reducing circumstance-related distress and/or symptoms of PTSD. However, trauma narrative work is predicated on the assumption that the death itself (or the circumstances surrounding the death) was experienced as inherently "traumatic." Although this may be true in many cases, some bereaved youth may experience severe grief-related distress that does not necessarily include symptoms of PTSD, such as separation distress (Kaplow et al., 2019, 2023). Thus, "trauma processing" activities such as creating a trauma narrative may not fully address the entire range of grief reactions that many bereaved youth tend to experience (Layne et al., 2017). For this reason, MGT includes the creation of a loss narrative that explicitly covers each of the dimensions of grief, including adaptive grief reactions, as described in multidimensional grief theory. For example, a child who exhibits elevations in separation distress can be encouraged to explore what he or she misses most about the deceased person and ways in which he or she still feels connected (Kaplow et al., 2019). Similarly, if a child demonstrates elevations in existential or identity distress, he or she can be asked to describe how life circumstances or goals and aspirations have changed since the death. This typically includes an exploration of secondary adversities, important lessons learned, and future goal setting that may involve carrying on the legacy of the deceased (Kaplow et al., 2023).

Cognitive coping, restructuring, and meaning making

Almost all of the aforementioned evidence-based treatments for bereaved youth contain a cognitive coping and/or cognitive restructuring component in which the clinician helps the client to identify, challenge, and modify maladaptive or unhelpful thoughts about the death or the deceased person. Some treatments focus explicitly on making connections between loss reminders and bereavement-related thoughts, feelings, behaviors, and consequences (e.g., Kaplow et al., 2023; Saltzman et al., 2017). Helping bereaved youth to identify personal loss reminders and understand how they may lead to grief reactions allows them to feel more "in control" as they become better able to predict when and how grief reactions may arise (Kaplow et al., 2019, 2023). Cognitive coping activities can also help youth deal with some of the more difficult thoughts and feelings that occur in the context of traumatic or stigmatized deaths (e.g., homicide, suicide), such as anger, remorse, guilt, or shame, and identify more helpful replacement thoughts (e.g., "It wasn't my fault").

In the CBT Griefhelp treatment, cognitive restructuring is central to the second task of "Regaining confidence in yourself, other people, life, and the future." The therapist helps the child to detect negative thoughts that may block this task, such as negative thoughts about oneself, guilt and responsibility, or fearful cognitions about one's grief; then, simple questions are discussed to test if cognitions are true and helpful and behavioral experiments are designed to test specific negative predictions that underly the child's negative feelings and avoidant tendencies. For instance, a child may avoid social situations due to the prediction: "If I tell my friends how I feel, then they will respond unfavorably." Then, a behavioral experiment can be designed in which the child shares thoughts and feelings about the loss with someone who feels trustworthy to test whether a negative reaction actually occurs and, if so, to explore strategies to respond to that effectively. The child is also taught to seek distraction when negative thoughts continue to come up and to reformulate negative thoughts into positive, helpful ones.

In CBT Griefhelp and MGT (as well as various other approaches), unhelpful cognitions are explicitly addressed and challenged to modify current unhelpful thinking, but also, or even more so, to equip the child with skills to identify and challenge underlying cognitions in future situations involving intense emotions. In addition, particularly with older adolescents, it can be beneficial to engage in a more reflective exchange of thoughts about attribution of meaning to the loss. The death of a parent, sibling, or friend during adolescence can profoundly disrupt previously unquestioned assumptions about the meaning of life and challenge fundamental beliefs about fairness, safety, predictability, and trust. This is especially true in cases of sudden or traumatic loss. It is essential for the therapist to acknowledge these disruptions and support the adolescent in reflecting on them from different perspectives—while being cautious not to prematurely debate the validity of specific assumptions.

Ongoing connection and symbolic interactions

Memorializing activities, or practice elements that involve facilitation of an ongoing connection to the deceased, can be found across a number of evidence-based interventions for bereaved youth. Research has shown that reminiscing about the deceased person, engaging in mourning rituals, and identifying mementos are associated with positive adaptation after loss (Siddaway et al., 2015; Stroebe et al., 2010). Memorializing activities are typically designed to help youth renegotiate his or her relationship with the deceased from one of physical presence to one of memory or, for some, spiritual presence (Kaplow et al., 2023; Saltzman et al., 2017). Youth often require assistance from caregivers and other adults in finding healthy ways of connecting to the deceased. For example, a caregiver may offer the child something tangible to hold on to that once belonged to the deceased person (e.g., a necklace, a treasured item, etc.). These practice elements that are designed to strengthen continuing bonds can be difficult for some families in which members have markedly different ways of dealing with separation distress. For example, some family members may wish to visit the grave site regularly, or look at photos of the deceased, whereas other family members may be more comfortable finding other ways of feeling connected. Often the treatment itself involves facilitating discussions between the child and caregiver (or other family members) about ways in which they can each feel connected to the deceased, while honoring their individual differences.

Symbolic interactions with the lost person can be included in treatment and may help to establish a healthy ongoing connection with the deceased. The child may be guided in writing a letter to the lost person, in order to, e.g., express unresolved thoughts, saying goodbye one more time, seek permission to focus less on the loss and more on other aspects of life, or tell about new experiences and events that happened since the loss took place. With the same objectives, a therapist may help a child to engage in an imaginary conversation with the loss person.

Reengagement in valued activities

It is normal and understandable that the loss of a loved one may lead children to withdraw from activities that were previously enjoyable and meaningful, such as socializing with friends, participating in sports, and attending school. However, the tendency to withdraw from activities or social situations may also persist. This could happen if, for example, the child believes that activities will no longer be fun or possible without the lost person, or if the child feels that engaging in enjoyable activities is not permissible, due to a sense of survivor guilt, as the deceased can no longer participate in such experiences. The child may also fear that peers will perceive them differently or more negatively now that they have experienced loss. Like how social withdrawal and inactivity in depression can contribute to a self-perpetuating cycle of negative cognitions and emotions, avoidance of activities and social interactions following a loss may reinforce and exacerbate grief. Against this background, several therapeutic approaches described here explicitly emphasize the gradual increase of enjoyable and fulfilling activities. For example, in the Family Bereavement Program, parents are taught strategies to encourage their children to engage in more positive activities. Similarly, the CBT Griefhelp program includes a structured approach to replacing depressive avoidance with an increase in pleasurable activities, as part of Task 4 (Continuing activities that you used to enjoy), and TF-CBT explicitly focuses on recommitting to ongoing and new relationships.

Parental grief facilitation

A primary consideration when distinguishing adult- versus child-focused treatments for prolonged or traumatic grief is the essential role of parents or caregivers as grief facilitators. Consistent with evidence documenting the important role played by parents in facilitating children's adaptive grief reactions (Alvis et al., 2022; Haine et al., 2008; Howell et al., 2016; Shapiro et al., 2014), a number of interventions for bereaved youth incorporate a parenting or parent-child dyadic component. The structure and content of parenting sessions vary from treatment to treatment. Typical intervention objectives include general enhancement of parenting skills (Sandler et al., 2010) and parent-child communication (Kaplow et al., 2023). Some of these practice elements include (1) reviewing session activities with the parent/caregiver as a means of translating the skills to home (e.g., Cohen et al., 2004; Kaplow et al., 2023; Spuij et al., 2013) and (2) parental grief facilitation skill-building activities that involve identifying and naming specific parenting behaviors that may either promote or inhibit children's adaptive grief reactions (Kaplow et al., 2023). Another key component of parental grief facilitation involves preparing the parent for dyadic sessions, both in terms of content as well as helpful responses they can provide to the child, and ensuring that they feel emotionally equipped to bear witness to the child's grief (while presumably grappling with their own grief reactions). If parents are not ready to engage in this way, another caregiver may be called into the session to provide support to the child.

Developmental and cultural considerations

Bereaved children vary in many respects, and although there are many common practice elements across different treatments, the way in which interventions are applied should also be adjusted to align with the child's emotional and cognitive development level. So, although it is a critical common element to expose children to the reality and pain of the loss, this is mostly done in more playful, creative, and sometimes reiterative ways with younger children and more directly with older children. For example, young children often have a difficult time grasping the permanency of the loss and/or the body's lack of functioning after death and may therefore need to revisit the circumstances of the death repeatedly before they are able to fully accept the reality of the loss. For children at a lower developmental level, unhelpful cognitions are typically addressed by introducing more positive ways of thinking, whereas for older youth, a Socratic, reflective, or philosophical approach may be more appropriate to target unhelpful thinking patterns.

Apart from the child's developmental and emotional level, therapists should consider the child's cultural background. Thus, when working with children from different cultural backgrounds, therapists should be sensitive to the mourning customs and potential spiritual beliefs of the child's culture, aware of any potentially complex historical contexts related to the child's country of origin, and adaptable in their use of language and metaphors to explain key concepts. Several studies have shown that different therapeutic approaches addressed in this chapter (e.g., expressive writing, Kalantari et al., 2012; TF-CBT, Dorsey et al., 2020) have yielded positive outcomes when applied to non-Western groups. A recent review of (mostly uncontrolled) CBT-based treatments for PGD also reported favorable outcomes for this approach in children of different ethnicities (Saladino et al., 2023). There is therefore no reason to be hesitant in applying the approaches described in this chapter to children from a non-Western background, provided that sensitivity to the children's cultural, ethnic, and religious background is always maintained.

Future directions, research, and conclusions

The field of childhood bereavement is in a relatively nascent state compared to the fields of adult bereavement and trauma/posttraumatic stress. Although we have made progress with regard to the development of valid measures of grief (see Chapter 12) and the development of theoretically-driven interventions as outlined above, the childhood bereavement field remains in need of research that identifies and rigorously evaluates mechanisms of therapeutic change responsible for producing therapeutic benefit, while also eliminating less helpful and potentially harmful practice elements (Kaplow et al., 2019). We are also in need of "best practice guidelines" for risk screening, assessment, and triage of bereaved youth, to ensure that youth are matched to the most appropriate type of support (e.g., peer support vs. individual psychotherapy; trauma-focused practice elements versus grief-focused practice elements) based on their unique bereavement-related mental health needs and circumstances. It is important to gain a clearer understanding of which interventions can effectively prevent a problematic course of grief in high-risk children and which interventions are effective as curative treatments for children already suffering from PGD and additional difficulties. It is also critical to investigate the extent to which the effects of interventions are moderated by factors such as the circumstances of the loss, the relationship to the deceased, and community-based or socio-economic contexts. Finally, future research should help us to better understand the ways in which culture plays a role in how children grieve and, relatedly, how to tailor treatments to ensure that they harness the important strength-based, cultural aspects of mourning.

References

Alvis, L., Oosterhoff, B., Giang, C., & Kaplow, J. B. (2024). A pilot open trial of an individualized adaptation of trauma and grief component therapy (TGCT) in children and adolescents. *Child & Youth Care Forum*, *53*(4), 893–908. https://doi.org/10.1007/s10566-023-09776-3

Alvis, L., Zhang, N., Sandler, I., & Kaplow, J. (2022). Developmental manifestations of grief in children and adolescents: Caregivers as key grief facilitators. *Journal of Child and Adolescent Trauma*, *28*, 1–11.

Boelen, P. A., Lenferink, L. I. M., & Spuij, M. (2021). CBT for prolonged grief in children and adolescents: A randomized clinical trial. *American Journal of Psychiatry*, *178*(4), 294–304. https://doi.org/10.1176/appi.ajp.2020.20050548

Breen, L. J., Greene, D., Rees, C. S., Black, A., Cawthorne, M., & Egan, S. J. (2023). A co-designed systematic review and meta-analysis of the efficacy of grief interventions for anxiety and depression in young people. *Journal of Affective Disorders*, *335*, 289–297. https://doi.org/10.1016/j.jad.2023.05.032

Clow, S., Olafson, E., Ford, J., Moser, M., Slivinsky, M., & Kaplow, J. (2023). Addressing grief reactions among incarcerated adolescents and young adults using trauma and grief component therapy. *Psychological Trauma: Theory, Research, Practice and Policy*, *15*(Suppl 1), S192–S200. https://doi.org/10.1037/tra0001364

Cohen, J. A., Mannarino, A. P., & Deblinger, E. (2017). *Trauma-focused CBT for children and adolescents: Treatment applications*. Guilford Press.

Cohen, J. A., Mannarino, A. P., & Knudsen, K. (2004). Treating childhood traumatic grief: A pilot study. *Journal of the American Academy of Child & Adolescent Psychiatry*, *43*(10), 1225–1233. https://doi.org/10.1097/01.chi.0000135620.15522.38

Cohen, J. A., Mannarino, A. P., & Staron, V. R. (2006). A pilot study of modified cognitive-behavioral therapy for childhood traumatic grief (CBT-CTG). *Journal of the American Academy of Child & Adolescent Psychiatry*, *45*(12), 1465–1473. https://doi.org/10.1097/01.chi.0000237705.43260.2c

Currier, J. M., Holland, J. M., & Neimeyer, R. A. (2007). The effectiveness of bereavement interventions with children: A meta-analytic review of controlled outcome research. *Journal of Clinical Child and Adolescent Psychology*, *36*(2), 253–259. https://doi.org/10.1080/15374410701279669

Dorsey, S., Lucid, L., Martin, P., King, K. M., O'Donnell, K., Murray, L. K., Wasonga, A. I., Itemba, D. K., Cohen, J. A., Manongi, R., & Whetten, K. (2020). Effectiveness of task-shifted trauma-focused cognitive behavioral therapy for children who experienced parental death and posttraumatic stress in Kenya and Tanzania: A randomized clinical trial. *JAMA Psychiatry*, *77*(5), 464–473. https://doi.org/10.1001/jamapsychiatry.2019.4475

Grassetti, S. N., Herres, J., Williamson, A. A., Yarger, H. A., Layne, C. M., & Kobak, R. (2015). Narrative focus predicts symptom change trajectories in group treatment for traumatized and bereaved adolescents. *Journal of Clinical Child and Adolescent Psychology*, *44*(6), 933–941. https://doi.org/10.1080/15374416.2014.913249

Haine, R. A., Ayers, T. S., Sandler, I. N., & Wolchik, S. A. (2008). Evidence-based practices for parentally bereaved children and their families. *Professional Psychology: Research and Practice*, *39*(2), 113–121. https://doi.org/10.1037/0735-7028.39.2.113

Hanauer, C., Telaar, B., Rosner, R., & Doering, B. K. (2024). The efficacy of psychosocial interventions for grief symptoms in bereaved children and adolescents: A systematic review and meta-analysis. *Journal of Affective Disorders, 350*, 164–173. https://doi.org/10.1016/j.jad.2024.01.063

Herman, J. L. (1997). *Trauma and recovery.* Basic Books.

Herres, J., Williamson, A. A., Kobak, R., Layne, C. M., Kaplow, J. B., Saltzman, W. R., & Pynoos, R. S. (2017). Internalizing and externalizing symptoms moderate treatment response to school-based trauma and grief component therapy for adolescents. *School Mental Health, 9*(2), 184–193.

Hill, R., Oosterhoff, B., Layne, C., Rooney, E., Yudovich, S., Pynoos, R., & Kaplow, J. (2019). Multidimensional grief therapy: Pilot open trial of a novel intervention for bereaved children and adolescents. *Journal of Child and Family Studies, 28*(11), 3062–3074.

Howell, K. H., Barrett-Becker, E. P., Burnside, A. N., Wamser-Nanney, R., Layne, C. M., & Kaplow, J. B. (2016). Children facing parental cancer versus parental death: The buffering effects of positive parenting and emotional expression. *Journal of Child and Family Studies, 25*(1), 152–164.

Kalantari, M., Yule, W., Dyregrov, A., Neshatdoost, H., & Ahmadi, S. J. (2012). Efficacy of writing for recovery on traumatic grief symptoms of Afghani refugee bereaved adolescents: A randomized control trial. *Omega, 65*(2), 139–150. https://doi.org/10.2190/OM.65.2.d

Kaplow, J. B., Layne, C. M., & Pynoos, R. S. (2019). Treatment of persistent complex bereavement disorder in children and adolescents. In M. Prinstein, E. Youngstrom, E. Mash, & R. Barkley (Eds), *Treatment of disorders in childhood and adolescence* (4th ed., pp. 560–590). Guilford Publications, Inc.

Kaplow, J. B., Layne, C. M., Pynoos, R. S., & Saltzman, W. (2023). *Multidimensional grief therapy: A flexible approach to assessing and supporting bereaved youth.* Cambridge University Press.

Kaplow, J. B., Layne, C. M., Saltzman, W. R., Cozza, S. J., & Pynoos, R. S. (2013). Using multidimensional grief theory to explore the effects of deployment, reintegration, and death on military youth and families. *Clinical Child and Family Psychology Review, 16*(3), 322–340. https://doi.org/10.1007/s10567-013-0143-1

Kaplow, J. B., Saunders, J., Angold, A., & Costello, E. J. (2010). Psychiatric symptoms in bereaved versus non-bereaved youth and young adults: A longitudinal epidemiological study. *Journal of Child and Adolescent Psychiatric Nursing, 49*(11), 1145–1154. https://doi.org/10.1016/j.jaac.2010.08.004

Layne, C. M., Kaplow, J. B., Oosterhoff, B., Hill, R., & Pynoos, R. (2017). The interplay of trauma and bereavement in adolescence: Integrating pioneering work and recent advancements. *Adolescent Psychiatry, 7*(4), 266–285.

Layne, C. M., Pynoos, R. S., Saltzman, W. R., Arslanagić, B., Black, M., Savjak, N., Popović, T., Duraković, E., Mušić, M., Ćampara, N., Djapo, N., & Houston, R. (2001). Trauma/grief-focused group psychotherapy: School-based postwar intervention with traumatized Bosnian adolescents. *Group Dynamics: Theory, Research, and Practice, 5*(4), 277–290. https://doi.org/10.1037/1089-2699.5.4.277

Layne, C. M., Saltzman, W. R., Poppleton, L., Burlingame, G. M., Pašalić, A., Duraković, E., Mušić, M., Ćampara, N., Dapo, N., Arslanagić, B., Steinberg, A. M., & Pynoos, R. S. (2008). Effectiveness of a school-based group psychotherapy program for war-exposed adolescents: A randomized controlled trial. *Journal of the American Academy of Child & Adolescent Psychiatry, 47*(9), 1048–1062. https://doi.org/10.1097/CHI.0b013e31817eecae

Layne, C. M., Warren, J. S., & Saltzman, W. R. et al. (2006). Contextual influences on post-traumatic adjustment: Retraumatization and the roles of distressing reminders, secondary adversities, and revictimization. In L. A. Schein, H.I. Spitz, G. M. Burlingame, & P. R. Muskin (Eds.), *Group approaches for the psychological effects of terrorist disasters* (pp. 235–286). Haworth.

Lechner-Meichsner, F., Spuij, M., & Boelen, P. A. (2025). Sudden gains in the treatment of children and adolescents with prolonged grief. *Journal of Consulting and Clinical Psychology, 93*(1), 14–26. https://doi.org/10.1037/ccp0000932

O'Donnell, K., Dorsey, S., Gong, W., Ostermann, J., Whetten, R., Cohen, J. A., Itemba, D., Manongi, R., & Whetten, K. (2014). Treating maladaptive grief and posttraumatic stress symptoms in orphaned children in Tanzania: Group-based trauma-focused cognitive–behavioral therapy. *Journal of Traumatic Stress, 27*(6), 664–671. https://doi.org/10.1002/jts.21970

Pynoos, R. S., Steinberg, A. M., Layne, C. M., Liang, L.-J., Vivrette, R. L., Briggs, E. C., Kisiel, C., Habib, M., Belin, T. R., & Fairbank, J. A. (2014). Modeling constellations of trauma exposure in the National Child Traumatic Stress Network Core Data Set. *Psychological Trauma: Theory, Research, Practice, and Policy, 6*(Suppl 1), S9–S17. https://doi.org/10.1037/a0037767

Rosner, R., Kruse, J., & Hagl, M. (2010). A meta-analysis of interventions for bereaved children and adolescents. Centre for Reviews and Dissemination (UK). https://www.ncbi.nlm.nih.gov/books/NBK78573/

Rynearson, E. K. (2001). *Retelling violent death.* Brunner-Routledge.

Saladino, V., Verrastro, V., Calaresi, D., & Barberis, N. (2023). The effectiveness of cognitive behavioral therapy for prolonged grief symptoms in children and adolescents: A systematic review. *International Journal of Stress Management, 31*(1), 66–85. https://doi.org/10.1037/str0000301

Salloum, A. (2008). Group therapy for children experiencing grief and trauma due to homicide and violence: A pilot study. *Research on Social Work Practice, 18*(3), 198e211. doi:10.1177/1049731507307808

Salloum, A., & Overstreet, S. (2008). Evaluation of individual and group grief and trauma intervention for children post disaster. *Journal of Clinical Child & Adolescent Psychology, 37*(3), 495–507. https://doi.org/10.1080/15374410802148194

Salloum, A., & Overstreet, S. (2012). Grief and trauma intervention for children after disaster: exploring coping skills versus trauma narration. *Behaviour Research and Therapy, 50*(3), 169–179. https://doi.org/10.1016/j.brat.2012.01.001

Saltzman, W., Layne, C. M., Pynoos, R. S., Olafson, E., Kaplow, J. B., & Boat, B. (2017). *Trauma and grief component therapy for adolescents: A modular approach to treating traumatized and bereaved youth.* Cambridge University Press.

Sandler, I., Tein, J.-Y., Wolchik, S., & Ayers, T. S. (2016). The effects of the family bereavement program to reduce suicide ideation and/or attempts of parentally bereaved children six and fifteen years later. *Suicide and Life-Threatening Behavior, 46*(S1), S32–S38. https://doi.org/10.1111/sltb.12256

Sandler, I. N., Ayers, T. S., & Wolchik, S. A. et al (2003). The family bereavement program: Efficacy evaluation of a theory-based prevention program for parentally bereaved children and adolescents. *Journal of Consulting and Clinical Psychology, 71*(3), 587–600. https://doi.org/10.1037/0022-006X.71.3.587

Sandler, I. N., Ma, Y., Tein, J.-Y., Ayers, T. S., Wolchik, S., Kennedy, C., & Millsap, R. (2010). Long-term effects of the family bereavement program on multiple indicators of grief in parentally bereaved children and adolescents. *Journal of Consulting and Clinical Psychology, 78*(2), 131–143. https://doi.org/10.1037/a0018393

Sandler, I. N., Wolchik, S. A., Ayers, T. S., Tein, J.-Y., & Luecken, L. (2013). Family bereavement program (FBP) approach to promoting resilience following the death of a parent. *Family Science*, *4*(1), 87–94. https://doi.org/10.1080/19424620.2013.821763

Shapiro, D., Howell, K., & Kaplow, J. (2014). Associations among mother-child communication quality, childhood maladaptive grief, and depressive symptoms. *Death Studies*, *38*(3), 172–178.

Siddaway, A. P., Wood, A. M., Schulz, J., & Trickey, D. (2015). Evaluation of the CHUMS child bereavement group: A pilot study examining statistical and clinical change. *Death Studies*, *39*(2), 99–110. https://doi.org/10.1080/07481187.2014.913085

Spuij, M., van Londen-Huiberts, A., & Boelen, P. A. (2013). Cognitive-behavioral therapy for prolonged grief in children: Feasibility and multiple baseline study. *Cognitive and Behavioral Practice*, *20*(3), 349–361. https://doi.org/10.1016/j.cbpra.2012.08.002

Stroebe, M., Schut, H., & Boerner, K. (2010). Continuing bonds in adaptation to bereavement: Toward theoretical integration. *Clinical Psychology Review*, *30*(2), 259–268. https://doi.org/10.1016/j.cpr.2009.11.007

Chapter 14

Psychotherapy for prolonged and traumatic grief in older adults

Katrine B. Komischke-Konnerup and Maja O'Connor

Older people (≥65 years) constitute the age group mostly confronted with bereavement (Hansson & Stroebe, 2007). *Grief,* a natural reaction to the death of a close other, involves emotional, existential, cognitive, behavioral, social, and physical reactions. Across adulthood, adaptive coping with bereavement involves coming to terms with the reality of the loss itself but also reorientating oneself in the changed present world (Stroebe & Schut, 1999, 2010). Stressors in bereavement can be related to the loss itself, but may also encompass secondary loss-related stressors and more general stressors in one's life such as increased physical vulnerabilities and mortality in older age (Stroebe & Schut, 2016). If the bereaved persons experience an overload of stressors, that is when coping demands for a longer period exceed ones coping resources, it may activate and intensify feelings of weakness, pressure, anxiety, and distress interrupting the coping process (Stroebe & Schut, 2016).

Stressors in old age bereavement

Older adults may have an increased risk of overload when coping with loss due to multiple stressors they face – both related to their loss but also associated with their general life circumstances (Hansson & Stroebe, 2007; Thiemann et al., 2021). In terms of loss-related stressors, older adults may experience bereavement overload (i.e., multiple losses of close relatives within a short period of time) and may have several medical conditions themselves (Stroebe & Schut, 2016). Due to multiple losses, the size of their social network may be reduced, which fewer close relatives to seek support from when coping with grief (Hansson & Stroebe, 2007). Moreover, older adults may lose crucial attachment figures (e.g., life partner), which their self-identity and everyday life may be constructed around and they frequently describe such loss as losing a central part of themselves (Maccallum & Bryant, 2013).

DOI: 10.4324/9781003429777-18

In terms of secondary loss-related stressors, an indirect result of losing a close relative such as a long-term spouse may also mean losing important practical, cognitive, and financial resources in one's daily life (Hansson & Stroebe, 2007). One must learn new practical skills that the deceased previously took care of (e.g., cooking, initiating social activities, keeping track of finances). Due to the potential financial consequences of the loss, one may have to save costs and rehouse (Stroebe & Schut, 2016).

Finally, older individuals face stressors related to their life situation in general that may increase the experience of overload. This includes loss of close relationships and social networks, loss of income, increased risk of serious illness and chronic medical conditions, and age-related physical and cognitive decline (O'Connor & Elklit, 2022). For example, while *crystallized intelligence* (i.e., the ability to draw on knowledge and skills acquired over the lifespan) remains relatively stable into older age, *fluid intelligence* (i.e., abstract reasoning, information processing speed, and episodic memory) declines with age (Atalay & Staneva, 2020; Verhaeghen, 2011), potentially making significant changes in life circumstances difficult to manage. While older age is associated with a decline in certain cognitive and physical abilities, bereavement may further impair cognitive abilities such as information processing speed and working memory performance (i.e., fluid intelligence; Atalay & Staneva, 2020) and undermine physical health such as increasing risk of cardiovascular events (Carey et al., 2014). This decline may affect their ability to cope with loss-related and secondary stressors related to their loss, making them particularly vulnerable.

Resilience versus vulnerability

Despite these challenges associated with older age, most older adults cope well with bereavement (O'Connor, 2010). Longitudinal studies of older bereaved populations found that 64–66% show resilient grief-trajectories, while only 6.8–23.6% show persistent symptoms of depression or prolonged grief disorder (PGD) (Galatzer-Levy & Bonanno, 2012; Lundorff et al., 2020). Studies suggest that older age may be a predictor of adverse bereavement outcomes such as PGD (e.g., Comtesse et al., 2024; Kersting et al., 2011; Lundorff et al., 2017; Newson et al., 2011). However, a recent review and meta-analysis of 120 studies of risk factors for developing symptoms of PGD did not find age as a statistically significant risk factor (Buur et al., 2024). It is important to recognize that older bereaved individuals constitute an especially heterogeneous group in terms of psychological, physical, and social abilities (James, 2010). In spite of age-related physical and cognitive challenges, older people generally manage their daily lives well, and many describe older age to include the best decade of their life

(Mehlsen, 2005). Older people can be said to have unique resources that may help them cope well with bereavement. For example, older people generally have higher satisfaction with life and higher levels of well-being than younger people (Jensen et al., 2019) and, besides the increasing prevalence of dementia, also less mental illness (Kessler et al., 2012). They often had many experiences with bereavement and thus may know how to cope with grief when they are bereft again later in life (Hansson & Stroebe, 2007). Older people often have experiences with temporary and chronic physical illness and pain, and many have learned to consider such as an expected part of life (Laidlaw & Pachana, 2009; Laidlaw et al., 2003). The ability to accept what you cannot change may lead to a greater ability to also accept the pain of loss and grief as a part of life. In many ways, older people as a group are proficient at coping with loss and finding ways of adapting to the changed life circumstances that loss often causes. That said, variations in physical, mental, and social in older age are considerable (Hansson & Stroebe, 2007; Stuart-Hamilton, 2011). Coping with bereavement will therefore largely differ from one older individual to the next. This means that bereavement care professionals must investigate variations in personal capacities, challenges, and motivations when meeting older clients.

Prolonged and traumatic grief

Over the course of a person's life span, the risk of dying due to natural causes such as age-related cardiovascular diseases or cancer increases. This means that the odds of experiencing a loss due to natural causes are relatively higher in older age, while the odds of losing someone to a sudden, unnatural cause are relatively larger for younger adults (Hansson & Stroebe, 2007; Treml et al., 2022). Thus, *traumatic grief*, which, according to Smid et al. (2015), refers to the co-occurrence of PGD, posttraumatic stress disorder (PTSD), and/or depression as a result of losses due to traumatic deaths (e.g., homicide), is likely not as frequent in older adults as in younger adults. However, older age losses due to illness can also involve traumatic experiences, e.g., finding the loved one dead after a sudden heart attack or witnessing the loved one in extreme pain, hallucinating, falling, or choking. Such experiences can lead to PTSD symptoms or a mixture of PGD, PTSD, and/or depression symptoms (Hansson & Stroebe, 2007; Komischke-Konnerup et al., 2023; O'Connor, 2010). Based on population- or register-based studies with a majority of non-traumatic deaths, approximately 5–14% of older people showed clinically relevant PGD symptoms, 4–8% experienced depressive symptoms, and 5–16% showed symptoms of PTSD (Komischke-Konnerup et al., 2023; Lundorff et al., 2021; O'Connor, 2010; Treml et al., 2022). Due to high co-occurrence and intertwined temporal relationships between PGD, depression, and PTSD post-loss, the term *complicated grief reactions* has been proposed by the authors of this chapter to capture these diverse symptom profiles in bereaved individuals, irrespective of whether the loss has happened due to traumatic deaths or natural deaths (e.g., Komischke-Konnerup et al., 2021; Larsen et al., 2018). The term complicated grief reactions is an umbrella term that captures PGD as defined in the ICD-11 and DSM-5-TR diagnostic manual as well as other common bereavement-related disorders such as PTSD, depression, anxiety, and additional co-occurrent manifestations of these syndromes. This term may be particularly relevant in the older population because although deaths due to unnatural, traumatic causes are not common, co-occurrence between these syndromes still is (Hansson & Stroebe, 2007; O'Connor, 2010). Furthermore, distress may also manifest itself as somatic complaints in older adults (Hansson & Stroebe, 2007). For example, a study of 324 bereaved older adults found higher PGD symptoms in individuals with high pain compared to those with low pain (Ghesquiere et al., 2020).

Psychotherapy for older bereaved individuals

One relatively recent meta-analysis of psychological interventions for PGD symptoms in adults found that age did not statistically significantly moderate the effect post-intervention (Johannsen et al., 2019). At follow-up, studies with older participants even had larger effects than those with younger. Older individuals are therefore likely to also benefit from psychological interventions, but their change trajectories may have a slower pace. Still, the pooled effect was relatively small ($g = 0.41$; Johannsen et al., 2019), indicating a need for optimizing treatment of PGD in adults across age groups.

PGD treatments based on cognitive behavioral therapies (CBTs) have been suggested to be particularly beneficial for bereaved adults (Doering & Eisma, 2016), and a recent meta-analysis of grief-focused CBTs found an overall moderate effect for PGD symptoms ($g = 0.65$), which was not moderated by age (Komischke-Konnerup et al., 2024). Evidence suggests that CBT may be a helpful treatment in older age in general (see e.g., meta-analysis by Pinquart et al., 2007), because it focuses on specific problems and enhancing skills to deal with challenges in the here-and-now (Laidlaw & McAlpine, 2008). Two narrative reviews of treatment studies for older bereaved people (defined as mean sample age ≥ 65 years) concluded that the strongest available evidence for effective treatments for PGD symptoms in older age is complicated grief treatment (CGT; a treatment which is heavily based on CBT methods such as exposure and behavioral activation), interventions based on the dual-process model, and behavioral interventions with a restoration-oriented focus (Davidow et al., 2022; Roberts et al., 2019). The dual process model is a theoretical model of coping with grief that includes a loss-oriented process (coping with changes in emotions and (continuing) bond to the deceased), a restoration-oriented process (coping with secondary consequences of the loss such as changes in daily routines, economy, and social roles), and an integrative process of oscillating between the two types of challenges (Stroebe & Schut, 1999, 2010; see Chapter 4 for details on the dual-process model). Furthermore, evidence suggests that treatment can be delivered effectively in both a group and individual format to older adults (see e.g., Nam, 2016; Shear et al., 2014; Supiano & Luptak, 2014). However, sufficiently powered RCTs of grief-focused CBTs specifically adapted to treating PGD in older age are still needed and may even be more effective in targeting the specific problems relevant to older bereaved people (Davidow et al., 2022; Komischke-Konnerup et al., 2024; Roberts et al., 2019). A recent qualitative study by Buur et al. (2025) found that older adults treated with a manualized grief-focused CBT for PGD symptoms and other complicated grief reactions (CBTgrief), experienced the treatment as helpful, but also highlighted suggestions for adaptions for interventions better tailored to their individual needs. Recently, a preliminary study further evidenced the feasibility of CBTgrief specifically tailored to older adults in a naturalistic clinical setting (Komischke-Konnerup et al., 2025), and its effectiveness is now being tested in a larger RCT carried out by the authors of this chapter and pre-registered at www.clinicaltrials.gov (identifier: NCT04694807). Tailoring the treatment specifically to a given older client may potentially lead to better treatment outcomes.

Adapting cognitive behavioral therapy for older adults

As the older age group constitutes a highly heterogeneous group both in terms of cognitive and physical function as well as socially, therapists must be attentive to individual needs of clients when adjusting the treatment in general (James, 2010; Laidlaw & McAlpine, 2008). Some older individuals may be both physically and cognitively impaired, thus greater adjustments of the treatment are warranted, whereas others may have high levels of physical and cognitive functioning, and adjustments of standard treatment may not be needed (James, 2010). For this reason, it is important to thoroughly assess the nature of the older individual's problems, weaknesses, and resources both psychologically, biologically, and socially before initiating therapy and take this into account when deciding whether and what adjustments are needed (Laidlaw & McAlpine, 2008). For example, if severely physically impaired, home visits may be needed.

Structure, socialization, and therapeutic style

Keeping a clear structure, socializing the client to therapy, focusing on concrete and present-oriented problems, and collaborative efforts between the therapist and older client are core elements of CBT (Laidlaw et al., 2003).

However, reinforcing these elements may be important when working with older clients with physical and cognitive decline (O'Connor & Elklit, 2022), and providing a clear structure for the therapy sessions with concrete goals, and using simple materials and forms becomes vital (James, 2010). Older clients who received CBTgrief (Komischke-Konnerup et al., 2025) also expressed an extra need for external materials to aid their memory (Buur et al., 2025). For example, the therapist could use visual aids and give the client a handout with the agenda for the session, provide handouts with examples of the homework, or take a picture of the whiteboard at the end of the session.

Therapists need to be particularly aware of potential cohort effects and consider the clients' historical context and societal changes (James, 2010; Laidlaw & McAlpine, 2008). Older individuals did their schooling in a more authoritarian classroom than younger people and are often used to taking a more passive recipient role also when talking to professionals. This could challenge the therapeutic alliance in CBT-based treatments because they commonly use an active and collaborative therapeutic style (Laidlaw & McAlpine, 2008). Furthermore, historical differences in gender roles may be important to be aware of. Older men may have less experience in talking about their feelings, whereas older women may experience more trouble taking charge of their lives and making important decisions about, e.g., financials on their own. However, again with large variations from one individual to the next, significant individual variations are also likely to be present concerning gender roles. Furthermore, older clients may tend to have wandering thoughts and may not be used to concentrating and focusing on talking about a specific topic for longer periods of time and may need extra help staying focused in therapy (Laidlaw & McAlpine, 2008). Here, it becomes crucial to spend time on socializing the older clients to the CBT method. For example, to clearly state that the treatment is focused on present problems and what maintains them, rather than focusing on the client's past life. In CBTgrief, a clear framework for the therapy is presented as a way of socializing to the method and increasing motivation. CBTgrief centers around three key tasks of grieving which are explained to clients as a part of the initial: (1) confronting the loss and the difficult feelings connected to it, (2) keeping or regaining confidence in oneself, others, life, and the future, and (3) engaging in activities that promote adjustment to the new life situation (Komischke-Konnerup et al., 2025). Furthermore, a more directive therapeutic style and more strict turn-taking in groups may be needed to keep the client on track and not get stuck in memories from the past. Older clients who received CBTgrief found this therapeutic style particularly helpful.

> ... you really need someone who, so to speak, takes control and gives you directions (...). So, I don't like the word authoritarian, but right there at

> that point in my life, I thought it was great that someone took me by the hand and said that this is the way we must go
>
> (Buur et al., 2025).

Specific techniques

Psychoeducation

Psychoeducation about grief is essential for bereaved persons to be able to understand and accept their grief reactions (Boelen et al., 2006). When treating older adults this may be even more central due to the historical changes in the understanding of adaptive and pathological grief reactions during the last decades as well as changing cultural norms in society (Prigerson et al., 2021). Psychoeducation in CBTgrief focuses on the framework of the dual process of coping with bereavement (Stroebe & Schut, 1999, 2010) and a cognitive-behavioral conceptualization of PGD (Boelen et al., 2006; see also Chapters 4 and 5). Giving the older clients insight into newer understandings of grief may lead to the normalization of their grief reactions as well as a greater acceptance of different feelings in grief. After being treated with CBTgrief one client expressed it as:

> It was helpful to talk about my anxiety during therapy and to be told, well, there is nothing unusual about this. It was legitimized. To be told that it's natural to have anxiety due to what you've been through
>
> (Buur et al., 2025).

Furthermore, it may be relevant to provide information on how memory can be affected by grief (O'Connor & Seeley, 2022). Older clients may experience fears of dementia when experiencing reductions in memory function and cognitive abilities, which are common during bereavement, making psycho-educating about the grieving brain important (Buur et al., 2025).

Grief- and trauma-focused exposure

Exposure is a core method in CBTgrief and involves the client gradually confronting the avoided internal and/or external loss-related stimuli that are assumed to hinder an adaptive grieving process (Boelen et al., 2006; see also Chapter 6). Different types of exposure can be used depending on the client's problem and what he/she is trying to avoid (Komischke-Konnerup et al., 2025). Examples of the different types of exposure are presented in Table 14.1. While these types of exposure are used across adulthood, some adjustment may be needed for some older adults with physical or cognitive impairments. For example, if the older adult is not able to write, then audio recordings can be used to document the farewell letter to the deceased. Also, music, pictures, and other sensory aids may be important to enhance memory and the potential effects of the exposure.

In a focus group, older clients highlighted exposure as one part of CBT-grief that they found particularly helpful, although it, at the same time, was challenging. One client who received group CBTgrief expressed:

> They asked every time I went to therapy, did you scatter the ashes? Every time… In the end, I had to do it. It was group pressure but in a good way.
>
> (Buur et al., 2025)

Writing letters to the deceased was also highlighted as helpful (Buur et al., 2025). In CBTgrief, letter writing is used flexibly as exposure to target core avoidance behaviors (Komischke-Konnerup et al., 2025). It is often used as exposure to the reality of the loss and associated feelings, by writing a farewell letter to the deceased. However, it can also be a symbolic interaction – a way to construct a new and adaptive connection with the deceased (see also Chapter 8). This may be particularly helpful for older clients who lost their life partner and often experience loneliness related to the absence of their loved one (Bennet & Victor, 2012).

> What was absolutely crucial for me, was that I was told for half an hour a day for five days, I had to write a letter to my husband. I really felt that something important happened. I felt I was in contact with him and at the same time I was fully aware that he was gone[…] Something unfulfilled in me became fulfilled
>
> (Buur et al., 2025).

The use of a Subjective Units of Distress Scale (SUDS) to monitor distress before, during, and after exposure to exercise is recommended.

Cognitive interventions

Cognitive restructuring is a core CBT method that aims to aid clients in identifying unhelpful negative cognitions, testing the utility and validity of cognitions, and formulating more helpful alternative cognitions (Boelen et al., 2006; see also Chapter 7). When working with older clients, it remains particularly important to keep a simple and slow focus and pace (James, 2010). In CBTgrief for older adults, the Cognitive Diamond, a conceptual tool to examine one's *thoughts*, *feelings*, *bodily sensations*, and *behaviors* and how they relate to each other, was added as a supplement to

Table 14.1 Types of exposure and examples

Type of exposure	*Examples*
Exposure to the irreversibility of the loss and painful emotions.	*During therapy*: Leonard, a 75-year-old man who lost his wife Ruth a year ago, and the therapist discussed what is missed most now that Ruth is dead while looking at a picture of Ruth. The therapist put special effort into talking about Ruth in the past tense and repeatedly mentioning that Ruth is dead to exposure to the reality of the loss. *Homework*: Write a farewell letter to Ruth.
Imaginary exposure to traumatizing moments related to the death.	*During therapy*: Mary, 82 years old, who lost her twin sister Sophie two years ago, and the therapist were zooming in on the period of sickness leading up to Sophie's death giving special attention to the most traumatizing moments. The therapist gently guided Mary, helping her reexperience the death by verbalizing sensory inputs, feelings, and thoughts in the present tense. *Homework*: Mary listened to the audio recording several times between sessions and wrote down her distress level before, during, and after listening to the recording.
Exposure to specific stimuli that are avoided and hinders adjustment to life after the loss.	*During therapy*: Leonard and the therapist were making a hierarchical exposure plan to confront the church where Ruth was buried. Leonard used to go to church but after the loss of Ruth, he stopped doing so. He was terrified that he would be paralyzed by grief. *Homework*: Take the first step of looking at the church from the outside until the anxiety decreases.
Diminish compulsive proximity-seeking behaviors that function as avoidance of the reality of the loss and its painful emotions.	*During therapy*: Mary and the therapist discussed the pros and cons of visiting Sophie's grave for several hours each day of the week. *Homework*: Mary agreed to ultimately reduce her time spent at the grave to two weekly visits of approximately 30 minutes.

the traditional cognitive diary (see Figure 14.1). As older clients often mix up thoughts and feelings, psychoeducation about the differences between these is especially important (Laidlaw et al., 2003). Further, it may be helpful to include examples of how the homework forms can be filled out aided

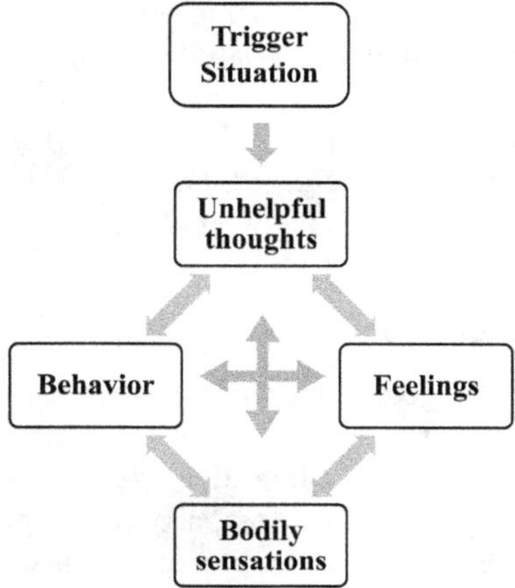

Figure 14.1 The cognitive diamond. Adapted from the Generic CBT (James, 2010).

by questions such as "What was going through your head in that situation?" (Thoughts), "How did your body feel?" (Bodily sensations), "What feelings were present: Anger, fear, sadness, disgust?" (Feelings), and "What did you do?" (Behavior).

The first step in cognitive restructuring is to identify an emotionally stressful situation (a "hot-spot") and examine *negative automatic cognitions* or, as formulated in CBTgrief, to identify and examine *unhelpful thoughts* (Komischke-Konnerup et al., 2025). Sometimes identifying these thoughts may be enough for the older adults to get the needed insights to change their unhelpful cognitions. Older adults often face a lot of challenges such as an increased risk of getting a serious illness or losing other relatives. Therefore, it may be more effective to focus on *helpful* re-evaluations instead of pure *rational* evaluations (James, 2010). Abstract problem-solving may be challenging for some older adults (declining fluid intelligence; Atalay & Staneva, 2020). Thus, it is recommended to draw on older people's tendency for concrete thinking and problem-solving. For example, identifying a concrete everyday situation from last week that was experienced as emotionally difficult.

Behavioral experiments specially designed for the client's problem may be a supportive tool in changing unhelpful thoughts (Laidlaw et al., 2003). There are several reasons for this. First, they involve gathering concrete experiences from the older client's life, which may provide convincing and direct evidence against the unhelpful cognitions (Laidlaw et al., 2003). Second, this may be helpful when there is uncertainty about the nature of the problem (Laidlaw & McAlpine, 2008). For example, is it physical impairment or unhelpful catastrophizing thoughts that are stopping the client from confronting situations related to the loss? Third, behavioral experiments can provide a sense of empowerment through clear evidence that change is possible, especially when combined with monitoring increases and decreases in distress using, e.g., SUDS, which is important when the older client is feeling hopeless (Laidlaw et al., 2003).

Behavioral activation and goal work

Behavioral activation and goal work aim to increase the older client's activity level and commitment to more valuable and enjoyable activities (Eisma et al., 2015; Papa et al., 2013). In older age bereavement, where long-lasting close relationships often are lost, a point to pay attention to is the way clients perceive their self-identity, life, and future without the deceased and what they enjoy. This is important, as many years of habit and systems for leading the daily life may be lost with the death of a close other, and new habits must be learned (cf. Maccallum & Bryant, 2013). A longitudinal study found that the experience of one's identity after the loss as being closely entwined with the deceased relative was a predictor of PGD symptoms, whereas one's perception of one's pre-loss self as being closely merged with the deceased was not (Harris et al., 2023). Thus, it is important to foster the older client's sense of self-identity post-loss. This may concern what are important values to the client, what the client enjoys spending time on, how plans can be rethought and adjusted to the client, but also learning new practical skills and roles. In a focus group an older client mentioned the following about the emotional challenges when she had to make decisions for her life after the loss:

> I've always had someone by my side to discuss things with. Suddenly, I was all alone. So, I really needed help to say "I". I had to rethink things. What do I know? And what can I do? And what should my life look like? I am still learning
>
> (Buur et al., 2025).

If older clients do not know what they enjoy without their loved one, it is useful to start brainstorming and making a list of possible activities (Laidlaw et al., 2003), with a focus on potentially enjoyable activities that did not historically involve the deceased. Psychoeducation about the connection between mood and activities may enhance the client's motivation for working with activation and goal work. If the client is troubled by negative sabotaging cognitions (e.g., "*If I go to the theater, I will be overwhelmed by such an intense sorrow that I will paralyze*"), it would be relevant to frame the activities as a part of a behavioral experiment to test the negative predictions.

Finding the right balance between highly valued and realistic goals is important to maximize functioning and minimize loss experiences (Laidlaw & McAlpine, 2008). *The model of selective optimization with compensation* by Baltes and Baltes (1990) can be used as a guide for the selection of realistic and achievable goals and activities. Here, the older person's potentially reduced functional and cognitive repertoire is taken into account, but at the same time strives for the optimal level of functioning by focusing on the older client's resources and limits (Laidlaw & McAlpine, 2008). For example, a client who wants to go to a theater club once every month, but whose financial resources and physical health are limited, may need to give up other less important but costly activities (selection) and make driving arrangements with friends to compensate for the difficulties walking (compensation).

It may also be helpful to include supportive others in the treatment both to aid the commitment to goals and to foster close connections to persons that could be a source of supporting the older client's life. An RCT by Nam (2016) found that CGT with a supportive other led to statistically significant larger reductions in PGD symptoms among older adults than CGT without a supportive other. This was also something extra that the older adults requested in a focus group of CBTgrief (Buur et al., 2025).

Concluding remarks

Although older people are confronted with many stressors related to their life circumstances and multiple losses of close persons, most older people cope well with bereavement. Still, an important minority experiences complicated grief reactions associated with functional impairment and requires effective treatment. Older individuals with PGD and loss-related PTSD and depression are likely to profit from grief-focused psychotherapy such as CBT. As the older age group is highly diverse – both physically, socially, and psychologically – resources and challenges of each client must be taken into consideration when planning treatment. Some older individuals may require adaptions of interventions, but this is not the case for all.

References

Atalay, K., & Staneva, A. (2020). The effect of bereavement on cognitive functioning among elderly people: Evidence from Australia. *Economics & Human Biology*, *39*, 100932. https://doi.org/10.1016/j.ehb.2020.100932

Baltes, P. B., & Baltes, M. M. (1990). Psychological perspectives on successful aging: The model of selective optimization with compensation. *Successful Aging: Perspectives from the Behavioral Sciences*, *1*(1), 1–34.

Bennet, K. M., & Victor, C. (2012). 'He wasn't in that chair': What loneliness means to widowed older people. *International Journal of Ageing and Later Life*, *7*(1), 33–52. https://doi.org/10.3384/ijal.1652-8670.127133

Boelen, P. A., van den Hout, M. A., & van den Bout, J. (2006). A cognitive-behavioral conceptualization of complicated grief. *Clinical Psychology: Science and Practice*, *13*(2), 109–128. https://doi.org/10.1111/j.1468-2850.2006.00013.x

Buur, C., Zachariae, R., Komischke-Konnerup, K. B., Marello, M. M., Schierff, L. H., & O'Connor, M. (2024). Risk factors for prolonged grief symptoms: A systematic review and meta-analysis. *Clinical Psychology Review*, *107*, 102375. https://doi.org/10.1016/j.cpr.2023.102375

Buur, C., Mackrill, T., Hybholt, L., Nissen, E. R., & O'Connor, M. (2025). Older bereaved individuals' experiences of cognitive-behavioral therapy for complicated grief reactions: A qualitative multistage focus group approach. *Cognitive and Behavioral Practice*, 32, 56–69. https://doi.org/10.1016/j.cbpra.2024.06.002

Carey, I. M., Shah, S. M., DeWilde, S., Harris, T., Victor, C. R., & Cook, D. G. (2014). Increased risk of acute cardiovascular events after partner bereavement: A matched cohort study. *JAMA Internal Medicine*, *174*(4), 598–605. https://doi.org/10.1001/jamainternmed.2013.14558

Comtesse, H., Smid, G. E., Rummel, A.-M., Spreeuwenberg, P., Lundorff, M., & Dückers, M. L. A. (2024). Cross-national analysis of the prevalence of prolonged grief disorder, *Journal of Affective Disorders*, *350*, 359–365, https://doi.org/10.1016/j.jad.2024.01.094

Davidow, J. B., Zide, B. S., Levin, L. L., Biddle, K. D., Urizar, J. C., & Donovan, N. J. (2022). A scoping review of interventions for spousal bereavement in older adults. *The American Journal of Geriatric Psychiatry*, *30*(3), 404–418.

Doering, B. K., & Eisma, M. C. (2016). Treatment for complicated grief: State of the science and ways forward. *Current Opinion Psychiatry*, *29*(5), 286–291. https://doi.org/10.1097/yco.0000000000000263

Eisma, M. C., Boelen, P. A., van den Bout, J., Stroebe, W., Schut, H. A. W., Lancee, J., & Stroebe, M. S. (2015). Internet-based exposure and behavioral activation for complicated grief and rumination: A randomized controlled trial. *Behavior Therapy*, *46*(6), 729–748. https://doi.org/10.1016/j.beth.2015.05.007

Galatzer-Levy, I. R., & Bonanno, G. A. (2012). Beyond normality in the study of bereavement: Heterogeneity in depression outcomes following loss in older adults. *Social Science & Medicine*, *74*(12), 1987–1994. https://doi.org/10.1016/j.socscimed.2012.02.022

Ghesquiere, A., Bagaajav, A., Ito, M., Sakaguchi, Y., & Miyashita, M. (2020). Investigating associations between pain and complicated grief symptoms in bereaved Japanese older adults. *Aging & Mental Health*, *24*(9), 1472–1478. https://doi.org/10.1080/13607863.2019.1594166

Hansson, R. O., & Stroebe, M. S. (2007). *Bereavement in late life: Coping, adaptation, and developmental influences* (1st ed.). American Psychological Association. http://www.loc.gov/catdir/toc/ecip0611/2006009891.html

Harris, C. B., Brookman, R., & O'Connor, M. (2023). It's not who you lose, it's who you are: Identity and symptom trajectory in prolonged grief. *Current Psychology*, *42*(13), 11223–11233. https://doi.org/10.1007/s12144-021-02343-w

James, I. A. (2010). *Cognitive behavioural therapy with older people: Interventions for those with and without dementia.* Jessica Kingsley Publishers.

Jensen, R. A. A., Kirkegaard Thomsen, D., O'Connor, M., & Mehlsen, M. Y. (2019). Age differences in life stories and neuroticism mediate age differences in subjective well-being. *Applied Cognitive Psychology*. *34*(1), 3–15. https://doi.org/10.1002/acp.3580

Johannsen, M., Damholdt, M. F., Zachariae, R., Lundorff, M., Farver-Vestergaard, I., & O'Connor, M. (2019). Psychological interventions for grief in adults:

A systematic review and meta-analysis of randomized controlled trials. *Journal of Affective Disorders, 253*, 69–86. https://doi.org/10.1016/j.jad.2019.04.065

Kersting, A., Brähler, E., Glaesmer, H., & Wagner, B. (2011). Prevalence of complicated grief in a representative population-based sample. *Journal of Affective Disorders, 131*(1), 339–343. https://doi.org/10.1016/j.jad.2010.11.032

Kessler, R. C., Petukhova, M., Sampson, N. A., Zaslavsky, A. M., & Wittchen, H. U. (2012). Twelve-month and lifetime prevalence and lifetime morbid risk of anxiety and mood disorders in the United States. *International Journal of Methods in Psychiatric Research, 21*(3), 169–184. https://doi.org/10.1002/mpr.1359

Komischke-Konnerup, K. B., O'Connor, M., Hoijtink, H., & Boelen, P. A. (2023). Cognitive-behavioral therapy for complicated grief reactions: Treatment protocol and preliminary findings from a naturalistic setting. *Cognitive and Behavioral Practice. 32*(1), 29–43. https://doi.org/10.1016/j.cbpra.2023.11.001

Komischke-Konnerup, K. B., Vang, M. L., Lundorff, M., Elklit, A., & O'Connor, M. (2023). Do early symptoms of prolonged grief disorder lead to symptoms of posttraumatic stress disorder and depression? A longitudinal register-based study of the two first years of bereavement. *Journal of Psychopathology and Clinical Science. 132*(8), 996–1006. https://doi.org/10.1037/abn0000859

Komischke-Konnerup, K. B., Zachariae, R., Boelen, P. A., Marello, M. M., & O'Connor, M. (2024). Grief-focused cognitive behavioral therapies for prolonged grief symptoms: A systematic review and meta-analysis. *Journal of Consulting and Clinical Psychology, 92*(4), 236–248. https://psycnet.apa.org/doi/10.1037/ccp0000884

Komischke-Konnerup, K. B., Zachariae, R., Johannsen, M., Nielsen, L. D., & O'Connor, M. (2021). Co-occurrence of prolonged grief symptoms and symptoms of depression, anxiety, and posttraumatic stress in bereaved adults: A systematic review and meta-analysis. *Journal of Affective Disorders Reports, 4*, 100140. https://doi.org/10.1016/j.jadr.2021.100140

Laidlaw, K., & McAlpine, S. (2008). Cognitive behaviour therapy: How is it different with older people? *Journal of Rational-Emotive & Cognitive-Behavior Therapy, 26*, 250–262.

Laidlaw, K., & Pachana, N. A. (2009). Aging, Mental Health, and Demographic Change: Challenges for Psychotherapists. *Professional Psychology: Research and Practice, 40*(6), 601–608. https://doi.org/10.1037/a0017215

Laidlaw, K., Thompson, L. W., Gallagher-Thompson, D., & Dick-Siskin, L. (2003). *Cognitive behaviour therapy with older people.* John Wiley & Sons.

Larsen, L., Lauritzen, L. R., & O'Connor, M. (2018). Kompliceret sorg og vedvarende sorglidelse: begrebsmæssig adskillelse og sammenhæng. *Psyke & Logos, 39*(1), 15–36.

Lundorff, M., Bonanno, G. A., Johannsen, M., & O'Connor, M. (2020). Are there gender differences in prolonged grief trajectories? A registry-sampled cohort study. *Journal of Psychiatric Research, 129*, 168–175. https://doi.org/10.1016/j.jpsychires.2020.06.030

Lundorff, M., Holmgren, H., Zachariae, R., Farver-Vestergaard, I., & O'Connor, M. (2017). Prevalence of prolonged grief disorder in adult bereavement: A systematic review and meta-analysis. *Journal of Affective Disorders, 212*, 138–149. https://doi.org/http://dx.doi.org/10.1016/j.jad.2017.01.030

Lundorff, M., Johannsen, M., & O'Connor, M. (2021). Time elapsed since loss or grief persistency? Prevalence and predictors of ICD-11 prolonged grief disorder using different applications of the duration criterion. *Journal of Affective Disorders, 279*, 89–97. https://doi.org/10.1016/j.jad.2020.09.116

Maccallum, F., & Bryant, R. A. (2013). A cognitive attachment model of prolonged grief: Integrating attachments, memory, and identity. *Clinical Psychology Review*, *33*(6), 713–727. https://doi.org/10.1016/j.cpr.2013.05.001

Mehlsen, M. Y. (2005). Den paradoksale livstilfredshed i alderdommen. *Psyke & Logos*, *26*(2). 609–628..

Nam, I. (2016). Complicated grief treatment for older adults: The critical role of a supportive person. *Psychiatry Research*, *244*, 97–102. https://doi.org/10.1016/j.psychres.2016.07.044

Newson, R. S., Boelen, P. A., Hek, K., Hofman, A., & Tiemeier, H. (2011). The prevalence and characteristics of complicated grief in older adults. *Journal of Affective Disorders*, *132*(1-2), 231–238. https://doi.org/10.1016/j.jad.2011.02.021

O'Connor, M. (2010). A longitudinal study of PTSD in the elderly bereaved: Prevalence and predictors. *Aging & Mental Health*, *14*(3), 310–318. https://doi.org/10.1080/13607860903228770

O'Connor, M., & Elklit, A. (2022). Treating PTSD symptoms in older adults. In U. Schnyder & M. Cloitre (Eds.), *Evidence based treatments for trauma-related psychological disorders: A practical guide for clinicians* (2nd ed., pp. 443–459). Springer. https://doi.org/10.1007/978-3-030-97802-0_21

O'Connor, M.-F., & Seeley, S. H. (2022). Grieving as a form of learning: Insights from neuroscience applied to grief and loss. *Current Opinion in Psychology*, *43*, 317–322. https://doi.org/10.1016/j.copsyc.2021.08.019

Papa, A., Sewell, M. T., Garrison-Diehn, C., & Rummel, C. (2013). A randomized open trial assessing the feasibility of behavioral activation for pathological grief responding. *Behavior Therapy*, *44*(4), 639–650. https://doi.org/10.1016/j.beth.2013.04.009

Pinquart, M., Duberstein, P. R., & Lyness, J. M. (2007). Effects of psychotherapy and other behavioral interventions on clinically depressed older adults: A meta-analysis. *Aging & Mental Health*, *11*(6), 645–657. https://doi.org/10.1080/13607860701529635

Prigerson, H. G., Kakarala, S., Gang, J., & Maciejewski, P. K. (2021). History and status of prolonged grief disorder as a psychiatric diagnosis, *Annu Rev Clin Psychol*, *17*, 109–126, https://doi.org/10.1146/annurev-clinpsy-081219-093600

Roberts, K. E., Walsh, L. E., Saracino, R. M., Fogarty, J., Coats, T., Goldberg, J., Prigerson, H., & Lichtenthal, W. G. (2019). A systematic review of treatment options for grieving older adults. *Current Treatment Options in Psychiatry*, *6*(4), 422–449. https://doi.org/10.1007/s40501-019-00191-x

Shear, M. K., Wang, Y., Skritskaya, N., Duan, N., Mauro, C., & Ghesquiere, A. (2014). Treatment of complicated grief in elderly persons: A randomized clinical trial. *JAMA Psychiatry*, *71*(11), 1287–1295. https://doi.org/10.1001/jamapsychiatry.2014.1242

Smid, G. E., Kleber, R. J., de la Rie, S. M., Bos, J. B. A., Gersons, B. P. R., & Boelen, P. A. (2015). Brief eclectic psychotherapy for traumatic grief (BEP-TG): Toward integrated treatment of symptoms related to traumatic loss, *European Journal of Psychotraumatology*, *6*, 11, https://doi.org/10.3402/ejpt.v6.27324

Stroebe, M., & Schut, H. (1999). The dual process model of coping with bereavement: Rationale and description. *Death Studies*, *23*(3), 197–224. https://doi.org/10.1080/074811899201046

Stroebe, M., & Schut, H. (2010). The dual process model of coping with bereavement: A decade on. *Omega: Journal of Death and Dying*, *61*(4), 273–289. https://doi.org/10.2190/OM.61.4.b

Stroebe, M., & Schut, H. (2016). Overload: A missing link in the dual process model. *OMEGA-Journal of Death and Dying*, *74*(1), 96–109.

Stuart-Hamilton, I. (2011). *An introduction to gerontology*. Cambridge University Press.

Supiano, K. P., & Luptak, M. (2014). Complicated grief in older adults: a randomized controlled trial of complicated grief group therapy. *The Gerontologist*, *54*(5), 840–856. https://doi.org/10.1093/geront/gnt076

Thiemann, P., Street, A. N., Heath, S. E., Quince, T., Kuhn, I., & Barclay, S. (2021). Prolonged grief disorder prevalence in adults 65 years and over: a systematic review. *BMJ Supportive & Palliative Care*. https://doi.org/10.1136/bmjspcare-2020-002845

Treml, J., Linde, K., Engel, C., Glaesmer, H., Hinz, A., Luck, T., Riedel-Heller, S., Sander, C., & Kersting, A. (2022). Loss and grief in elderly people: Results from the LIFE-Adult-Study. *Death Studies*, *46*(7), 1621–1630. https://doi.org/10.1080/07481187.2020.1824203

Verhaeghen, P. (2011). Cognitive processes and ageing. In I. Stuart-Hamilton (Ed.), *An introduction to gerontology* (pp. 159–193). Cambridge University Press. https://doi.org/10.1017/CBO9780511973697.006

Chapter 15

Psychotherapy for prolonged and traumatic grief in migrants and refugees

Franziska Lechner-Meichsner, Clare Killikelly, and Jeroen W. Knipscheer

A cultural perspective on prolonged and traumatic grief

The father of Aziz, a 36-year-old refugee, was killed five years ago when their town was attacked by members of a terrorist group. Knowing their lives were in danger, Aziz and his brother fled the country immediately and without holding a funeral for their father. During the flight, the brothers became separated when they needed to go with different traffickers to avoid captivity. Aziz has not heard from his brother since then and keeps wondering if he is still alive. He is also plagued by intrusive images of his dead father, has frequent headaches and troubles concentrating, and he blames himself for not being home that day and able to defend his father. He yearns to be able to speak to his father again and feels that he is lost without his guidance.

Lina, the only child of Gita, a 45-year-old Indonesian woman currently living in the Netherlands, was killed during the MH 17 plane crash/attack in 2014. Gita has great difficulty to accept the death of her daughter and longs for her every minute of the day. She blames herself for not having prevented the death as she had some bad feelings about this trip, but her daughter insisted on visiting her grandparents in Indonesia. Gita has horrific images of the moments that Lina was struggling for her life. She rationally knows that Lina will never return but cannot accept it emotionally and constantly ruminates "why" this had to happen. Gita sometimes experiences Lina's presence in her bedroom at night and is overwhelmed with feelings of guilt. Ever since Lina died, life has lost its meaning and Gita hardly engages in social and work-related activities anymore.

Refugees and migrants like Aziz and Gita can develop problems adjusting to bereavement that can be complicated by migration-related stressors or cultural incongruities between their country of origin and host culture. The rate of bereavement among refugees is high and in recent studies between 28% and 92% of the participants reported the death of a loved one (Lechner-Meichsner et al., 2024) that often occurs under traumatic circumstances

DOI: 10.4324/9781003429777-19

and/or is part of a sequence of traumatic events and losses (e.g., Bryant et al., 2020, 2021a). Many refugees also experience ambiguous loss due to the disappearance of their loved ones and uncertainty about their fate (e.g., Comtesse et al., 2022). In Syria alone, an estimated 102,000 people have forcibly disappeared since 2011 (Syrian Network For Human Rights, 2021) and not knowing what happened to their loved ones can add additional grief and stress (see Chapter 11).

The prevalence rates of mental disorders in refugees generally exceed those found in samples from Western countries. With a pooled prevalence of 31%, posttraumatic stress disorder (PTSD) is among the most common disorders (Patanè et al., 2022). Prolonged grief disorder (PGD) has been investigated in fewer studies, but elevated prevalence rates between 15.1% and 36.8% in bereaved refugees have been reported (Bryant et al., 2020, 2021a, 2021b). Bereaved migrants have also been shown to experience more stress-related symptoms than locals (Smid et al., 2018). Symptoms of PGD and PTSD often co-occur in refugees after traumatic loss (Comtesse & Rosner, 2019; Nickerson et al., 2014).

Explanations of the higher prevalence can be related to the inability to perform rituals (e.g., Hinton & Good, 2016), acculturative demands and stress (e.g., Smid et al., 2018), and cultural incongruence (Bhugra & Becker, 2005; see also Chapter 3). Additionally, variable prevalence rates may also be the result of culturally incongruent measurement tools. For example, a study of bereaved Balinese used questionnaires that were developed in Western European settings and found a prevalence rate of 0% for PGD (Djelantik et al., 2021). This is attributed to access to supportive bereavement rituals, but it could also be that the questionnaires did not ask the most culturally relevant or clinically predictive questions (Kokou-Kpolou, 2021).

The generally high prevalence of prolonged grief reactions underscores the importance of including inquiries about the death or disappearance of loved ones and the circumstances of the loss in intake assessments (see also Chapter 2). This should be done in a way that takes culture into account.

Culture-specific symptoms

It is well established that bereavement rituals and expressions of grief differ between cultures (Stroebe & Schut, 1998), and there is increasing acknowledgment that culture can also shape the experience and expression of mental health problems, including PGD (e.g., Hinton & Lewis-Fernández, 2011). The duration of bereavement and mourning is strongly bound to cultural norms. For example, in German-speaking countries, the *Trauerjahr* (year of mourning) is commonly observed, whereas 40 days of mourning may be expected in Arabic-speaking cultures (Rosenblatt, 2008). Worldwide, unique symptoms of grief are increasingly reported, including in refugee and humanitarian migrant groups. A narrative review found that grief-related symptoms unique to particular groups were found to be an important predictor of PGD symptoms: Dreams of the deceased were associated with PGD symptoms in Cambodian refugees, whereas imitating the behavior of the deceased was reported as a common experience for Kurdish refugees (Killikelly et al., 2018). Without this important cultural information, a Western-based clinician might consider these symptoms to be indicative of a serious mental health disorder such as psychosis. Cultural concepts of distress (CCD) were introduced in the DSM-5 in order to capture culturally specific symptoms, explanatory models, and cultural syndromes (American Psychiatric Association, 2013) that may be particularly important for clinical decision making.

Presently, CCD related to bereavement has not been officially documented in the DSM, but the introduction of the cultural caveat in the diagnostic criteria for PGD is an important step forward. In order to account for the contribution of culture to grief symptoms, in both ICD-11 and DSM-5-TR criteria for PGD, the grief reaction must exceed "expected social, cultural, or religious norms for the individual's culture and context" (American Psychiatric Association, 2022; World Health Organization, 2019). To date there is a lack of clear clinical guidance on how to operationalize the cultural caveat, particularly in clinical settings working with diverse cultural groups. Most studies that assessed PGD in refugee samples relied on established instruments that were developed among samples from Western countries, but culturally adapted measures have been shown to yield even higher prevalence estimates and additional symptoms (Killikelly et al., 2018). There have been recent advances in the development of assessment measures that may reliably and effectively assess the role of culture in PGD diagnosis and treatment planning. The International Prolonged Grief Disorder Scale (IPGDS) was developed in two parts: part 1 (standard scale) aims to capture the established ICD-11 criteria for PGD and includes 13 items based on the specific diagnostic criteria (Killikelly et al., 2020). Part 2 (cultural supplement) aims to assist treatment planning by assessing common culturally specific symptoms of grief. Presently, part 2 has been adapted to assess unique symptoms of PGD in Chinese, Japanese, Swiss, Syrian, and Arabic-speaking cultural groups. Guidance on how to use the cultural supplement including cultural adaptation is available for clinicians and researchers (Killikelly & Maercker, 2023). For example, following key informant interviews with refugees from Syria unique symptoms such as "emotional outburst" and "weariness" were identified (Killikelly et al., 2021).

Alongside the development of a questionnaire, the Bereavement and Grief Cultural Formulation Interview (BG-CFI; Groen et al., 2022; Smid et al., 2018) was developed to provide clinicians and patients with a shared understanding of grief, culture, and the relevance for treatment planning.

We recently assessed the feasibility and acceptability of the BG-CFI in a brief pilot study with a group of 11 displaced people from different countries and three clinicians from Switzerland. Thematic analysis found that patients determined the interview experience to be comfortable, easy to understand, and provided the opportunity to express oneself. Clinicians also identified the usefulness of the interview protocol in helping to redefine diagnosis and guide treatment planning.

Recognizing culturally specific symptoms of grief is essential for conducting a reliable and valid assessment of PGD in refugee groups and has been shown to improve therapeutic rapport, yield more effective treatment planning, and produce better patient outcomes (Kohrt et al., 2014; Lewis-Fernández et al., 2017).

Postmigration stressors

Refugee mental health is not only affected by premigration factors such as prior exposure to traumatic events, but also by ongoing postmigration stressors (Miller & Rasmussen, 2017). Postmigration stressors include all hardships related to migration that refugees face in their host country, including problems with the asylum procedure, housing difficulties, unemployment, separation from family, or discrimination. These stressors can have a significant impact because they are daily stressors over which refugees have little or no control (Miller & Rasmussen, 2017), and they are also related to prolonged grief symptoms (Lechner-Meichsner et al., 2023). Studies have shown that, for example, an uncertain residence status (Comtesse & Rosner, 2019), experienced discrimination (Bryant et al., 2019), or a lack of social support (Comtesse et al., 2022) are associated with higher PGD symptoms. Additionally, non-personal losses that occur as part of flight or migration, such as disruptions of role and identity, and erosion of interpersonal bonds and networks (Tay et al., 2019) or the loss of culture and support (Nickerson et al., 2014), can also have a negative impact on grief reactions.

Depending on the culture of origin, mourning rituals involving the community are also an important part of bereavement, and a lack of shared mourning can hinder adaptation to the loss (Lechner-Meichsner & Comtesse, 2022; Smid et al., 2018). In an interview study with refugees from Arabic-speaking countries and sub-Saharan Africa about illness beliefs regarding PGD, participants described the importance of religious or spiritual rituals as well as sharing grief in the community in a ritualized way (Lechner-Meichsner & Comtesse, 2022). Being unable to perform or participate in rituals due to the flight or not being able to return home when the death occurred was perceived as a possible cause of PGD by a quarter of participants (Lechner-Meichsner & Comtesse, 2022). This association was also shown in a study with immigrants and refugees to Belgium and France, where those who had not taken part in bereavement rituals reported higher levels of guilt, emptiness, and despondency (Kokou-Kpolou et al., 2017).

Help-seeking

In general, psychological interventions developed in Western Europe and North America are grounded in Western epistemological and philosophical traditions that might be culturally incongruent for people of non-Western descent. For example, the act of visiting a clinic or hospital to discuss bereavement or mental health more generally may be considered inappropriate or intrusive (Killikelly et al., 2021). As a result, help-seeking from mental health services might be lower among these populations than other ethnic groups, leading to more severe clinical profiles at treatment initiation and an increased likelihood of poor treatment outcomes or treatment dropout (Boettcher et al., 2021).

In many cultures, grief support is located within the private sphere, i.e., from local or grassroot support groups, religious leaders, family, and friends. In the above-mentioned study with Arabic-speaking and sub-Saharan African refugees, the majority of participants thought social support most adequate to alleviate PGD symptoms, but also named the completion of rituals, and spiritual or religious cures (Lechner-Meichsner & Comtesse, 2022). About half of the participants also considered seeking help from mental health professionals, and many participants named behavior changes or cognitive changes that align with elements of evidence-based treatment for PGD (e.g., changing unhelpful beliefs, expressing painful emotions, pursuing goals). However, some participants also voiced doubts whether mental health professionals with a Western background can help if they are not familiar with the bereavement-related traditions of the patient's culture. In addition, participants mentioned stigma associated with mental illness and explained that seeking psychotherapy because of grief reactions could be considered as "crazy". Similarly, in focus groups and key informant interviews with Syrian refugees (Killikelly et al., 2021), many expressed concern over the acceptability of PGD as a mental health disorder. For example, participants were concerned that the label of PGD would be stigmatized and lead to discrimination in the community. The understanding of mental health disorders as an explanation for distress is a Western-centric view that may not be helpful or accepted in other contexts. Practitioners need to be aware that this can also influence help-seeking behavior.

Psychotherapy with migrants and refugees

Some key aspects need to be considered when providing psychotherapy for migrants and refugees. In a broader sense, psychotherapy constitutes a cultural encounter between the patient and practitioner that is sometimes

Table 15.1 Recommendations for practice

Clinical encounter	*Clinical tools*
• Explore and reflect on grief and psychotherapy in general, including stigma • Reflect on your own cultural norms, beliefs and values, own privileges and biases, and how they might differ from the patient's • Ensure access to supervision, debriefing, and self-reflection for dealing with complex cases and intense emotional distress	• Construct a shared explanatory model including key elements such as rituals, access to support, and beliefs about grief and mental health • Incorporate culturally-sensitive assessment instruments • Take time to explain the treatment rationale • Provide and elicit recommendations for local support, religious support, and social support • Prepare to work with multiple losses and multiple traumas

accompanied by a language barrier and that may involve an exploration of the role of the patient's and therapist's cultural identity. More specifically, psychotherapy for prolonged and traumatic grief involves cultural identity in relation to bereavement and grief, that is particularly salient when beliefs and expectations differ between the culture of origin and the host culture. Table 15.1 summarizes recommendations for practice.

Cultural sensitivity

Cultural sensitivity includes the tailoring of an intervention to a cultural context (Hall, 2001), as well as knowledge, awareness, and understanding on the side of the practitioner (Foronda, 2008). Next to organizational and therapist-related adaptations (such as ethnic matching of therapists to patients, and professional competencies like knowledge, awareness, attitude, and skills), content-related adaptations are of particular interest (Hinton et al., 2012). Cultural adaptation has been defined as the systematic modification of evidence-based interventions to consider language, culture, and context so that the interventions are congruent with the cultural background of the patient (Bernal et al., 2009). Domains in intervention-related adaptations are: language, metaphors, content, goals, concepts, methods, and context (e.g., Bernal & Sáez-Santiago, 2006; Heim et al., 2021).

Practitioners need to be aware how their own culture of origin has shaped their worldview and that this can differ in their patients. Relatedly, cultural identity can be understood as the identity shaped by incorporated norms and values that also determine what someone perceives as right or wrong or appropriate or inappropriate, while these norms and values are negotiated within a group to which the individual belongs (Groen et al., 2018). This is largely implicit, but worth being openly addressed in case of different cultural backgrounds of practitioner and patient. Inquiring about expectations regarding mourning and grief, being open to understanding the significance of rituals, and asking about traditional help-seeking behaviors, can contribute to the patient being understood and incorporating important elements into the treatment. In the case of Aziz, this is how the therapist learned about the significance of holding funeral rites for the deceased.

Cultural sensitivity also extends to being aware of culturally specific symptoms and being attentive to them during the assessment. Culturally-sensitive assessment instruments such as the IPGDS and the BG-CFI can be valuable tools. Including Aziz's headaches in the assessment revealed that medical examinations have failed to identify an underlying medical condition, but that his headaches were most severe when he was reminded of the traumatic events. This was also seen in the case of Gita, who suffered from different severe somatic symptoms that she initially did not relate to her grief reaction. While not inherently a cultural factor, postmigration factors relating to general daily stressors as well as to the loss experience more directly, should also be explored during intakes and assessments.

Subsequently, the assessment results should inform the formulation of a shared explanatory model (see below).

Working with interpreters

Refugees and migrants who have arrived in the host country only fairly recently or who suffer from severe PTSD symptoms (Schiess-Jokanovic et al., 2021) may not speak the language well enough to engage in psychotherapy. If the patient cannot be matched to a practitioner who speaks their language, therapy needs to be conducted with an interpreter. Although there can be challenges regarding cultural, bureaucratic, and practical aspects, the quality of the translation, and working in a triadic setting, interpreter-assistant treatments can be delivered successfully (e.g., d'Ardenne et al., 2007; Lechner-Meichsner et al., 2022). Including an interpreter can also have additional benefits because the interpreter can serve as a cultural broker and increase understanding between the patient and therapist. Table 15.2 summarizes a few key points for working with interpreters. Further information can be found elsewhere (e.g., Kluge, 2020; Martin et al., 2020).

Psychoeducation and development of a shared explanatory model

Psychoeducation about prolonged and traumatic grief needs to be combined with the patient's perception and explanations of the grief reaction. This is important because arriving at a shared understanding of the complaints and the explanatory model (i.e., the explanation for the complaints or symptoms) is the foundation of a successful treatment (Heim et al., 2021;

Table 15.2 Tips for working with interpreters

- The interpreter needs to be a professional who has undergone training, ideally including interpreting in a health care context.
- Preferably, the therapist should provide the interpreter with information about the most relevant aspects of the treatment, such as information about prolonged and traumatic grief as well as rationale and procedures for key interventions.
- Gender, ethnicity, and political sensitivities need to be considered when selecting an interpreter.
- The same interpreter needs to be used throughout the whole treatment, unless there are reasons that make a change necessary.
- Confidentiality, as part of the formal professional obligation, needs to be clearly addressed. If possible, there should also be no contact between the patient and interpreter outside the therapy session, although this can be difficult to achieve for members of small language groups that may encounter the same interpreter in different contexts.
- Therapists and interpreters should plan for regular debriefing after the sessions.

see also Chapter 5). To achieve this, the conversation between therapist and patient can go back and forth between inquiring how the patient and their community perceive and explain the grief reaction, and offering psychoeducation on the disorder and theoretical models on the part of the therapist. If not offered by the patient themselves, therapists should also inquire about traditions and rituals surrounding a death, and if they could be completed. For Aziz, for example, not having been able to hold a funeral for his father played a major role in explaining his symptoms because this caused guilt and a sense of "unfinished business". Therapists also need to be aware of the stigma discussed above and explore if such concerns exist.

Brief eclectic psychotherapy for prolonged and traumatic grief

Although there is a body of research on the treatment of PTSD in refugees, so far, only Brief Eclectic Psychotherapy for Prolonged and Traumatic Grief (BEPPTG; de Heus et al., 2017) specifically addresses prolonged and traumatic grief in refugees. It consists of 16 sessions and four phases that can be provided individually or integrated into a day patient treatment setting aimed at dealing with high levels of intervening stressors. In a pilot study that evaluated the effectiveness of this day patient treatment in 16 patients, rates of completion were high (81%). At the end of treatment, symptoms of PTSD and rates of diagnosable PTSD and prolonged grief (i.e., persistent complex bereavement disorder as included in DSM-5) were markedly reduced (de Heus et al., 2017). Therapists also valued BEPPTG as an effective treatment. An uncontrolled study with a larger sample of 81 patients found medium effects on the reduction of PTSD and prolonged grief symptoms, while the presence of postmigration stressors was associated with a slightly lower reduction in prolonged grief symptoms (Djelantik et al., 2020). Important elements of BEPPTG are described below.

Grief- and trauma-focused exposure

Before starting exposure sessions, it is important to explain the rationale and prepare the patient for intense bodily sensations that may occur. It should be considered that in some cultures repressing or avoiding intense emotions is favored above bearing or expressing them. Consequently, arousal during exposure might be highly increased, and the window of tolerance may be smaller (Zayfert, 2008). It is then important to increase affect tolerance by providing emotion regulation techniques before entering the exposure phase. In the case of Gita, exposure was related to images in which Lina was struggling for her life. This was very difficult for Gita, and while being confronted with these images, she was afraid she would faint, become "totally mad" or lose control. The therapist therefore first invested in teaching emotion regulation techniques which gave her more confidence so that she could bare the physical sensations during the exposure sessions.

During general exposure with Aziz, the therapist asked him about his father, the circumstances of the death, and what he misses most. When Aziz described this, the therapist also asked him to name the emotions and thoughts associated with first realizing that his father was gone. This was followed by imaginal exposure about the worst moment. For Aziz, this was coming home and seeing his father's dead body lying in the street, surrounded by a crowd of neighbors. Aziz told this story chronologically with closed eyes, while the therapist asked him to name sensory experiences, thoughts, and emotions. Aziz also told crucial parts of the memory—e.g., an exchange with a neighbor who told him what happened—in his native language to reach full memory activation.

Attribution of meaning, reengaging, and activation

Information from the BG-CFI may help practitioners to distinguish between avoidance and cultural context, and ensure that interventions are adapted to the cultural context. The information may for instance increase understanding why a patient still dresses in black months after a death, or it may enable the therapist and patient to investigate whether reducing mourning behavior is possible while the cultural context into account.

Attribution of meaning relates to evaluating implications of the loss, i.e., how the death of the loved one affects the bereaved person's view on themselves, others, the future, and the relationship with the deceased. The therapist aims to foster self-compassion, acceptance of emotions, reengagement with people and activities, and a revised connection with the deceased.

Regarding the latter, imaginary conversations and other symbolic interactions (see below) can be used.

Symbolic interactions

When coping with loss, many survivors participate in activities related to spiritual, religious, or moral traditions, such as prayer, meditation, visits to spiritual or religious gatherings, or conversations with religious or spiritual leaders (Hinton et al., 2013). This can be experienced as helpful in processing the loss and dealing with feelings of guilt. Family, friends, or others may suggest other types of help. The BG-CFI provides insight into cultural rituals and practices related to grief, allowing practitioners to assess what is appropriate within the person's specific culture. This insight into cultural norms of mourning makes it possible to estimate how the treatment can be tailored to suit the patient best. The BG-CFI encourages practitioners to explore alternative ways in which grief and mourning can be expressed, with an emphasis on enabling emotional expression, for instance, whether it is allowed to talk about or with the deceased, why this is or is not allowed, or inappropriate.

Mourning rituals in particular may often shape and define culturally specific ways to grieve (Smid et al., 2018). These rituals may include various prescribed practices, such as designated time frames for expressing grief, specific activities (such as holding a wake, annual commemorations, or ways to handle the body of the deceased). They may also outline conditions regarding when and how it is appropriate to mourn or communicate with the deceased (Cacciatore & DeFrain, 2015). When a bereaved person describes experiences of contact with the deceased loved one (such as when the person who died is being seen, felt, or smelt, or when the bereaved person is speaking to the deceased), it is essential to consider cultural interpretations, in close tuning with the bereaved and their system. Mourning rituals can also serve as a way to restore balance or express apologies and gratitude to the deceased (Smid et al., 2018).

The therapist and Gita discussed which specific rituals her family in Indonesia would do (Wojtkowiak et al., 2021) and planned how she could perform these activities with food, music, and dance with her loved ones in honor of Lina. These experiences of support meant much to her and made her feel less anxious, which was evidenced in the decrease of nightmares and feelings of guilt.

The empty chair technique was also introduced with Gita. She was guided through a conversation with her daughter and encouraged to express all the feelings she had, including negative ones. As Gita was affiliated with the Islamic religion, it was particularly difficult to address the feelings of anger she had toward her daughter because they had been quarrelling before the journey, and their farewell had not gone well. She was reluctant to engage in the exercise and afraid that by expressing bad thoughts to her, Lina would not find peace in the afterlife. By exploring her fears and inviting her to reflect on the essence of the Islamic religion, Gita gradually could look differently and realized she was guided by fear and superstition as the true Islamic religion fosters love. She then could engage in the exercise, in which she came to terms with her daughter. Following this, the experiences of being aware of her daughter in her bedroom decreased and were no longer frightening.

Aziz was distressed by the fact that he had not been able to say goodbye to his father and participate in the funeral. This was addressed using imagery rescripting (Arntz et al., 2013). First, Aziz relived the memory until the moment he found his father's body, but was then guided to imagine a course of events that allowed him to complete rituals. He imagined washing the blood of his father's body, dressing him in clean clothes, and holding a traditional funeral. This reduced feelings of guilt, sadness, and anger, but Aziz still expressed the need to say goodbye. The therapist then guided him into an imagery conversation with his father. Aziz told his father how lost he feels without his guidance, and the father answered that he is proud of the path Aziz has found for himself and that he will be alright.

Future directions and conclusions

Despite advances in studying mental health in refugees and migrants as outlined in this chapter, 90% of mental health research to date has been conducted in Western European contexts and is susceptible to particular biases and assumptions that may not apply to the rest of the world (Henrich et al., 2010). Consequently, there has been considerable debate about the adaptability of Western psychological interventions that are based on specific cultural conceptions of mental disorders, and whether such interventions might be efficacious only when delivered in a congruent cultural context (e.g., Kleinman et al., 2006). There is increasing recognition of a need for a paradigm shift toward research that prioritizes the experiences and perspectives of those outside of the North American-European context (Mills, 2013).

Refugees and migrants have a heightened risk to develop prolonged and traumatic grief. Practitioners need to be aware that grief reactions can manifest in the form of additional culturally specific symptoms and that culturally diverse help-seeking intentions, explanations of psychological reactions, and grief-related rituals also call for adaptations of treatments developed based on Western practices.

References

American Psychiatric Association (2013). *Diagnostic and statistical manual of mental disorders* (5th ed.). Author.

American Psychiatric Association (2022). *Diagnostic and statistical manual of mental disorders, fifth edition, text revision (DSM-5-TR)*. Author.

Arntz, A., Sofi, D., & van Breukelen, G. (2013). Imagery rescripting as treatment for complicated PTSD in refugees: A multiple baseline case series study. *Behaviour Research and Therapy*, *51*(6), 274–283. https://doi.org/10.1016/j.brat.2013.02.009

Bernal, G., Jiménez-Chafey, M. I., & Domenech Rodríguez, M. M. (2009). Cultural adaptation of treatments: A resource for considering culture in evidence-based practice. *Professional Psychology: Research and Practice*, *40*(4), 361–368. https://doi.org/10.1037/a0016401

Bernal, G., & Sáez-Santiago, E. (2006). Culturally centered psychosocial interventions. *Journal of Community Psychology*, *34*(2), 121–132. https://doi.org/10.1002/jcop.20096

Bhugra, D., & Becker, M. A. (2005). Migration, cultural bereavement and cultural identity. *World Psychiatry: Official Journal of the World Psychiatric Association (WPA)*, *4*(1), 18–24.

Boettcher, V. S., Nowak, A. C., & Neuner, F. (2021). Mental health service utilization and perceived barriers to treatment among adult refugees in Germany. *European Journal of Psychotraumatology*, *12*(1), 1910407. https://doi.org/10.1080/20008198.2021.1910407

Bryant, R. A., Edwards, B., Creamer, M., O'Donnell, M., Forbes, D., Felmingham, K. L., Silove, D., Steel, Z., McFarlane, A. C., van Hooff, M., Nickerson, A., & Hadzi-Pavlovic, D. (2020). A population study of prolonged grief in refugees. *Epidemiology and Psychiatric Sciences*, 29, e44. https://doi.org/10.1017/S2045796019000386

Bryant, R. A., Bawaneh, A., Giardinelli, L., Awwad, M., Al-Hayek, H., & Akhtar, A. (2021a). A prevalence assessment of prolonged grief disorder in Syrian refugees. *World Psychiatry*, *20*(2), 302–303. https://doi.org/10.1002/wps.20876

Bryant, R. A., Edwards, B., Creamer, M., O'Donnell, M., Forbes, D., Felmingham, K. L., Silove, D., Steel, Z., McFarlane, A. C., Van Hooff, M., Nickerson, A., & Hadzi-Pavlovic, D. (2021b). Prolonged grief in refugees, parenting behaviour and children's mental health. *Australian & New Zealand Journal of Psychiatry*, *55*(9), 863–873. https://doi.org/10.1177/0004867420967420

Cacciatore, J., & DeFrain, J. (Eds.). (2015). *The world of bereavement: Cultural perspectives on death in families*. Springer International Publishing. https://doi.org/10.1007/978-3-319-13945-6

Comtesse, H., Lechner-Meichsner, F., Haneveld, J., Vogel, A., & Rosner, R. (2022). Prolonged grief in refugees living in Germany confronted with ambiguous or confirmed loss. *Anxiety, Stress, and Coping*, *35*(3), 259–269. https://doi.org/10.1080/10615806.2021.1967936

Comtesse, H., & Rosner, R. (2019). Prolonged grief disorder among asylum seekers in Germany: The influence of losses and residence status. *European Journal of Psychotraumatology*, *10*(1). 1591330. https://doi.org/10.1080/20008198.2019.1591330

d'Ardenne, P., Ruaro, L., Cestari, L., Fakhoury, W., & Priebe, S. (2007). Does interpreter-mediated CBT with traumatized refugee people work? A comparison of patient outcomes in East London. *Behavioural and Cognitive Psychotherapy*, *35*(3), 293–301. https://doi.org/10.1017/S1352465807003645

de Heus, A., Hengst, S. M. C., de la Rie, S. M., Djelantik, A. A. A. M. J., Boelen, P. A., & Smid, G. E. (2017). Day patient treatment for traumatic grief: Preliminary evaluation of a one-year treatment programme for patients with multiple and traumatic losses. *European Journal of Psychotraumatology*, *8*(1), 1375335. https://doi.org/10.1080/20008198.2017.1375335

Djelantik, A. A. A. M. J., Aryani, P., Boelen, P. A., Lesmana, C. B. J., & Kleber, R. J. (2021). Prolonged grief disorder, posttraumatic stress disorder, and depression following traffic accidents among bereaved Balinese family members: Prevalence, latent classes and cultural correlates. *Journal of Affective Disorders*, *292*, 773–781. https://doi.org/10.1016/j.jad.2021.05.085

Djelantik, A. A. A. M. J., de Heus, A., Kuiper, D., Kleber, R. J., Boelen, P. A., & Smid, G. E. (2020). Post-migration stressors and their association with symptom reduction and non-completion during treatment for traumatic grief in refugees. *Frontiers in Psychiatry*, *11*, 407. https://doi.org/10.3389/fpsyt.2020.00407

Foronda, C. L. (2008). A concept analysis of cultural sensitivity. *Journal of Transcultural Nursing*, *19*(3), 207–212. https://doi.org/10.1177/1043659608317093

Groen, S. P. N., Menninga, M. C., Cath, D. C., & Smid, G. E. (2022). Let's talk about grief: Protocol of a study on the recognition and psychoeducation of prolonged grief disorder in outpatients with common mental disorders. *Frontiers in Psychiatry*, *13*, 944233. https://doi.org/10.3389/fpsyt.2022.944233

Groen, S. P. N., Richters, A., Laban, C. J., & Devillé, W. L. J. M. (2018). Cultural identity among Afghan and Iraqi traumatized refugees: Towards a conceptual framework for mental health care professionals. *Culture, Medicine, and Psychiatry*, *42*(1), 69–91. https://doi.org/10.1007/s11013-016-9514-7

Hall, G. C. N. (2001). Psychotherapy research with ethnic minorities: Empirical, ethical, and conceptual issues. *Journal of Consulting and Clinical Psychology*, *69*(3), 502–510. https://doi.org/10.1037/0022-006X.69.3.502

Heim, E., Mewes, R., Abi Ramia, J., Glaesmer, H., Hall, B., Harper Shehadeh, M., Ünlü, B., Kananian, S., Kohrt, B. A., Lechner-Meichsner, F., Lotzin, A., Moro, M. R., Radjack, R., Salamanca-Sanabria, A., Singla, D. R., Starck, A., Sturm, G., Tol, W., Weise, C., & Knaevelsrud, C. (2021). Reporting cultural adaptation in psychological trials – The RECAPT criteria. *Clinical Psychology in Europe*, *3*(Special Issue), e6351. https://doi.org/10.32872/cpe.6351

Henrich, J., Heine, S. J., & Norenzayan, A. (2010). Most people are not WEIRD. *Nature*, *466*, 29. https://doi.org/10.1038/466029a

Hinton, D. E., & Good, B. J. (Eds.). (2016). *Culture and PTSD: Trauma in global and historical perspective*. University of Pennsylvania Press. https://doi.org/10.9783/9780812291469

Hinton, D. E., & Lewis-Fernández, R. (2011). The cross-cultural validity of posttraumatic stress disorder: Implications for DSM-5. *Depression and Anxiety*, *28*(9), 783–801. https://doi.org/10.1002/da.20753

Hinton, D. E., Peou, S., Joshi, S., Nickerson, A., & Simon, N. (2013). Normal grief and complicated bereavement among traumatized Cambodian refugees: Cultural context and the Central role of dreams of the dead. *Culture, Medicine, and Psychiatry*, *37*(3), 427–464. https://doi.org/10.1007/s11013-013-9324-0

Hinton, D. E., Rivera, E. I., Hofmann, S. G., Barlow, D. H., & Otto, M. W. (2012). Adapting CBT for traumatized refugees and ethnic minority patients: Examples from culturally adapted CBT (CA-CBT). *Transcultural Psychiatry*, *49*(2), 340–365. https://doi.org/10.1177/1363461512441595

Killikelly, C., Bauer, S., & Maercker, A. (2018). The assessment of grief in refugees and post-conflict survivors: A narrative review of etic and emic research. *Frontiers in Psychology*, *9*, 1957. https://doi.org/10.3389/fpsyg.2018.01957

Killikelly, C., & Maercker, A. (2023). The cultural supplement: A new method for assessing culturally relevant prolonged grief disorder symptoms. *Clinical Psychology in Europe*, *5*(1), e7655. https://doi.org/10.32872/cpe.7655

Killikelly, C., Ramp, M., & Maercker, A. (2021). Prolonged grief disorder in refugees from Syria: Qualitative analysis of culturally relevant symptoms and implications for ICD-11. *Mental Health, Religion & Culture*, 1–18. https://doi.org/10.1080/13674676.2020.1825361

Killikelly, C., Zhou, N., Merzhvynska, M., Stelzer, E.-M., Dotschung, T., Rohner, S., Sun, L. H., & Maercker, A. (2020). Development of the international prolonged grief disorder scale for the ICD-11: Measurement of core symptoms and culture items adapted for Chinese and German-speaking samples. *Journal of Affective Disorders*, *277*, 568–576. https://doi.org/10.1016/j.jad.2020.08.057

Kleinman, A., Eisenberg, L., & Good, B. (2006). Culture, illness, and care: Clinical lessons from anthropologic and cross-cultural research. *FOCUS*, *4*(1), 140–149. https://doi.org/10.1176/foc.4.1.140

Kluge, U. (2020). The role of the interpreters in intercultural psychotherapy. In M. Schouler-Ocak & M. C. Kastrup (Eds.), *Intercultural psychotherapy* (pp. 93–101). Springer International Publishing. https://doi.org/10.1007/978-3-030-24082-0_7

Kohrt, B. A., Rasmussen, A., Kaiser, B. N., Haroz, E. E., Maharjan, S. M., Mutamba, B. B., de Jong, J. T., & Hinton, D. E. (2014). Cultural concepts of distress and psychiatric disorders: Literature review and research recommendations for global mental health epidemiology. *International Journal of Epidemiology*, *43*(2), 365–406. https://doi.org/10.1093/ije/dyt227

Kokou-Kpolou, C. K. (2021). Letter to the editor: Prolonged grief disorder, posttraumatic stress disorder, and depression following traffic accidents among bereaved Balinese family members: Prevalence, latent classes and cultural correlates. *Journal of Affective Disorders*, *295*, 1–2. https://doi.org/10.1016/j.jad.2021.08.007

Kokou-Kpolou, C. K., Mbassa Menick, D., Moukouta, C. S., Baugnet, L., & Kpelly, D. E. (2017). A cross-cultural approach to complicated grief reactions among Togo–Western African immigrants in Europe. *Journal of Cross-Cultural Psychology*, *48*(8), 1247–1262. https://doi.org/10.1177/0022022117721972

Lechner-Meichsner, F., & Comtesse, H. (2022). Beliefs about causes and cures of prolonged grief disorder among Arab and sub-Saharan African refugees. *Frontiers in Psychiatry*, *13*, 852714. https://doi.org/10.3389/fpsyt.2022.852714

Lechner-Meichsner, F., Comtesse, H., & Olk, M. (2023). Prevalence, comorbidities, and factors associated with prolonged grief disorder, posttraumatic stress disorder and complex posttraumatic stress disorder in refugees: A systematic review. *Conflict and Health*, *18*(1), 32. https://doi.org/10.1186/s13031-024-00586-5

Lechner-Meichsner, F., Ehring, T., Krüger-Gottschalk, A., Morina, N., Plankl, C., & Steil, R. (2022). Using imagery rescripting to treat posttraumatic stress disorder in refugees: A case study. *Cognitive and Behavioral Practice*. https://doi.org/10.1016/j.cbpra.2022.06.002

Lewis-Fernández, R., Aggarwal, N. K., Lam, P. C., Galfalvy, H., Weiss, M. G., Kirmayer, L. J., Paralikar, V., Deshpande, S. N., Díaz, E., Nicasio, A. V., Boiler, M., Alarcón, R. D., Rohlof, H., Groen, S., Van Dijk, R. C. J., Jadhav, S., Sarmukaddam, S., Ndetei, D., Scalco, M. Z., & Vega-Dienstmaier, J. M. (2017). Feasibility, acceptability and clinical utility of the cultural formulation interview: Mixed-methods results from the DSM-5 international field trial. *British Journal of Psychiatry*, *210*(4), 290–297. https://doi.org/10.1192/bjp.bp.116.193862

Martin, W. B., Benedetto, N. N., Elledge, D. K., Najjab, A., & Howe-Martin, L. (2020). Beyond the language barrier: Recommendations for working with interpreters in individual psychotherapy. *Professional Psychology: Research and Practice*, *51*(6), 623–629. https://doi.org/10.1037/pro0000350

Miller, K. E., & Rasmussen, A. (2017). The mental health of civilians displaced by armed conflict: An ecological model of refugee distress. *Epidemiology and Psychiatric Sciences*, *26*(2), 129–138. https://doi.org/10.1017/S2045796016000172

Mills, C. (2013). *Decolonizing global mental health: The psychiatrization of the majority world*. Routledge.

Nickerson, A., Liddell, B. J., Maccallum, F., Steel, Z., Silove, D., & Bryant, R. A. (2014). Posttraumatic stress disorder and prolonged grief in refugees exposed to trauma and loss. *BMC Psychiatry*, *14*(1), 106. https://doi.org/10.1186/1471-244x-14-106

Patanè, M., Ghane, S., Karyotaki, E., Cuijpers, P., Schoonmade, L., Tarsitani, L., & Sijbrandij, M. (2022). Prevalence of mental disorders in refugees and asylum seekers: A systematic review and meta-analysis. *Global Mental Health*, *9*, 250–263. https://doi.org/10.1017/gmh.2022.29

Rosenblatt, P. C. (2008). Grief across cultures: A review and research agenda. In M. S. Stroebe, R. O. Hansson, H. Schut, & W. Stroebe (Eds.), *Handbook of bereavement research and practice: Advances in theory and intervention* (pp. 207–222). American Psychological Association. https://doi.org/10.1037/14498-010

Schiess-Jokanovic, J., Knefel, M., Kantor, V., Weindl, D., Schäfer, I., & Lueger-Schuster, B. (2021). Complex post-traumatic stress disorder and post-migration living difficulties in traumatised refugees and asylum seekers: The role of language acquisition and barriers. *European Journal of Psychotraumatology*, *12*(1), 2001190. https://doi.org/10.1080/20008198.2021.2001190

Smid, G. E., Drogendijk, A. N., Knipscheer, J., Boelen, P. A., & Kleber, R. J. (2018). Loss of loved ones or home due to a disaster: Effects over time on distress in immigrant ethnic minorities. *Transcultural Psychiatry*, *55*(5), 648–668. https://doi.org/10.1177/1363461518784355

Smid, G. E., Groen, S., de la Rie, S. M., Kooper, S., & Boelen, P. A. (2018). Toward cultural assessment of grief and grief-related psychopathology. *Psychiatric Services*, *69*(10), 1050–1052. https://doi.org/10.1176/appi.ps.201700422

Stroebe, M., & Schut, H. (1998). Culture and grief. *Bereavement Care*, *17*(1), 7–11. https://doi.org/10.1080/02682629808657425

Syrian Network For Human Rights. (2021, June 20). On World Refugee Day: More Than Half of the Syrian People Remain Forcibly Displaced, Either as IDPs or Refugees, and Are Unable to Return. *Syrian Network for Human Rights*. https://snhr.org/blog/2021/06/20/56415/

Tay, A. K., Rees, S., Tam, N., Kareth, M., & Silove, D. (2019). Defining a combined constellation of complicated bereavement and PTSD and the psychosocial correlates associated with the pattern amongst refugees from West Papua. *Psychological Medicine*, *49*(9), 1481–1489. https://doi.org/10.1017/S0033291718002027

Wojtkowiak, J., Lind, J., & Smid, G. E. (2021). Ritual in therapy for prolonged grief: A scoping review of ritual elements in evidence-informed grief interventions. *Frontiers in Psychiatry*, *11*, 623835. https://doi.org/10.3389/fpsyt.2020.623835

World Health Organization. (2019). *International statistical classification of diseases and related health problems* (11th Revision). https://icd.who.int/browse11/l-m/en

Zayfert, C. (2008). Culturally competent treatment of posttraumatic stress disorder in clinical practice: An ideographic, transcultural approach. *Clinical Psychology: Science and Practice*, *15*(1), 68–73. https://doi.org/10.1111/j.1468-2850.2008.00111.x

Epilogue

Hannah Comtesse, Geert E. Smid, and Paul A. Boelen

The loss of a loved one is one of the most common stressful life events affecting individuals, families, and communities, and is associated with grief as a universal and natural response. However, a significant minority of bereaved individuals develop debilitating and persistent grief reactions, namely prolonged grief disorder (PGD). PGD is included as a new disorder in both the International Classification of Diseases (ICD-11; WHO, 2022) and the text revision of the fifth edition of the Diagnostic and Statistical Manual of Mental Disorders (DSM-5-TR; APA, 2022). Although clearly distinct from related conditions of posttraumatic stress disorder (PTSD) and depression, PGD often co-occurs with these conditions, particularly after a traumatic death, constituting traumatic grief.

Spurred by the introduction of diagnostic criteria for PGD, the field of bereavement research has accumulated substantive knowledge on risk factors for the development and maintenance of PGD, diagnostic instruments for the assessment of PGD symptoms and other loss-related concepts (e.g., grief-related negative appraisals), and effective treatments for PGD. The chapters in this book describe the basis for understanding prolonged and traumatic grief, relevant risk and protective factors and diagnostics, and approaches to grief support and treatment in different settings, ages, and cultural groups.

Summary of the chapters in this book

The DSM-5-TR and ICD-11 diagnostic criteria for PGD overlap in the core symptoms (yearning and preoccupation), but differ in the content and number of additional symptoms and in the time criterion, leading to different prevalence rates (mostly higher rates for PGD as defined in ICD-11). Prevalence estimates based on representative samples have recently become available and indicate that between 2% and 8% of bereaved people in the general population of different countries develop PGD. Psychiatric comorbidity of PGD is high, most commonly with

DOI: 10.4324/9781003429777-20

PTSD and depression, which can be differentiated from PGD in terms of cognitive, emotional, behavioral, and physiological responses. Much higher rates of PGD are consistently found after unnatural, mostly traumatic deaths, a major risk factor for PGD. Several other factors may also increase the risk of PGD, including older age, attachment insecurity, a closer relationship to the deceased, low social or relational support, and perceived stigma. In addition to such immutable factors, several theoretical approaches include various internal psychological processes and coping styles that influence the adaptation to loss. At the core is the premise that one's self-concept needs to be revised in ways that acknowledge the physical absence of the deceased and the permanence of the separation, and that allow for the development of new sources of meaning and purpose. To overcome the limitations of a dichotomous classification of normal and disordered grief, an emerging stage typology of PGD has been introduced that could possibly provide a framework for understanding the longitudinal development of grief, the factors influencing this progression, and interventions to address both normal and disordered grief responses, in a stepped care or "tired" approach.

For the treatment of prolonged and traumatic grief, cognitive-behavioral therapy (CBT) approaches are most effective and usually follow stages. Psychoeducation about normal and disordered grief reactions, fostering motivation for change and treatment, and developing individual goals are essential. Grief-focused exposure can be used to reduce avoidance and mitigate separation distress by encouraging patients to confront both internal and external stimuli associated with the loss. Exposure to memories, thoughts, and feelings connected to other emotional experiences (e.g., anxiety, guilt, anger) can help foster emotional processing of broader events and threats related to the loss. Negative, unhelpful cognitions associated with loss and grief are also identified, challenged, and changed. Attribution of meaning, reengagement with activities and others, and activation processes focus on making sense of the loss and reintegrating into a life and future without the deceased. Symbolic interactions, using methods such as writing, imagery, rescripting, and rituals, address unresolved or painful issues and help to further process the loss. Evidence on pharmacological treatments for PGD is limited, but the available evidence suggests that pharmacotherapy may be helpful in managing comorbid symptoms of depression and PTSD. Internet-based interventions are increasingly available and could improve access for disadvantaged groups and support the implementation of a stepped care approach. In addition, culture- and developmental-sensitive and loss-specific approaches are available to provide tailored assessments and interventions for children and adolescents, older adults, and people with conflict and displacement experiences and those experiencing ambiguous loss.

Agenda for future research and practice

Based on the areas and topics covered in the chapters of this book, there are a number of challenges that need to be addressed in the field of bereavement research and the translation of findings into practice. Particular challenges in relation to the staging typology of grief and a stepped care approach have been outlined in Chapter 1.

Dissemination of knowledge about prolonged and traumatic grief

The introduction of PGD in the DSM-5-TR and ICD-11 helps to distinguish more clearly between people who are stuck in their grief and need professional help, and those for whom grief reactions may be intense but not impairing and for whom interventions are not indicated. There are many misconceptions about grief in general and about prolonged and traumatic grief in particular. An important misconception is that the use of such a label means that normal grief is medicalized and stigmatized. However, all kinds of labels for mental illness carry this risk. Indeed, experimental research has shown that labelling disordered grief reactions as PGD is stigmatizing, but no more so than labelling them as depression (Gonschor et al., 2020). This means that we should be careful about labelling grief reactions, and only say that someone has PGD when this has been determined by a clinician. Careful use of labels and appropriate diagnostics and indication could even help to counteract the medicalization of grief, for example, by recommending psychotherapy to people with PGD as the first-line treatment rather than prescribing antidepressants. Moreover, recognizing exactly what constitutes disordered grief could also help to avoid unnecessarily labelling people who are going through a normal grieving process as having a mental disorder (Johnson et al., 2009).

More work needs to be done to disseminate knowledge about prolonged and traumatic grief to relevant stakeholders who have a role to play in identifying early signs of disordered grief, educating about PGD, and providing treatment. These include first responders, social workers, general practitioners, spiritual counsellors, as well as psychotherapists and psychiatrists. In the field of psychotraumatology, a comorbid diagnosis of PTSD in traumatically bereaved patients should not lead clinicians to focus on treating PTSD and ignore PGD. Greater awareness that bereavement in most cases does not lead to PGD, may also help to serve all those bereaved persons who are actually in need of treatment but currently do not receive it. It has been found that about one in five people bereaved by a road traffic accident wanted help but did not receive it (Lenferink et al., 2020). For some of these people this was due to the limited availability of care, for others it was due to their own beliefs such as "I think my problems will go away on their own", "I don't think anyone can help me", or "I think it's also too painful to talk about the loss". Therefore, education about prolonged and traumatic grief is also needed for people suffering from PGD. In addition to making care more accessible, this can reduce the treatment gap.

Improvement of diagnostic instruments

A prerequisite for the identification and correct classification of prolonged and traumatic grief is the availability of valid instruments for the screening and diagnosis of PGD. Much progress has been made with screening tools in recent years. An important development is the availability of the Traumatic Grief Inventory-Self-Report plus (TGI-SR+; Lenferink et al., 2022), which captures symptoms according to both DSM-5-TR and ICD-11 and allows for assessing the severity of PGD symptoms and probable diagnostic status. The International Prolonged Grief Disorder Scale (IPGDS; Killikelly et al., 2023) assesses PGD according to ICD-11 and provides a culturally sensitive approach by also capturing possible culture-specific grief reactions. Both instruments have been researched, although more data are needed on their validity and clinical usefulness. These and all other self-report instruments discussed in Chapter 2 of this book have been developed in countries of the Global North. However, there is also a need to take other contexts in account, particularly in the developmental phase of criteria and measures (Mazza et al., 2024). The same applies to interviews administered by clinicians to assess the diagnosis of PGD. PGD is not included in a transdiagnostic interview for mental disorders, and we need specific interviews that are valid and clinically useful to ensure correct diagnostics. The Aarhus Structured Clinical Interview for Prolonged Grief Disorder in ICD-11 and DSM-5-TR (A-PGDi; O'Connor et al., 2024) is an important new development that has been evaluated with trained clinicians in a clinical sample, pointing to its relevance.

Early detection and prevention of PGD

As the concept of PGD and measurement tools becomes more widely available and accepted, and as the burden of disease becomes clearer, more attention will be paid to early detection and prevention. The self-report measures described in Chapter 2 can be used for early identification of people at risk for PGD. Importantly, intense PGD symptoms in the first year after a loss are strongly associated with severe PGD symptoms beyond that first year (when the DSM-5-TR diagnosis can be given; Boelen & Lenferink, 2020, 2022). However, more research is needed on how to define the time criterion after which a diagnosis can be made, particularly across cultural settings, and how this might affect diagnostic rates (e.g., Haneveld et al., 2022; Redican et al., 2025). An internet-based intervention may help to prevent the exacerbation and chronicity of PGD for those with severe symptoms in the first year after the loss (i.e., indicated prevention). This has been shown in studies involving individuals who had suffered a loss 3 to 6 months earlier (Litz et al., 2014), people who had recently suffered a loss during the COVID-19 pandemic (Reitsma et al., 2023), and women who had lost a child before birth (Eklund et al., 2022; Fernández-Férez et al., 2021; Kersting et al., 2013). For people at high risk of developing PGD following the death of a loved one (e.g., because of high levels of pre-loss grief, depression, or caregiver stress), communication between palliative care providers and mental health professionals crucially supports timely intervention. Establishing *bereavement care networks* bridges gaps between end-of-life and grief care providers, fostering collaboration and information sharing, providing a structured framework for community engagement, and benefiting public health (Killikely et al., 2021; Lichtenthal et al., 2024).

Improvement of treatment approaches

CBT-based treatments are available and have been shown to be effective, compared to both waitlist and other active treatments (Bryant et al., 2024; Rosner et al., 2024). Nevertheless, a substantial number of persons with PGD benefit insufficiently from available treatments. This is especially true for persons with PGD with high comorbidity, but also other factors that have not been sufficiently studied. For example, one could speculate that this might be the case for persons with strong avoidance and reservations against distressing exposure exercises. However, we need more research on what forms of treatment work in what intensity for whom, and also how do they work (Elinger et al., 2023) or whether comorbid problems should be addressed in a particular order (Neimeyer et al., 2022). In addition, there is now sufficient evidence and an urgent need to develop treatment guidelines for PGD. Such guidelines could help to facilitate the dissemination of evidence-based treatments to therapists in routine care.

There are many more topics for a research agenda. Several chapters in this book outline the need for more knowledge about different target groups (children, older adults, refugees) and causes of death (e.g., homicide, suicide, disaster). More knowledge is also needed about the impact of multiple losses and ambiguous loss, and the long-term effects of early loss. One major challenge is that most research on PGD still comes from countries of the Global North and is based on samples of white, educated, industrialized, rich, and democratic populations (Heinrich et al., 2010). Diagnostic criteria and measures have mostly been developed in this context and applied or adapted to other groups from low- and middle-income countries. But the extent to which measures are culturally equivalent and measurement invariant needs to be tested. This would help to ensure the generalizability of research findings across different cultural settings. Although bereavement care has improved in countries of the Global North, research on local and community-based approaches in other parts of the world is still scarce. The COVID-19 pandemic provided a lesson for the field: many researchers raised scientifically based concerns that the pandemic would lead to an increase in PGD cases (e.g., Eisma et al., 2020a, b; Killikelly et al., 2021). This was based on the high number of deaths associated with the COVID-19 pandemic and the number of associated risk factors (e.g., unexpectedness of loss or lack of physical social support). However, such an increase is unlikely to have occurred, suggesting that the majority of bereaved people are resilient (e.g., Bonanno et al., 2002). This underlines the importance of the emerging typology of PGD that also focuses on protective factors after bereavement and could thus enable us to be more prepared for rapid action in case of possible future pandemics.

Conclusion

Loss and grief are important and universal themes in life. The inclusion of PGD in international classification systems is a recognition of the fact that grief does not always subside or pass, but can sometimes be associated with severe suffering and impairment for long periods of time. It is striking that traumatic death is associated with a significantly increased risk of PGD and traumatic grief. It seems fair to say that not every loss leads to a mental disorder, but when a disorder is present, the loss often plays an activating or aggravating role. The last three decades have seen a rapidly growing body of research into normal and disordered grief. As a result, we now have a much better understanding of how disordered grief can manifest itself, what factors are involved, and what support is indicated and when. Finally, we are able to outline the contours of a possible staging, profiling, and stepped care model for PGD. The inclusion of PGD in leading classification systems will hopefully provide a further boost to all valuable efforts aimed at improving bereavement research and care—to alleviate the suffering of those experiencing loss, both within and outside of traumatizing circumstances.

References

American Psychiatric Association [APA]. (2022). *Diagnostic and statistical manual of mental disorders, Fifth Edition, Text Revision (DSM-5-TR)*. APA. https://doi.org/10.1176/appi.books.9780890425787

Boelen, P.A. & Lenferink, L.I.M. (2020). Symptoms of prolonged grief, posttraumatic stress, and depression in recently bereaved people: Symptom profiles, predictive value, and cognitive behavioural correlates. *Social Psychiatry and Psychiatric Epidemiology*, *55*, 765–777. https://doi.org/10.1007/s00127-019-01776-w

Boelen, P. A. & Lenferink, L. I. M. (2022). Prolonged grief disorder in DSM-5-TR: Early predictors and longitudinal measurement invariance. *Australian and New Zealand Journal of Psychiatry*, *56* (6), 667–674. https://doi.org/10.1177/00048674211025728

Bonanno, G. A., Wortman, C. B., Lehman, D. R., Tweed, R. G., Haring, M., Sonnega, J., Carr, D., & Nesse, R. M. (2002). Resilience to loss and chronic grief: A prospective study from preloss to 18-months postloss. *Journal of Personality and Social Psychology*, *83*(5), 1150–1164. https://doi.org/10.1037/0022-3514.83.5.1150

Bryant, R. A., Azevedo, S., Yadav, S., Cahill, C., Kenny, L., Maccallum, F., … & Dawson, K. S. (2024). Cognitive behavior therapy vs mindfulness in treatment of prolonged grief disorder: A randomized clinical trial. *JAMA Psychiatry*, *81*(7), 646–654. https://doi.org/10.1001/jamapsychiatry.2024.0432

Eisma M. C., & Tamminga A. (2020). Grief before and during the COVID-19 pandemic: Multiple group comparisons. *Journal of Pain and Symptom Management*, *60*(6), e1–e4. https://doi.org/10.1016/j.jpainsymman.2020.10.004

Eisma, M. C., Boelen, P. A., & Lenferink, L. I. (2020). Prolonged grief disorder following the Coronavirus (COVID-19) pandemic. *Psychiatry Research*, *288*, 113031. https://doi.org/10.1016/j.psychres.2020.113031

Elinger, G., Hasson-Ohayon, I., Bar-Shachar, Y., & Peri, T. (2023). Narrative reconstruction therapy for prolonged grief disorder: Basic interventions and mechanisms of change. *Death Studies*, *47*(10), 1082–1093. https://doi.org/10.1080/07481187.2022.2164633

Eklund, R., Eisma, M.C., Boelen, P.A., Arnberg, F.K. & Sveen, J. (2022). My Grief app for prolonged Grief in bereaved parents: A pilot study. *Front Psychiatry*, *13*, 872314. https://doi.org/10.3389/fpsyt.2022.872314

Fernández-Férez, A., Ventura-Miranda, M.I., Camacho-Ávila, M., Fernández-Caballero, A., Granero-Molina, J., Fernández-Medina, I.M., Requena-Mullor, M.D.M. (2021) Nursing Interventions to Facilitate the Grieving Process after Perinatal Death: A Systematic Review. *International Journal of Environmental Research and Public Health*, *18*(11), 5587. https://doi.org/10.3390/ijerph18115587

Gonschor, J., Eisma, M. C., Barke, A., & Doering, B. K. (2020). Public stigma towards prolonged grief disorder: Does diagnostic labeling matter?. *PloS One*, *15*(9), e0237021. https://doi.org/10.1371/journal.pone.0237021

Haneveld, J., Rosner, R., Vogel, A., Kersting, A., Rief, W., Steil, R., & Comtesse, H. (2022). Same name, same content? Evaluation of DSM-5-TR and ICD-11 prolonged grief criteria. *Journal of Consulting and Clinical Psychology*, *90*(4), 303–313. https://doi.org/10.1037/ccp0000720

Henrich, J., Heine, S. J., & Norenzayan, A. (2010). The weirdest people in the world?. *Behavioral and Brain Sciences*, *33*(2-3), 61–83. https://doi.org/10.1017/S0140525X0999152X

Johnson, J. G., First, M. B., Block, S., Vanderwerker, L. C., Zivin, K., Zhang, B., & Prigerson, H. G. (2009). Stigmatization and receptivity to mental health services among recently bereaved adults. *Death Studies*, *33*, 691–711. https://doi.org/10.1080/07481180903070392

Kersting, A., Dolemeyer, Steinig, J., Walter, F., Kroker, K., Baust, K., et al. (2013). Brief internet-based intervention reduces posttraumatic stress and prolonged grief in parents after the loss of a child during pregnancy: a randomized controlled trial. *Psychotherapy and Psychosomatics*, *82*, 372e381. http://dx.doi.org/10.1159/000348713

Killikelly, C., & Maercker, A. (2023). The cultural supplement: A new method for assessing culturally relevant prolonged grief disorder symptoms. *Clinical Psychology in Europe*, *5*(1), e7655. https://doi.org/10.32872/cpe.7655

Killikelly, C., Smid, G. E., Wagner, B., & Boelen, P. A. (2021). Responding to the new International Classification of Diseases-11 prolonged grief disorder during the COVID-19 pandemic: a new bereavement network and three-tiered model of care. *Public Health*, 191, 85–90. https://doi.org/10.1016/j.puhe.2020.10.034

Lenferink, L.I.M., de Keijser, J.,Eisma, M.C., Smid, G.E. & Boelen, P.A. (2020). Treatment gap in bereavement care: (Online) bereavement support needs and use after traumatic loss. *Clinical Psychology & Psychotherapy*, *28*, 907–916. https://doi.org/10.1002/cpp.2544

Lenferink L.I.M., Eisma M.C., Smid G.E., de Keijser J. & Boelen P.A. (2022). Valid measurement of DSM-5 persistent complex bereavement disorder and DSM-5-TR and ICD-11 prolonged grief disorder: The Traumatic Grief Inventory-Self Report Plus (TGI-SR+). *Comprehensive Psychiatry*, *112*, 152281. https://doi.org/10.1016/j.comppsych.2021.152281

Lichtenthal, W. G., Roberts, K. E., Donovan, L. A., Breen, L. J., Aoun, S. M., Connor, S. R., & Rosa, W. E. (2024). Investing in bereavement care as a public health priority. *The Lancet Public Health*, *9*(4), e270–e274. https://doi.org/10.1016/S2468-2667(24)00030-6

Litz, B., Schorr, Y., Delaney, E., Au, T., Papa, A., Fox, A.B., Morris, S., Nickerson, A., Block, S., & Prigerson, H. (2014). A randomized controlled trial of an Internet-based therapist-assisted indicated preventive intervention for prolonged grief disorder. *Behaviour Research and Therapy*, *61*, 23–34. https://doi.org/10.1016/j.brat.2014.07.005

Mazza, A., Maercker, A., Forstmeier, S., Müller, M., & Killikelly, C. Toward centrality evaluation of yearning symptoms for prolonged grief disorder: A cross-cultural approach. *Psychopathology*, 1–11. https://doi.org/10.1159/000541321

Neimeyer, R. A., Breen, L. A., & Milman, E. J. (2022). The effectiveness of grief therapy: A meta-analytic perspective. In Steffen, E. M., Milman, E., & Neimeyer, R. A. (Eds.). *The Handbook of Grief Therapies* (pp. 29–35). Sage.

O'Connor, Maja & Vang, Maria & Bryant, Richard & Buur, Christina & Komischke-Konnerup, Katrine & Frostholm, Lisbeth & Ladegaard, Nicolai. (2024). The Aarhus PGD interview. Development and validation of the Aarhus Structured Clinical Interview for Prolonged Grief Disorder in ICD-11 and DSM-5-TR (A-PGDi). Preprint available at: https://doi.org/10.13140/RG.2.2.30066.93126

Redican, E., Shevlin, M., Ben-Ezra, M., Karatzias, T., & Hyland, P. (2025). Are 'time' and 'culture' useful and necessary diagnostic requirements for ICD-11 Prolonged Grief Disorder? A cross-national study. *Death Studies*, 1–12. https://doi.org/10.1080/07481187.2025.2468822

Reitsma, L., Boelen, P. A., de Keijser, J., & Lenferink, L. I. M. (2023). Self-guided online treatment of disturbed grief, posttraumatic stress, and depression in adults bereaved during the COVID-19 pandemic: A randomized controlled trial. *Behaviour Research and Therapy*, 163, 104286. https://doi.org/10.1016/j.brat.2023.104286

Rosner, R., Rau, J., Kersting, A., Rief, W., Steil, R., Rummel, A. M., Vogel, A., & Comtesse, H. (2024). Grief-specific cognitive behavioral therapy vs present-centered therapy: A randomized clinical trial. *JAMA Psychiatry*. https://doi.org/10.1001/jamapsychiatry.2024.3409

World Health Organization [WHO]. (2022). *International Classification of Diseases Eleventh Revision (ICD-11)*. WHO. https://icd.who.int/browse11/l-m/en

Index

Note: Page references in *italics* denote figures and in **bold** tables.

For Product Safety Concerns and Information please contact our EU representative GPSR@taylorandfrancis.com
Taylor & Francis Verlag GmbH, Kaufingerstraße 24, 80331 München, Germany

www.ingramcontent.com/pod-product-compliance
Lightning Source LLC
Chambersburg PA
CBHW050630280326
41932CB00015B/2586

* 9 7 8 1 0 3 2 4 6 4 8 0 0 *